Wessex from AD 1000

1

A Regional History of England

General Editors: Barry Cunliffe and David Hey
For full details of the series, see pp. xii–xiii.

Wessex
from AD 1000

J. H. Bettey

Longman
London and New York

Longman Group Limited
Longman House, Burnt Mill, Harlow
Essex CM20 2JE, England
Associated companies throughout the world

Published in the United States of America
by Longman Inc., New York

First published 1986

British Library Cataloguing in Publication Data
Bettey, J. H.
  Wessex from AD 1000. – (Regional history of England)
  1. Wessex (England) – History
  I. Title   II. Series
  942.3   DA670.W4
  ISBN 0-582-49208-4 ppr
  ISBN 0-582-49207-6 csd

Library of Congress Cataloging in Publication Data
Bettey, J. H.
  Wessex from AD 1000.
  (Regional history of England)
  Bibliography: p.
  Includes index.
  1. Wessex – History.   I. Title.   II. Series.
DA670.W48B475   1986   942.2′735   85–5924
  ISBN 0-582-49207-6
  ISBN 0-582-49208-4 (pbk.)

Set in Linotron 202 10/12 pt Sabon Roman
Produced by Longman Singapore Publishers (Pte) Ltd.
Printed in Singapore.

Contents

Wessex from AD 1000

List of plates

List of figures

List of tables

General preface

England cannot be divided satisfactorily into recognisable regions based on former kingdoms or principalities in the manner of France, Germany or Italy. Few of the Anglo-Saxon tribal divisions had much meaning in later times and from the eleventh century onwards England was a united country. English regional identities are imprecise and no firm boundaries can be drawn. In planning this series we have recognised that any attempt to define a region must be somewhat arbitrary, particularly in the Midlands, and that boundaries must be flexible. Even the South-West, which is surrounded on three sides by the sea, has no agreed border on the remaining side and in many ways, historically and culturally, the River Tamar divides the area into two. Likewise, the Pennines present a formidable barrier between the eastern and western counties on the Northern Borders; contrasts as much as similarities need to be emphasised here.

The concept of a region does not imply that the inhabitants had a similar experience of life, nor that they were all inward-looking. A Hull merchant might have more in common with his Dutch trading partner than with his fellow Yorkshireman who farmed a Pennine smallholding: a Roman soldier stationed for years on Hadrian's Wall probably had very different ethnic origins from a native farmer living on the Durham boulder clay. To differing degrees, everyone moved in an international climate of belief and opinion with common working practices and standards of living.

Yet regional differences were nonetheless real; even today a Yorkshireman may be readily distinguished from someone from the South East. Life in Lancashire and Cheshire has always been different from life in the Thames Valley. Even the East Midlands has a character that is subtly different from that of the West Midlands. People still feel that they belong to a particular region within England as a whole.

In writing these histories we have become aware how much regional identities may vary over time; moreover how a farming region, say, may not coincide with a region defined by its building styles or its dialect. We have dwelt upon the diversity that can be found within a region as well as upon common characteristics in order to illustrate the local peculiarities of provincial life. Yet, despite all these problems of definition, we feel that the time is ripe to attempt an ambitious scheme outlining the history of England's regions in 21 volumes. London has not been included – except for demonstrating the many ways in which it has influenced the provinces – for its history has been very different from that of the towns and rural parishes that are our principal concern.

In recent years an enormous amount of local research both historical and archaeological has deepened our understanding of the former concerns of ordinary men and women and has altered our perception of everyday life in the past in many significant ways, yet the results of this work are not widely known even within the regions themselves.

This series offers a synthesis of this new work from authors who have themselves been actively involved in local research and who are present or former residents of the regions they describe.

Each region will be covered in two linked but independent volumes, the first covering the period up to AD 1000 and necessarily relying heavily on archaeological data, and the second bringing the story up to the present day. Only by taking a wide time-span and by studying continuity and change over many centuries do distinctive regional characteristics become clear.

This series portrays life as it was experienced by the great majority of the people of South Britain or England as it was to become. The 21 volumes will – it is hoped – substantially enrich our understanding of English history.

Barry Cunliffe
David Hey

A Regional History of England

General Editors: Barry Cunliffe (to AD 1000) and David Hey (from AD 1000)

The regionalisation used in this series is illustrated on the map opposite.

*The Northern Counties to AD 1000   *Nick Higham*
The Northern Counties from AD 1000   *Norman McCord & Richard Thompson*

The Lancashire/Cheshire Region to AD 1000   *G. D. B. Jones with Denise Kenyon & Nick Higham*
The Lancashire/Cheshire Region from AD 1500   *John Smith*

Yorkshire to AD 1000   *T. G. Manby*
Yorkshire from AD 1000   *David Hey*

The Severn Valley and West Midlands to AD 1000   *R. T. Rowley*
The West Midlands from AD 1000   *Marie B. Rowlands*
The Welsh Borders from AD 1000   *R. T. Rowley*

The East Midlands to AD 1000   *Jeffrey May*
The East Midlands from AD 1000   *J. V. Beckett*

The South Midlands and Upper Thames to AD 1000   *David Miles*
The South Midlands and Upper Thames from AD 1000   *John Broad*

The Eastern Counties to AD 1000   *W. J. Rodwell*
The Eastern Counties from AD 1000   *B. A. Holderness*

The South West to AD 1000   *Malcolm Todd*
The South West from AD 1000   *Bruce Coleman & R. A. Higham*

Wessex to AD 1000   *Barry Cunliffe*
*Wessex from AD 1000   *J. H. Bettey*

The South East to AD 1000   *Peter Drewett*
The South East from AD 1000   *Peter Brandon & Brian Short*

*already published

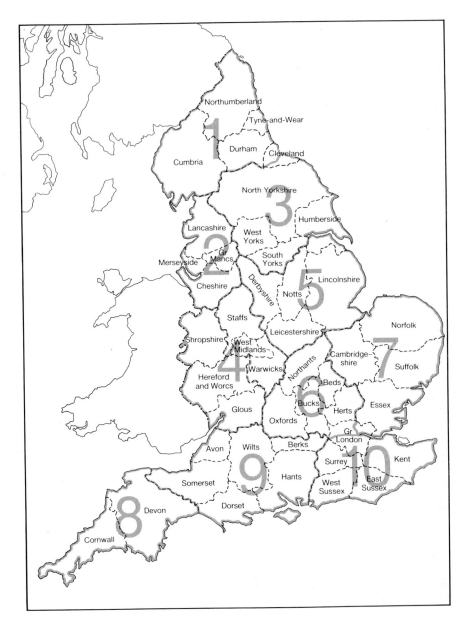

1. The Northern Counties
2. The Lancashire/Cheshire Region
3. Yorkshire
4. The Severn Valley and West Midlands
5. The East Midlands
6. The South Midlands and the Upper Thames
7. The Eastern Counties
8. The South West
9. Wessex
10. The South East

Acknowledgements

Any general survey of this sort must depend heavily upon the detailed research of others on specific subjects and localities, and a list of the major studies and articles which have been consulted will be found in the references and the bibliography. The General Editor, Dr David Hey, has been a constant source of encouragement and guidance, and I am grateful to him for all his perceptive comments upon earlier drafts of each chapter. I also acknowledge with thanks the help and advice of numerous friends and colleagues, in particular Michael Aston, Dr Robert Dunning and Bernard Lane each read and commented upon various sections of the book. I am also grateful to Michael Aston for all his work on the maps, in particular for drawing Figure 2.2, and for his generous help, and to several other people for their assistance, advice over illustrations, and help in other ways, including Alan Andrew, Patrick Brown, Christopher Clay, Michael Costen, John Crook, Jim Hancock, Gordon Kelsey, Rosemary Johnston, and Robert Machin. Many of the subjects explored and illustrated on the following pages have been discussed at length with students on courses of the University of Bristol Department of Extra-Mural Studies. Their ideas and contributions have been very helpful. The aerial photographs (Plates 2.1 & 2.4) are from the superb record of Wessex sites and landscapes compiled over many years by Jim Hancock, and I acknowledge with thanks all his help as well as his permission to use the material from his collection. I am also grateful to the following for their specific permission to reproduce plates which appear in the text: Alan Andrew (7.3, 7.5, 7.6 & 8.1); Patrick Brown (6.3 & 6.4); John Crook (1.1); *Farmers Weekly* (7.4); Gordon Kelsey (3.4); The Museum of English Rural Life, Reading (7.7); *The Wiltshire Times* (6.1); A. Wright (7.2); and The Yeovil Museum (7.1). Mrs J. Morrison also provided me with invaluable help in the drafting of the caption for Plate 7.6.

J. H. Bettey
University of Bristol.

Introduction

This book is concerned with the history and development of southern England over the past ten centuries. The region covers the whole of central-southern and western England from the Thames valley to Exmoor, from the Severn estuary and the Bristol channel to the Isle of Wight and the English Channel coast between Lyme Regis and Portsmouth, and it comprises the ancient counties of Berkshire, Hampshire, Dorset, Wiltshire and Somerset, and the city and county of Bristol, as they existed before the boundary changes of 1974. Within this large area there are great contrasts in geology and landscape. It includes the fertile countryside of the Thames valley, the Vale of the White Horse, and the rich farmlands of the vales of Taunton Deane and of west Dorset, as well as the windswept, barren uplands of Exmoor rising to 1,700 feet at Dunkery Beacon, the rugged coastline of west Somerset and the poor, acid soils of the heathlands of Hampshire and Dorset. The landscape, towns, villages and farms of the chalk downlands which dominate the central core of the region are quite different from the lush pastures and neat villages of the Thames valley, the wooded claylands of north Wiltshire, east Somerset and west Dorset, or the marshlands of central Somerset. A traveller through the region cannot fail to notice the frequent and often dramatic changes in scenery; the observant will also notice the different ways in which each landscape has been adapted and changed by human activity, the contrasts in the size, shape and frequency of villages and towns, the varieties of farming practice, the different field shapes, road patterns and the evidences of former industries. It is the purpose of this book to describe the history of the communities which have lived within the region from the time of the Norman Conquest to the twentieth century, and to show how the environment and landscape have been modified and developed by human activity, by economic pressures, religious movements, political changes and military requirements, and above all by long centuries of toil by many generations of farmers.

The name 'Wessex', which is used here as a convenient description of the central and western parts of southern England, originally denoted the old kingdom of the West Saxons, with all its associations with King Alfred, with

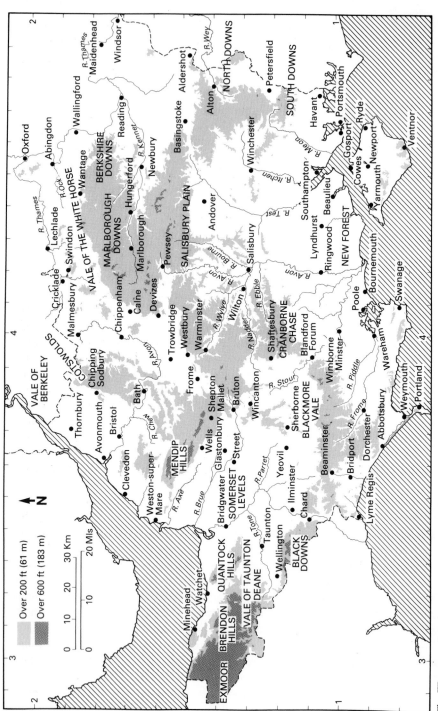

The Wessex region

stalwart resistance to the Danish invasions during the ninth and tenth centuries, and with the creation of an English kingdom and culture. But the modern use of the term derives largely from its revival by the novelist and poet, Thomas Hardy, during the later nineteenth century, and its current popularity and widespread use is evident from the large number of commercial firms and enterprises within the region which have adopted it as part of their name.

The central, dominating feature of the Wessex region, which gives it a unity it would otherwise lack, is the large expanse of chalk downland at its heart. The high chalk downs rising in places to over 900 feet, with their deeply cut river-valleys, extend from the Dorset coast between Abbotsbury and Portland through central Dorset and Cranborne Chase to Salisbury Plain, which is the essential core of Wessex, and on to the Marlborough and Berkshire Downs in the north and to the Hampshire Downs in the east. This range of chalkland is surrounded by older, harder rocks, clays and greensand. To the west, in Somerset and west Dorset, are the heavy clays of the Somerset levels and of the Marshwood and Blackmore vales, the carboniferous limestone of Mendip, and the Devonian slates and red sandstones of the Quantock, Brendon and Blackdown hills and the majestic sweep of Exmoor. To the north the chalk downs fall sharply away to the claylands of north Wiltshire, the Vale of Pewsey, the Vale of the White Horse and the valleys of the Kennet and the upper Thames; while to the south the chalk gives way to the low-lying gravels, sands and clays of the Hampshire basin, through which flow the rivers from the chalklands with their characteristic fast-flowing, clear streams, draining into the English Channel through Poole Harbour, Christchurch, Southampton Water and the Solent. Running across the region from Portland to the Cotswolds and beyond is a belt of Jurassic oolitic limestone which provides some of the finest building stone in England. The high-quality, white stone from Portland was used during the Middle Ages and has been extensively quarried since the seventeenth century; the golden upper lias limestone from Ham Hill in south Somerset can be seen to perfection in such buildings as Sherborne Abbey and Montacute House; the Chilmark quarries in south Wiltshire provided the stone for Salisbury Cathedral; Doulting quarries near Shepton Mallet in central Somerset produced the stone for Glastonbury Abbey, Wells Cathedral and many other churches in that area, while the great oolite quarries and stone mines at Corsham and Box in north-west Wiltshire produced the famous Bath stone.

Apart from the central chalk downlands, still sparsely settled though with a wealth of evidence for prehistoric occupation and land-use, the Wessex region has no natural centre. The Hampshire basin and the surrounding Hampshire chalklands look naturally towards Southampton, the Solent and the English Channel coast; the Marlborough and Berkshire Downs, drained by the Kennet and upper Thames are drawn towards Reading and London; while the western part of the region is focused towards Bristol. Nonetheless the easy cross-country communications provided by the well-drained chalklands, and especially by the ancient ridgeway tracks, have provided a unifying influence throughout the whole Wessex region. Winchester, Old Sarum and Bath were important centres in the Roman road network, and later roads from London to the Channel ports, to Exeter and to Bristol, provided important links between various parts of Wessex. The junctions where the prehistoric ridgeway routes cross the river-valleys determined where the future towns such as Cricklade, Wallingford, Reading, Wilton, Malmesbury and many others would develop. Bristol grew up by the lowest bridge over the Avon, and Winchester, the great centre of West Saxon government, Church life and culture, developed at the junction of Roman roads and at the place where a ridgeway crossed the Itchen.

In all parts of Wessex, and especially in the chalklands, the extensive and dramatic signs of prehistoric settlement and evidence of long centuries of human activity can be seen, and the impact of prehistoric farmers upon the landscape can more easily be appreciated here than anywhere else in England. In later centuries the region has been notable for its wealth and for the number and size of its monastic houses, churches, market towns, great estates and royal palaces. The latter range from the Saxon royal palaces such as those at Winchester and Cheddar, through the residences of medieval kings at Windsor and Clarendon, to the villa-retreat of Queen Victoria and Prince Albert at Osborne House on the Isle of Wight. Apart from the coal of Somerset and Kingswood, lead from Mendip, a few locally important deposits of iron-ore, copious supplies of good building stone, and good ports and harbours such as those at Portsmouth, Southampton, Poole and Weymouth or at Bristol, Bridgwater and Minehead, much of the region lacks natural resources. It does, however, have a generally fertile and easily worked soil, excellent communications by land and water, a good water supply, extensive forests and woodland, and a mild climate which encourages the growth of grass and has fostered the livestock farming upon which so much of the region has traditionally depended for its livelihood. Everywhere in Wessex there are the signs of the unremitting toil of countless generations. The results of their labours show in fields, hedges, buildings, churches and chapels, farms and barns, ports and harbours, military fortifications, great country houses, roads, bridges, canals and railways. The following chapters will explore these developments and examine the varying fortunes of the societies which created them.

Chapter 1

The Early Middle Ages: Conquest and Civil War

By the year 1000 central-southern England, the heartland of the kingdom of Wessex, was already an ancient, settled land, where the long centuries of work by prehistoric settlers, the efficiency of Romano-British farmers, Roman land-surveyors and road builders, and the efforts of Saxon pioneers had laid out the landscape with a framework of estates and villages, towns and parishes, administrative boundaries and ecclesiastical divisions. The roots of much of this framework are to be sought in Roman or even earlier estate boundaries and administrative units; many parish boundaries in Wessex correspond to the bounds of Anglo-Saxon land grants, and modern research increasingly shows the antiquity of manorial, parish, township and other divisions, and the persistence of land-units from prehistoric times (Gelling 1978: 191–214). Wessex had already been divided into shires, with a system of local administration through hundreds, before the end of the eighth century. Somerset was the territory of the people who were referred to by *The Anglo-Saxon Chronicle* in 845 as the *Sumorsaete*, who looked to Somerton as their administrative and military centre; Dorset had its centre at the old Roman provincial capital of Dorchester; Wiltshire was dependent upon Wilton, then the most important town in the shire with its wealthy Benedictine nunnery founded by King Alfred; Hamwic, the Saxon predecessor of Southampton, was the capital of Hampshire. The only one of the central-southern counties not to be named after the people of its principal town was Berkshire, which, according to Asser, the Welsh monk who wrote a biography of King Alfred and who was to become Bishop of Sherborne, was 'called Bearrocscire, which district is so called from the Berroc wood where the box-tree grows most abundantly'. Wallingford, at a major crossing-point of the Thames, was for long the chief urban centre of Berkshire, although the Saxon shire court met in the open on a mound by the Ridgeway at Scutchamer Knob in East Hendred, high up on the Berkshire Downs.

By the year 1000 monastic houses at Glastonbury, Shaftesbury, Malmesbury, Abingdon, Winchester and several other places were already long-established institutions.

Place-name endings such as 'ley', 'leigh', 'hay' or 'hurst', signifying clearings or enclosures, already bore abundant witness to the inroads made by Saxon farmers upon the woodland cover of the region, although this slow laborious process of clearing was to continue throughout the Middle Ages. From the evidence of late Saxon charters and from royal and ecclesiastical estate records it is possible to obtain a picture of the landscape and settlement pattern of the region during the eleventh century, but even where documentary sources are lacking, the evidence of the landscape, the surviving pattern of fields and roads, boundaries and settlements, can be used to show how well-established most features of the landscape were by the time of the Norman conquest. For example, the typical pattern of parish and manorial boundaries to be found on the chalklands of Dorset, Wiltshire, Hampshire and Berkshire, with long narrow areas of land running across the valleys of the chalkland streams and extending far up on to the surrounding downland is clearly described in numerous Saxon charters, and is also marked by pre-Conquest boundaries often running continuously for several miles across the chalklands (Bonney 1976: 72–82; Taylor 1970: 51–66). Likewise in the Vale of Wrington on the borders of Somerset and Avon, where low-lying pastures rise up to the bleak carboniferous limestone slopes of Mendip, a whole series of clearly defined estates dating from the Roman period are recorded in charters of the tenth century, each carefully aligned across the Vale and evidently the result of deliberate, careful planning (Fowler 1972: 45–6, 132). Similar evidence of the antiquity and planned nature of parish, manorial and estate boundaries is to be found throughout the region and has obvious links with the complex pattern of boundaries marked by banks and ditches which can be discerned on the chalklands and which were already in existence in Wessex long before the coming of the Romans. All modern research continues to confirm that the arrangement of the Wessex landscape and its administrative divisions and estate boundaries had already been in existence for many centuries before the Norman Conquest, and that many of the settlements in Wessex are much older than was hitherto supposed (Bonney 1976).

The Towns

Evidence concerning the towns of Wessex during the century before the Norman Conquest comes from *The Anglo-Saxon Chronicle* and from the remarkable document known as the Burghal Hidage dating from the early years of the tenth century, which lists some thirty *burhs* or fortified places established by King Alfred before his death in 899. The *burhs* formed a defensive system for Wessex against Viking raids; some were on the sites of former Roman towns where defences were already available such as Winchester, Portchester, Bath and Dorchester; others were newly fortified, notably Wareham, between the rivers Frome and Piddle, where the impressive earth banks with which three sides of the town were surrounded are a dramatic survival. Wareham is the best place in the region to appreciate the defensive potential of Alfred's system of *burhs*. Malmesbury was easily defended on its promontory overlooking the river Avon, while at Cricklade and Wallingford the burghal defences can still be seen, enclosing both towns with rectangular earthen banks, as at Wareham. Other *burhs* in the region included Southampton (Hamwic), Twynham, Watchet, Langport, Lyng and Wilton. The existence of the *burhs* and their surviving defences are themselves impressive evidence of the administrative system operating within the region, which could organise such complex and labour-intensive work and could arrange for the maintenance of such a defensive system (Hill 1969). By the year 1000 other towns and market-places were also important in Wessex. Bristol was established by the lowest bridge across the river Avon, and on a well-defended position above the point where the river Frome joined the Avon, providing a safe anchorage for ships, well inland from the mouth of the river. By the early eleventh century Bristol, which the Anglo-Saxon chronicler called 'Brycgstow' or 'the holy place of the bridge', had a mint and fortifications. Its inhabitants were engaged in overseas trade, notably with Ireland, and when in 1051 Earl Godwin, Earl of Wessex, and his sons, including Harold who was later to be King, revolted against Edward the Confessor, it was from Bristol that Harold and his brother Leofwine took ship and fled to Ireland. Possibly there was also at Bristol a religious community established across the river Frome where St Augustine's monastery was later to be founded. Certainly there was an important ecclesiastical centre nearby at Westbury-on-Trym which was in existence at least by the ninth century (Dickinson 1976).

Archaeological evidence suggests that the port which was to develop into the later Southampton may have been the largest urban settlement in Wessex before the Viking invasions, but although it provided an admirably sheltered harbour between the rivers Test and Itchen and at the head of what is now Southampton Water, it was in a vulnerable position, open to raiders from the English Channel. It was ravaged by Viking attacks during the ninth and tenth centuries, and thereafter recovered only slowly, although it remained sufficiently important to give its name to the shire (Platt 1973; Hinton 1977).

The evidence of the Domesday Survey makes it clear that numerous other places in Wessex had some claim to be regarded as urban centres, or at least possessed markets and market traders and were thus differentiated from the surrounding rural settlements by the early eleventh century. There were traders outside the gates of the wealthy monastery at Abingdon, and no doubt other large monastic houses such as Glastonbury, Shaftesbury, Romsey and several others fostered the growth of trade by their presence, but it is not until Domesday that we have firm evidence. Bedwyn in Wiltshire developed as an urban centre during the tenth and eleventh centuries probably because of the proximity of the *burh* at Chisbury, since the hill-fort itself was too difficult of access to be useful as a market. Early in the tenth century Bishop Denewulf of Winchester bought privileges from the Crown which were to make Taunton a profitable market town as well as the centre of the rich Winchester estates in Somerset. Other places with some claim to be regarded as towns in the first half of the eleventh century include Andover, Basingstoke, Bruton, Crewkerne, Frome, Milborne Port, Amesbury, Calne, Chippenham and Warminster.

By far the most important of all the towns of Wessex in the century before the Norman Conquest was Winchester. The recent intensive programme of archaeological and historical investigation at Winchester has transformed our knowledge of this royal town of the West Saxon kings. It is clear that within the Roman defences a large and complex city had developed by the tenth century,

---

Plate 1.1 Winchester Cathedral. The longest cathedral in Europe, and a powerful reminder of Winchester's status as the capital of Wessex and the royal centre of Anglo-Saxon England. The great Saxon church, the Old Minster, was demolished to make way for the Norman cathedral which was begun by Wakelin, the first Norman bishop, in 1079. The substantial remains of the Norman work are now overlaid by successive rebuildings and alterations, including the nave and west front which are illustrated here. The nave was remodelled during the fourteenth century, mainly under two notable bishops, William of Edington (Bishop 1346–66), and William of Wykeham (Bishop 1367–1404).

with a regular lay-out of streets and lanes, and with numerous crafts and trades. Winchester was the largest of the Alfredian *burhs*, with a fortified area of 144 acres, and was the royal capital of Anglo-Saxon England. Cnut, his wife Emma and their son Harthacnut were all buried in the Old Minster at Winchester, and it was there that the line of English kings was restored by the coronation of Edward the Confessor on Easter Day, 1043 (Biddle 1976: 449–70). The still-operative system of Roman roads made Winchester the natural centre of communications over a wide area, and by the ninth century a stone bridge over the Itchen brought traffic from the east through the Roman gateway into the walled area of the city. The main entrance to the city from the west was also through a Roman gateway, and the road through the city linking the east and west gates is still the main street; the evidence of a tenth-century charter shows that the street was then already known as 'Cheap Street', that is 'market' street. Archaeological evidence reveals that this and other streets were being regularly surfaced during the tenth century, which must mean that there was a well-developed system of government in the city. By the eleventh century an important annual fair was already being held at Winchester and within the city was the principal royal palace of the Saxon kings and the major ecclesiastical centre in Wessex.

The rapid growth of the city during the tenth century is shown by the development of the built-up area within its walls and by the spread of suburbs beyond. By the time of the Norman Conquest there were ten or more parish churches as well as important monastic communities, and the range of crafts to be found could hardly have been matched in any other English city. Winchester formed a market and focus for a large area of the surrounding chalklands, and within its walls could be found workers in leather, wood, bronze and iron, moneyers, goldsmiths, jewellers, potters, artists and musicians. Winchester was also dominated by three great monastic foundations, whose buildings and precincts occupied more than a quarter of the area within the walls of the city. Here the kings of Wessex were crowned and here they were buried, while it was here that the remarkable reform of the Saxon Church during the tenth and early eleventh centuries was initiated and sustained (Biddle 1976).

The Pre-Conquest Church in Wessex

It was primarily from Wessex that the monastic revival and ecclesiastical reforms of the tenth and eleventh centuries sprang, for Dunstan – the originator of much of the reforming movement – was born in Somerset in *c.* 909 and educated at Glastonbury; he became Abbot of Glastonbury in 943 and Archbishop of Canterbury 960–988. At Glastonbury Dunstan created a strictly organised and tightly controlled community of monks, and the influence of this reformed monastic house soon spread throughout Wessex. The effect of the Church revival was seen in Wessex during the tenth and eleventh centuries in ecclesiastical art and architecture and in the great flowering of Saxon craftsmanship and artistic excellence which reached its peak in the productions of the Winchester school of artists. Something of the vigour and enthusiasm of this revival can still be felt in the fragments of work that remain, even though most of the Saxon architectural achievements of the eleventh century were swept away by the Norman conquerors to make way for churches in their own style. Thus the Old Minster at Winchester which had been rebuilt on a grand scale with an imposing tower during the years 971–994 was demolished to make way for the Norman cathedral. At Sherborne, Glastonbury and Bath large Saxon structures were replaced by Norman buildings, and there were numerous less dramatic examples of the replacement of recently built Saxon churches by new ones in the Norman style. Enough Saxon church architecture and stone-carving survives in Wessex, however, to show the freshness, liveliness and inventive genius of the buildings, sculpture and decoration produced by the Church revival. The most eloquent testimony to the vigour of the Church is at Breamore in the valley of the Hampshire Avon, mid-way between Salisbury and Ringwood. Above the entrance to this Saxon church is the figure of the crucified Christ, carved in stone, with body twisted in the agony of crucifixion, still a powerfully moving work of art in spite of the mutilation it received at the hands of reformers during the sixteenth century. Above an arch inside the church is the deeply-cut inscription HER SPVELAD SEO GECPYDRAEDNES DE 'In this place the Word is revealed unto thee' (Bettey and Taylor 1982: 14–27).

The most characteristic product of the Church revival in Wessex was the book-production and manuscript illumination which is associated above all with the school at Winchester. Here, from the middle of the tenth century onwards, works of the very highest quality were produced, able to rank with the finest output of contemporary continental craftsmanship. Among the best-known of these productions was the *Benedictional of St Ethelwold*, the most sumptuous of Anglo-Saxon books to be produced at Winchester, and the output also included missals, service books, psalters including chants and a form of musical notation known as 'tropes', lives of the saints, and the *Liber Vitae* produced at the New Minster between 1016 and 1020 which includes a famous drawing of the Last Judgement. The Church revival in Wessex also developed a new religious literature in the vernacular language, and in the works of Aelfric, addressed to laymen, Anglo-Saxon prose reached its highest point. Aelfric was a monk at the Old Minster at Winchester where he studied under Ethelwold. In 987 he went as novice-master to the new foundation at Cerne in Dorset, and in the seclusion and quiet of the monastery at Cerne he produced many of his principal works including *Catholic Homilies*, *Lives of the Saints*, devotional works, school books, and biblical translations, works which have established Aelfric as the most considerable scholar of the late Saxon Church (Wormald 1959).

In its teaching, literature, manuscript illumination, architecture, carving in stone, bone and ivory, metalwork, needlework, music and other ecclesiastical art the late Saxon Church in Wessex, and especially at Winchester, was superbly rich and vigorous, and showed beyond doubt the depth of the revival which had occurred in religious life (Godfrey 1962; Loyn 1962).

The Norman Conquest

Like the rest of England, Wessex was profoundly affected by the Norman victory at Hastings. In the ten weeks which elapsed between his victory at Hastings and his coronation in London, William marched his victorious army westward through Guildford and Basingstoke to Winchester which surrendered under the influence of Edith, the widow of Edward the Confessor, thence north to Wantage and eastward to the Thames at Wallingford where Archbishop Stigand, who had been one of Harold's leading supporters, came and swore fealty to William. This great march of the invading Norman army during November and December 1066, in a wide circle around London, eventually intimidating the city into submission, may have been a masterly military tactic, but for the towns and villages along the route, the impact of the march was horrific. The Norman army could only sustain itself by taking cattle, corn and provisions from the people through whose towns and villages they passed, and so great was the damage caused that twenty years later it was still reflected in the reduced values of those places along the line of the march (Welldon Finn 1971: 19–23).

The invading force moving towards Winchester seems to have concentrated around Basingstoke, where it was joined by reinforcements from Normandy. Their movement up the Meon valley was still marked in 1086 by the declined value of the manors in that area. When Winchester surrendered, the army moved on, probably in at least three separate contingents to subdue Berkshire, and their route between Winchester and Wallingford is likewise marked by the destruction they caused and by the decline in the value of the places through which they passed. The main body seems to have crossed the Kennet near Newbury, and then to have proceeded by way of the royal manor of Wantage. Another part of the army went by way of Great Shefford and then up the Lambourn valley; while a third column proceeded along the western border of Berkshire, possibly penetrating into Wiltshire as far as Highworth before turning east along the Vale of the White Horse (Welldon Finn 1971).

The destruction and devastation in Wessex did not end with William's coronation in London on Christmas Day 1066, for apart from the heavy taxes which were imposed by the victorious Normans, the replacement of Saxon landowners by William's followers, and the heavy labour services required for building the Norman castles, Wessex also saw a number of defiant but futile rebellions against the imposition of Norman rule, risings which were ruthlessly suppressed and punished by the Norman armies with a deliberate ferocity designed to deter further resistance. A revolt at Exeter in 1068 was sufficiently serious to bring William himself at the head of a Norman army through the region to subdue the city and suppress disaffection in Devon and Cornwall. Later in 1068 three illegitimate sons of King Harold descended on Bristol with a raiding party from Ireland. They plundered the neighbourhood and tried unsuccessfully to raise a force along the coast of Somerset against the Normans.

Resistance to the Norman Conquest persisted strongly in south Somerset and north Dorset, and was fanned into flame by the castle at Montacute built in *c.* 1068 by Robert count of Mortain – half-brother of the Conqueror – for this was a spot with particularly hallowed associations for the English. It was here on top of the conical hill, the *Mons Acutus*, that earlier in the eleventh century a fragment of the Holy Cross was said to have been discovered, a discovery which was subsequently commemorated in the feast of the Invention of the Holy Cross. The estate at Montacute belonged to the wealthy Saxon land-owner, Tofig, who also possessed an estate at Waltham in Essex where he built a church to receive the holy relic found on his Somerset lands. Later Earl Harold, the future King, richly endowed a religious house dedicated to the Holy Cross at Waltham, and the Holy Rood of Waltham became an object of popular veneration and pilgrimage. 'Holy Cross' was the battle-cry of Harold's successful army at Stamfordbridge and of the defeated English at Hastings. After Hastings it was to Waltham that Harold's body was taken for burial. The building of a Norman castle on the very spot where the legendary relic had been found was seen as a final insult to a defeated race, and produced a fierce local reaction. The castle was besieged by the English during 1069, and a considerable force had to be assembled to relieve it by the Norman bishop Geoffrey of Coutances whose large grants of land in the south-west were directly threatened by the insurrection (Stenton 1947: 595). The ferocity with which the attack on Montacute was suppressed and the devastation in the surrounding area which followed the English defeat may explain why so many manors in south Somerset are recorded in the Domesday Survey as having decreased in value (Darby and Finn 1967: 170). Likewise the Domesday Survey shows a string of manors between Salisbury and Dorchester whose values had declined following the Conquest and it is reasonable to suppose that this is connected with the movement of troops from Winchester and Salisbury in 1069 in order to suppress the rising at Montacute, and possibly also other smaller risings in Dorset (Welldon Finn 1971: 285).

The Effects of the Norman Conquest

The Norman castles

One of the most dramatic effects of the Norman Conquest was the building of castles, a new kind of military fortification. These were quite different in form and concept from the Saxon *burhs* or fortified towns, for the *burhs* were essentially communal efforts, collectively built and maintained, and designed to protect the whole community against attack by strangers or foreigners coming from a distance. The Norman castles were private fortifications to protect the lord and his armed men, built for men who were in an essentially hostile environment, and with the wider purpose of over-awing the local population, deterring their attempts at rebellion, and providing a base from which a small body of mounted soldiers could dominate the surrounding area for many miles around.

Soon after the Conquest castles were built at Chepstow and Berkeley, dominating the Severn valley and providing a symbol of Norman rule against the Welsh, at Exeter where William himself chose the site for the castle after suppressing the rebellion there, and at Montacute. Early castles were also built at Wallingford where William had crossed the Thames in 1066 and where the Domesday Book entry later recorded that eight house-plots had been destroyed to accommodate the castle, and at Winchester. William realised the importance of demonstrating his mastery in the ancient royal capital of Winchester, and within two months of the surrender of the city the south-west corner was embanked to form the site for a Norman castle, many houses being swept away in the process. By 1072 the castle at Winchester had progressed sufficiently to have a richly appointed chapel and to be the site of an important Easter meeting of the King's council. By the time of the Domesday Survey in 1086 castles had also been built on a high *motte* or earth mound at Carisbrooke in the Isle of Wight, at Corfe on the dramatic site controlling the gap through the Purbeck Hills, the main route to the Isle of Purbeck, and at Old Sarum within the ramparts of the Iron Age hill-fort, an ideally defensive site to which in 1075 the bishopric of Sherborne was transferred and where a cathedral was also built inside the defences of the prehistoric earthwork. At Dunster, another good defensive site on a hillside overlooking the Bristol Channel and well-placed to dominate the western part of Somerset, a castle was built by William de Mohun, the Sheriff of Somerset. Bristol, already an important port, was an obvious site for a castle, to protect the town and to dominate the lower valleys of the Severn and the Avon, and Bristol Castle was in existence by 1086 or soon afterwards on a well-defended site on a ridge enclosed by a loop of the river Frome just before it joined the Avon.

During the century following the death of William the Conqueror in 1087, and especially during the period of confusion and conflict during the anarchy of the twelfth century, numerous other castles and lesser military fortifications were built in the region, far too many to attempt to list them all. As the writer of *The Anglo-Saxon Chronicle* bitterly expressed it in 1137:

> For every great man built him castles and held them against the King; and they filled the whole land with these castles. They sorely burdened the unhappy people of the country with forced labour on the castles; and when the castles were built, they filled them with devils and wicked men.

The Norman castles and military fortifications in Wessex ranged from hastily constructed small mottes or minor earthworks like the ring-ditch and drystone walled enclosure at Ashton Keynes (Wilts) or the earthwork at Castle Neroche (Somerset) to the moated site with square tower and rectangular gatehouse at Bishops Waltham (Hants) or the great rectangular stone keep of the castle at Christchurch. At Windsor a twelfth-century motte and bailey with timber fortifications received stone walls during the early thirteenth century and thereafter a complex series of enlargements, alterations and additions until it was the largest and most impressive castle in England. Similarly the royal castle at Portchester grew to be one of the strongest fortifications along the south coast. Southampton was developed by the Normans as one of the vital links between England and Normandy, and a castle was built in the north-west corner of the town to dominate the harbour. As a result of the growth in cross-Channel traffic with Normandy, Southampton grew to be one of the leading ports in the country by the early thirteenth century. Many smaller towns in Wessex were also dominated by motte and bailey earthworks or by stone castles in the years after the Conquest, and the evidence for these structures and the way in which they have influenced the shape and development of the towns can still be clearly seen. At Devizes the concentric semi-circular fortifications around the former castle have fundamentally shaped the plan of the town and the pattern of its streets and markets. The dramatic artificial motte at Marlborough now towers over the grounds of Marlborough College; mottes, baileys and other earthworks are still a feature of towns such as Nether Stowey, Castle Cary, Stogursey and Taunton (Somerset), Sherborne, Corfe Castle, Sturminster Newton and Wareham (Dorset), and Downton (Wilts), Wallingford, Faringdon, Newbury and Reading (Berks) (Renn 1968).

The Norman castles towering over towns, harbours, river crossings and other key points in the landscape were the most obvious signs that new and energetic governors had arrived and were determined to rule; they symbolised the changes in lordship which substituted new Norman masters for the Saxon lords; likewise the forcible employment of great numbers of English labourers upon the work of castle building must have given many their first intimate acquaintance with their new Norman overlords.

The royal forests

Another effect of the Norman Conquest which influenced the lives of many people in the region was the creation of very large areas of royal forest. Kings and noblemen of Wessex had loved hunting long before the Normans came. It was while hunting at Cheddar in *c.* 943 that King Edmund appointed Dunstan to take charge of the religious community at Glastonbury, and so initiated the Church reforms of the tenth and eleventh centuries. Saxon charters have references to deer-parks and game enclosures, the laws of Cnut had laid heavy penalties on those who hunted in a district reserved for the King's own pleasure, and Domesday records that Edward the Confessor had given land at Chippenham to his huntsman, Wulfgeat, while another huntsman, Alvric, held land of the King in Burbage, Savernake and elsewhere. But it was the Norman kings with their passionate involvement with hunting who introduced the forest laws and greatly extended the areas of royal forest. Such areas were not necessarily wooded, but were outside the common law and subject instead to the special forest laws. Many of the favourite hunting places of the Norman kings were in Wessex, and very large areas of the region were given over to royal forests. The great forest of Windsor was already in existence by the time of Domesday Book where it is mentioned by name and referred to as *foresta regis*; during the Middle Ages it extended over much of eastern Berkshire as well as parts of Surrey, Buckinghamshire and Middlesex. In Wiltshire by the thirteenth century royal forests extended all along the south-east border of the county, and included Savernake, Chute, Clarendon (where there was an important royal palace), and Melchet on the Hampshire border. Between the valleys of the rivers Wylye and Nadder lay the forest of Groveley, while royal forests covered large tracts of country around Chippenham and Melksham (*VCH Wilts* IV, 1959: 391–460). Large areas of Dorset were subject to forest law, and by the twelfth century there were royal forests at Powerstock in the west of the county, in the Blackmore Vale, at Gillingham where there was another royal palace and where substantial remains of the park enclosure survive, in Cranborne Chase and in the Isle of Purbeck. Royal forests in Somerset included the great expanse of Exmoor, Neroche forest on the slopes of the Blackdown hills, Quantock, Mendip and the very large and ancient forest of Selwood along the Wiltshire border. Covering much of what was then south Gloucestershire, the forest of Kingswood stretched out for several miles across the broken country north-east of Bristol and came up to the bounds of the town itself. Hampshire contained the forests of Alice Holt and Woolmer in the east, the forest of Bere north of Portsmouth harbour and the great expanse of the New Forest in the south-west of the county (Young 1979).

More detail survives about the creation of the New Forest than about any other royal forest, and there are many persistent myths concerning the destruction involved and the forcible eviction of large numbers of inhabitants in order to provide secluded shelter for the king's deer. As late as 1951 the medieval historian A. L. Poole could write that 'The making of the New Forest and the injury it caused to the inhabitants is a familiar fact of history' (Poole 1951: 30). There is no doubt that this was one of the earliest and most important of the royal forests created by William the Conqueror, and a separate section of Domesday Survey is devoted to it. Chroniclers and annalists of the twelfth century castigated the Conqueror for the high-handed way in which they claimed he had reduced a previously flourishing and prosperous district to waste and had ruthlessly driven out the inhabitants to make his forest. The writer of *The Anglo-Saxon Chronicle* saw this as among the most wicked of William's misdeeds, and turned to verse to describe it in an often-quoted passage:

> He caused castles to be built
>
> Which were a sore burden to the poore.
> A hard man was the king
> And took from his subjects many marks
> In gold and many more hundreds of pounds in silver.
> . . . . .
> He set apart a vast deer preserve and imposed
> Laws concerning it.
> Whoever slew a hart or a hind
> Was to be blinded.
> He forbade the killing of boars
> Even as the killing of harts.
> For he loved the stags as dearly
> As though he had been their father.

Later chroniclers lamented the villages laid waste and the people driven from their homes. When William Rufus was killed in an hunting accident in the New Forest in 1100, some contemporaries saw the hand of God at work and viewed the incident as divine retribution for the hardship caused by the making of the Forest. Florence of Worcester wrote that

> Doubtless, as common report has it, this was verily the righteous
> vengeance of God. For in days of old, that is in the days of King Edward
> and other Kings of England before him, that land flourished plentifully
> with country-folk, with worshippers of God and with churches; but at

the bidding of King William the elder, the men were driven away, their houses thrown down, their churches destroyed, and the land kept as an abiding-place for beasts of the chase; and thence, it is believed, was the cause of the mischance.

(Thorpe 1848–49, I, 44–5)

Modern research into the Domesday Survey and later records, coupled with the evidence of geology, gives a somewhat different account. Most of the area is covered by poor sands and gravels, and the infertile soil could never have supported a large population. Some thirty to forty settlements, most of them small, were placed under the forest law by William the Conqueror, perhaps 100,000 acres in all, but there is no evidence of mass eviction of the inhabitants. Some certainly remained at the time of the Domesday Survey; Brockenhurst, for example, in the heart of the Forest, still had $3\frac{1}{2}$ plough-teams with 10 men on its arable land in 1087. No doubt upheaval and dislocation was caused by the creation of the forest, and no doubt there was some justification for the chroniclers' indignation; just across the Wiltshire border at Downton there were 'two hides from which the inhabitants have fled because of the king's forest', but nonetheless it does seem as though the earlier legends of wholesale eviction and destruction were greatly exaggerated (Darby and Campbell 1962, 324–38).

Within the forests, protection was given to the red, roe and fallow deer, to the boar, and to the woodland, pasture and undergrowth that sheltered and fed them. During the early Middle Ages wolves were also to be found within the forests and as late as 1210 King John gave 15 shillings to two huntsmen who killed two wolves at Gillingham and another at Clarendon, although the fact that they were given so much may suggest that by then it was an unusual incident. A year earlier two foals belonging to the bishop of Winchester had been devoured by wolves on his estate at Merdon, south-west of Winchester.

Those unfortunate enough to live within the extensive royal forests were subject to many vexatious restrictions and to harsh punishments for their infringement. They were also at the mercy of the petty tyrannies of foresters and verderers, whose exactions were a standing grievance throughout the Middle Ages, a fact which is illustrated by the complaint of the dwellers within the forest of Mendip in 1279, that they were not even allowed to collect firewood without being fined by the foresters.

It was not only the kings who were obsessed by love of hunting and hawking; during the twelfth and thirteenth centuries deer-parks were established throughout the region by the nobility, clergy and others. Within the parks deer could be preserved and could be released for hunting; they could also be easily caught to provide a source of fresh meat during the winter. The Bishops of Winchester had a park at Billingbear in east Berkshire, the Abbots of Reading had a park at Whitley south of the town, the Bishops of Salisbury had a park beside their castle at Sherborne and the Abbots of Glastonbury had parks at Pilton, Ditcheat, Sharpham and Marksbury. In 1230 Alan Basset was granted leave to make a park at Wootton Basset within the royal forest of Braydon, and in 1246 Simon de Montfort, Earl of Leicester, obtained licence to enclose and impark an area of woodland called 'Bantley' in his manor of Hungerford. William de Valence, who had a park within the royal forest of Chute, was granted a licence in 1256 to have a deer-leap so that deer could get into his park but not out again. Much survives in the modern landscape as a reminder of the forests and deer-parks. The remains of the former royal hunting palaces, where the kings could lodge and conduct business of state as well as indulge their passion for the chase, remain at Gillingham, at Bagden Lodge in Savernake Forest and Groveley Lodge near Wilton. Little now survives of what was once the greatest of all such palaces, the former royal residence at Clarendon east of Salisbury. The deer-parks with their great earthen banks have left their imprint upon the landscape in many places, and have affected the pattern of roads, the shapes of later fields and place-names. They range in size from a few acres to the 3,000 acres of Windsor Great Park. Harbin's Park in Tarrant Gunville parish near Blandford Forum covers 115 acres and is still completely enclosed by a massive bank with an internal ditch, a prominent and evocative reminder of former land-use. The park surrounding the former palace at Clarendon was more than three miles in diameter, while the bank along the south side of John of Gaunt's deer-park at Kings Somborne is still 12 feet high. The bank and ditch which formerly surrounded the 145 acre deer-park of Milton abbey is still remarkably well-preserved in the thick woodland of an isolated valley to the east of the former monastery. The carefully constructed bank is still 3–4 feet high and has remained intact although the medieval town of Milton Abbey has disappeared from the landscape and the former Benedictine abbey has been transformed. The banks and fences of deer-parks needed constant repair, and a thirteenth-century custumal of Glastonbury Abbey lists three days' work each year on the park fences at Pilton as one of the obligations of its tenants there.

The Domesday Survey: Wessex in 1086

Another result of the Norman Conquest was the Domesday Survey which was ordered by King William while he held court at Gloucester during Christmas 1085; the results of this painstaking enquiry, the outcome of William's understandable curiosity about his realm, were eventually housed in the Royal Exchequer at Winchester. Despite the vast amount of patient research that has been done on the Domesday Survey, its detailed interpretation remains beset by difficulties and doubtful meanings. Its purpose was to record tenurial rights and financial duties, and it records only indirectly and imperfectly the settlement pattern and ecclesiastical organisation of the time. Nonetheless the information it provides, used in conjunction with other documents and with archaeological evidence, does give an invaluable picture of the region during the eleventh century. Above all it reveals the scale on which a new and militarily organised foreign aristocracy had replaced the English landowners, and it shows the devastation caused by the Conquest and by the passage of the Norman armies, and the depression in the status and prosperity of the population of Wessex. Wessex appears in the Domesday Book as already an area of large estates and great landowners, a characteristic which was to survive down the centuries. Much land was in the hands of the King himself, the *terra regis*; much also belonged to the great ecclesiastical estates. For example, in Hampshire the lands of the Church were even more widespread than those of the King; while in Dorset nearly forty manors were in the hands of the King, who was the largest single landowner. After him came Robert, Count of Mortain, the King's half-brother, whose Dorset lands were only a small part of his vast estates. Most of the rest of Dorset was held by Norman barons, with only a few Englishmen remaining in possession of small estates. Of the lands of the Church in Dorset, by far the greater part belonged to the Bishop of Salisbury. Between 1075 and 1078 the bishopric of Sherborne was transferred to the larger and more populous town of Old Sarum, where a new cathedral was built beside the castle within the prehistoric earthwork. The extensive endowments of the former Bishop of Sherborne were transferred to the new bishopric, including lands in and around Sherborne and the rich estate at Netherbury and Beaminster in west Dorset. Church lands in Dorset also included the estates of the great nunnery of Shaftesbury, and the possessions of the monasteries at Sherborne, Cerne, Milton, Abbotsbury, Cranborne and Horton. In addition the monasteries of Glastonbury and Winchester and the Dean and Chapter of Wells all possessed lands in the county.

Wessex in 1086 was an area of large, consolidated manors, with many villages belonging to a single lord, and with a peasantry bound to labour service. In Wiltshire, for example, many of the manors were very large; fifty-three estates were assessed at more than twenty hides or units of taxation, ten of them exceeded fifty hides. Some of these large manors comprised numerous subsidiary settlements, like the Bishop of Winchester's huge Somerset manor of Taunton Deane which extended for several miles and included many villages. The Bishop of Winchester's properties, together with those of the monks of Winchester formed one of the most remarkable estates in the whole region, the ancient patrimony of the most important church in the capital city of Wessex. These estates lay in nine counties stretching from Somerset to Cambridgeshire, but the bulk were in Hampshire, Wiltshire and Somerset. They included properties in the towns of Winchester, Taunton, Oxford and Wallingford, the large and valuable manors of Chilcombe in Hampshire, Taunton Deane in Somerset and Downton in Wiltshire, and comprised land for 970 plough-teams, with more than 1,300 villeins, almost as many bordars and some 500 serfs. There were more than 100 mills, and the total Domesday valuation of the land came to £1,325 (Lennard 1959: 75–84).

Throughout Wessex the less prosperous elements in the population were numerous, and there were far fewer of the free peasantry who were such a feature of eastern England. The number of serfs or *servi* is high, and their proportion is much greater in Wessex than elsewhere. The general impression therefore is of a substantial downgrading of the peasantry as a result of the Norman Conquest.

Table 1   Classification of the recorded population of Wessex in 1086

County	Villeins	Bordars	Serfs	Coscets	Cottars	Coliberts	Miscel- laneous	Total
Berkshire	2,687 43.6%	1,868 30.3%	804 13.1%	— —	734 11.9%	— —	67 1.1%	6,160
Hampshire	3,575 40.5%	3,558 40.3%	1,535 17.4%	— —	— —	— —	167 1.9%	8,835
Isle of Wight	360 33.7%	461 43.2%	237 22.2%	— —	— —	— —	10 0.9%	1,068
Wiltshire	3,418 35.1%	2,766 28.4%	1,550 15.9%	1,384 14.2%	276 2.8%	233 2.4%	108 1.1%	9,735
Dorset	2,569 35.0%	3,032 41.3%	1,243 16.9%	182 2.5%	196 2.7%	—	122 1.7%	7,344
Somerset	5,239 40.7%	4,743 36.9%	2,106 16.4%	—	390 3.0%	208 1.6%	172 1.3%	12,858

(Darby and Welldon Finn 1967: 28, 90, 162; Darby and Campbell 1962: 258, 314)

The picture of the landscape and of the patterns of settlement in Wessex in the later eleventh century which can be discerned in the Domesday Survey shows the sort of sharp contrasts which might be expected in a region of such diverse geology and topography. The most striking comparison is between the thickly settled, evidently prosperous areas on the better-drained, fertile lands and the impoverished settlements situated in unfavourable conditions on poor soils, or within the royal forests. The most prosperous, well-populated areas with numerous settlements were to be found in northern Berkshire, especially in the rich pastures along the Vale of the White Horse, where there was already evidence of specialised dairy farming, in the manors of the Thames valley and along the valleys of the Kennet and the Loddon; also in Hampshire along the Test, the Itchen and the Meon, and in the rich hilly lands of the southern part of the Isle of Wight; other prosperous districts included the clay vales of north and west Dorset and west Wiltshire and the rich lands of the vale of Taunton Deane in Somerset. Areas with fewer and far less populous settlements included the parts of the region which were now within the royal forests, especially on the light, acid soils of the New Forest and the forests of Windsor and Kingswood; also the Dorset heathland, the wet clays and sterile gravel soil of the northern part of the Isle of Wight, much of the high chalk downland of Salisbury Plain and the Hampshire, Dorset and Berkshire Downs; the frequently flooded lands of the Somerset levels which appear to have been shunned by farmers and where little drainage work had as yet been carried out; and the bleak uplands of Mendip and Exmoor.

The effect of the forest laws can be clearly discerned in Berkshire where in the northern vales there were generally some 3 or 4 plough teams per square mile and a recorded population of between 11 and 14 peasants per square mile, while in the south-east of the county where the law of Windsor Forest lay heavily on the land the density of plough-teams was everywhere below 3 per square mile and the recorded population nowhere rose above 7 per square mile and over most of the area was much lower. A similar comparison can be made between parts of north and west Wiltshire and the forest areas of Savernake, Chute, Clarendon and Melchet in the east (Lennard 1959).

Farming
Tenth- and eleventh-century charters provide evidence of common field agriculture at several places in the region. Land is described as lying in common at Ardington (Berks) in 961, at Curridge (Berks) in 953, and at Winterbourne (Wilts) in 963; references to intermixed acres are found at Harwell (Berks) in 985 and at Kingston Bagpuize (Berks) in 1032, and a charter for Avon (Wilts) speaks of three hides of land 'in a mixture here and there in common land' (Finberg 1972: 488–9). The Domesday Survey, however, adds little to our knowledge of farming methods, and the figures for the distribution of arable land, plough-teams, pasture and meadow in the region are broadly what might be expected. Districts with little arable in the survey and less than one plough-team per square mile included the Somerset Levels, Exmoor, the Selwood district, the Dorset heathland and the areas of royal forest in Wiltshire, Hampshire and Berkshire. The most intensively farmed arable areas included, predictably, the rich lands of the vale of Taunton Deane, the vale of Pewsey, the river valleys of the Bristol Avon and the Salisbury Avon, the lands along the Thames valley and the slopes of the vale of the White Horse. The largest areas of meadow listed were in the Somerset lowlands, in the Chew valley of north Somerset, along the valleys of the streams that cut through the chalk downs, the Wylye, Nadder, Ebble, Stour, Piddle, Frome, Test and Itchen.

The Exeter text of Domesday Book gives information about livestock on the demesne lands for Somerset and Dorset, and although the record is partial and incomplete, and probably lists only a small proportion of the total livestock in each county, yet it does give some indication of the sort of animals kept and of their relative importance in the rural economy. Sheep were obviously of major importance in both counties, and were probably already

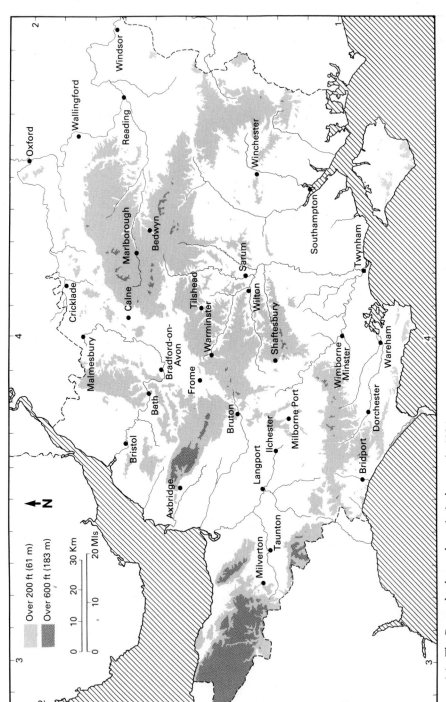

Figure 1.1 The Domesday boroughs: principal towns in 1086

Over 200 ft (61 m)

Over 600 ft (183 m)

30 Km
20 Mls

N

Bristol
Axbridge
Milverton
Taunton
Langport
Ilchester
Milborne Port
Bruton
Bath
Bradford-on-Avon
Frome
Malmesbury
Cricklade
Calne
Marlborough
Bedwyn
Tilshead
Warminster
Wilton
Sarum
Shaftesbury
Wimborne Minster
Wareham
Bridport
Dorchester
Oxford
Wallingford
Reading
Windsor
Winchester
Southampton
Twynham

valued for their capacity to fertilise the corn-lands with their dung as well as for their wool, since the largest flocks were to be found on the lighter arable lands; in Dorset almost all the sheep listed were in the chalklands. Some very large flocks were kept on royal manors in Dorset, including flocks of 1,600 at Puddletown, 1,037 at Cranborne, 900 at Portland and 826 at Ashmore. In Somerset there were 800 sheep at Chewton Mendip, 700 at Keynsham and large numbers at Doulting, Shepton Mallet, Croscombe and Pilton in the hilly country of the north-eastern part of the county. Goats were numerous throughout Wessex, and were obviously kept for milk and cheese production. Cows were however important in some areas, and in Berkshire the Domesday Survey has references to specialised dairy farms (*vaccaria*) and to cheese-making at three places in the Vale of the White Horse. Clearly some farmers on the rich pasture lands in this well-watered vale were already concentrating on the dairy farming for which the area was later to become famous. Thirteen cows were recorded at West Stafford (Dorset) in the lush grassland of the Frome valley providing some evidence that dairy-farming was already being carried on there. Pack horses or rounceys were widely distributed, and the 'unbroken mares' (*equae indomitae*) and the 'forest mares' (*equae silvaticae*) no doubt included the ancestors of the hardy, free-ranging ponies of Exmoor and of the Dorset heathlands. Swine were also important in the rural economy, and some large herds are mentioned, such as 70 at Ashill (Somerset), 70 at Pitcombe (Somerset) and 60 at Puddletown (Dorset).

Towns

The following Wessex boroughs are recorded in the Domesday Book:

Berkshire	*Hampshire*
Wallingford	Winchester
Windsor	Southampton
Reading	Twynham
Wiltshire	*Dorset*
Malmesbury	Dorchester
Wilton	Bridport
Cricklade	Wareham
Bedwyn	Shaftesbury
Warminster	Wimborne Minster
Tilshead	
Salisbury	*Somerset*
Bradford-on-Avon	Langport
Calne	Axbridge
Marlborough	Frome
	Bruton
South Gloucestershire	Milborne Port
Bristol	Ilchester
	Milverton
	Bath
	Taunton

Berkshire

As well as Wallingford, Windsor and Reading, other places which possessed markets included Abingdon, Faringdon, Newbury and possibly also Thatcham. At Abingdon we are specifically told of ten traders (*mercatores*) dwelling in front of the door of the church of the great abbey, an excellent example of the way in which an important monastery could give rise to a town. Wallingford was a market and administrative centre with a probable population of between 2,000 and 3,000 people, and with numerous dependent villages. Reading was primarily an agricultural community with 62 plough-teams, numerous mills and fisheries, and with 64 villeins and 38 bordars, but it also had a small urban community, and its position on the Thames and on an important route to the west gave it a considerable commercial importance.

Hampshire

The Domesday Survey contains no detailed account of Winchester, although it was the ancient capital and the home of the royal treasury where the Domesday Survey was eventually housed. The facts concerning Winchester were no doubt collected, but were either lost or for some reason were never copied into the final manuscript, although a space was left for them. Southampton had some 200 households, possibly as many as 230, so that its total population was at least 1,000 and was probably a good deal more. The inhabitants included 65 Normans who are described in the Survey as 'Frenchmen', and this may be an indication of its trade with the continent and of its important position as a link between England and Normandy. Twynham, the modern Christchurch, situated at the mouth of the Avon, was a small town set in the midst of a large agricultural area. It had 22½ plough-teams with some 60 villeins, bordars and others, and 39 burgesses. This total of 99 heads of households must therefore indicate a population of at least 500 but clearly the agricultural element outnumbered the urban. Basingstoke, Neatham and Titchfield were also said to have markets.

Wiltshire

Information about most of the ten Wiltshire boroughs is very sparse. Four were situated in large royal manors – Bedwyn, Calne, Tilshead and Warminster; two were on ecclesiastical manors – Bradford-on-Avon which belonged to the nunnery at Shaftesbury, and Old Sarum which belonged to the bishop; Wilton was specifically described as a borough, while Cricklade and Marlborough apparently also had burghal status. Only Malmesbury is described in detail, with many subsidiary settlements in the surrounding district, a mint, and 100 burgesses, so that its total population was probably well over 500.

Dorset

Shaftesbury was the largest of the Dorset boroughs with a probable population of about 1,000. Dorchester and Wareham probably had about 700 people each, while at Bridport the population has been estimated to have been no more than 500. All four of these boroughs had mints, and coins from all four survive from the reigns of William the Conqueror and William Rufus. Wimborne Minster, although not classed as a borough in the Domesday Survey, is said to have had burgesses and no doubt therefore also had a market. It was smaller than the other Dorset towns with a population of no more than some 400 people.

Somerset

In addition to the nine boroughs listed for Somerset, Yeovil and Watchet may also be regarded as embryo towns since they had burgesses or a market or a mint; Somerton and Cheddar may perhaps also have had markets. Some of these places were, however, very small, and ceased to be boroughs during the twelfth century. Bath was the largest borough with 178 burgesses, Ilchester had 107, Taunton 64. The urban centre at Taunton was part of the Bishop of Winchester's large manor of Taunton Deane, and was the administrative focus of a large surrounding area of rich countryside.

Bristol

The Domesday Survey says little about the town of Bristol which was part of the royal manor of Barton, but there is no doubt that it was an important port. It paid an annual render to the King of £84, which ranks with such towns as York, Lincoln and Norwich. Dominating the town was the royal castle overlooking the harbour and the bridge across the Avon (Darby 1973: 39–74).

Again, one point which emerges very clearly from the Domesday Survey is the extent of the devastation caused in the towns of Wessex by the Norman Conquest and subsequent events. The building of castles caused great damage in several towns, such as Winchester, Wallingford and Wareham, while the passage of armies apparently devastated other places. In Dorset of the 172 houses in Dorchester in 1066 only 88 remained standing in 1086, at Shaftesbury 61 houses had been destroyed, and at Bridport 20, while the building of the castle at Wareham had apparently destroyed 150 houses. Most of the destruction in the Dorset towns must be attributed to the havoc wrought by the Norman army on its way to besiege Exeter in 1068, and to the upheaval caused by the suppression of the rebellion at Montacute in 1069 (Darby 1973: 39–74).

Industries and Resources

The Domesday Book says nothing of lead mining on Mendip, nor does it mention the stone quarries which the surviving evidence in Wessex churches shows were being extensively worked at that time. Salt production along the south coast is referred to at several places, and twelve manors had a total of 22 salt-pans along the Hampshire coast, most of them around Southampton Water and in the shallow parts of Portsmouth and Langstone harbours. Salt-pans or salt-workers are also recorded at five places in Dorset, each with several salt-pans; 56 salt-workers are mentioned so clearly this was an important industry along the Dorset coast.

Coastal fisheries or fishermen are seldom mentioned, but along the rivers and in the marshes fisheries were sufficiently important to be listed in many places. There were 34 such fisheries in Berkshire, especially along the Thames, the Kennet and the Loddon. In Hampshire 23 fisheries were listed, and 10 in Somerset, although in view of the large areas of lake and marshland in the Somerset levels it is probable that many more fisheries went unrecorded.

Water-mills were common along the fast-flowing rivers of the chalklands. Hampshire had 172 mills, Wiltshire 197, Dorset 166; Somerset had 250 mills although none was to be found in the central part of the county where the slow rivers of the levels were unsuitable. Of the 192 settlements in Berkshire listed in Domesday Book, 94 had mills, and some indication of the elaboration of water-mills which had been achieved by the eleventh century is seen at Old Windsor where archaeological excavation has revealed that there was a mill with three water-wheels, turned by water brought along a massive artificial channel, 20 feet wide and 12 feet deep, and running for nearly a mile across a bend in the Thames. Water-mills were obviously a familiar feature of the landscape, and in the late tenth century the Wessex monk Aelfric could liken the motion of the heavens around the earth to a water-wheel, confident that his readers would grasp his meaning.

Vineyards were listed at Bisham (Berks), Durweston and Wootton (Dorset), and there was a fruit-orchard at Orchard in Church Knowle (Dorset). Five vineyards are recorded in Somerset, three of them on the lands of Glastonbury Abbey; and four vineyards in Wiltshire, where in the description of Wilcot in the vale of Pewsey even the usually dry and formal words of the Domesday Book manage to show the place as pleasingly prosperous and fertile, for it had *ecclesia nova, domus optima et vinea bona* (a new church, an excellent house and a good vineyard).

Royal Power and Local Administration, 1066–1350

Most of the Norman and Angevin kings spent a good deal of time in Wessex. William I established the custom of keeping his Easter court at Winchester, and it was at Winchester that the royal treasury was housed. Winchester itself was transformed in the decades after the Conquest. The castle was built in the south-west corner of the city, many houses being swept away in the process. Soon after 1070 the Saxon royal palace in the centre of the city was enlarged to twice its former size, again involving the destruction of numerous houses and encroaching upon the precinct of the New Minster. In 1079 the Saxon cathedral, the old Minster of St Swithin, which had been completed barely a century before, was demolished and rebuilt on a scale much greater than anything previously seen in England. All this represents a conscious policy of impressing Norman power and domination upon the ancient capital. Other frequently used royal residences, castles and hunting lodges in Wessex included Clarendon Palace and the castles at Marlborough and Ludgershall in Wiltshire, Portchester in Hampshire, Corfe Castle in Dorset, and hunting lodges at Gillingham and Powerstock (Dorset), and Warnford and Romsey (Hants). The largest and most opulent of all was the great castle at New Windsor. At the time of the Conquest the Saxon settlement and royal palace was at Old Windsor three miles down the Thames. In about 1070 however a new castle was built upstream on the chalk hill which dominates the river valley and the surrounding countryside for several miles around; but it was not until 1110 that *The Anglo-Saxon Chronicle* records that Henry I 'held his court for the first time in the New Windsor'. This rapidly became one of the most important of all royal residences and the town grew up beside the castle to serve its needs during the urban expansion of the twelfth century (Bond 1970).

The great royal forests of the region also drew successive monarchs to Wessex. Two of the Conqueror's sons, William Rufus and Richard of Beorn, were killed while hunting in the New Forest, and both were buried in Winchester Cathedral. When Rufus died in 1087 it was to Winchester that his brother and successor Henry I came to secure the royal treasury, and it was from the nunnery at Romsey, where she had been brought up under the care of her aunt, that he took his English wife, Edith, the great-grand-daughter of Edmund Ironside, and thereby linked himself to the old royal house of Wessex. The rich Cluniac abbey at Reading was founded by Henry I in 1121 and became his favourite monastic establishment, and he was buried there in 1135. The great abbey church at Reading was consecrated in 1163 by Archbishop Thomas Becket in the presence of Henry II, one of the last occasions when the King and Archbishop met amicably.

Both Henry II and Henry III greatly enlarged the royal palace at Clarendon within the former royal forest, two miles east of Salisbury. This favourite residence of early medieval kings was not fortified, but was arranged as an opulent palace, intended for comfortable living, with a great hall, apartments for the King and the Queen, chapels, kitchens, stables and numerous other buildings. The palace covered an area of about 6 acres and consisted of a series of single storey buildings linked by walkways. The roofs were covered with wooden shingles and many of the floors with finely decorated tiles. Many twelfth- and thirteenth-century royal documents were

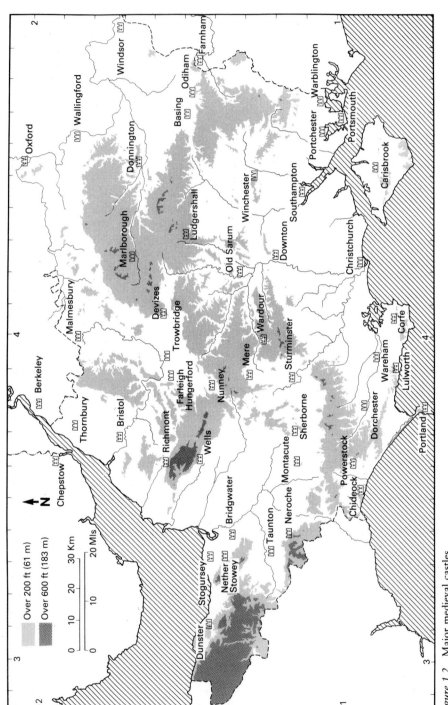

Figure 1.2 Major medieval castles

issued from Clarendon, including the Constitution of Clarendon (1164) and the Assize of Clarendon (1166), and there are frequent references to building work there. King John made much use of Clarendon throughout his reign and stayed there frequently, and royal accounts of the early thirteenth century frequently refer to the carriage of wine and provisions to Clarendon. Henry III ordered many alterations and enlargements, including work on the chapels and royal apartments, and woodwork, marble pillars, tiled floors and painted glass for the windows. He gave careful instructions as to how the chambers were to be decorated with wall-paintings, including the Wheel of Fortune, the Tree of Jesse, the four Evangelists and various other religious themes, and ordered that 'all these paintings are to be done with good and exquisite colours' (Salzman 1952: 37, 160, 385). Several documents of Edward I are dated from Clarendon, and in 1317 Edward II assembled a Parliament to meet there. In 1331 Edward III's eldest daughter, Isabella, was born at Clarendon; and following the victory at Poiters in 1356 King John of France and King David of Scotland were both brought as prisoners to Clarendon, each with a numerous retinue. In 1358–59 the great hall was rebuilt by Edward III in Chilmark stone. Clarendon Palace continued to be used by English monarchs throughout the Middle Ages, but with the disafforestation of the royal forest it was abandoned and fell into ruin, so that today only a fragment of walling remains above ground of what was one of the greatest of medieval royal palaces, and the site is overwhelmed by trees and undergrowth.

Wessex suffered more of the fighting, turmoil and destruction of the reign of Stephen (1135–54) than any other part of England. Revolts against Stephen began as early as 1136 when Baldwin de Redvers led an unsuccessful rising at Exeter, and from there fled to his lands in the Isle of Wight. From his stronghold at Carisbrooke Castle he organised a pirate fleet which preyed upon the commerce of Southampton, Portsmouth and the south coast. It is not necessary to follow in detail the chesslike war of castles and sieges, accompanied by local devastation, pillage and suffering which marked the course of the long struggle between Stephen and Henry I's daughter, the Empress Matilda; but since the main strongholds of Matilda's chief supporter, her half-brother Robert, Earl of Gloucester, lay at Bristol and Gloucester, and since the powerful magnate Roger Bishop of Salisbury, who also favoured Matilda, held the castles of Sherborne, Malmesbury, Salisbury and Devizes, a great deal of fighting inevitably occurred in Gloucestershire, Wiltshire, Berkshire, Somerset and Dorset. The battles and sieges in which first one side and then the other gained the ascendant, moved from one castle to another throughout the west country, accompanied by pillaging, burning of towns and massacres. The various Somerset castles which were besieged included Dunster in the west, Castle Cary which commanded the roads from Bristol and Bath to Sherborne and beyond, and Richmont Castle which dominated the area south of Bristol and controlled the road from Bristol over Mendip to Wells and the south-west. In Dorset there were sieges at Corfe Castle, Wareham, Sherborne and Powerstock near Bridport, in Wiltshire at Malmesbury, Marlborough and Trowbridge, and in Berkshire at Wallingford where the castle with its stone walls and water defences controlled the point at which the route to the west crossed the Thames. Pitched battles took place at Wilton in 1143 when the rich nunnery was plundered, and in 1141 at Winchester, where Stephen's brother, Henry of Blois, was Bishop. Stephen himself was imprisoned within the massive stone keep of Robert, Earl of Gloucester's castle at Bristol after his capture at Lincoln in February 1141, and was later released in exchange for the Earl of Gloucester who was captured at Stockbridge after Matilda's forces had been defeated in fierce fighting at Winchester in September 1141. The seven weeks' fighting in Winchester during August and September 1141 did great damage to the city which was sacked by the victorious army; Hyde Abbey was burnt to the ground and the nunnery severely damaged. Our detailed knowledge of the events of the long war and of the suffering which it caused owes much to the descriptions by two of the most famous of the medieval chroniclers of Wessex. A graphic account is given by the anonymous author of *Gesta Stephani*, who was possibly Robert of Lewes, Bishop of Bath (1136–66); he certainly knew Wessex well and describes the events which occurred in the region, and especially in the neighbourhood of Bath, in great detail. The *Gesta Stephani* provides abundant evidence of the horrors of the war and of the suffering endured by the people of Wessex as fortune favoured first one side and then the other, and as undisciplined mobs of soldiers roamed the countryside. The author was at first a staunch supporter of Stephen and did not conceal his hatred for the followers of Matilda, as in the following description of the misdeeds of the army which the Earl of Gloucester had assembled at Bristol in 1138:

> Bristol is almost the richest city of all in the country, receiving merchandise by sailing-ships from lands near and far. It lies in the most fertile part of England and is by its very situation the most strongly fortified of all its cities. . . .
> Into this they [the Earl of Gloucester and other leading supporters of Matilda] summoned a stream of horsemen and their dependants on foot, or to be more accurate a torrent of robbers and brigands, on so huge and extraordinary a scale that to those who beheld it, it seemed not only great and formidable but appalling beyond belief. For they appeared from different countries and districts and went there in all the greater numbers and all the greater joy inasmuch as they were allowed, under a rich lord and from a very strongly fortified castle, to commit against the most fertile part of England whatever seemed most pleasing to their eyes. . . .
> So the people of Bristol, unrestrained in the commission of every crime, wherever they heard of lands or property belonging to the king or his supporters rushed thither greedily and quickly like starving and

ravening dogs on a corpse that lies in their way; yokes of oxen, flocks of sheep, any object of desire that the eye beheld or the covetous heart yearned for they seized and carried off, sold and consumed. . . .

(Potter and Davis 1976: 57–63)

The other distinguished twelfth-century chronicler was William of Malmesbury who recorded many of the events of the Civil War in his *Historia Novella*. He was born in *c.* 1090 and spent most of his life as a monk at Malmesbury Abbey. His great history, the *Gesta Regum* which described events in England from the coming of the Saxons, was followed by the *Historia Novella* describing contemporary events, and ending in 1142 shortly before the author's death. Like the *Gesta Stephani*, William of Malmesbury's work is not an impartial account, for his patron was the Earl of Gloucester and his chronicle strongly supports the followers of Matilda (Potter 1955).

The long struggle finally ended in 1152 when Stephen failed to take the castle at Wallingford, one of the most important and strategic strongholds of the opposing party. He was at last persuaded to recognise Matilda's son Henry as his heir, by a treaty agreed at Winchester in November 1153.

One important effect of the Civil War upon Wessex was that it greatly weakened the link between Winchester and the monarchy, so that under Henry II Winchester effectively ceased to be a royal capital. The regular Easter crown-wearing at Winchester had been abandoned under Henry I, and the burning of the royal palace in 1141 ended the close tie between the city and the royal house. The royal treasury remained at Winchester for much of the twelfth century, but the place of the king in the city was largely taken by the bishop, especially under the powerful Henry of Blois, who greatly enlarged the bishop's palace at Wolvesey in the south-east corner of the city with its notable Great Hall, and also founded and endowed the Hospital of St Cross. The ancient importance and prestige of Winchester as the capital of Wessex was not completely forgotten, however, for it was to Winchester that Richard I returned in 1194 to seek a second coronation after the disasters he had suffered on his crusade. A great procession led the King from Winchester Castle to the Cathedral where, after a ceremonial bathing, Richard was again crowned as King of England. This was to be the last such occasion at Winchester, although English monarchs continued to visit the city, and during the 1230s Henry III commissioned Elias de Dereham to design and supervise the building of the Great Hall of the castle which remains one of the finest medieval halls in the country (Colvin 1963).

Under Henry II (1154–89) and his two sons Richard I (1189–99) and John (1199–1216) royal power was exercised through sheriffs who were the main local agents of the Crown for securing law and order. The administrative system of counties, each divided into hundreds and tithings, which the Normans had largely inherited from the late Saxon kings, remained the backbone of local government, although during the twelfth and thirteenth

31

centuries the system was far from tidy or precise, and there were many anomalies. Because of ancient tenurial bonds, some counties had detached portions lying within other counties, such as Kingswood and Minety, both of which were inside Gloucestershire but belonged to Wiltshire, or the group of lands many miles inside Berkshire, lying to the east of Reading, which included part of Wokingham and several adjacent villages, all of which were regarded as part of Wiltshire. Holwell in the Blackmore Vale of Dorset was a detached part of Somerset, and there were similar discrepancies and confusions in the hundred boundaries. For example, a group of Glastonbury Abbey manors in south Wiltshire formed the hundred of Damerham, but a further group of Glastonbury manors in the north-west of the county became known as North Damerham and were treated as a hundred. Several hundreds had detached portions within other hundreds, while the hundreds themselves varied enormously in size. Many boroughs, liberties and townships claimed to be outside the system altogether, like the area around Bristol Castle, or the towns of Devizes and Marlborough which each came under the authority of the keeper of the royal castles. The great growth in the number of boroughs during the thirteenth century also helped to complicate the system further.

Under Henry I sheriffs were increasingly drawn from the ranks of royal servants rather than from the great barons, although the process of change was slow and received a great setback during the reign of Stephen. By 1100 the king's official, William Pont de l'Arche, who was later to be Chamberlain of the Treasury, was Sheriff of Wiltshire and Hampshire. From 1160 to 1179 the Wiltshire sheriff was Richard the Clerk who was also one of the itinerant royal justices. Robert Maudit who was Sheriff of Wiltshire from 1178 to 1187 was also a royal official, but by 1199 the office had passed into the hands of the great magnate William Longspee who held it until his death in 1226. He was succeeded by his wife, Ela, who remained in the office until 1232 when she entered the nunnery which she had herself founded at Lacock. For much of the Middle Ages Somerset and Dorset had a joint sheriff, and so did Berkshire and Oxfordshire (*VCH Wilts* V, 1957: 5–14).

The first general instructions to the royal itinerant justices were issued from the royal palace at Clarendon in 1166, laying down the manner in which felons indicted by the hundred juries should be brought by the sheriffs before the justices. The increase in royal administration and royal justice during the twelfth and thirteenth centuries brought more and more importance to the office of the sheriff, and ever more various tasks concerning the defence of the realm, the collection of royal revenues and taxes, the administration of justice, the punishment of offenders, the supervision of royal property, and from the late thirteenth century onwards the oversight of parliamentary elections. Some idea of the varied nature of the sheriff's duties can be seen from the following examples. In 1213 the Sheriff of Dorset was ordered to come to Portsmouth with all haste bringing with him hay, oats and provisions for the fleet and ropes for the military engines. He was also ordered to command to 'be made at

Bridport day and night cordage great and small for ships', and there is interesting reference to the existence of rope-making there at that time. In 1215 the Sheriff of Berkshire was ordered to bring hogs and grain for the provisioning of the royal castle at Wallingford. In 1221 the Sheriff of Hampshire was ordered to have repaired the hall, chamber and cellar of the castle at Winchester and to build an oven there. The Sheriff of Berkshire was ordered to repair the gaol in Wallingford Castle. In 1223 the Sheriff of Dorset was ordered to obtain timber for repairing the hall of the king's castle at Sherborne. In 1225 the Hampshire sheriff was to cause the image of St Christopher with Christ in his arms and the image of St Edward the King to be painted in the Queen's Chapel at Winchester (Morris 1927).

The litigation in the courts might involve a trial before royal justices sitting with sworn juries of local men, or it could involve judicial combat. In Wiltshire in 1199 a victorious champion felled his adversary, and then complained that a certain Robert Block came and seized the fallen man's weapon and set about the winner. This was denied by the knights who had been appointed to supervise the combat. The deficiencies of trial by jury were exposed in Hampshire in 1248 when a local jury refused to convict some highway robbers who had forcibly taken the goods of two Brabant merchants at Alton on the road between Southampton and Winchester (Cam 1930: 31).

The sort of cases which came before the King's justices can be seen from the Wiltshire court meeting at Wilton in 1249. The majority of cases concerned disputes over land or the inheritance of land; others concerned theft, violence, rape or personal injury. Typical is the following case of sheep-stealing and its sequel at Downton:

> Roger de Fonte came to the sheep pen of the bishop of Winchester, and there he trussed up a sheep and tried to carry it away by stealth. Walter the bishop's shepherd, seeing this, chased him to try to take the sheep from him. Roger struck Walter with a staff and Walter retaliated, striking Roger so that he died at once. . . . The jurors say that Roger was a thief and went there to steal the sheep. Walter seeing him chased him and raised the hue and Roger, fearing the hue, ran upon Walter and struck him. Walter, in defence, struck Roger so that he killed him but not by felony, rather in self defence. So Walter is acquitted . . .
>
> (Meekings 1961)

It is not necessary here to enter into details of the struggles between the King and barons during the thirteenth century, nor to describe the gradual development of Parliaments and the machinery of national and local governments, but the great castles of Wessex, Windsor and Wallingford, Corfe, Devizes, Marlborough, Bristol and many others were naturally key factors in many of the wars and civil disturbances of the period. King John made great use of the castles at Corfe, Bristol and Devizes, both as prisons and as strongholds in the course of his last conflicts with his barons and during the French invasion of England. Bristol Castle was used by John for the life-long detention of the tragic figure, Princess Eleanor, sister of John's nephew Arthur of Brittany who was brutally murdered in 1203. Eleanor remained a prisoner until her death in 1241, when her body was taken for burial to the nunnery at Amesbury. Magna Carta was signed at Runnymede, just down the Thames from Windsor Castle on 17 June 1215; it was in Devizes Castle that Henry III's powerful justiciar, Hubert de Burgh, was imprisoned after his overthrow in 1232, a movement led by the influential Bishop of Winchester, Peter des Roches (Bishop, 1205–38), who had crowned Henry III in 1216; and it was at Marlborough Castle in 1267 that Henry III and the Lord Edward, the future Edward I, held the great council which issued the Statute of Marlborough binding the King to significant changes in the government of the realm. But these and numerous other well-known events, involving the magnates and bishops, castles and towns of Wessex, are part of national rather than of regional history. Important though they were, it was the slow procession of the agricultural year, the painful progress of bringing new land under cultivation and maintaining the fertility of the soil, the development of new towns, markets and fairs and the expansion of trades and industries which were of much greater consequence to most of the people of Wessex, and it is these aspects of the history of the region which must now be considered.

Chapter 2

Economic Life, Society and the Church, 1066–1350

Farming

In spite of wars and civil strife, the period between the Conquest and the Black Death was one of great expansion in Wessex. The area of cultivated land was enlarged, agricultural production was increased, population rose, settlements were extended, old towns developed and new towns were founded, while foreign trade and internal commerce increased substantially.

Much of Wessex was dominated by great estates, by the lands of the Crown, of the bishoprics of Winchester, Salisbury and Wells, and of the great monastic houses, and most of the documentary evidence for farming and other aspects of rural life in this period comes from the records of such estates, especially from the fine collections of the Bishops of Winchester and of the Abbots of Glastonbury. These sources are naturally biased towards the sort of farming conducted on the great estates, and tell us less about the much larger number of peasant farmers, but they do give a detailed picture of rural life and society in the region during the early Middle Ages. By the thirteenth century when abundant documentary evidence becomes available, common arable fields were already well established over most of the chalklands, and were to be found in many parts of the clay vales. Most of the villages in the valleys of the chalk downs of Dorset, Hampshire, Wiltshire and Berkshire had two-field systems for farming their arable land so that half the land was left untilled each year to be grazed by the cattle and to recover its fertility. Some of the more fertile manors along the Vale of the White Horse and in the valley of the Salisbury Avon had three-field systems, whereby one third of the arable land lay fallow each year. The three-field system was also common in some of the rich claylands, such as in north and west Dorset, although here, as in many parts of the claylands and in the hilly country of west Somerset, there were large numbers of dairy and stock-raising farms with few arable fields and with most of the land already divided and enclosed by hedges into small fields (Miller and Hatcher 1978: 87–90; *VCH Wilts* IV, 14–15). Some richer land near the villages which could conveniently be dressed with dung from the

Plate 2.1 Medieval fields on the island of Portland, Dorset. The most notable survival of a medieval field system in the region, the common fields still cover some 150 acres and show better than anywhere else in Wessex what a medieval arable landscape was like. On the royal manor of Portland the custom of partible inheritance continued until the early twentieth century, so that many people had rights in the fields and this effectively prevented any enclosure.

farmsteads was ploughed every year, like the two acres at Potterne near Devizes which were described in 1176 as 'cultivated each year' ('*excoluntor singulis annis*').

The process which started long before the Norman Conquest and continued through the Middle Ages by which large areas of forest, marshland and heath in north and west Wiltshire, south-east Somerset, east Berkshire, west Dorset and in other parts were slowly claimed for agriculture is still clearly marked in the landscape. Many of the scattered farmsteads, joined by narrow winding lanes between thick hedge-banks and surrounded by small irregular fields were no doubt in existence long before the coming of the Normans, although precise evidence for this is rare. At Povington in the parish of Tyneham on the Dorset coast a demesne farm worked by eight serfs together with smaller tenements worked by four villeins and five bordars are recorded in Domesday Book. Here, on the edge of the heathland, there was still one large farm in the early nineteenth century, four smaller farms of between 40 and 70 acres, and eight or nine smallholdings of between 5 and 15 acres. Professor W. G. Hoskins has suggested that here we have the demesne farm of Domesday Book, the four holdings of the villeins and the smallholdings of the bordars, the latter slightly increased in number by medieval encroachments upon the surrounding heathland. This means that the farms were in existence by 1086, and probably for long before that (Hoskins and Stamp 1953).

In the Marshwood Vale of west Dorset and in the north of the county in the Blackmore Vale many areas are without nucleated settlements, but isolated farms are set amongst small irregular fields with massive winding hedges, and many of the farm names end in 'hay', meaning enclosure, and incorporate a pre- or immediate post-Conquest personal name, such as in Bluntshay, Denhay, Swinhay, Manshay, Gummershay and many others. Similarly Professor Barry Cunliffe and others have described the expansion of the original arable lands of Chalton in east Hampshire by the creation, probably during the twelfth and thirteenth centuries, of colonist holdings around the eastern and southern fringes of the fields of the village. Some of these holdings created out of the waste and woodland have names such as Woodhouse, Woodhouse Ashes and Woodcroft which vividly suggest the process of forest clearance which preceded their creation (Taylor 1970: 68–70, 98–100; Cunliffe 1972: 1–12; Addyman and Leigh 1972: 1–25).

In clayland or hilly areas of scattered hamlets and isolated farmsteads, where dairying, stock-raising and pasture-farming predominated, manorial control was generally weak, and few detailed documentary sources survive, whereas in the nucleated villages of the chalklands, where corn-growing was the main object of farming, and where the continuous programme of work on the arable fields demanded a large and disciplined labour force, manorial control was much stronger and documentation is more abundant.

Inevitably a detailed picture of early medieval life and society in any part of the region must rely very heavily upon the documentary evidence which survives from the great monastic houses, bishoprics and royal estates, but there is no reason to suppose that the picture we get of the manor of Fontmell, on the Dorset chalklands near Shaftesbury, from two surveys of *c.* 1135 and *c.* 1175 is in any way untypical. The manor was part of the extensive lands of the wealthy nunnery at Shaftesbury, and the Survey of *c.* 1135 shows that Fontmell was a populous village with sixty-five tenants and four mills. Twenty-two villeins each held a yardland of probably some 40 acres, and nineteen others held half a yardland each; the rest of the community were cottagers with small amounts of land. Labour services and other dues required from the tenants are set out very clearly. Each villein did three days' work a week, paid 7½*d.* per annum in rent, ploughed an acre and a half on the nuns' demesne, harrowed an acre, and in return for wood to repair his house paid 10*d.* and a measure of corn. A generation later in *c.* 1175 the second survey reveals several important changes. The population had increased and more land had been brought under cultivation. There were now eighty tenants, twenty-eight with a yardland and twenty-seven with a half-yardland, besides the cottagers; the four mills remained unchanged. The most significant difference however was that most of the tenants' labour services had been commuted for money payments. Rents of 1s. 3d. 2s. 0d. or 2s. 6d. were now being paid, in addition to some work at harvest and some duties in carrying produce to Shaftesbury or to nearby markets. The low level of prices for agricultural produce in the mid-twelfth century, as well as the unfavourable and unstable conditions created by political anarchy and Civil War, meant that many landowners retreated from active involvement in farming and preferred instead to lease their demesnes and take a money rental instead of labour services from their tenants (Stenton 1952: 139–41).

A custumal of Glastonbury Abbey lands in 1189 shows that on the Wiltshire estates of the abbey more than a dozen leases of demesne land had been made, at Nettleton, Kington St Michael, Damerham, Winterbourne Monkton, Christian Malford, Grittleton and elsewhere. Many of these had been granted during the abbacy of Henry of Blois (1126–71) who was also Bishop of Winchester, and who, as the brother of King Stephen, was himself very actively involved in the Civil War. The account rolls of the bishopric of Winchester reveal the same situation; for example at Downton in 1208, leases of the former demesne lands had been granted to thirteen tenants (*VCH Wilts* IV: 7–8). This process was to be reversed in the more prosperous farming conditions of the early thirteenth century, as population expanded and prices rose, and many of the great estates took their demesnes into their own hands once more and revived the old labour services. Thus the Glastonbury Abbey lands leased out in 1189 were shown to be in the abbots' hands again in a mid thirteenth-century custumal and an early thirteenth-century rent roll of the Bishops of Winchester shows that on their widespread estates in Hampshire and Wiltshire lands and tenements which had formerly been leased out for a money rent were now being brought back into the demesnes and labour services were once again being imposed upon the tenants instead of the money rent which had earlier replaced work service (Hall 1903; Holt 1964; Titow 1969). This resumption of farms, reimposition of labour services and the renewed farming of demesne lands by estate owners was widespread throughout the region during the early decades of the thirteenth century, as a response to the changed conditions and increasing profits to be derived from agricultural produce. The evidence for the rise in the price of agricultural produce during the thirteenth century can be seen in Table 2, in the series of accounts from the lands of the Bishops of Winchester where increases of the following order are recorded:

Table 2   Price increases, 1208–1349

Commodity	Percentage increase in price
Wheat	58
Wool	63
Oats	64
Oxen	67
Barley	69
Salt	92

(Titow 1972)

The inflationary leap of prices at the opening of the thirteenth century and the longer upward movement continuing into the first quarter of the fourteenth century had far reaching consequences. Landlords turned from leasing to direct farming and to producing for the market on a grand scale. Peasants were given opportunities for enrichment by the sale of surplus produce. The rapid growth of a market economy, and of internal trade in agricultural produce is as characteristic of the central Middle Ages as are the increase in people and the expansion of land under cultivation.

Evidence of the prosperity and profitability of demesne farming during the thirteenth century survives in the landscape in the great barns which were built by some of the monastic houses to store their produce. At Great Coxwell the magnificent thirteenth-century barn which belonged to Beaulieu Abbey remains as impressive evidence of monastic wealth. The barn is 152 feet long and 51 feet high with a noble roof covered with stone tiles. The Great Coxwell barn uses an elaborate and sophisticated system of roof construction, and is clearly the work of highly skilled carpenters. The dating of the barn to the first half of the thirteenth century has been confirmed by radio-carbon tests on the massive roof timbers. The grange at Great Coxwell served as the centre for the extensive Beaulieu estates in the Faringdon region including Faringdon itself, Great and Little Coxwell, Wick, Inglesham, Little Faringdon and Shilton. The huge barn was used to store the produce of the monks' estates before it was taken to local markets or on the long journey to Beaulieu. The permanent staff on the grange at Great Coxwell included eight ploughmen, two carters, a hayward, forester, baker, cheese-maker, porter, swineherd, a cook and his boy, cowherd and three shepherds (Horn and Born 1965).

Equally remarkable, although slightly later in date, is the barn at Tisbury, one of the granges belonging to the wealthy nunnery at Shaftesbury. The Tisbury barn is the largest in England, nearly 200 feet long with an immense thatched roof. Other surviving barns of Shaftesbury Abbey include those at Bradford-on-Avon and Kelston near Bath, while fine monastic barns remain at Glastonbury, Abbotsbury, Titchfield, Haseley in the parish of Arreton on the

Isle of Wight and at St Leonards near Bucklers Hard in Hampshire where the remains of the barn, part of another grange of Beaulieu, date from the first half of the thirteenth century. The St Leonards barn, of which only a fragment survives, was 216 feet long; the largest of all was the barn at Cholsey belonging to Reading Abbey: this was 303 feet long, and survived until 1815.

On the estates of the bishopric of Winchester the detailed account rolls of the thirteenth century record recurrent expenditure upon farm buildings of all sorts, barns, sheep-houses, ox-stalls and dairies, and illustrate the concern of landowners to benefit from this period of rising prices and to produce the maximum profits from their estates. For example when a new area of 47 acres in the bishop's manor of Downton was cleared and brought into arable cultivation in the years *c.* 1250–53, the account rolls show expenditure on making and fencing a farmyard and providing it with a ditch and wooden gates, on erecting buildings in the yard including an ox-shed with stalls for the oxen, a sheep-house and a large barn, and money was also spent on wooden ploughs with iron shares and coulters, harrows, carts, wheels, pickaxes and shovels (*VCH Wilts* IV, 1959: 11–13).

The rising prices of the thirteenth century and the consequent profit-conscious approach to demesne land also saw numerous improvements in

---

Plate 2.2   Great Coxwell barn, near Faringdon. This huge thirteenth-century barn was at the centre of the estates around Faringdon given by King John to the Cistercian monks of Beaulieu Abbey in Hampshire. The stone-built barn, roofed with stone slates, is 152 ft long and 51 ft high; within the barn a dramatic series of wooden pillars resting on stone piers supports the roof and divides the interior into a nave and side aisles like a great cathedral. This impressive building, like the numerous other abbey barns in the Wessex region, is a remarkable witness to the immense wealth and widespread estates of the medieval monastic houses.

farming and attempts to increase productivity, as well as a centralisation of estate management and manorial control. At Glastonbury under the notable Abbot Michael of Amesbury (1235–52) the area of arable land was extended, land was enclosed and reclaimed from the sea and from the marsh, new barns, sheep houses, dairies and dovecotes were constructed and stock was increased until there were some 1,400 cattle and over 7,000 sheep (Knowles 1948: 44–6). The vast estates spread over Somerset, Dorset, Wiltshire and beyond were closely controlled from Glastonbury, with the bailiffs on each manor rendering detailed accounts of farming operations, expenses and profits. On the Glastonbury manors of Buckland Newton and Sturminster Newton in Dorset for example, arable farming concentrated on the production of wheat which was sent to Glastonbury for consumption by the monks. Sheep, cattle and pigs were also regularly sent from the Dorset estates to Glastonbury, and sheep flocks were moved and interchanged between manors in a complex system, some sheep being sent from Dorset to Somerset estates of the Abbey such as Butleigh or Pilton, other sheep flocks coming to Buckland Newton from the Wiltshire manors of Damerham where there was a large wool store.

On the Bishop of Winchester's estates during the thirteenth century attempts were made to improve the fertility and productivity of the land by the use of marl and by the introduction of legumes into crop rotations. The proportion of arable under legumes grew from less than 1 per cent in 1208 to over 8 per cent in 1345, while the account rolls show that the bishop and his very large household were supplied by his manors with grain, pigs, fowls, cheese, eggs, fish, eels and cider. These were consumed either at his manor houses, Marwell, High Clere, Bishop's Waltham, Downton, Farnham and elsewhere, or at his palace at Wolvesey to which most of the produce was sent, even the bacon which had been cured at his centralised plant at Bishop's Waltham (Holt 1964).

From the ploughing services demanded from villeins on some of the monastic estates, it is clear that strenuous efforts were made during the period of high prices for agricultural produce in the thirteenth century to increase yields. During the late twelfth century the practice of ploughing the demesne lands three times before sowing was introduced on some of the Malmesbury Abbey estates and on those of Glastonbury. Attempts to conserve and increase the fertility of the soil explain the references in the thirteenth-century custumal of the Bishop of Winchester's manor of Downton to the fact that each virgator had to carry from 13 to 25 loads of dung onto the demesne lands each year, while cottars had to spread up to 50 loads each. Similar demands were made on the tenants of the nunnery at Lacock. References are also found to marl and marl-pits on the Brendon Hills in west Somerset, and to the use of marl as a dressing at Bratton, East Knoyle, Monkton Deverill, Downton and elsewhere (*VCH Wilts* IV: 12–15). At Downton where a new piece of arable ground was cultivated in 1250–53 the account rolls for 1252 refer to five men with ten horses being employed for 43 days in marling the new land at $1\frac{1}{2}d$. per day each; 2,040 heaps of marl were spread at a cost of 2½*d.* per heap, and three men were paid for 83 days' work in digging marl at 3½*d.* per day.

The main crops grown in the common arable fields were wheat, the autumn sown crop, and barley and oats which were sown in the spring either single or mixed together as 'dredge' or 'drage' corn. Very little rye was grown, but some peas and beans were cultivated in parts of the region, especially in richer lands like those in south Somerset around Martock, or in north and west Wiltshire around Wanborough and Trowbridge (*VCH Wilts* IV: 16). The importance of corn on the chalklands and the fact that this was essentially a crop grown for the market can be seen from the grain accounts of the Bishop of Winchester which begin in 1208. From 50 to 90 per cent of the wheat grown was sold, and from 30 to 60 per cent of the barley. The account book of Beaulieu Abbey near Southampton for the year 1270 also shows that the corn produced on its granges throughout Hampshire and Wiltshire was normally sold and the money sent to Beaulieu. The totals and proportions of the various crops grown on the granges were as follows:

Table 3   Corn production on the Beaulieu Abbey granges, 1270

	Wheat	Barley	Oats	Rye	Vetch	Peas	Beans
Total in quarters	2,898	712	3,281	224	218	127	97
Percentage	38	9	44	3	3	2	1

The production of the Beaulieu granges is unusual in the high proportion of oats grown, much of it on the poorer lands formerly within the New Forest, and the correspondingly small proportion of barley (Hockey 1974).

A similar picture emerges from the detailed late thirteenth-century accounts of a layman, Adam de Stratton, who possessed a group of manors in Berkshire and Wiltshire. The bulk of the income from his estates came from the sale of produce which accounted for 53 per cent of the total; most of this was grain. Only 13 per cent of the income came from wool sales and the rest came from rents. Services rendered by the tenants included work on the demesnes and carriage of corn and wool to market (Farr 1959).

By the end of the thirteenth century there were signs that the boom years of demesne farming were coming to an end. Productivity and profits were falling, and several years witnessed harvest failures and famines. Poor harvests were experienced in 1272, 1277, 1283, 1292, 1311 and especially in 1315–18 and 1321. The consequences of this decline in the profitability of demesne farming will be considered in the next chapter (Postan 1966: 556–9; Titow 1969: 52–4; Titow 1972: 12–33).

One consequence of the thirteenth-century emphasis upon demesne pro-duction for the market, and upon centralised control and storage was that on many manors services in carrying goods formed an important part of tenants' obligations. The duties of Robert Tac, a tenant of the Glastonbury Abbey manor of Burton in the north Dorset parish of Marnhull, are set out in the detailed custumnal of 1250; in addition to his annual rent of 6s. 0d. for a virgate tenement of about 40 acres, he was bound to work on the demesne for several days each week, and 'he ought for the whole year to carry the lord's corn with his beast as well from Niweton [Sturminster Newton] as from Burton to Glastonbury or elsewhere at the lord's will'. Glastonbury was more than twenty miles distant, so this service was no light task. Perhaps as a consolation the custumal goes on to specify the tenant's rights, including a dinner to be provided by the abbot on Christmas Day, 'the lord to find him food on Christmas Day, to wit bread, cheese, pottage, and two dishes of meat'. The tenant, however, 'shall take with him a plate, mug and napkin if he wishes to eat off a cloth, and he shall bring a faggot of brushwood to cook his food, unless he would have it raw' (Bettey 1974: 124).

A survey of Littleton in Hampshire in 1265/66, a manor which belonged to the Abbey of St Peter in Gloucester, shows the typical labour service demanded of a tenant holding a virgate of land. Mathias of Schottesdene paid 5s. 0d. per annum in rent for his house and land, he had to plough twice a year on the demesne lands, harrow the demesne for the Lent sowing until all the corn was sown, weed the corn for three days, make and carry hay on the demesne, plant beans, help to wash and shear the demesne sheep, reap $2\frac{1}{2}$ acres of demesne corn each week in autumn, help carry and thrash the demesne corn, gather nuts for half a day, and finally carry the demesne produce to the markets at Andover or Ludgershall (Titow 1969: 149).

On the manors of Durrington and Combe Bisset in Wiltshire tenants had to carry produce to markets all over Wiltshire, and on the Glastonbury Abbey manor of Christian Malford the tenants were obliged to take three loads of grain each year for sale to Bristol, a distance of some twenty-five miles. Such services are additional evidence of the importance of grain crops on these chalkland manors, and of the practice of selling a substantial proportion of each year's crop.

To produce good corn crops on the thin chalkland soils the fertility provided by the sheep-fold was essential, and very large common flocks were accordingly kept, as much for their dung as for their wool. By the thirteenth century when detailed figures are available enormous sheep flocks were being kept throughout the chalklands. Many demesne flocks contained more than 1,000 sheep and the common flocks kept by the tenants were even larger. The importance of sheep in the farming economy of Wiltshire can be seen from the figures in Table 4 taken from an assessment roll drawn up in 1225 to aid the collection of a tax on moveable property in south-west Wiltshire (*VCH Wilts* IV: 28).

On the lands of the great estates such as those of the bishopric of Winchester or of the great abbeys, sheep flocks were subject to a system of

Table 4   Sheep flocks on some Wiltshire Manors

Manor	Total number of tenants	Tenants owning sheep	Number of sheep owned by tenants
Bower Chalke	40	33	851
Alvediston	28	20	510
Bridmore	16	16	669
Tisbury	87	33	853
West Hatch	21	3	233
Donhead	137	45	1,491
Semley	37	5	108
Dinton	42	12	324
Teffont Magna	37	24	419
Damerham	122	61	1,265
Martin	85	77	2,585

centralised control, and sheep were regularly moved between different manors on the estate. As early as 1208 the Bishop of Winchester's flocks were being improved by the introduction of long-woolled Lincolnshire rams, and later in the thirteenth century wool from all the Bishop's manors was collected at the Bishop's Palace at Wolvesey in Winchester for sale. Wool from the granges at Faringdon and Great Coxwell in Berkshire was conveyed back to the wool store or *Bergerie* at Beaulieu where it was washed, graded and packed for the market. From the *Bergerie* the large flocks in all the distant granges, some over fifty miles from the abbey, were controlled and managed (Hockey 1974). The sheep provided lambs, mutton, wool, milk and, above all, dung for the cornlands; without the richness imparted to the thin chalkland soils by the folds of sheep, corn crops would have been very poor.

The Cistercian Abbey of Kingswood was involved in sheep-farming and wool-production on a large scale during the thirteenth century, and was noted for the quality of its wool. Wool was eagerly bought from Kingswood by merchants from Italy and the Low Countries, and there was a scandal in 1214 when the lay-brothers at the Abbey were accused of buying wool from elsewhere to sell again at as high a price as Kingswood demesne produce. At Quarr Abbey, the Cistercian foundation on the Isle of Wight, the sheep flocks were of great importance and were valued for their dung, their milk and their wool. There are thirteenth-century references from Quarr to the ewe flocks being kept at night in 'Bercaries' constructed of stone, and to the excellence of the cheese produced. In *c.* 1280 Robert Carpenter, describing the de Insula estates on the Island, wrote that twenty-five ewes on a good pasture would produce as much cheese as four cows, and that cheesemaking lasted from Easter to Michaelmas. Wool from the Quarr flocks was sold to Italian merchants; it was collected in the wool-store at the grange of Claybrook before being sent from Medina to Southampton for shipment (Hockey 1970).

Behind the farming changes of the thirteenth century lay a massive growth in population. Some idea of this increase in population and in wealth in the region can be gained from various sources. A comparison of the tax assessments of 1225 and 1334 reckoned in terms of shillings per square mile in Table 5 shows the pattern of growth in wealth in all the counties:

Table 5   Tax assessments in 1225 and 1334

County	Assessment per sq. mile in 1225	Assessment per sq. mile in 1334
Berkshire	17.0	27.8
Dorset	8.1	16.5
Hampshire	9.3	15.1
Somerset	7.5	16.0
Wiltshire	11.4	22.7

(Donkin 1976: 78–9)

The scattered evidence of court rolls, manorial surveys and custumals from all over the region also shows the same trend of rising population from the late twelfth century onwards, and of the consequent extension of settlements and of the cultivated area (*VCH Wilts* IV: 9–11). But the most impressive and definite evidence of population growth comes from the Bishop of Winchester's large manor of Taunton Deane. In this manor a fine of one penny per annum was levied on each male over the age of twelve years, and the record of these fines survives, covering the years 1209 to 1311. In 1209 there were 612 males in the manor while by 1311 the number had grown to 1,448, thus representing an annual growth in population of 0.85 per cent (Titow 1961). It was this increase in population and the growing demand for food which stimulated both the resumption of demesne farming which has already been described and the renewed attack on woodland, waste, moorland and marsh in an effort to bring more land under cultivation. This thirteenth-century extension of arable and pasture land throughout the region has had a profound effect upon the Wessex landscape.

Drainage

The largest single area which was available for reclamation and improvement was the Somerset Levels, where many thousands of acres of marsh and swamp produced only fish, wild-fowl, rough pasture and peat. It was on some of the 'islands' of slightly higher land in these marshes that early monks found ideally secluded sites such as Athelney and Muchelney for the establishment of their monasteries, just as King Alfred had found there a secure hiding place and refuge from the Danes.

By the thirteenth century the greater part of the Levels was controlled by the Dean and Chapter of Wells, and by the monks of Glastonbury, Athelney and Muchelney, and through their drainage schemes the first really significant improvements were made in these potentially rich and fertile lands. The 'island' of Sowy which contained the villages of Middlezoy, Othery and Westonzoyland, was extended and enlarged by ditching and draining so that by about 1240 nearly a thousand acres had been added to the productive land. At the same time drainage work and sea-walls secured much land along the north Somerset coast around Portbury and Wraxall and further south at Berrow, South Brent and Lympsham from regular inundation by the sea (Williams 1970: 25–75; Helm 1949). Major drainage work and land reclamation was also carried out during the thirteenth century by the Abbey of Malmesbury in the low-lying lands of the Avon valley in north Wiltshire, especially under the energetic leadership of William of Colerne (Abbot 1260–96) (*VCH Wilts* IV, 1959: 11).

Assarts and the Extension of Cultivation

Throughout the region during the thirteenth century land was being cleared and brought under the plough. Among the commonest landscape features of the chalklands of Wessex are the *strip lynchets*, the terraces by which cultivation was extended up the hillsides thereby enabling much more land to be ploughed. Whole series of such terraces survive right across the chalklands, for example at Maiden Newton, Bincombe, Worth Matravers in Dorset, Mere, Combe Bisset and all around the Deverills in Wiltshire, along the vale of the White Horse in Berkshire, and in many other places. These terraces are very difficult to date, but it is clear that the great labour involved in constructing them would not have been undertaken without a considerable pressure on the available arable and an increased demand for food; and many were made during the population explosion of the thirteenth century. Evidence of thirteenth-century land hunger is also seen in the *assarts* or clearance of forest and waste to create small enclosed arable fields which are to be found throughout the region. The fields resulting from the long process of forest clearance or from the reclamation of waste, moorland marsh and heath, can be recognised by their irregular shape, small size and substantial hedges; many thousands of acres of such fields survive in the landscape. Their irregular shape reminds us of the way in which they were laboriously hacked out of thick woodland and slowly cleared of tree-stumps, stones and other obstacles to the plough. Other assart fields, more regular in shape, were formed in the Somerset levels and along the coast by the process of drainage and by the construction of sea-defences. Documentary evidence is not lacking for this long process of assarting. At Whiteparish in south-east Wiltshire, which lay within the royal forest of Melchet, the Forest Eyres or lists of fines for making assarts show a continuing process of encroachment upon woodland and waste, with constant references to small enclosures being hacked out of the forest. These consist of little fields, seldom more than two or three acres in extent, each enclosed by a bank and hedge. Nearly 1,000 acres were cleared on the Bishop of Winchester's manor of Wargrave in Berkshire during the first half of the thirteenth century, and a further 680 acres between 1256 and 1306 (Titow 1962: 8). Waverley Abbey in Surrey paid £882 during the period 1171–81 for encroachments in the royal forest, while Stanley Abbey in Wiltshire paid £667 for similar encroachments in the royal forest of Chippenham during 1203–4. All classes of medieval society were engaged in this slow process of land reclamation, and only the extent of the land involved distinguishes the rich assarter from the poor. For example in 1314 Ingelram de Berenger, who was steward of the royal forest of Blackmore in Dorset, was granted permission to 'reduce to cultivation' 184½ acres of land in Hermitage parish within the royal forest; in 1269 the Abbot of Abbotsbury held 30 acres of recently enclosed land at Hilton; while at the bottom of the social ladder, the Court Rolls of the royal manor of Gillingham record in 1302 that 'Walter atte Wodeseyned gives to the Lady Queen twelve pence for a perch and a half encroachment opposite his gate, paying for rent due a penny a year'. In many parts of Somerset and Dorset the number of farm, field and place names ending in 'ley' or 'leigh' (meaning a woodland clearance) or 'hay' (meaning an enclosure), is itself a reminder of this origin (Taylor 1967: 86–90; and 1970: 96–100).

Towns and Trade

The prosperity and growth which characterised the later-twelfth and much of the thirteenth century, fuelled by increasing population and rising prices, gave rise to the far-reaching changes in rural society, and also led to the rapid expansion of towns, to the establishment of numerous new urban centres, new markets and fairs, and to the growth of industries, trade and commerce. This in turn greatly affected the network of communications within the region and was responsible for the building of new bridges, the opening of new routes and the development of new ports and harbours.

There are substantial difficulties in any attempt to measure the growth in the number of towns, because of the different definitions of a town which have been used for different purposes, and this is especially acute in the west country where many towns remained small and were distinguished from surrounding villages only by the possession of a weekly market and perhaps by a slightly

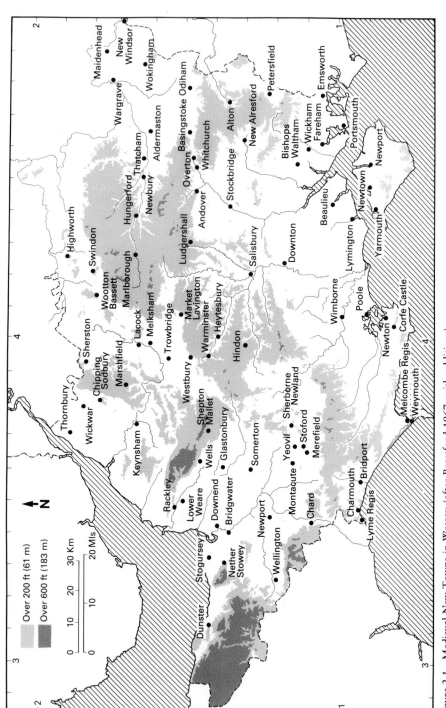

Figure 2.1 Medieval New Towns in Wessex (after Beresford 1967, with additions)

greater range of crafts and services. But some indication of the growth which had taken place can be seen by comparing the number of boroughs listed in the Domesday Survey of 1086 with the list of places which possessed burgage tenure ('the lowest common denominator of boroughs') by the mid-fourteenth

Table 6   Medieval boroughs

Domesday boroughs	*Additional boroughs listed by mid-14th century*	
Berkshire		
Abingdon	Aldermaston	Lambourn
Old Windsor	Bray	Newbury
Reading	Cookham	Thatcham
Wallingford	Faringdon	Wargrave
	Hungerford	Windsor
Dorset		
Bridport	Blandford	Newton (in Purbeck)
Dorchester	Charmouth	Poole
Shaftesbury	Corfe Castle	Sherborne Newland
Wareham	Lyme Regis	Weymouth
Wimborne Minster	Melcombe Regis	Whitechurch Canonicorum
South Gloucestershire (now Avon)		
Bristol	Chipping Sodbury	Thornbury
	Marshfield	Wickwar
Hampshire		
Portchester	Alresford	Overton
Southampton	Alton	Petersfield
Winchester	Andover	Portsmouth
	Basingstoke	Romsey
	Fareham	Stockbridge
	Lymington	Twynham (Christchurch)
	Newport	Whitchurch
	Newton (Burghclere)	Yarmouth
	Newton (Franchville)	
Somerset		
Axbridge	Bridgwater	Somerton
Bath	Chard	Stoford
Bruton	Downend	Stogursey
Ilchester	Dunster	Templemead
Langport	Merryfield	Watchet
Milborne Port	Milverton	Weare
Taunton	Montacute	Wellington
	Nether Stowey	Wells
	Newport (North Curry)	Wiveliscombe
	Rackley	Yeovil
	Redcliff	

(continued overleaf)

Table 6   cont.

Domesday boroughs	Additional boroughs listed by mid-14th century	
Wiltshire		
Bedwyn	Amesbury	Ludgershall
Bradford-on-Avon	Chippenham	Marlborough
Calne	Cricklade	Mere
Malmesbury	Devizes	Salisbury
Old Sarum	Downton	Sherston
Tilshead	Heytesbury	Trowbridge
Warminster	Highworth	Westbury
Wilton	Hindon	Wootton Bassett
	Lacock	

century, compiled by M. W. Beresford and H. P. R. Finberg in 1973 (see Table 6).

The south and west of England has been from the early Middle Ages a region of numerous small market towns, described by Maitland in his seminal study, *Domesday Book and Beyond* (1897) as 'the classical land of small boroughs'. The reasons for this predominance of small boroughs and little market towns in the south and west are far from clear, but among the causes may be the proliferation of late Saxon *burhs*, many of which later became towns, the importance of industry, economic activity and marketing within the region, especially the wool and woollen cloth trades and the consequent growth of markets, fairs, guilds and urban centres around this industry, agricultural productivity and the demand for markets for corn, cattle, sheep and wool, the number of great landowners and estates, lay and ecclesiastical, which fostered the growth of towns and markets on their lands and also were involved in demesne farming aimed at producing crops for the markets; finally the numerous small but locally important sea and river ports which developed into towns. Towns also grew up around royal castles and the numerous wealthy monasteries of the region.

Some of the established towns and ports prospered and grew very rapidly during the twelfth and thirteenth centuries. Southampton profited from the extensive cross-Channel traffic which grew up with Normandy following the Norman conquest, and later had important trade in the export of wool to Flanders and the import of wines from Gascony. The importance of this cross-Channel trade was marked by the settlement of a group of French or Norman traders in the town soon after the Conquest with their own quarter around French Street and their own church dedicated to St Michael, the patron saint of Normandy. Royal interest and patronage, were demonstrated by expenditure on the great royal castle, guarding the harbour, and by the frequent use which the royal ships made of the port. The growth in the trade and prosperity of Southampton during the later twelfth century led to the construction of the great defensive system of town walls. The building of these

Plate 2.3 The Bargate, Southampton. A remarkably fine and complete town gateway, which was begun in the twelfth century and enlarged during the later Middle Ages. The whole of the upper floor is occupied by the medieval Guildhall. The adjacent town walls were demolished during the 1930s to make way for modern traffic, but enough survives to show the medieval wealth and importance of the port and the great strength of its defences.

great stone walls and impressive gateways was to continue throughout the thirteenth century and beyond. The scale of the surviving defences at Southampton, together with the impressive entrance at Bargate dating from *c.* 1200, one of the finest medieval town gateways in the country, are dramatic reminders of the extent of urban wealth and prosperity in the region during the thirteenth century. The increasing wealth of Southampton is also shown in the amount of building work undertaken during the period *c.* 1200–1350, merchants' houses, cellars and store-houses built of expensively imported stone from the quarries on the Isle of Wight at Quarr and Binstead, from Purbeck along the coast in Dorset, or high-quality stone from the quarries across the Channel at Caen. The remarkable number of surviving stone-built houses or remains of houses in Southampton dating from this period also emphasises the wealth of the town's merchants. Surviving documentary evidence shows that many of the principal merchant families who dominated the trade of Southampton used their wealth to build themselves fine houses during this period. Some of their names, such as Wallis le Fleming, James le Fleming, and Roger le Tankerville, reflect the importance of trade with the Low Countries or with France; other wealthy burgess families included the

Bonhaits, Isembards, Barbfletes and the powerful Bulehouse family. Notable among the early houses of Southampton are the so-called 'King John's house' and 'Canute's palace', both combining dwelling house and warehouse. The building boom of the first half of the thirteenth century established the plan and the pattern of streets which Southampton still retains; the details were little changed until further population increase in the seventeenth and eighteenth centuries led to expansion beyond the limits of the medieval town.

Equally impressive evidence of the wealth and life-style of the merchants of thirteenth-century Southampton has been revealed by the excavation of the house of Richard of Southwick, who died *c.* 1290. He was not one of the wealthiest burgesses of the town, but the range and quality of his possessions show an extraordinarily high standard of living and a wide range of contacts. He possessed fine wine jugs, pewter and ceramic tableware imported from France and Spain; silk imported from Persia, glass from Venice, fine wines, glazed windows and tiled floors. Evidence of foodstuffs included beef and mutton, eggs, fish, shell-fish, fruit including imported fruits and nuts. He had fashionable and good quality clothes and his household included cats and dogs and a small African pet monkey. Richard of Southwick lived in an age of urban expansion when there were numerous opportunities for profitable investment in trade and commerce through a thriving port like Southampton. The remarkable range of his possessions preserved in a rubbish pit behind his house shows that he, like many other merchants in Southampton during the thirteenth century, was not slow to take advantage of these opportunities (Platt 1973; Platt and Coleman Smith 1975).

Likewise in Winchester there is evidence of substantial growth during the thirteenth century. The city had declined from the position of a royal capital, and even before the accession of Stephen in 1135 and the start of the Civil War which wrought so much destruction in the town, Henry I had abandoned the regular annual crown-wearing at Winchester and royal visits to the city had become less frequent. In 1141 the royal palace in the city was destroyed by fire during bitter fighting, and with it was destroyed any possibility of a revival of the city's position as one of the ancient capitals of the realm. Henceforward the principal figure in the city was to be the bishop. It was one of the greatest of the bishops of Winchester, Henry of Blois, who established the bishopric as a major political and economic, as well as religious, power in the region. Henry of Blois was the brother of King Stephen, and one of the outstanding medieval prince-bishops, wealthy, powerful, scholarly, generous and ceaselessly energetic. He was Bishop of Winchester for forty-two years, from 1129 to 1171, and was also Abbot of Glastonbury. His wealth enabled him to build on a lavish scale; his palace at Wolvesey in the south-east corner of Winchester used materials from the ruined royal palace, and included a magnificent hall which could be used for public functions. He also spent lavishly on episcopal palaces at Merdon, Farnham and Bishop's Waltham, and on his most enduring monument the Hospital of the Holy Cross, for the relief of the poor just outside Winchester which, better known as St Cross, was to become one of the most famous almshouses in the country. Henry of Blois was also a patron of the arts and did much to encourage the great flowering of artistic work at Winchester during the twelfth century, a movement which produced fine architecture, metal and enamel work, rich vestments and superbly illuminated manuscripts including the famous Winchester Psalter and Winchester Bible.

It was Henry of Blois who caused a detailed survey of Winchester to be made in 1148, which provides much information about the city. The survey reveals that already by 1148 Winchester contained more than 8,000 souls, and was the largest town in the region. Traders within the walls included tanners, weavers, dyers, fullers, gold and silver smiths, shoemakers, butchers and dealers in agricultural produce from the surrounding region. There was a merchant guild, a guildhall and a developed system of civic government whereby the roads and walls were maintained and trading standards enforced. Encroachments on the High Street, the principal market street linking the two main gates of the city on the Roman line, were strictly controlled. In 1155 the customs and liberties of the burgesses were ratified by a charter of Henry II. Most important of all for the economic life of Winchester was the great fair held each year on St Giles's Hill to the east of the city. This was one of the greatest fairs of medieval England, and by far the most important fair in southern England; only St James's fair at Bristol approached it in importance. The Winchester fair was under the control of the bishop and the tolls provided one of the regular sources of episcopal income. It lasted for sixteen days, and attracted merchants from all over England and from Europe. The main trade was in wool, cloth and livestock, and Winchester became the most important centre of the west-country wool and cloth trade during the thirteenth century. In 1224 for example, merchants from Spain, Toulouse, Normandy and the towns of Flanders and Germany came to the fair at Winchester, as did merchants from all over England (Biddle 1976).

Bristol also grew rapidly during the twelfth and thirteenth centuries, both as a port and as a manufacturing and market centre. The port of Bristol had trading links with Ireland, Spain and Gascony; wool for export came from the Cotswolds, from the Wiltshire downs and by way of the Severn from the Midlands and the Welsh Marches, cloth, hides, corn, lead came from the Mendips and iron from the Forest of Dean. Salt was imported from France, fish, dyestuffs, especially woad from Picardy, and wine. The first royal charter was granted to Bristol in 1155 confirming its commercial liberties, and in 1373 Bristol was given the status of a county, independent both of Gloucestershire and of Somerset. The trading links between Bristol and Ireland were of great importance, and Bristol had especially close ties with Dublin. An idea of the way in which Bristol operated as the export centre for a very wide area can be gained from a record of a voyage in 1171 when six Bristol ships carried supplies for Henry II's expedition to Ireland. Among the cargo were victuals which had

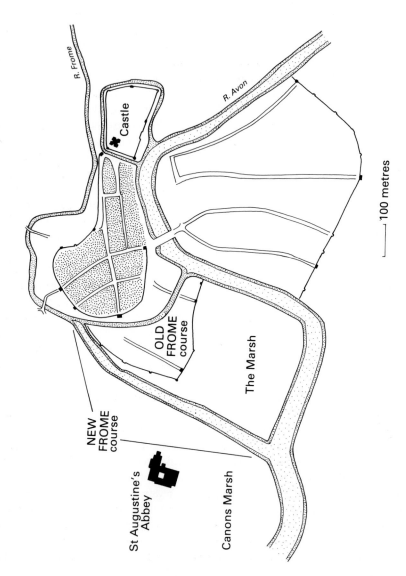

Figure 2.2 Plan of the diversion of the River Frome in Bristol, *c.* 1240

come down the Severn by barge from Gloucester, wine which had been brought from Winchester, and cheeses from Abingdon and Newbury. Wine dominated the medieval import trade of Bristol. The fine series of Constables Accounts of Bristol Castle record receipts from tolls on wine during the later thirteenth century, and clearly indicate the vigorous wine trade of the port. In 1275 duty was paid on 2,055 tons, by 1285 this had risen to 2,787 tons, and by 1293 the tonnage had increased to 3,862. Thereafter war with France interfered with the trade, but it recovered rapidly during the early fourteenth century (Sharp 1982).

Bristol's growing prosperity is reflected in the development of the suburbs, especially Redcliffe and Temple Fee where much of the cloth production of the town was based and where weavers, dyers and fullers were at work. The town's growing wealth is also reflected in the number of monastic institutions, hospitals and parish churches which were founded during the twelfth and thirteenth centuries, notable among them the house of Augustinian canons founded by Robert Fitzharding in *c.* 1140 and destined in the sixteenth century to become the cathedral. On the north side of the town Robert, Earl of Gloucester had founded in 1129 the Benedictine priory of St James as a dependent cell of Tewkesbury Abbey, and the fair at Bristol which was granted to the monks became important throughout the west of England.

By the mid-thirteenth century Bristol already had a piped water supply, a developed system of local government, merchant guilds and a vigorous religious life. The castle, now in royal hands, was one of the chief strongholds of England, and a centre of local administration. The growth in the size of the city was marked by the extension of its boundaries to include the rapidly growing Temple and Redcliffe Fees and the walls of the town were extended to include these suburbs during the 1230s. The best evidence of growing wealth and commercial activity in the port of Bristol comes in *c.* 1240 with the improvement of the harbour facilities, a remarkable example of medieval civic engineering. By the thirteenth century the port facilities of Bristol were inadequate to cope with the shipping needed for its expanding trade. The quay on the Avon was small and inconvenient, and because of the very high rise and fall of the river, ships were left stranded at low tide on the stony bottom of the river Avon and suffered damage to their timbers. The ambitious and formidable task was therefore undertaken of diverting the tributary river, the Frome, into a new and deeper channel some 750 yards long; thus providing, at its new junction with the Avon stone quays, a deep channel and a soft muddy bottom for ships to lie safely when the tide was out. The new channel also made it much easier to turn ships. The work was done during the years 1239–47 at the enormous cost of £5,000. The enterprise was encouraged by the Crown, and by a writ of 1240 Henry III ordered the men of Redcliffe to take their full share in the construction of 'a certain trench in the marsh of St Augustine, that ships coming to our port of Bristol may be able to enter or leave more freely and without impediment' (Little 1954: 42–4).

After the new channel was finished and the water from the Frome was diverted into its new course, Bristol Bridge was rebuilt. By 1350 Bristol had outstripped Winchester and Southampton and was the wealthiest provincial town in England.

Royal castles and the numerous wealthy monastic houses of the region also fostered the growth of towns and markets beside them. The town of New Windsor grew up in the shadow of the great castle, and Corfe Castle, Wallingford, Portchester and Devizes all owed their development to the existence of royal castles. The great castle built at Devizes by Bishop Roger of Salisbury early in the twelfth century to replace the original Norman castle which was destroyed by fire in 1113 was said to be one of the largest in Europe and certainly played an important role in the conflicts of the twelfth century. The feature which makes Devizes so notable among the towns of the region is the way in which it has preserved the medieval street pattern; the curving pattern of streets and the shape of the two market-places still reflect the way in which the town was laid out in two stages around the castle.

Likewise the wealthy monastic houses created demand for foodstuffs, labour and services, and brought visitors and pilgrims, thereby encouraging the growth of towns at their gates. Towns grew up around the monastic houses at Abingdon, Glastonbury, Shaftesbury, Malmesbury, Bruton, Lacock, Wimborne, Old Sarum, Romsey, Reading and elsewhere. At Reading the great Benedictine abbey was founded by Henry I in 1121 with extensive endowments, including the already-existing borough of Reading, so that in size and wealth it ranked high among the major abbeys of England. The favourable position of Reading on a well-drained ridge near the junction of the Kennet and Thames, with good communications and at the centre of a rich agricultural region, ensured the rapid development of the town. The abbey also brought a stream of pilgrims since it soon acquired an impressive collection of relics, including the hand of St James.

New Towns of the Twelfth and Thirteenth Centuries

To the developing older towns of the region were added, during the period of rapid population growth in the twelfth and thirteenth centuries, a new and numerous group of 'planted' towns, created by bishops, abbots, the Crown and other lay landowners for the profits they would bring. Such towns can often still be recognised by the regularity of their plan, since they were generally laid out on new sites or on empty land adjacent to an existing settlement. Good examples of such new towns may be seen all over the region. At Chipping Sodbury, which was founded by William le Gras in 1218 in a corner of Sodbury parish, the place-name element 'Chipping' meaning market gives a clue to its origin, as does its single wide street, and the former market-place through which the old road has been diverted with the burgess plots on either side. Marshfield, with its classic straight street, and a wide market-place in front of the parish church, was granted a charter in 1265. In Wiltshire there are several excellent and easily recognisable examples of 'planted' towns, among them Sherston with its market-place laid out on a well-drained spur overlooking the river Avon, Warminster where a new market was developed in the thirteenth century along the wide, straight street south-east of the original settlement and the ancient parish church, Wootton Bassett where a market charter was granted to Alan Bassett in 1219, Swindon founded as a market, 'Chipping Swindon', by the de Valence family during the thirteenth century, Lacock, Highworth, and Heytesbury for which Walter de Dunstanville obtained a charter in 1214 granting weekly markets and an annual fair. Two new towns were founded at Downton and Hindon in Wiltshire by the Bishop of Winchester during the early thirteenth century. At Downton, south of Salisbury, the new town was founded in 1208 and laid out in a broad, straight street along the west bank of the river Avon, away from the older settlement around the parish church on the east side of the river. The wide street of the 'planted' thirteenth-century new town of Downton is still called 'The Borough', as is the former market-place of another planned medieval town, Montacute in south Somerset, which was founded beside the original settlement in *c.* 1240 by the prior of the Cluniac priory there. Perhaps the best example of all in the region is Hindon, which was founded by the Bishop of Winchester in 1220 on a new site in the parish of East Knoyle in south Wiltshire at a point where a number of well-used routes met. Hindon can never have completely fulfilled the expectations of its founder, for it remained small and still consists only of a single long wide street, lined on either side by what are obviously the burgage plots of 1220. At Hindon the whole concept and plan of a medieval new town can be readily understood.

The most successful of the six new towns founded by the Bishops of Winchester during the thirteenth century was at New Alresford in Hampshire, seven miles from Winchester along the road to Alton. Here also the planned lay-out of the town with its wide street, the site of the market, at right angles to the main road can easily be recognised, and the burgage plots are still evident on either side of the market-place. The origin of New Alresford is well-documented in the episcopal account rolls; it is clear that Bishop Godfrey de Lucy obtained the first charter for a market, 'novum forum', in 1200 and two years later King John also granted him the right to hold a fair. In order to attract burgesses to his new town the Bishop provided a fulling mill, a market hall, a communal over and a boulting house for sifting flour. But much more spectacularly, the Bishop also built a great dam across the valley of the river Alre creating a 200-acre pond which gave a powerful head of water to drive fulling and grist mills and possibly also provided water to flow into the river

Itchen thus creating a navigable canal to Winchester. Whether the canal project was ever a really practical proposition is in doubt, but the huge dam certainly provided unlimited power for water mills and has been described as 'one of the largest secular earthworks surviving from medieval England' (Beresford 1959). The great dam still carries the road from New Alresford to the original settlement at Old Alresford, and although silting has made the pond much smaller than its original 200 acres, the whole project remains as remarkable evidence of the energy and optimism of the early thirteenth century. Within a decade of its foundation New Alresford had attracted forty burgesses, and as well as their rents the bishop was also receiving a substantial income from tolls paid by stall-holders in the market-place and at the annual fairs as well as the profits from his courts which dealt with the inevitable disputes over commercial transactions. By the fourteenth century New Alresford was one of the greatest wool markets in Hampshire, a collecting point for wool from the extensive downland to the east and north-east of Winchester (Beresford 1959; and 1967).

Another highly successful new town was Portsmouth, founded on Portsea Island by Richard I in 1194 as a deep-water harbour for royal ships which could not proceed up the estuary to Portchester. The new town was granted the right to weekly markets and an annual fair, and a series of streets was laid out on a grid pattern facing the harbour. As a trading port Portsmouth was over-shadowed by Southampton, but it was increasingly used by royal ships as a place of assembly and for repairs (Hoad 1981: 1–32). During the thirteenth century the Bishops of Winchester founded new towns in Hampshire at Newtown in the parish of Burghclere and at Overton, while in the Isle of Wight the Bishops founded Newtown alias Franchville.

The Bishop of Salisbury, Richard Poore, founded the most successful of all the new towns in the region when he transplanted the hill-top town of Old Sarum down to the meadow land in the Avon valley at Salisbury in 1219. The situation of Old Sarum was constricted within its Iron Age fortifications which contained both a cathedral and a castle, and the town had spread across the hillside to the east of the hill-fort. Quarrels between the cathedral clergy and the inhabitants of the castle, difficulties for townsmen caused by lack of space and shortage of water, and the bleak, exposed site, all led to support for a move to a new site. The new town of Salisbury was carefully planned and laid out on a regular grid pattern, with a large close surrounding the new cathedral on which work was started in 1220, with parish churches, market-place and the burgage plots arranged in rectangles or 'chequers', and the streets watered from the Avon. The town rapidly became very successful, attracting industries such as cloth-working, tanning and malting, and forming the market centre for a very prosperous area. It was favoured by abundant supplies of water, and by good communications, especially after the building by Bishop Bingham of a great stone bridge of ten arches over the Avon at Harnham in 1244 thus providing a direct route from Salisbury to the south. This effectively by-passed the old town and market centre of Wilton only three miles to the west and the remnant of the town which survived at Old Sarum (Chandler 1983). Wilton did not totally decay, but its fortunes were very much affected by the rapid rise of Salisbury, and its market was severely diminished by the success of its new neighbour. Not all the new towns were successful. Somerset has several examples of failures, including Stoford, south of Yeovil where two parallel streets were laid out in the thirteenth century by a ford across the river Yeo and at the boundary of Somerset and Dorset, but the planned town failed to achieve the success hoped for by its founders or to compete with the nearby market at Yeovil, and has reverted to a small village. Another Somerset failure was at Rackley or Radeclive on the former course of the Axe about two and a half miles west of Axbridge. In 1189 Reginald, Bishop of Bath and Wells, obtained a charter from Richard I authorising him to set up a port on the river 'that he may make a borough on his own land of Radeclive . . . with a market and other free customs and liberties that any borough has that is in our land in England'. The Bishop no doubt hoped to export lead from his Mendip mines through this new port, and for a time the port was indeed a success, for a dispute of 1390 concerning the place mentions cargoes of salt, iron and fish, and barges carrying goods inland along the watercourses of the Somerset levels. Drainage works and other changes in the water-levels may have spelled the end of this

Table 7 A list of new towns founded in the region during the twelfth and thirteenth centuries (based on Beresford 1967 with additions).

County	Date of foundation or first recorded reference to a town
Berkshire	
Aldermaston	1298
Cookham	1225
Hungerford	1170
Lambourn	late 12th century
Maidenhead	by 1270
Newbury	1189
New Windsor	1130
Thatcham	by 1300
Wargrove	1225
Wokingham	late 12th century
Dorset	
Corfe Castle	*c.* 1215
Charmouth	1320
Melcombe Regis	by 1268
Newton (in Purbeck)	1286
Poole	1170–90
Sherborne Newland	1227
Weymouth	by 1244

(continued overleaf)

Table 7 cont.

County	Date of foundation or first recorded reference to a town
South Gloucestershire	
Chipping Sodbury	1218
Marshfield	1265
Thornbury	*c.* 1250
Hampshire	
Beaulieu	1204
New Alresford	1200
New Lymington	1184–1216
Newport (Isle of Wight)	1177–84
Newtown (Burghclere)	1218
Newton (Franchville, Isle of Wight)	1255
Overton	1217
Petersfield	1182
Portsmouth	1194
Stockbridge	*c.* 1200
Yarmouth (Isle of Wight)	*c.* 1170
Somerset	
Chard	1234
Downend (in Puriton)	1159
Dunster	1197
Milverton	*c.* 1280
Montacute	*c.* 1240
Nether Stowey	*c.* 1225
Rackley (Radeclive)	1179
Stoford	1273
Stogursey	*c.* 1225
Weare (Lower Weare)	1225
Wellington	*c.* 1215
Wiltshire	
Devizes	1135
Downton	1208
Highworth	mid-13th century
Hindon	1219
Lacock	1232
New Salisbury	1219
Sherston	mid-13th century
Swindon	12th century
Wootton Bassett	1219

port; certainly the site is now beside a small stream and is covered by an apple orchard, giving little indication that it was ever a port or that ships could ever have reached it (Aston and Leech 1977).

Four new ports were developed in Dorset during the thirteenth century, at Lyme Regis, Weymouth, Melcombe Regis and Poole, all of which prospered and grew rapidly. Dorset also saw an ambitious plan for a new town which ended in total failure. This was Newton on the southern shores of Poole Harbour; it was a project of Edward I and was intended as a port from which Purbeck marble, then in great demand for church memorials and as a building stone, could be shipped. A charter was granted to the proposed town in 1286, providing for two weekly markets and an annual fair, and the new town was planned with a harbour, market-place, church and burgage plots. Merchants were to be attracted by generous privileges. But in spite of royal support and backing, the whole project collapsed and little of the grand scheme was actually built.

The Woollen Cloth Trade

Of all the industries of the region, the manufacture of woollen cloth has been by far the most important and widespread. By the end of the twelfth century the west-country textile industry had already been changed by the introduction of the complex horizontal loom, superseding the ancient and primitive upright loom. The new looms were capable of producing cloths up to two yards wide and over twenty yards in length, instead of the much smaller cloths produced by the upright looms. During the thirteenth century another significant development in the west-country industry was the widespread use of the water-powered fulling mill, a technical revolution which had a profound effect upon the fortunes and location of the industry. Fulling, or 'tucking' as it was called in many parts of the west country, was an essential process in the production of cloth, especially the long, heavy broadcloth which was a staple product of the region, and involved beating or compressing the cloth in water with fuller's earth to scour, shrink and felt it. Until the thirteenth century this laborious process was done by hand or by trampling the cloth with the feet in a trough. The fulling mill used water power to turn a water-wheel which by a series of cogs alternately raised and dropped heavy wooden hammers to pound and full the cloth; this was the first mechanised process in the textile industry, and for centuries it was to remain the only part of cloth production not done by hand. The earliest references to fulling mills occur in the late twelfth century. A survey of the Templars' lands in 1185 mentions one at Guiting Power in the Cotswolds, and a 'molendinum fullericum' belonging to the Cistercian Abbey of Stanley near Chippenham in Wiltshire is referred to in 1189. Stanley was a daughter house of Quarr Abbey on the Isle of Wight and the Cistercian monks at Quarr had a fulling mill in operation on their grange at Heasley on the river

Yar by 1198. The fulling mill at Heasley was very profitable to the monks, and they went to great trouble to secure ownership of the lands upstream which gave them control of the watercourse supplying the mill. By the early thirteenth century there were half a dozen more fulling mills on the Island (Hockey 1970: 50–3). The idea of water-powered fulling mills spread rapidly. By *c*. 1200 there was a fulling mill at the other end of the region, in the north Berkshire village of Seacourt on the Thames near Oxford where Robert de Sevecowrthe (Seacourt) granted the tithes of his two fulling mills to the nunnery at Godstow. A fulling mill on royal land at Elcot just outside Marlborough was in existence by the early thirteenth century, and was rebuilt on the orders of Henry III in 1237. The cost was £4 17*s*. 4*d*. and timber for the mill was brought from the royal forest of Savernake. The earliest account roll of the Bishops of Winchester dating from 1208–9 refers to episcopal fulling mills at Bishops Waltham, Sutton, Brightwell and at New Alresford. By 1215 the Bishop of Winchester also had a fulling mill at Downton, and another on the great episcopal manor of Taunton Deane by 1218. The episcopal fulling mill at Taunton was situated on the river Tone below the Bishop's castle and near the corn mill. The cost of its construction was £16 4*s*. 5½*d*., but this capital outlay was rapidly recovered and the mill began to make substantial profits for the bishop. The earliest annual rental was £3 13*s*. 4*d*. for the year 1219–20; this rapidly rose to £6 13*s*. 4*d*. by 1220–21, and to £8 13*s*. 4*d*. by 1225–26. Other local landowners were clearly impressed by such a profitable investment and began to copy it, for from 1231–32 the annual income from the episcopal mill at Taunton declined considerably and this was explicitly stated to be due to the competition from other fulling mills which had been built nearby (Carus-Wilson 1941: 39–60; Pelham 1944: 52–6).

It is clear from these and numerous other references during the thirteenth century that water-powered fulling mills were rapidly replacing the older process of fulling by hand or foot. At the beginning of the thirteenth century the main centres of the cloth industry were in towns such as Bristol, Winchester, Marlborough, Bedwyn, Cricklade, Wallingford, Abingdon, Andover and Reading. During the thirteenth century the industry became much more widespread as weavers and dyers, escaping from the guild restrictions and high taxation of the towns, began to settle around the fulling mills.

An area in which the medieval migration of the textile industry into the countryside can be appreciated is in the river valleys radiating south from the Bristol Avon and covering the Somerset–Wiltshire borders.

The most important river valley was probably that of the Frome, which flows north from the town of Frome to join the Avon near Bath. The visitor who wanders along its deserted banks today would not at first think that it was once one of the main industrial areas in England, but the evidence remains in the weirs and mill streams that were built to drive the water-wheels for the fulling mills. One finds them at Freshford, Iford, Farleigh Hungerford, Stowford, Tellisford, Rode, Lullington and other now deserted parts between. The history of the West of England cloth trade could be written as the economic history of this river valley.

(Ponting 1957: 26)

No one explanation will totally account for the changes in the cloth industry from the thirteenth century, and the industry was not only affected by the introduction of fulling mills, but also by the movement of workers into the countryside to escape the restrictive guild regulations and the high costs of the towns, and by foreign imports of high-quality cloth which stimulated the home production of less expensive cloths such as burels and russets, which were the main output of the rural weavers. Nonetheless the fulling mills undoubtedly were an important factor in changing the industry and Professor E. M. Carus-Wilson has argued convincingly that they were of great advantage to the west country, with its abundance of fast-flowing, easily-harnessed streams, and that the fulling mills were a primary reason for the enormous growth of the west of England cloth industry (Carus-Wilson 1954: 183–210).

There is no doubt that the towns were badly affected by the changes. Complaints from Winchester during the second half of the thirteenth century speak of the decline of trade and decay of tenements, and of the large numbers of cloth-workers who had left the town; and at Bristol the craft ordinances of the cloth-workers attempted to stop cloth being sent out of the town for fulling, and forbade the finishing of cloth in Bristol which had been fulled elsewhere. Some towns managed to retain a cloth industry however, and the trade in coarser cloths continued to thrive at Romsey, Newbury, Trowbridge, Castle Combe, Frome, Malmesbury, Shepton Mallet and most notably at Salisbury where the cloth trade remained very prosperous. Salisbury had the advantage of good communications and of a situation which lent itself to the development of fulling mills in or near the city. Mills had been constructed at Stratford-sub-Castle by 1277, at West Harnham (where a medieval mill building survives) by 1299, and on a royal estate not far from the city at Steeple Langford by 1294. David Hinton has made the interesting observation that a college which was established at Salisbury in 1262 might have developed into a university if the town's success with its cloth production had not kept rents high, whereas a university grew up at Oxford because of the commercial decline which kept rents low so that students could afford to live there (Hinton 1977: 181; Chandler 1983: 181).

The Church in Wessex, c. 1100–1350

The Norman Conquest and the imposition of Norman rule had a profound effect upon the Church in Wessex, remodelling its structure, giving a fresh impetus to the building or reconstruction of parish churches and encouraging the rapid spread of new monasteries and other religious institutions. Throughout the Middle Ages the region was divided between four dioceses: Winchester which stretched from the Isle of Wight to the south bank of the Thames at Southwark and covered the counties of Hampshire and Surrey; Salisbury which included the counties of Dorset, Wiltshire and Berkshire; Bath and Wells which consisted of the county of Somerset; and the southernmost part of the great diocese of Worcester which included Gloucestershire and Bristol. The Bishopric of Winchester was one of the best endowed in England, with vast estates stretching from the large, rich manor of Taunton Deane to the Bishop's estate at Southwark and including numerous manors, villages, towns, castles and houses in Hampshire and Surrey, including the episcopal palace at Wolvesey in Winchester. From the middle of the tenth century Benedictine monks had been established in the cathedral priory of St Swithin in Winchester, and one of the consequences which followed upon the Norman Conquest was the building of the great new cathedral in Winchester, one of the most impressive visual demonstrations of the impact of the Conquest upon Wessex. The large Saxon cathedral which had been completed less than a century before was demolished during the episcopate of the first Norman bishop, Wakelin, and by 1093 the sacred relics of St Swithin were transferred to the new Norman cathedral, built on the grandest scale. By 1100 the building was sufficiently complete for William Rufus to be buried there. The wealth, antiquity and prestige of the Winchester Bishopric, and the magnificence of the cathedral led the powerful prince-bishop Henry of Blois (Bishop of Winchester, 1129–71) to propose that Winchester should become an archbishopric as the metropolitan see of the old Kingdom of Wessex. The scheme was not entirely fanciful, and might well have improved ecclesiastical administration, but it was rejected by Pope Innocent II.

Since 705 a Saxon cathedral had been established at Sherborne in Dorset, with an illustrious line of bishops reaching back to St Aldhelm who came from the Benedictine abbey of Malmesbury to be the first Bishop of Sherborne (705–709). In 1058 the sees of Ramsbury in Wiltshire and Sherborne had been united, and in 1075 the Council of London, as part of the Norman policy of transferring Saxon bishoprics to more populous centres, ordered that the see of Sherborne should be moved to Old Sarum. Here within the ramparts of the Iron Age hill-fort, which were already occupied by a royal castle, a small cathedral was built under the direction of St Osmund (Bishop, 1078–99), and was consecrated in 1092. The choice of Old Sarum as the new diocesan centre was curious, and struck William of Malmesbury as odd, being 'a castle rather than a city, an unknown place'. Old Sarum did however have several essential urban characteristics, a market, a mint, a defended situation and an important castle. But the site was constricted, bleak and windswept, and with hindsight it seems obvious that friction would develop between the cathedral clergy and the garrison of the castle forced to live side by side within the ramparts. The cathedral at Old Sarum, like its successor at Salisbury in the valley below which was begun in 1220, was served not by monks but by secular canons. After the transfer of the diocese in 1075 the old cathedral at Sherborne became a house of Benedictine monks. The medieval diocese of Salisbury stretched from Lyme Regis on the English Channel coast to the upper Thames valley, and contained the three counties of Dorset, Wiltshire and Berkshire; by the thirteenth century it was divided into four archdeaconries – Salisbury, Wiltshire, Dorset and Berkshire.

Plate 2.4 Bath (aerial view). The central area of Bath is the most remarkable example of continuity in the Wessex region. The well-preserved Roman Baths in the right foreground of the picture provide an impressive monument to the power and wealth of the Roman Empire in Britain; the Abbey and former Cathedral, which was once much larger, witnessed the Coronation of Edgar as King of all England in 973. The present abbey church reflects the wealth which Bath derived from the woollen-cloth trade during the later Middle Ages, and the Pump Room situated above part of the Roman Baths, and the Guildhall at the top left of the picture, show the position of Bath as a major eighteenth-century social centre and spa.

The Somerset bishopric had been established at Wells since 909, but the Norman bishop, John de Villula (1088–1122) moved the see to Bath, the largest town in the county. Here he became abbot of the ancient Benedictine abbey and rebuilt the old monastic church in which Edgar had been crowned King of all England in 973. The Norman abbey and cathedral church at Bath was on an enormous scale, but only fragments of the building survive within the much smaller late medieval church which now occupies the site. Some of the twelfth-century bishops returned to the cathedral at Wells, particularly Robert of Lewes (Bishop, 1136–66) who established a group of secular clergy at Wells under a dean, and secured twenty-four estates or prebends to provide an income for them. Bishop Robert also rebuilt much of the old cathedral at Wells. Eventually during the early thirteenth century the confusion and rivalry between the two diocesan centres was resolved by adopting the joint title, Bath and Wells, for the bishops and their diocese, and having two cathedral chapters, the monks at Bath and the canons at Wells. During the late twelfth century the present cathedral church at Wells was begun, on a different alignment from its predecessor, and in a revolutionary new style of architecture. Building work at Wells during the period *c.* 1180–1240 created what has been described as 'the most original treatment of space in architecture of which any country at that time was capable' (Pevsner 1958). This included the nave and south transept with their vigorous foliage decoration and figure carving. A later period of work at Wells, *c.* 1270–1340, produced the incomparable Chapter House as well as many of the buildings of the bishop's palace, which with its imposing mid-fourteenth-century walls and moat, and the remains of its remarkable thirteenth-century hall is the most potent reminder in the country of the wealth, power and influence of medieval bishops (Colchester 1982).

The Church in medieval Bristol was subject to episcopal government from the monastic cathedral of Worcester some sixty or more miles away to the north, although the bishops did possess an estate at Westbury-on-Trym just outside Bristol. Bishop Wulfstan (Bishop of Worcester, 1062–95), who had been the parish priest at Hawkesbury on the Cotswold escarpment a few miles north-east of Bristol before he became a monk at Worcester and eventually bishop there, knew Bristol well and visited the town on a number of occasions, preaching vigorously and successfully against the Bristol trade with Ireland in English-born slaves. Wulfstan established a community of monks on the site of an earlier religious house at Westbury; Bishop Walter de Cantilupe (Bishop of Worcester 1237–66) founded a college of secular canons there, and later bishops tried unsuccessfully to make Westbury a joint cathedral with Worcester and to create a diocese of Worcester and Westbury, in an attempt to redress the uneven balance of the diocese which had the important port and growing town of Bristol at its farthermost extremity.

The Norman Conquest also gave an enormous impetus to the spread and development of monastic institutions in Wessex. The new epoch saw a great increase in the number of monks, an extensive and costly programme of building in the older religious houses and the proliferation of new foundations, new monastic orders, monks, nuns and canons, and a great flood of wealth and property bestowed upon the monastic institutions by all classes of society. In 1066 there were thirty-five monasteries and nine nunneries in England, all of them Benedictine. Most of the richest and most ancient of these houses were in Wessex, and included the monasteries at Glastonbury, Muchelney, Abingdon, Malmesbury, Cerne Abbas, Abbotsbury, St Swithin's and the New Minster at Winchester. Nunneries included those at Shaftesbury, Wilton, Amesbury, Romsey, Wherwell and the Nunnaminster at Winchester.

The reformed, vigorous monasticism brought by the Normans was evidently regarded by the Conqueror as a powerful aid in the difficult task of imposing his rule upon the unwilling English. The monasteries were regarded as centres of English sentiment and accordingly the English abbots were rapidly replaced by Normans, a process not always accepted without protest by the monks. At Glastonbury in 1083 the new Norman Abbot, Thurstan, who had been brought from Caen to take charge of this stronghold of English monastic tradition, rapidly provoked a riot among his monks with his attempts to reform and change their services, chant, customs and ceremonial. Thurstan called upon his men-at-arms to impose his will upon the recalcitrant monks, whereupon the monks barricaded themselves in the chancel of their church. In the ensuing struggle two monks were killed and several others badly injured. As a result, Thurstan was deposed by the King and sent back to Caen in disgrace. This incident, unique in the violence which it engendered and the scandal which it caused among the laity, illustrates the strength of feeling and commitment to their divine offices and customary usages among the monks, and the importance with which they were regarded by contemporary society.

Other Norman abbots outraged the feelings of their English monks by disregarding the feasts of the old English saints or by refusing to venerate their relics. Abbot Athelelm of Abingdon refused to recognise the English saints Ethelwold and Edmund, although the latter was the object of especial veneration since he had been born in the town, and Abbot Warin of Malmesbury outraged his monks by contemptuously discarding the relics of English saints which had accumulated at that ancient foundation. But in spite of such quarrels there can be no doubt of the new and energetic spirit and the revived discipline which the Normans introduced into the Wessex monasteries, and the effect which this had upon recruitment, scholarship, culture and liturgy, as well as upon the monastic buildings (Knowles 1963: 100–27). The introduction of new styles in architecture and carving, and of new ideas in iconography can readily be appreciated at the ancient Benedictine abbey church of Malmesbury. The dramatic, unified composition which survives in the south porch is one of the finest pieces of Norman sculpture in the whole country; the carvings date from *c.* 1150–70, and although some of the figures are badly weathered, it is still possible to recognise the extent of the ambitious project. The outer doorway has scenes from the Old and New Testaments, the Creation, the story of Man's Fall and Redemption, the Life of Christ, the Passion, Crucifixion, and Resurrection. Within the porch on either side are the seated figures of the Apostles, and the tympanum over the inner door shows Christ in Majesty. The fine design and workmanship, as well as the ambitious concept of this remarkable porch at Malmesbury represent a great advance on anything that had previously been seen in the west country, and can only be equalled in expansive design by the great west front at Wells which was not built until a century later.

Above all, it was at Winchester where the overwhelming extent and effect of the new Norman rule was to be felt and observed. The grandiose Saxon cathedral, site of the coronation and burial of so many Saxon kings, where the Conqueror himself was crowned as well as in London, was no more than a century old when it was demolished to make way for the Norman cathedral. Built of stone from the Isle of Wight, the huge Norman structure was an outstanding symbol of the Conquest. It was begun in 1079 by Wakelin, the first Norman bishop, and by 1093 it was sufficiently advanced for the relics of the highly venerated Saxon bishop, St Swithin, to be transferred to the new building. In 1100 William Rufus was buried there. With the Norman castle, bishop's palace and great hall, the New Minster which survived beside the new cathedral until 1110, the many monastic buildings, the Norman parish churches and St Cross hospital founded by Bishop Henry of Blois in 1136, the ancient capital city of Winchester was very obviously dominated by the Church and by the new Norman rulers, with their new architecture, liturgical fashions and continental ideas of government, monasticism and scholarship. Among the notable early twelfth-century scholars in the region was William of Malmesbury (*c.* 1090–*c.* 1143), the chief English historian of his age, who spent most of his life in the ancient Benedictine abbey of Malmesbury. As well as his famous histories, *Gesta Regum Anglorum* (1120), *Gesta Pontificum Anglorum* (1125) and *Historia Novella*, which was unfinished at the time of his death, William of Malmesbury also produced several theological treatises.

An important new Norman religious house was founded at Montacute by the Count of Mortain in *c.* 1100. This was a Cluniac or reformed Benedictine priory and, as shown on p. 12, it was on a site of special significance for the English. By *c.* 1150 the priory of Montacute was sufficiently well established to found a daughter house at Holme in south-east Dorset. Benedictine priories were founded in west Somerset at Dunster (*c.* 1090), a daughter house of the Abbey of Bath, and Stogursey (*c.* 1100) where the Norman landowner gave the church and the surrounding lands to the Abbey of Lonlay in his native Normandy. The well-endowed Benedictine monastery at Reading was founded by Henry I in 1121 and was destined to become the most important religious house in the east of the region. It was also during the reign of Henry I that the intense new monastic force represented by the Cistercians, who were to be such an important influence in so many aspects of English life, were first established in Wessex. The monasticism of Wessex played an important part in the birth of the Cistercian movement, for the crucial figure in the early history of the new order, Stephen Harding, is reputed to have been born in Somerset and certainly was a monk of Sherborne. He left for Europe in search of learning and of a more rigorous form of monasticism, a search which led him to found the Cistercian order at the monastery of Citeaux in Burgundy, where he was abbot from 1109 to 1134, and where he produced the Cistercian rule, the *Carta Caritatis*, in 1119.

The Cistercians were introduced into England by Bishop William Giffard of Winchester (Bishop, 1100–29), who encouraged the order to found a monastery in the Winchester diocese at Waverley in Surrey, not far from the Hampshire border, and in just the sort of remote, wooded locality favoured by the White Monks. The Cistercian house at Waverley was founded in 1128. Later Cistercian foundations in the region included the important house at Quarr in the Isle of Wight (1132), Forde Abbey on the borders of Devon and Dorset founded from Waverley in 1141, Kingswood, then in Wiltshire, founded from Tetbury in *c.* 1147, Stanley near Chippenham in the thickly wooded claylands of north Wiltshire, founded as a daughter house of Quarr in 1151, Cleeve in west Somerset founded as a daughter house of Revesby in Lincolnshire 1198, and where impressive remains of the thirteenth-century domestic buildings and the gatehouse survive including the fine Dormitory and the Chapter House. Beaulieu was originally founded by King John in 1203 at Faringdon in Berkshire where it retained throughout the Middle Ages a large estate including the grange at Great Coxwell, but within the year the monks moved to a more agreeable site in the New Forest on the Beaulieu river in south Hampshire. By 1239 there were enough monks at Beaulieu and the house was sufficiently well-established to found a daughter house at Netley on Southampton Water. A house of Cistercian nuns was founded at Tarrant Crawford near Blandford Forum in Dorset by Bishop Richard Poore of Salisbury (Bishop, 1217–29). It was for the nuns of Tarrant Crawford that Bishop Poore compiled the *Ancren Riwle* or rules of conduct for the nuns, a work which had a wide popularity during the Middle Ages, with its eminently sensible, practical advice to the nuns on their life and conduct, and its warm, human touches, warning the sisters not to be too severe upon themselves, nor to impose unreasonable austerities; recognising that there were difficulties to be overcome, such as the insolence of 'Slurry the cook's boy who washes dishes in the kitchen', and containing the homely injunction, 'Ye shall not possess any beast, my dear sisters, save only a cat' (Morton 1853: 381, 417).

The Cistercian houses, established in remote places and with their emphasis on poverty, simplicity and hard work were a vital religious force in the region during the twelfth and thirteenth centuries, and with their numerous granges worked by lay brothers or *conversi* they had, as was shown earlier on pp. 52 and 59, an important influence on farming practice, sheep management and wool production, as well as upon the landscape.

The twelfth century also saw the spread of houses of secular canons, the

Plate 2.5 Tarrant Crawford Church, near Blandford Forum, Dorset. A nunnery, of which only the earthworks survive, was established here in 1230 by Richard Poore, Bishop of Salisbury. Bishop Poore wrote a set of Rules for the nuns, with much practical advice on their daily life and devotions. One of the rules ordered, 'Ye shall not possess any beast, my sisters, save only a cat'. The parish church illustrated here retains a remarkable series of fourteenth-century wall-paintings, showing the Annunciation, lives of the saints, and popular legends.

Augustinians. Some of these were established as missionary and preaching centres in towns or populous villages such as Taunton (*c.* 1120), Bruton in Somerset (1127), St Denys Southampton (1127), Portchester (1133), and Bristol (1142) where the church of this important Augustinian house was destined after the Reformation to become the cathedral of the newly founded diocese of Bristol. Augustinian canons were established at Christchurch (*c.* 1150) and at Keynsham (1167). Other Augustinian houses were in remote situations where the communities of secular priests lived a strict, semi-contemplative life, little different from that of the regular monks. In Wessex such comparatively remote houses of Augustinian canons included Breamore in Hampshire, founded in 1128, where the canons used the great Saxon minster church; Bradenstoke on a remote site in north Wiltshire, founded 1142; Maiden Bradley in Selwood forest on the borders of Wiltshire and Somerset which was established in 1154; Barlinch in the wooded valley of the river Exe near Dulverton in the far west of Somerset (1174); Sandleford in the heavily wooded area of south Berkshire near Newbury (1193); and Mottisfont on the river Test in Hampshire (1201) where the buildings, including the church, were converted into a dwelling house at the Dissolution. Bisham Abbey on the Thames near Maidenhead was founded by the Knights Templars, but became an Augustinian house in 1337. At Lacock in Wiltshire Ela, Countess of Salisbury, founded a house for Augustinian canonesses in 1229, and although the church has gone, more of the domestic buildings survive there than at any other English nunnery, including the elegant fifteenth-century cloisters with their lively and often irreverent roof bosses and figure carving.

The order which most directly owes its origin to the west country and whose foundations lie deep in a still isolated part of the Somerset countryside is the Carthusian. In many ways the strictest of all the orders, the Carthusians, named after the mother house of La Grande Chartreuse near Grenoble, had their first house in England at Witham in the remote fastness of Selwood Forest near Frome in east Somerset. This house, founded in 1179, was one of those established by Henry II as part of his penance after the murder of Thomas Becket in 1170. The early foundation at Witham nearly foundered through lack of planning and preparation, and the monks sent there from La Grande Chartreuse almost abandoned the attempt to live their solitary lives in such wild and uncivilised surroundings. The first two priors failed to provide the necessary leadership and drive to overcome the obstacles, but in *c.* 1180 Hugh of Avalon was sent, much against his will, from La Grande Chartreuse to take charge of the house at Witham. Later, as Bishop of Lincoln and eventually as St Hugh of Lincoln, he was to become one of the best known of medieval churchmen, but his earliest success was at Witham where he established the new house, organised the construction of the necessary buildings, and made this remote monastery the centre of an intense religious life. While at Witham, Hugh became closely acquainted with the King, Henry II and it was thus in 1186 after only six years at Witham that he was called upon to rule over the vast diocese of Lincoln, until his death in 1200; but he continued his connection with Witham and to the end of his life made annual visits to this remote Somerset house. Today only the simple church of the *conversi* survives at Witham together with a solitary dovecote, and of the monastic buildings of this once highly important religious centre nothing remains and only earthworks and the extensive fish ponds with their elaborately constructed system of dams and hatches now mark the site.

One other Carthusian house was established in the west country. This was at Hinton Charterhouse near Bath which was founded by Ela, Countess of Salisbury in 1232 on the same day as she founded the house of Augustinian canonesses at Lacock. The tradition is that she attended the ceremony at Lacock in the morning and then rode the twelve miles to Hinton for the foundation ceremony there in the afternoon. Later Ela herself entered the house at Lacock as a canoness. At Hinton Charterhouse the church and the cells of the monks have disappeared, although excavation has revealed their size and layout, but the thirteenth-century Chapter House survives; above it is the former library and above this in the three-storeyed building is a remarkably well-preserved dovecote. The former refectory, sacristy and gatehouse are now incorporated into a modern house and its outbuildings on the site.

As well as the major monastic institutions, there were a great number of smaller religious houses, nunneries, friaries, hospitals and chantries, so that as the result of the great outburst of monastic enthusiasm during the twelfth and thirteenth centuries, towns like Southampton, Winchester, Abingdon, Reading, Salisbury and Bristol were crowded with religious institutions of all kinds as well as with parish churches.

Medieval Bristol, for example, was dominated by its eighteen parish churches, and was surrounded by monastic houses including the great abbey of the wealthy Augustinian canons, the priory of St James, the Black Friars near Broadmead, the Grey Friars at Lewin's Mead, the Austin Friars near Temple Gate and the White Friars near the site of the present Colston Hall. There were also numerous hospitals in various parts of the town and its suburbs, and several chantry chapels including the chantry of the Assumption of Our Lady on Bristol Bridge which, as well as its religious obligations, was charged with the duty 'to keep and repair the Bridge of Bristol, piers, arches and walls, for the defence thereof against the ravages of the sea, ebbing and flowing daily under the same'.

Similarly at Abingdon the burgesses were surrounded by churchmen and ecclesiastical buildings. The great Benedictine abbey, one of the most important in the country, with its large church and complex range of buildings occupied the whole of the eastern part of the town, and throughout the Middle Ages the town remained under the control of the monks in spite of attempts by the townsmen during the fourteenth century to gain some degree of independence. The south of the town, on the bank of the Thames, was the site of the large parish church of St Helen, originally the minster for the surrounding area. The church of St Nicholas stood in the market-place at the abbey gateway and served the large lay population of the abbey. St John's Hospital was built during the twelfth century also at the abbey entrance; St Edmund's Chapel was founded in the thirteenth century, and the Almshouse of St Mary in the fourteenth century. There were also chapels at either end of the bridge over the river Ock, west of the town.

At Reading, which during the course of the Middle Ages became the major town in Berkshire, the wealthy abbey founded and liberally endowed by Henry I in 1121 remained the major feature of the topography and government of the town. In addition there were three parish churches, Chapels of All Saints and St Edmund, and Hospitals of St John the Baptist and St Mary Magdalen.

Even a small town like Bridport in Dorset, already in the thirteenth century dependent upon the trade in ropes, nets and twine for its livelihood, had in addition to the parish church of St Mary, a house of the Carmelites, or White Friars, a hospital or priory of St John the Baptist, a priory or small collegiate foundation of St Michael, a chapel of St Andrew, and, just outside the town, a leper hospital of St Mary Magdalen (Knowles and Hadcock 1953).

By the later thirteenth century some of the older Benedictine religious houses had begun to lapse from the austerities and enthusiasm which they had earlier displayed and which still characterised many of the new 'reformed' orders. Nowhere was this more in evidence than in Wessex with its many rich Benedictine houses, early foundations which by the thirteenth century were masters of wide estates and large annual incomes. A staff of servants to attend to the needs of the abbot and the choir monks came to be accepted as normal. At Abingdon, for example, during the later thirteenth century there were fifty monks and eighty-five servants including a porter, butler, larderer, cook, doorkeeper, scullion, numerous indoor and personal servants, as well as gardeners, carpenters, a tailor, laundryman, stableman and farm labourers.

Many of the Augustinian canonesses at Lacock were aristocratic ladies, unused to menial tasks, and although there were seldom more than twenty inmates in the house, they were attended by a small army of indoor and outdoor servants, as well as by three priests and a confessor to ensure their temporal and spiritual well-being. In other west-country monasteries the number of paid servants also frequently outnumbered the monks; at Glastonbury for example there were some sixty monks and eighty servants during the closing years of the thirteenth century. In spite of their large incomes many of the monasteries in the region were heavily in debt by the later thirteenth century, either through bad management, misfortune, or, more commonly, from their insatiable desire for ever more elaborate and costly buildings. In 1275 the debts of the Abbey of Reading were so considerable that in spite of its lavish endowments it was forced to apply to the tenants of the abbey to help with a subsidy because of its financial difficulties, and at a visitation in 1281 it was still reported to have an 'intolerable burden of debt', and the prior was unable to provide the basic necessities for the monks. The monks of Bath were reduced to borrowing from the local clergy, while at Milton in Dorset – where the abbey buildings suffered extensive damage by fire in 1309 when the wooden belfry of the church was struck by lightning – the debts of the house led to severe quarrels between the abbot and the monks and to a period of great depression in the fortunes of the abbey.

Even the very wealthy nunnery of Shaftesbury could not avoid falling into debt, for although the revenues from its extensive estates in Somerset, Wiltshire and Dorset were large, so too were the expenses of the house, and the competent management of the scattered estates was a task beyond many of the abbesses. Certainly from the mid-thirteenth century onwards the nunnery was constantly in debt. Part of the trouble with the nunneries lay in the fact that, unlike the monasteries, there was never any shortage of inmates or of applicants, and many nunneries were unable to support the large number of nuns which they had admitted. Constant complaints were made by the Bishops of Salisbury during their visitations of Shaftesbury for example that the house had more nuns than it could support and that the number should be limited to no more than one hundred.

In 1256 Amesbury nunnery had 76 nuns, by 1315 this number had risen to 100, and by 1318 to 117 nuns, together with 14 chaplains, as well as clerks, lay-brothers and household and estate servants. During the thirteenth century the nunnery at Romsey had 90 nuns and those at Wilton and Winchester had 80 each. In 1346 the nunnery of St Mary at Winchester, the Nunnaminster, was forced to appeal to the Pope for help, giving as reasons for the poverty of the house the sterility of their lands, the destruction of their woods, the diminution of their rents and the excessive number of nuns, and stating that they were unable to pay their debts or repair their buildings. In 1316 it was reported to the Archbishop of Canterbury that the small Cistercian nunnery at Hartley Wintney in north-east Hampshire was in decay through negligence and bad management and was in danger of speedy collapse. Until the house was reorganised the dozen nuns were forced to go to other nunneries for sustenance. It should be noted however that this was during the severe famine of *c.* 1315–18 which will be discussed in the next chapter, and the shortage of food at Hartley Wintney may well have been connected with this.

It is clear from the examples which have been quoted and from widespread evidence from all parts of the region, that by the later thirteenth century many monastic houses, especially the Benedictines, were losing that vigour and enthusiasm which had characterised them during the preceeding period. The management of their large and scattered estates took up more and more of their time and involved many of the monks in much travelling, keeping them away from choir and cloister, and the effort needed to sustain the major building projects indulged in by so many of the monastic houses increasingly occupied their energies. The surviving architecture does nonetheless bear eloquent witness to the scale of the monastic explosion in the region during the twelfth and thirteenth centuries. The thirteenth-century survivals amid the ruin of so much else at Glastonbury, the so-called 'Elder Lady Chapel' in the former Augustinian church at Bristol, now the cathedral, with its lively stone carving, the remains at Malmesbury, Beaulieu, Reading and Cleeve, the 'Chequer' at Abingdon and the 'Pilgrims Hall' at Winchester with its early hammer-beam roof, all in their different ways show the enthusiasm, confidence and dedication of the Wessex monasteries during the two centuries after the Norman Conquest.

The vitality and wealth of the Church can also be appreciated in the dramatic new cathedral churches at Salisbury and Wells. New Salisbury was transferred from the windswept, uncomfortable and cramped site within the Iron Age hill-fort at Old Sarum to the meadows below by Bishop Richard Poore (Bishop, 1217–29). Building work on the new cathedral began in 1220, using stone from the quarries at Chilmark ten miles away, and apart from the lofty spire which was not finished until the fourteenth century, the main structure was complete by *c.* 1280. This rapid construction and unified plan has produced the most homogeneous appearance of any English cathedral, and building on a completely new site meant that the cathedral could be placed within a spacious close so that it can be clearly seen from all sides. The new and elegant building, so different in style and concept from the Norman churches, provided the model for numerous parish churches which were rebuilt through-out the large Salisbury diocese during this prosperous period. Likewise the cathedral at Wells was reconstructed in Doulting stone from *c.* 1180, on a different alignment from its predecessor, providing another example of the new Gothic style, and of new ideas in construction, carving, and in the imaginative use of space, with fine figure-carving, deeply cut, naturalistic foliage, and the incomparable Chapter House. Most dramatic of all at Wells was the great west front of *c.* 1220–60, which marks the full emergence of English Gothic sculpture. The scheme was complex and ambitious, involving 176 full-length statues, 30 half-length angels, and 134 smaller reliefs, 85 panels with Christ in Judgement flanked by archangels and apostles, the whole front of the cathedral being used as a framework for the vast design. The statues themselves were originally richly coloured, with crimsons, greens, reds and yellows, and must have presented a spectacle that to modern eyes would probably have seemed garish and was certainly startling. The complex design, showing the story of Man from the Creation and Fall to the Redemption must have been the work of a learned theologian, skilled in iconography, open to influences from abroad and aware of contemporary developments in church building and decoration on the Continent. Perhaps it was the great and learned Bishop Joscelin (Bishop of Bath and Wells, 1206–42), but there is no surviving evidence to establish the facts. The statues were probably worked at the Doulting quarries and brought ready-finished to Wells; the scholarly theme and the high quality of its execution are an eloquent tribute to the designer and to the masons and carvers of the sculptural school at Wells during the thirteenth century.

Parish Churches and Church Life

By the time of the Norman Conquest or soon afterwards the parochial system was firmly established throughout Wessex, replacing the earlier organisation based on central or 'minster' churches. The memory of the former minsters and of their daughter-churches survives in Dorset place-names such as Yetminster, Charminster, Wimborne Minster, Beaminster and Iwerne Minster, and in Somerset at Ilminster, Bedminster, Misterton and elsewhere. The process by which daughter-churches gradually separated and acquired parochial status for themselves was a long one, and in many places was not completed until after the Reformation. Yetminster in north Dorset, for example, only gradually lost its surrounding circle of daughter churches as Ryme Intrinseca, Leigh,

Chetnole, Lillington and Beer Hacket became parishes in their own right. At the time of the Domesday Survey, Thatcham in Berkshire was listed as part of the royal estates in the county, with a well-endowed church and two priests. Possibly the minster at Thatcham served the whole of the large Thatcham hundred, with numerous daughter churches and dependent chapelries; gradually these became independent parishes, including the town of Newbury. The process was not completed until the nineteenth century when Midgham and Greenham achieved separate parochial status (Kemp 1967: 15–22).

Similarly through much of the Middle Ages Chewton Mendip retained its daughter churches at Farrington Gurney, Paulton, Emborough, Ston Easton and Easton Minor. At Crewkerne in south Somerset the parishioners of the former daughter church of Seaborough continued until recent times to bring the key of their church each year on the day of the patronal festival and solemnly lay it upon the high altar of the mother church. All this was part of the long process of the spread of Christianity and of churches into every part of the region. The number of parishes and parish churches therefore increased steadily through the Middle Ages. In the archdeaconry of Dorset, for example,

---

Plate 2.6 Winterborne Tomson Church, near Blandford Forum, Dorset. A good example of the sort of small village church which the Norman conquerors erected all over the region, replacing most of the Saxon churches. Built of local flint and rubble stone, it retains its apsidal east end, and the structure has been little altered since the twelfth century apart from the insertion of later windows. In most parishes such small Norman buildings were submerged by enlargements and extensions during the later Middle Ages, but at Winterborne Tomson the village failed to prosper and had declined to only a few farms by the fourteenth century, so there was never sufficient money to pay for major alterations. The church was carefully restored in 1936 in memory of Thomas Hardy, and money was raised by the sale of some of his manuscripts.

171 churches were listed in 1291, by 1341 the number had risen to 218, and by the end of the Middle Ages there were 234 (Bettey 1974: 94–5; *VCH Somerset* IV, 1978: 28–9).

For most of our knowledge of church life and of the attitude of parishioners towards their parish churches during the early Middle Ages we have to depend very heavily upon the evidence of the buildings themselves, their siting, structure and decoration, for there are few local documentary sources of information on services or on the day-to-day life in the parishes. While it is comparatively easy to trace the growth and functioning of the Church as an institution, we are dependent upon a few, pitifully inadequate glimpses of occasional, and often unusual incidents for our knowledge of church life in the parishes during the centuries after the Conquest. In the nature of the surviving sources, mention is seldom made of those parishes where all is well and where the clergy ministered dutifully and quietly to their congregations. The records tell only of the criminal or the weak.

It is clear from the evidence of the parish church buildings themselves, that powerful among the attitudes of parishioners towards their churches during the early Middle Ages was the certainty of the ever-present conflict between the forces of good and evil, and the absolute necessity for the protection of the Church and its sacraments if the assaults of the devil and his hosts upon the individual soul were to be resisted. This sense of the protection afforded by the Church to the otherwise helpless soul, and of the incessant conflict with the powers of darkness, is seen in many Norman carvings, for example in the battle between St Michael and the devil or dragon on the north wall of the church at Stoke-sub-Hamdon in south Somerset; in the demons, monsters, dragons and grotesques depicted on the notable fonts at Avebury in Wiltshire, Avington in Berkshire or at St Mary's, Southampton where the grotesque beasts are confronted by the symbols of the four Evangelists. The same conflict between good and evil is depicted in the Norman capitals of Romsey Abbey or on the great twelfth-century font of black Tournai marble in East Meon church, Hampshire which shows the story of the Temptation and Fall, amid a host of fearful dragons, birds and grotesque beasts. The essential protection provided by the sacraments is emphasised on the ornate Norman font at Lullington near Frome in Somerset with the inscription around its rim *'Hoc fontis sacro pereunt delicta lavacro'* ['In the sacred washing of this font are sins cleansed']. The conflict between the virtues and their contrary vices is depicted on the Norman fonts at Stanton Fitzwarren in Wiltshire and nearby at Southrop, just over the border in Gloucestershire. At Stanton Fitzwarren the virtues are shown trampling upon their corresponding vices; and at Southrop the figures of the vices each have their names carved in 'mirror' writing on the panels as a further indication of their wickedness, while around the top of the font, above the conflict, are depicted the heavenly mansions to which the soul may aspire by holding fast to the virtues through the help of the Church while eschewing the vices and all the works of the devil.

About the clergy and the other parish officials it is impossible to generalise, since they varied so much in their ability and efficiency. Details of those who behaved badly monopolise the surviving documentary evidence in bishops' registers and visitations, for the well-behaved are much less likely to appear in official, legal records. Such sources are full of evidence of clerical

Plate 2.7 Twelfth-century font at Lullington, near Frome, Somerset. One of the most highly decorated fonts in the region, giving a good indication of the power and vigour of the early-medieval church. Around the rim are the monsters, demons and grotesque creatures that lie in wait for the human soul, while below are the flowery mansions which can only be attained through the sacraments of the Church. The deeply cut inscription reads *Hoc fontis sacro pereunt delicta lavacro* (In the sacred washing of this font are sins cleansed).

lapses, pluralism, non-residence, or common human frailties. Many of the parochial clergy seem to have been local men who differed little in their outlook and life-style from their parishioners. They may have been slightly better educated but they were equally dependent upon the soil for their livelihood, and equally at the mercy of the agricultural uncertainties. There were many like Richard Fanellor, rector of Chilton Foliat in Wiltshire. He was a local man who kept in touch with his family, farmed his own glebe land, and when he died in 1397 directed that he should be buried in the chancel of his own church, that £5 10s. 0d. should be spent on his funeral, and left gifts and legacies to his three sisters, to his shepherd and other servants, and to the fabric of Salisbury cathedral and to his own church at Chilton Foliat (*VCH Wilts* III, 1956: 23).

By the thirteenth century there were often several priests attached to each church, even in small villages. Besides rectors or vicars there were frequently chaplains, assistant and unbeneficed clergy, and chantry priests, for private and guild chantries were commonly established inside parish churches or in chapels or aisles attached to parish churches. In the large church of Bitton near Bath a chantry chapel was founded in 1299 in the newly built north aisle by Thomas de Bitton, a local boy who rose through the Church to become Bishop of Exeter. At Stoke-sub-Hamdon in south Somerset a college or community of five priests was established by the Beauchamp family to say perpetual masses for the repose of their souls. A visitation of Sonning in Berkshire conducted by the Dean of Salisbury in 1220 revealed that there were seven curates or chaplains in this large parish as well as the vicar. Most of these men were found by the Dean to be very ill-educated, and few could understand the Latin of the Mass. The collegiate church of Heytesbury in Wiltshire in 1220 had four canons, three vicars, a deacon and a sub-deacon, a total staff of nine men for this thinly populated parish.

There is copious evidence of clerical lapses in the visitation records of the energetic bishop Simon of Ghent (Bishop of Salisbury, 1297–1315). The bishop was concerned with a host of minor human failings, missing books and ornaments, dilapidated churches, failure to provide all the services, charging unreasonable fees, neglect of parochial duties and similar faults. During the Bishop's visitation of Dorset in 1302 he had to warn the clergy of Stour Provost, Manston, Iwerne Courtney, Okeford Fitzpaine, Stoke Wake, Bishops Caundle and Pulham that they must ensure that their churches were properly consecrated. A year later a similar report was made on a group of churches in west Dorset. At Shaftesbury in 1311 the Bishop ordered that rough games in the churchyard should be stopped, and that animals should not be allowed to graze among the graves. The rector of Winterborne Stickland near Blandford Forum in Dorset was found to be a foreigner who could not speak English and was ordered to find a chaplain who could teach him the English language. The fact that so many churches or additions to churches were in need of consecration is in itself evidence of popular piety and concern for enlarging, rebuilding and beautifying the parish churches. In 1326, for example, Bishop Robert Petit, suffragan to Roger Mortival, Bishop of Salisbury, consecrated no fewer than fifty-three churches in the diocese after recent building work had been carried out. At one church, Urchfont in Wiltshire, there is dramatic evidence of the effect which a bishop's visitation could produce. In 1301 Simon of Ghent had visited Urchfont and severely reproved both the rector and the archdeacon of Wiltshire for allowing the chancel to get into such a bad state that it was virtually without a roof. Evidently the bishop's comments bore fruit for the church now has a remarkably fine vaulted chancel, which from its architectural style can be dated to the early years of the fourteenth century. In the absence of other evidence about the standards of life and work of most of the parochial clergy, perhaps the best testimony we have is the fact that, as will be shown in Chapter 3, so many of the parish clergy of Wessex perished in the plagues of the fourteenth century and were obviously in their parishes and in contact with the sick and dying during the onslaughts of the epidemic.

Because details of the life, commitment and standards of the great body of parish priests who carried on the work and teaching of the Church throughout the region during the early Middle Ages are so difficult to find, the intimate account provided by the twelfth-century life of St Wulfric of Hazelbury is especially valuable. This was written *c.* 1180 by John, Abbot of the Cistercian monastery of Forde, and describes the life of St Wulfric, an Englishman, the son of parents of modest means at Compton Martin in north Somerset. He became a priest and for a time was incumbent of one of the several parishes which take their name from the Deverill brook in Wiltshire. In *c.* 1125 he settled as a hermit or anchorite in a cell beside the parish church of Hazelbury Plucknett near Crewkerne in south Somerset, some eight miles from the site of Forde Abbey which was established in 1141. At Hazelbury Plucknett, confined to his cell and to worship in the adjoining parish church, Wulfric passed the rest of his life until his death in 1155. His piety, austerity and the miracles with which he was associated made him famous throughout the country, and a stream of penitents, suppliants and sufferers came to his window and sought his help, advice and prayers. Among his visitors were King Henry I and King Stephen; even the great St Bernard of Clairvaux, hearing of his sanctity, is said to have asked for his prayers. As well as recounting the life of this remarkable man, John of Forde's *Life of Wulfric* also includes fascinating glimpses of the parish priests at Hazelbury, for Wulfric maintained a close friendship with the priest Brichtric and with his successor Osbern. Brichtric was evidently a devout, hard-working and dedicated priest, and John of Forde describes him as follows:

> He was a man whose simplicity and humility were very like those of Blessed Wulfric, for he busied himself in the same way with psalms and prayers by day and by night and, so far as his ministry allowed him, gave himself up to perpetual watchings in his church.

   The Church had not yet completely enforced the regulation about clerical celibacy, and it provokes no surprise either in the author or the saint that Brichtric was married. His wife was named Godida, and their son, Osbern, became Wulfric's attendant and acolyte, and eventually succeeded his father as the parish priest of Hazelbury. Another neighbouring priest named Segar was also married and had four sons, all of whom entered the Cistercian house at Forde, three as monks and one as a lay-brother. The biography of Wulfric of Hazelbury shows the parish priests as comparatively unlearned, but as dedicated men, full of simple piety and deeply immersed in the pastoral care of their parishes. They are also shown to have a fund of practical common sense, for Wulfric confessed to one of them, probably Brichtric, that in a moment of ill-temper he had cursed a mouse for nibbling his clothing and that the creature had immediately fallen dead at his feet. The saint was filled with remorse at the incident, but the priest replied only that he wished Wulfric would curse all the mice in the district in the same way (Bell 1933).

Chapter 3

The Later Middle Ages, *c.* 1300–1500: Plague, Recession and Recovery

The fourteenth and fifteenth centuries saw the end of the long period of expansion in population, settlements, arable land, towns, trade and monasteries. Instead this was a period of population decline, of frequent poor harvests, recurrent plagues which reached a peak but did not end with the Black Death of 1348–49, of retreat from marginal lands, abandonment of settlements and of decline in the fervour of monasticism and in the popularity of the religious orders, while men concentrated upon individual salvation through the foundation of chantries and the extension, rebuilding and costly adornment of parish churches. There were throughout Wessex notable exceptions to the general recession; as will be shown later, the woollen cloth industry of the region underwent a massive expansion, the ports of Bristol and Southampton flourished during much of the fifteenth century, many cloth-producing towns and villages prospered from the overseas demand for English cloth, and the ornate fifteenth- and early sixteenth-century parish churches throughout the region, with their fine towers, elaborate stone-carving and expensive woodwork bear witness both to the available wealth and to the popular piety of the period. The profits to be made from trade and commerce, from wool and cloth production, from energetic pasture farming and careful estate management can also be appreciated in the numerous fine fifteenth-century merchants' dwellings, manor houses and castles of the region. But neither architectural achievement nor the copious evidence of individual wealth and religious zeal affect the basic fact that, compared with the expansion of the thirteenth century, this was a period of prolonged economic decline.

The contrasts between the booming years of the twelfth and thirteenth centuries and the recession which followed cannot be attributed to any single cause, and certainly cannot all be explained by the Black Death, devastating though its effects in the region undoubtedly were. The growth in population and the resultant pressure upon land had created before the end of the thirteenth century a situation in which many rural communities were ripe for calamity, where the marginal lands under the plough could produce satisfactory crops only in favourable years, and where the effects of a poor harvest were disastrous. Over-population on many manors meant numerous landless men were totally dependent upon wage-labour for their livelihood and were poorly equipped to withstand food shortages, while land-hunger had led to the proliferation of small tenements with insufficient land to support families, especially in poor years. On the estates of the Bishops of Winchester and the Abbots of Glastonbury up to a third of the men were landless, and the average holding per family was less than 2 acres. At Bishops Waltham the proportion of smallholders with less than 10 acres rose from 42.6 per cent of the landholders in 1259 to 51.5 per cent by 1332, while an average calculated from mid-thirteenth-century custumals of twenty-five manors in Hampshire, Wiltshire and Somerset belonging to the Bishop of Winchester shows that over 50 per cent of the tenants had holdings of less than 10 acres. On the Bishop's great manor of Taunton Deane 56 per cent of the tenants had under 15 acres in the mid-thirteenth century, while 13 per cent had less than 5 acres each. At Taunton the population of the manor more than doubled during the period 1209–1311, and by 1248 the amount of land per person on the manor was only some 3.3 acres; by 1311 the position had deteriorated even further and the amount of land per person was 2.5 acres (Titow 1962). Such people were obviously living dangerously close to subsistence level and rapidly succumbed to poor harvests, famine and disease (Titow 1969: 78–9). In most manors the arable land had reached the limit of its expansion, and all over the region there was a desperate extension of arable on to the most marginal of land. Thus the heavy clays of the Vale of the White Horse, the marshy lands of central Somerset and the thin soils of the chalk downlands alike were attacked by the plough. The strip lynchets above Mere in Wiltshire, on the high downlands around Maiden Newton or on the exposed hillsides at Worth Matravers in Dorset, and in many other places all over the chalklands, show the lengths to which thirteenth-century farmers were prepared to go in their search for arable land. Likewise on the bleak land at Longbarrow Warren above Winchester the thin chalk soil was ploughed during the thirteenth century, in an area which, five centuries later, struck William Cobbett as one of the most barren stretches of country he had ever encountered. Inevitably the stored-up fertility of such land was rapidly exhausted, and it is an indication of the fact that many people were living dangerously close to the subsistence level that a series of poor harvests during the late thirteenth and early fourteenth centuries should so rapidly be reflected in a rise in the death rate.

The real crisis years occurred during the period 1315–22. The weather during the summer of 1315 was unusually bad, with heavy rain and floods, producing widespread murrain among the sheep flocks, and the harvest was a disaster. All over England harvest failure was followed inevitably by famine, and the price of wheat in the south of England rose to as much as three times its previous average, while the death rate on the Winchester estates, as revealed by the number of heriots or death-taxes paid, went up by 10 per cent. The harvests of 1316 and 1317 were also bad, and not until the harvest of 1318 did matters improve, while there were further poor harvests and destructive plagues among cattle and sheep during the early 1320s (Postan and Titow 1959).

At Inkpen near Hungerford on the southern edge of Berkshire, the manor which belonged to the Premonstratensian monastery of Titchfield near Southampton, had 468 sheep in 1313, by 1317 the number had fallen to only 137. At Crawley on the Hampshire chalklands almost a fifth of the sheep flock was lost during the years 1312–15. On the whole of the vast and scattered Winchester estates there were 1,088 oxen during 1319–20, but by 1321 the number had fallen to only 500 (Kershaw 1973).

For much of the evidence for economic trends in the region during the early fourteenth century it is necessary to rely heavily on the incomparable series of records of the manors scattered through Hampshire, Wiltshire, Berkshire and Somerset belonging to the Bishopric of Winchester. The detailed analysis of these records by Postan, Titow and others forms the basis of much of what follows here. The Winchester evidence leaves no doubt that on many manors yields of corn were falling by the late thirteenth century and that as large-scale corn-growing became less profitable the acreage of land farmed directly as demesne was shrinking. Marginal lands brought under cultivation during earlier boom conditions were perhaps losing their fertility by the early fourteenth century and were either allowed to revert to grass or were leased to tenants. The process can be seen in the figures for the total demesne acreage on the Winchester estates; in the years 1310–15 this amounted to some 9,725 acres, in the years of poor harvests during 1315–17 it fell to 8,525 acres, and by 1325 was down to 8,282 acres (Kershaw 1973: 33; Titow 1969: 52–3). The decline in the arable acreage can be seen even more dramatically over a longer term on the Bishop of Winchester's manor of Downton in south Wiltshire. The figures for the demesne arable acres are as follows:

1208–9	838
1268	700
1282	600
1308	500
1319	400
1347	300
15th century	200

(*VCH Wilts* XI)

The same retreat from direct farming of the demesne land can be seen on the scattered manors of the Norman abbey of Bec, at Combe, an isolated manor south of Hungerford and just inside Berkshire, and in a group of manors in Wiltshire that formed part of the abbey's bailiwick of Ogbourne. Demesne farming was gradually giving way to leasing out of lands or of whole manors and to the collection of rents instead of the imposition of labour services (Morgan 1946: 97–118). On the Dorset lands of Glastonbury Abbey at Buckland Newton and Sturminster Newton yields of corn declined during the early fourteenth century and the size of the demesne was contracted by the leasing out of marginal lands. At the same time the income which the abbey derived from allowing its villeins to commute the labour services which they owed on the demesne lands for a money rental greatly increased. At Buckland Newton for example commutation of labour services in 1302 brought in 18*s*. 6*d*.; while by 1333 the amount had increased to £8 0*s*. 1*d*. (Keil 1965). Similarly on the Winchester estates, as direct farming of the demesne lands contracted and the lands were leased to tenants, so the income from the commutation of labour services increased; in 1221 the commutation of labour services brought in £14 14*s*. 6*d*., while by 1348 it had risen to £225 15*s*. 4½*d*. (Titow 1969: 61). A similar pattern can be observed on many manors in Wiltshire (*VCH Wilts* IV: 36–8).

Some of the former demesne lands in the marginal areas, such as the thin soils of the high chalk downs or on the waterlogged clays, reverted to grass, but much of it was leased to land-hungry tenants who in the over-populated manors of the early fourteenth century were only too willing to rent land which the great estates found unprofitable. Thus in 1330 John le Porter was willing to pay a fine of £13 6*s*. 8*d*. for 40 acres of demesne land of the Bishop of Winchester at Loscombe even though '20 (acres) had fallen out of cultivation and 20 could be sown, though it was not worth while for the lord to do so, for they were poor in themselves' (Titow 1962). Examples of former demesne lands which went out of cultivation and reverted to grass during the early fourteenth century are widespread. The taxation list of 1341, the *Nonarum Inquisitiones,* reveals the existence of abandoned arable and uncultivated lands in a large area of the Blackmore Vale south of Sherborne on a belt of acidic Cornbrash and Oxford Clay, along the eastern side of Southampton water, on the poor soils of east Wiltshire along the Hampshire borders, in the heavy clays of the Vale of the White Horse and in Berkshire on the thin soils of the Lambourn Downs.

Thus for several decades before the Black Death of 1348–49 there was already a substantial pause in the increase of population and a downturn in economic activity, and there is no doubt that the recession was already evident long before the onslaught of that terrible calamity. Nonetheless the impact of the Black Death upon the region was catastrophic.

The Black Death

It was probably through a ship arriving at the port of Melcombe Regis in June or July 1348 that the bubonic plague entered England and began its rapid spread through the country, and the Wessex region, being first affected, was also one of the hardest hit. From the records of numerous towns, villages and manors in the region it is possible to multiply again and again the horror stories of the death rates which the plague caused. The plague was active in Dorset throughout the autumn of 1348 and during 1349, and a good indication of the severity of its onslaught can be gathered from the episcopal registers of the diocese of Salisbury which show that as many as half the benefices in the county were made vacant during this eighteenth-month period. Although not all of these vacancies were caused by deaths from the plague a substantial majority undoubtedly were. In March 1349, for example, the episcopal registers record as many as two institutions a day to benefices vacant because their incumbents had died in the plague. At Winterborne Clenston four new rectors were instituted in late 1348 and during 1349, and at nearby Winterborne Houghton there were three new incumbents during the same period. At Wareham new vicars were instituted in October 1348, December 1348, May 1349 and June 1349. The same picture can be seen in parishes all over the county, especially along the coast and in the chalklands where the tightly packed, nucleated villages were no doubt more prone to the spread of infection than the scattered farms and hamlets of north and west Dorset.

The complete figures for institutions to Dorset benefices caused by the death of the previous incumbent during the plague period are as follows:

1348	October	4	1349	March	12
	November	17	(cont'd)	April	6
	December	28		May	9
1349	January	21		June	3
	February	12		July	11
				August	5

The previous average had been one institution per month. There is no reason to suppose that the mortality was any less severe among the laity.

As early as July 1349 the *Calendar of Fine Rolls* records that the King took note of the fact that at Bere Regis and Charminster 'the mortality of men in the present pestilence is so great that the lands thereof be untilled and the profits are lost'. Later, in 1352, the King ordered that all the men on the island of Portland should stay there for its safe-keeping, and that no crops or victuals should be drawn out of the island because it had been 'so depopulated on account of the late mortality in the time of the pestilence that the men left there will not be sufficient to defend the same against attacks'.

By the autumn of 1348 the plague was in Somerset. Again the figures for institutions to benefices in the diocese of Bath and Wells tell their own sorry story of the mortality among the clergy, and thus by implication among the laity also. Normally institutions to benefices averaged about nine per month. During the height of the plague the figures were:

1348	November	9	1349	March	36
1348	December	32	(cont'd)	April	40
1349	January	47		May	21
	February	43		June	7

Some of the clergy may have died from other causes, and some may have left their parishes to take up more lucrative livings made vacant elsewhere, but nonetheless the figures are an impressive witness to the virulence of the plague. It has been calculated that some 47.6 per cent of the beneficed clergy in the Bath and Wells diocese died of the Black Death, and it is unlikely that a smaller proportion of the laity died from its effects. In January 1349 Ralph of Shrewsbury, Bishop of Bath and Wells, issued a letter to the priests in his diocese in which he wrote:

> The contagious pestilence of the present day, which is spreading far and wide, has left many parish churches and other livings in our diocese without parson or priest to care for their parishioners. Since no priests can be found who are willing, whether out of zeal and devotion or in exchange for a stipend, to take on the pastoral care of these aforesaid places, nor to visit the sick and administer to them the Sacraments of the Church (perhaps for fear of infection and contagion), we understand that many people are dying without the Sacrament of Penance . . .
> (Ziegler 1969)

The Bishop went on to authorise the clergy to allow the dying to make their confession to laymen if no priests were available. A further indication of the effect of the plague in Somerset is that shortly afterwards the Carthusian houses of Witham and Hinton Charterhouse both petitioned to be allowed to hire labourers and servants from outside their enclosures because so many of their lay brothers had died in the pestilence, and their lands were uncultivated.

In Bristol between 35 and 40 per cent of the population fell victim to the disease, and a list of fifty-two members of the town council in 1349 has fifteen of the names struck through to show that they were dead. In Wiltshire the story is the same. Eighteen out of the forty-one tenants at Durrington near Salisbury died of the plague; no rents at all were collected at Tidworth as all the tenants were dead; the prior and thirteen out of the fourteen Augustinian canons at Ivychurch died of the plague. In Berkshire which was part of the diocese of Salisbury the figures from the Bishop's register for institutions to benefices from 1345 to 1351 tell their own story of the mortality:

1345	30	1349	145
1346	56	1350	93
1347	54	1351	66
1348	190		

Nearly 49 per cent of all the beneficed clergy died in Winchester diocese, the highest figure of all English dioceses, and one no doubt explained by the ease with which the plague could be brought in through the many ports and harbours of Hampshire, Surrey and the Isle of Wight. Again many examples can be found amongst manorial and other records of the devastation. At Bishops Waltham where 404 tenants were listed in 1332, there were 264 deaths in 1348–49 representing 65 per cent of the total, and a further 53 tenants died during a second visitation of the plague in 1361. Similarly 305 out of a total of 515 tenants on the Titchfield Abbey estates died during 1348–49, a mortality of nearly 60 per cent, and a further 92 tenants died in 1361 (Ziegler 1969; Shrewsbury 1970; Levett and Ballard 1916).

A survey of twenty-two of the manors belonging to Glastonbury Abbey, spread across Somerset, Wiltshire and Dorset, reveals that the average death-rate among the tenants during the Black Death was as high as 55 *per cent*. In many places lands were left untilled for want of labourers; for example at Bere Regis and Charminster in Dorset it was recorded as early as July 1349 that 'the mortality of men in the present pestilence is so great that the lands thereof be untilled and the profits are lost'. At Thatcham and Crookham in the Kennet valley near Newbury on the lands which the Countess of Salisbury obtained in 1349 on the death of her husband, it was found that all the labourers had died and the arable land had entirely gone out of cultivation in consequence (Bettey 1974: 46–7; Barfield I 1901: 40).

The massive mortality throughout the region caused by the Black Death and by subsequent visitations of the plague during the later fourteenth century, greatly accelerated the economic trends which have already been discussed such as the retreat from direct demesne farming and the leasing of lands by the great estates, the abandonment of arable farming on the marginal lands and the sale of labour services. The Black Death was also a powerful agent, though not the only factor, in other changes such as the shrinkage and desertion of villages, changes in social structure and developments in farming, which will be discussed later in this chapter.

The Late Medieval Church in the Region, *c.* 1300–1500

In spite of the decline in the fervour of monasticism and in the popularity of the monasteries, and notwithstanding the growing stream of criticism of many aspects of the teaching, ritual and clergy of the Church during the later Middle Ages, the buildings, estates and influence of the Church continued to dominate all parts of the region. The criticisms levelled against the Church as an institution did not stop the flow of contributions from the laity for the rebuilding, enlargement and decoration of their parish churches and for the foundation of chantries. After the Black Death the foundation of new monastic houses almost entirely came to an end, and it is indicative of the changed

Plate 3.1 The Street of the Vicars Choral, Wells. The College of Vicars Choral was founded at Wells in 1348, and the planned street of identical houses which was built for them survives on the north side of the Cathedral. It remains much as it was in the fourteenth century, with the Vicars' hall by the Cathedral at one end of the street, and the Chapel with the Vicars' library above it at the other, as is seen in this photograph.

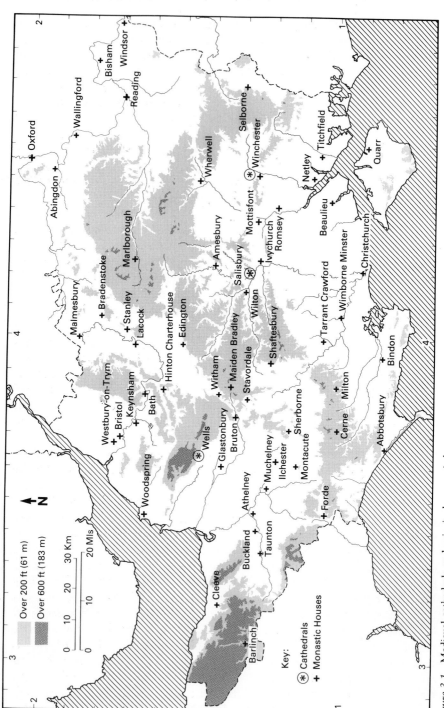

Figure 3.1 Medieval cathedrals and principal monastic houses

temper of the times and of the decline in the popularity of the monks that the typical late medieval foundations were schools, colleges, almshouses, hospitals and chantry chapels. Only the Carthusian houses such as those at Witham and Hinton Charterhouse with their proud boast of *nunquam reformata quia nunquam deformata* (never reformed because never deformed), retained undiminished their popularity with the laity, although the hardships of their austere life and rigorous discipline meant that they remained small.

Nonetheless the monastic houses continued to dominate the region with their vast estates. Their buildings towered over towns such as Abingdon and Reading, Malmesbury, Sherborne, Bath and many more, and the later Middle Ages saw the addition of sumptuous new buildings in many monasteries. In spite of all the destruction at the Reformation much survives as a reminder of this late medieval flowering of monastic architecture. It can be seen at its best in the great Perpendicular remodelling of the nave of the monastic cathedral at Winchester, in the cloisters at Forde Abbey, at Cerne Abbas in the fine gateway to the abbot's lodging, in the late medieval work at Sherborne, Bath, Christchurch and in the nunnery cloisters at Lacock.

Of the daily life in the monasteries, and especially of the regular performance of their central function, the maintenance of a continuous service of prayer and praise, day and night, there is surprisingly little evidence. Perhaps it was inevitable that with the passage of centuries some monastic houses should slip from the harsher austerities of their original routine. Some became very wealthy and, as at Glastonbury, the care of their vast estates occupied much of their attention and led to a highly developed bureaucratic system with separate revenues assigned to various officials such as the Sacrist, Precentor, Cellarer, Kitchener, Pittancer, Hosteler and Infirmarian. At Glastonbury also we can see the way in which increasing wealth generated the need for yet more. The abbot's kitchen which survives so dramatically amid the ruins at Glastonbury is a reminder of the splendour in which the late medieval abbots lived. Evidence of the way in which the comforts of the monks were increased and the way in which this increased the expenses of the abbey is seen in the way that parish churches over a wide area were 'appropriated' to the monastery which thus became the rector of the parish and took much of the income from its tithes, appointing a vicar to serve the spiritual needs of the parishioners. In 1391, for example, the parish church of Longbridge Deverill in Wiltshire together with its subsidiary chapelry at Monkton Deverill was appropriated by Glastonbury Abbey, and although Abbot Chinnock of Glastonbury in petitioning for Longbridge Deverill put forward the usual reasons of poverty brought on by plague, disease among the livestock, floods and poor harvests, the real reason was in order to improve the cash doles provided annually for each of the choir monks, although these were already the highest of any monastery in the country (Keil 1961–3). Evidence of the wealth and widespread possessions of Glastonbury Abbey and of the style in which the last abbots lived can be seen from the description of the abbey and its estates which the Royal Commissioners sent to Thomas Cromwell in September 1539 during the final dissolution of the abbey.

> The house is great, goodly, and so princely as we have not seen the like; with 4 parks adjoining, the furthermost of them but 4 miles distant from the house; a great mere, which is 5 miles compass, being a mile and a half distant from the house, well replenished with great pike, bream, perch and roach; 4 fair manor places, belonging to the late abbot, the furthermost but 3 miles distant, being goodly mansions; and also one in Dorsetshire, 30 miles distant from the late monastery.
>
> (Wright 1843)

Notwithstanding their widespread estates and large incomes, many monastic houses in the region impoverished themselves during the later Middle Ages by the scale and magnificence of their building work, not just on their churches, but also on their cloisters, and on fine residences for their abbots. The surviving remains of the prior's lodging at Montacute, the abbot's house at Muchelney and the abbot's gateway at Cerne Abbas, all of them on the grandest scale, certainly suggest that money was being spent even by the smaller houses in a way that only the richest could afford. Faced with the need for ever greater revenue some monastic houses attempted to exploit other sources of wealth. The Augustinian canons at Keynsham built up a considerable property-holding in nearby Bristol, with houses, shops, inns and warehouses. At Cerne Abbas the monastery constructed a whole row of shops at the abbey gate which were presumably intended for letting and of which a substantial part survive. At the ruins of the Augustinian house at Selborne excavations have revealed distilling apparatus and glassware which strongly suggest some industrial process and possibly the study of medicine and alchemy. The Somerset monasteries were much involved in schemes for drainage in the Somerset levels and also in lead mining on Mendip. The gradual abandonment of the earlier ideals of a life of poverty and abstinence is also to be observed in the increasing number of lay servants which were employed in the monastic houses. For example, during the fifteenth century Augustinian canonesses at Lacock employed besides day labourers and farm servants a janitor, hosteler, baker, brewer, larderer, swanherd, poulterer, dairymaid and cook. In 1536 the servants employed to look after the seventeen nuns at Lacock include 9 officers of the household, 3 waiting servants, 9 women servants, and 15 hinds. There were also 4 chaplains, a clerk and a sexton. A similar decline from the high ideals of its early years can be seen at Cleeve where in the dormitory range the remains of the bases for divisions between the sleeping quarters survive, a departure from the original arrangement of a communal dormitory and one which would have been greatly frowned upon in the early period of Cistercian enthusiasm for a life devoid of luxury, privacy or any ostentation. Likewise at

Cleeve the sumptuous refectory, rebuilt early in the sixteenth century, with its elegant windows and magnificent wagon roof decorated with angels, is far removed in spirit from the original Cistercian ideal of plainness and simplicity.

The nunneries were frequently in difficulties because the number of nuns was larger than the revenues of the houses could easily support. Even the great nunnery at Shaftesbury, the wealthiest in the country with its wide estates in Wiltshire and Dorset and an income at the Dissolution of £1,329 per annum, found itself in difficulties because of excessive numbers. As early as 1219 the Pope had forbidden the community at Shaftesbury to allow its numbers to rise above one hundred nuns because they were unable to support more or to give alms to the poor. But it proved impossible for the nuns to resist the pressure of local gentry families who wished to secure places for female members, and during the fourteenth century there are several references in the bishops' registers to the nunnery being allowed to grow too large for its revenues, and the house was constantly in debt, in spite of its vast estates and large annual income. Numbers declined however during the fifteenth century, and in 1441 there were 41 nuns and 14 novices; by 1460 there were 51 nuns, and at the dissolution in 1539 pensions were granted to the abbess, the prioress and 55 nuns.

In those places where the parish church was appropriated by a religious house, accommodation had to be provided by the monastery for the parish priest, and a fine example of a medieval priest's house survives largely unchanged at Muchelney in Somerset. The church was appropriated by the neighbouring Benedictine abbey, and in 1308 agreement was drawn up by Walter de Haselschawe, Bishop of Bath and Wells, specifying the vicar's rights and emoluments. The vicar, together with his curate or chaplain who served the neighbouring chapelry of Drayton, and their manservant, were to have the vicarage house with hall, parlour, buttery, kitchen and chambers above, together with the outbuildings. The vicar was also to have

> a monk's bread of 60s weight and two gallons of best conventional ale from the cellarer of the abbey; a dish of flesh meat each Sunday and Tuesday, and a dish of eggs or fish on other days, from the monastic kitchen; £4 yearly from the sacrist in support of charges; all Sunday offertories at the church of Muchelney and at the chapel of Drayton thereto annexed; all oblations at burials, both at first and second mass, and any bequests and money left for masses for the deceased; all bread, eggs, and other oblations on Good Friday and Easter Day; oblations at confessions, marriages and purifications. On the other hand, to the abbot are reserved oblations at the said church and chapel on Christmas Day, Easter, the Feast of SS Peter and Paul, St Peter ad Vincula, St Catherine and the Purification, and on the feast of the dedication; also all tithes and unspecified receipts.
>
> (Schofield 1927: 46)

Plate 3.2 The Priest's House, Muchelney, near Langport, Somerset. This charming house dates from the fourteenth and fifteenth centuries; it stands beside the parish church and close to the ruins of the great Benedictine abbey. The earliest part of the house was built soon after 1308 when an agreement was drawn up fixing the emoluments to be received by the vicar of Muchelney. In addition to the house, he was to have the offerings in the parish church, bread and two gallons of best conventual ale weekly from the cellarer of the abbey, and he was to receive a meal each day from the monastic kitchen.

Other medieval vicarages or priest's houses survive at Horton, Congresbury, Trent and Wimborne Minster (Pantin 1957).

It is not difficult to find examples of scandalous neglect, abuses or of bad behaviour in the monastic houses of the region during the later Middle Ages, but it has to be remembered that while there were many monks the criticisms concern only a few, and that the visitations which provide most of this evidence were concerned only with reporting faults and were silent about the many houses where all was well. In some places, however, the fall from the original monastic ideal had been dramatic. At the Cistercian house of Bindon in Dorset there were frequent reports during the fourteenth century of debt, disorder, internal strife and scandals. In 1331, for example, one of the monks, John de Monte Acuto, collected a mob of local people and attacked the abbey, carrying away cattle and sheep, books, chalices, charters, deeds and other possessions. At the Augustinian abbey of Bruton a visitation by Bishop Beckington of Bath and Wells in 1452 revealed that the canons took part in 'confabulations and conspiracies, and sometimes drinking bouts and gluttonous feasts ... so that ... divine offices are performed negligently'. A visitation of Malmesbury Abbey in 1527 revealed that there had been quarrels and violence among the monks, that several monks had broken out at night, there was no reading in the refectory, women of doubtful reputation were allowed into the house, services were neglected, the food was bad and the community had become completely disordered and demoralised. At the nunnery of Romsey where the church with its magnificent Norman architecture and even earlier Roods survives and is the finest nunnery church in England, there were frequent scandals during the later Middle Ages. In 1492 it was said that the nuns went into the town and frequented taverns, that the services were badly conducted and the nuns made an unseemly noise in the choir, that the roofs had been allowed to fall into disrepair 'so that if it happened to rain, the nuns were unable to remain in the choir in the time of divine service, or in their beds'. The funds of the nunnery it was alleged had been squandered by the abbess on Master Bryce, the vicar, and there was grave scandal about their relationship.

Most of the late medieval treasures of the Wessex monasteries have vanished or perished, especially the illustrated and illuminated service books, most of which were destroyed at the Reformation. One great treasure does however survive to give some indication of the wealth of material which has been lost; this is the Sherborne Missal of *c.* 1400. The Missal is one of the finest surviving English medieval manuscripts. It was commissioned for use on the high altar of Sherborne Abbey by Richard Mitford, Bishop of Salisbury 1396–1407, and Robert Brunning, Abbot of Sherborne 1385–1415. The calligraphy was the work of John Whas, a monk of Sherborne, and the illumination was done by John Sifrewas, a Dominican friar from Ilchester. As well as being a superb work of devotional art and craftsmanship, the Sherborne Missal is also full of interest for the contemporary scenes portrayed so skilfully by John Sifrewas. The missal contains numerous portraits of the Bishop and the Abbot and of Whas and Sifrewas themselves; there are also many architectural drawings, religious processions, scenes from contemporary life, from the lives of the saints, and heraldic devices. Most delightful of all are the large number of birds which decorate the pages, chaffinches, bullfinches, swallows, wagtails, pheasants, peacocks, herons, jays and many others. The Calendar of Saints' days also includes several saints who were especially venerated at Sherborne, among them St Aldhelm, the first bishop, and most notably St Juthware, a Saxon virgin who was said to have been martyred at Halstock near Sherborne and whose martyrdom is realistically depicted in the Missal (Fowler 1951).

The Cathedrals

Like the monasteries, the three great cathedrals of the region dominated the towns in which they were situated. Wells and Salisbury were served by secular canons; Winchester by Benedictine monks; all three were supported by the income from extensive estates and numerous properties. The impact, wealth and power of a cathedral and the complexity of its organisation, with its clergy, officers and all the associated institutions, is obvious at Winchester with its huge cathedral church, the longest in Europe, and at Salisbury where the great spire presides over the city and is visible all over the countryside for miles around; but the atmosphere of a late medieval cathedral close can perhaps best be appreciated at Wells where beside the cathedral church with its superb West Front, its cloisters and incomparable Chapter House, is the moated and fortified bishop's palace, the finest and most idyllic of all such palaces in England, making it abundantly clear that the bishop was a great medieval lord as well as a spiritual leader. Also beside the cathedral at Wells are the dwellings for the canons and the mid-fourteenth-century street of houses for the vicars choral. The manor houses and estates of the bishop were scattered throughout Somerset, at Chew Magna, Banwell, Wiveliscombe and Evercreech. Similarly the immensely wealthy bishops of Winchester had their palace at Wolvesey, as well as manor houses at Farnham, Bishops Waltham, Bishops Sutton, Clere, Downton, Merdon and a large London residence in Southwark.

The Parish Churches

The most remarkable expression of late medieval piety as well as of the wealth available in the region during the later Middle Ages is to be found in the parish churches. The splendour and elegance of the perpendicular architecture, and the surviving evidence of late medieval furnishings in woodwork, glass, paintings, plate and images leave no doubt of the way in which money was lavished upon these buildings during the century and a half before the Reformation. Medieval churchwardens' accounts and the few surviving building contracts make it clear that in most parishes the money for rebuilding or enlarging the parish church was raised by the parishioners themselves. In a few places the churches were rebuilt on a grand scale by one or more wealthy benefactors. The fine church at Wellow near Bath is reputed to have been built at the cost of Sir Thomas Hungerford who had been the first Speaker of the House of Commons; North Cadbury church in south Somerset was rebuilt and greatly enlarged at the expense of Lady Elizabeth Botreaux who intended to establish there a college of secular priests and accordingly made a large and elegant chancel to accommodate them. The nave of Newbury parish church which was rebuilt in *c.*1500 was paid for by the wealthy clothier John Smallwood. Steeple Ashton church in Wiltshire, one of the finest in the county, was paid for by the Long and Lucas families, both of whom had grown rich through the woollen cloth trade. The ornate tower of St Stephen's church in the

Plate 3.3 'The Green Man', Crowcombe, Somerset. This figure forms one of the bench-ends in Crowcombe church in west Somerset and dates from 1534. Similar figures are to be found carved in churches throughout the west country, many of them dating from the end of the Middle Ages. Originally the Green Man represented the pre-Christian god of vegetable fertility, and the survival of so many examples of this and other pagan symbols is a tribute to the tenacity of the old beliefs and superstitions, particularly in rural areas.

centre of Bristol beside the former quay along the Frome was paid for during the mid-fifteenth century by John Shipward, a prosperous merchant and a former Mayor of Bristol. There are numerous other examples, but such churches are in a minority, for most places had no single wealthy benefactor, and the enlargement and adornment of the parish church rested entirely upon the parishioners. It is clear from those places for which medieval churchwardens' accounts survive, such as Croscombe, Tintinhull, St Michael's Bath, Yatton and Pilton in Somerset, St Edmund's and St Thomas's in Salisbury, St Laurence's at Reading and several other places, that the money was raised by the parishioners themselves through 'church ales', gifts, collections and other fund-raising activities, and that the building work was arranged and supervised by the churchwardens. For example, the building of a fine new spire at Bridgwater in 1366 at a cost of £137 was financed by parish collections, gifts and bequests, and the whole process from the money-raising to the completion of the building work was organised by the churchwardens. Another example of communal effort comes from the records of the parish of Dunster in west Somerset where the parishioners decided in 1442 to add a new tower to their church. The contract for this survives, made between a local mason, John Marys of Stogursey, and the churchwardens of Dunster, and it is evident that the whole project was a communal enterprise masterminded by the churchwardens on behalf of the entire parish. The money was raised by the parishioners both to pay John Marys and to purchase the necessary materials, stone, timber and scaffolding. The wording of the contract suggests that very few men were to be involved in the building work, and that there was little mechanical assistance, for the stipulation was made that if any of the stones was so large that John Marys and his two or three workmen could not lift it then the parishioners were to provide the necessary additional muscle-power,

> Allso if there by any stone y-wroughte of such quantity that ii men or
> iii at moste may not kary hym, the saide parish shall helpe hym.

According to the terms of the contract, John Marys was to be paid for his work on the tower at the rate of 13*s.* 4*d.* per foot, excluding the materials (Salzman 1952: 514–15).

Above all the parish church towers which dominate the landscape throughout the whole region emphasise more than anything else the universal power and presence of the medieval church even in the remotest and most isolated corners. By the end of the Middle Ages few places in the region were far from the view of a church tower and nowhere was out of earshot of the church bells.

At the same time that parishes were lavishing money on the structure of their churches, they were also engaged in other expensive work on decoration and furnishings. Evidence for the way in which additions to the interior furnishings of a parish church were made throughout the later Middle Ages can be seen from the remarkably full and detailed churchwardens accounts for the parish of Yatton between Bristol and Weston-super-Mare. The accounts begin in 1440 and reveal a very active church life with tremendous fund-raising by the little community. The money was spent on the enlargement, decoration and maintenance of their ornate parish church. In 1446 the Yatton churchwardens started upon a new project, one which was carried out in almost all west-country parish churches during the fifteenth century, the construction of an elaborate rood-screen dividing off the chancel from the nave, and surmounted by the Rood – the figure of the crucified Christ with the attendant figures of the Blessed Virgin and St John. At Yatton the large screen went across both the nave and the two aisles, and had a large loft above the screen on which an organ was later mounted. The first task of the churchwardens, once it had been decided to build a rood screen, was to examine other screens in the locality to get ideas as to the form and shape which would best suit their church. Their accounts record expenses incurred in travelling to local churches including those in Bristol and Easton-in-Gordano, to view the screens. Next, timber had to be purchased, and oak was obtained from as far away as the forest of Selwood on the borders of Somerset and Wiltshire. The work itself was en-trusted to a local craftsman, John Crosse who, with his apprentice ('hys childe') worked for several years on the construction and carving of the elaborate screen. From time to time Crosse was encouraged in his work, not just by money payments, but as in 1454 by 'ale gevyn to Crosse at certyn tymis yn hys worke to make hym well wellede'. When the screen was finished and erected in the church it had then to be painted, and the accounts record large expenditure on paint in Bristol and payments to the painter for his work and for his accommodation. Finally, sixty-nine statues of the Saints were bought to stand on the rood screen. The whole project was an enthusiastic communal effort by the parishioners directed towards the beautifying and adornment of their church.

At Yatton, as in many other places, another expensive late medieval project was the provision of seats and pews throughout the church. No sooner had seats appeared in the naves of parish churches than churchwardens saw in them an opportunity of raising funds, and the custom of charging rents for the right to sit in particular pews was started. The churchwardens' accounts of St Laurence's, Reading, show a regular income from pew rents from the mid-fifteenth century. At Yeovil there was a large regular income from the pew rents during the late Middle Ages; a tariff was fixed, so that seats in the front and near the pulpit cost 18*d.* per annum while those at the back cost 6*d.* or less.

From the evidence which survives in the parish churches themselves, as well as from documentary sources, it is possible to make the difficult imaginative leap which is necessary to recreate a picture of the decoration, furnishing and rich colour of a typical late medieval parish church. The fifteenth-century churchwardens' accounts of St John's, Glastonbury show that the church had a staff of five clergy, that it was decorated with numerous images of the saints including the Blessed Virgin and St Erasmus, St George, St

Plate 3.4 Fifteenth-century brass candelabrum, Bristol Cathedral. This beautiful and rare example of a late medieval candelabrum was formerly in the Temple, the church established by the Knights Templar in Bristol. The church was destroyed by bombing during the Second World War, although its leaning tower survives, and the candelabrum now hangs in the Berkeley chapel in Bristol Cathedral. At the top is a statue of the Virgin and Child, and below is the figure of St George slaying the Dragon, while the arms for the candles are decorated with brass leaves. It illustrates the sort of lavish and expensive treasures with which the pre-Reformation churches were adorned, especially in a wealthy port like Bristol, and it is a reminder of the mass of artistic treasures which were lost in the upheavals and destruction of the Reformation.

Catherine and St Nicholas (Dunning 1976).

Perhaps the most difficult aspect of the late medieval parish churches to imagine is the colour, since many churches must have been a riot of colour, with painted stone and woodwork, wall paintings and stained glass. Enough survives in a few churches, however, to show what most must once have been like. Fine wallpaintings survive at Sutton Bingham and Ditcheat (Somerset), at Tarrant Crawford and Gussage St Andrew (Dorset), at Hurstborne Tarrant, Idsworth, Catherington and Stoke Charity (Hants), and Aldermaston, Enborne, Hampstead Norris and Ashampstead (Berks).

The most characteristic religious foundations of the later Middle Ages were the chantry chapels or endowments whereby a priest was employed to sing masses for the soul of the founder. By the fifteenth century all the larger churches in the region and many of the smaller ones had at least one chantry, each with its chantry priest. For example two chantries were established in St Mary Recliffe, Bristol by the wealthy and pious merchant William Canynges in 1466 and 1467; and a chantry was founded at St Mary's, Southampton by Joan Holmhegge, widow of Nicholas Holmhegge, a wealthy merchant and former Mayor of Southampton. Other evidence for such foundations survives in the elegant chapels which are such a prominent feature of the cathedrals, like the six major chantries in Winchester Cathedral, or in the specially built aisles and side chapels, often of the most lavish and elaborate construction, in many parish churches, such as the Beauchamp Chapels at Bromham and St John's, Devizes in Wiltshire, the Morton Chapel at Bere Regis, Dorset, the remains of the guild chantries in St Thomas's Church, Salisbury, the Brocas Chapel at Sherborne St John near Basingstoke, and countless others (Wood-Legh 1965).

The Guilds also vied with each other in the opulence of their chapels and in the lights, tapestries, paintings, statues, and carving with which they were decorated. The Chantry Chapel of the Guild of Merchant Tailors in Bristol, for example, occupied the whole of the south aisle of St Ewen's Church; it was separated from the nave by carved wooden screens, and an inventory of 1401 shows that the chapel was decorated with fine tapestries showing scenes from the life of St John the Baptist, their patron saint, numerous frontals and other hangings for the altar and vestments for the chantry priest, chalices, plate, processional banners or 'pageants', one of them decorated with the *Agnus Dei*, candlesticks, linen and a quantity of smaller articles. In late medieval Bristol, as in many other towns, church and civic life were inextricably bound together. Merchants' guilds and craft fellowships contributed lavishly to the parish churches, founded the chantries and maintained the almshouses.

Some of the numerous Bristol guilds were primarily religious in purpose, most notably the Guild of Kalendars, an ancient association of clergy and laity which existed to offer masses and intercessions for their brethren, living and dead, and to engage in charitable works towards those who were old or sick. The Guild of Kalendars met in All Saints' Church. The Fraternity of Mariners was founded in 1445 in the Hospital of St Bartholomew, and consisted of a priest and twelve poor mariners whose duty it was to pray for the well-being and safety of those at sea. They were maintained by a levy on all cargoes coming into the port of Bristol. Other religious guilds also had a practical purpose, like the guild associated with the chapel of Our Lady on Bristol Bridge. This was charged with the task of maintaining the bridge

> to keep and repair the Bridge of Bristol, piers, arches and walls, for the defence thereof against the ravages of the sea, ebbing and flowing daily under the same.

Collegiate Foundations

Even grander and more opulent than the chantries were the collegiate foundations where a community of priests was employed to say daily masses. An example of this was the college of priests founded at Tormarton north of Bath by Sir John de Riviere in 1334, for a warden and four chaplains who were to maintain a perpetual round of masses according to a detailed plan carefully prepared by the founder whose mutilated tomb survives in the chancel, showing him holding a model of the church. A less ambitious collegiate foundation was established at Bridport by a local merchant John Munden in 1361. Munden's chantry was set up in the chapel of St Michael at Bridport and consisted of two priests who lived together in a nearby chantry house, a building which had previously been occupied by Munden himself. This was no different from scores of other similar foundations, but what distinguishes Munden's chantry is that one of the chantry priests, William Savernak, kept a careful account of the daily expenditure of the household for the years 1453–60. This shows in minute detail the amounts spent on food for the two priests, their visitors and their servant, on the upkeep of the chantry house with its garden, orchard and dovecote, on the maintenance of the chapel and on the properties in Bridport from which the income of the foundation was derived. Savernak's account book therefore provides an almost unique record of the daily life in this small chantry. The picture which emerges from the accounts is of a quiet, regular life, with few disturbances to the tranquil routine of the two elderly chantry priests other than those provided by the feasts and fasts of the Church's year. There is of course no way of judging the devotion of the priests, nor of knowing whether the services were performed devoutly or perfunctorily; but the chantry, like many other town chantries, was subject to an annual visitation by the civic authorities, and it was probably for these visitations that William Savernak kept his elaborately detailed account book (Wood-Legh 1953).

An incomparably grander collegiate foundation was established in St George's Chapel at Windsor during the fourteenth century, consisting of a college of secular canons which comprised a Dean, twelve canons, thirteen priest-vicars as well as clerks and choristers.

Hospitals, Almshouses and Schools

Also characteristic of the later Middle Ages were the charitable endowments designed both to perpetuate the memory of the founder and to provide for the sick, the old, the poor, and for the education of scholars and the training of the clergy. The most famous of such foundations in the region is the Hospital of St Cross at Winchester. This was originally founded in 1136 by Bishop Henry of Blois, and the massive church of the hospital was begun in the twelfth century and finished in the thirteenth, but the attractive hospital buildings which survive with their cloister, kitchens, dining hall and range of individual lodgings for the bedesmen are the result of a complete rebuilding by Cardinal Beaufort about 1445. A medieval almshouse survives at Sherborne where the Hospital of St John the Baptist and St John the Evangelist was established in 1437 for twelve poor men and four poor women, with a matron and chaplain to attend to their bodily and spiritual well-being. The hospital with its beautifully preserved chapel and refectory is still used for its original purpose, although it was considerably enlarged during the nineteenth century. At Abingdon Christ's Hospital was founded in 1446 and the much restored buildings survive together with later almshouses to form a charming group in the churchyard of St Helen's Parish Church. Bishop Richard Poore of Salisbury was an active patron of the Hospital of St Nicholas at Salisbury which was charged with the duty of caring for the poor, the sick and travellers. This hospital also survived the Reformation and continues to function. Two other medieval hospitals were founded in Salisbury, the Hospital of St John the Baptist and St Anthony established in the thirteenth century, and the Hospital of the Holy Trinity established in the fourteenth century. Other medieval towns of the region saw a similar proliferation of late medieval charitable foundations.

The educational foundation destined to become by far the most famous in the region was the school established at Winchester by Bishop William of Wykeham in the late fourteenth century. This like other medieval schools was intended primarily to supply educated recruits to the ranks of the clergy, but Wykeham's genius encompassed the idea not only of his school at Winchester but also of his foundation of New College, Oxford in the first English example of a coherent, graduated educational system. Winchester College was founded

Plate 3.5 St Cross, Winchester. The hospital was founded by Bishop Henry of Blois in 1136, and the great church, of which the eastern end is shown here, was begun soon afterwards. The massive Norman architecture and large size of the church reflects the wealth of the medieval bishops of Winchester and the grandiose plan proposed for his hospital by Henry of Blois.

in 1382 and teaching began in 1394. The original foundation consisted of a warden, a headmaster, ten fellows, three chaplains, one usher, three chapel clerks, seventy 'poor and needy scholars', sixteen choristers and ten commoners or fee-paying scholars. Not only were William of Wykeham's foundations educationally far-sighted and radical, but architecturally they were also planned on the grandest scale, arranged around a quadrangle based upon the monastic idea of the enclosed cloister with a common chapel and dining hall for the scholars and their teachers.

Critics of the Church

Because of the wealth, power, and splendour of the late medieval Church in the region, and because of the scale and number of the surviving buildings, it is easy to forget that there were many vociferous critics of the Church, and that such critics were particularly strong in the Wessex region. John Wycliffe himself was instituted to a prebend in the collegiate foundation at Westbury just outside Bristol in 1362, but apart from his institution there is no evidence that he ever came to Westbury again, and he appears to have found substitutes to perform his duties there. Bristol, however, on the edge of the dioceses of Worcester and of Bath and Wells, with many craftsmen and traders and with trading links with London, and up the valleys of the Severn and the Avon to the cloth-working areas of Gloucestershire, Coventry and the Midlands, was very favourably situated to become an active centre of religious dissent, and an underlying current of Lollard opinions was to be a feature of the town throughout the later Middle Ages.

In the Lollard revolt of 1414 some forty weavers and other cloth-workers from Bristol marched to join the forces of Sir John Oldcastle at St Giles's Fields, the largest single contingent in that motley and ill-fated army. Heretical beliefs, often of a crude, inarticulate kind continued to be held by many people in the region throughout the fifteenth century, and heretics were occasionally tried for attacking the authority of the Pope and the bishops, or for preaching against such things as pilgrimages, veneration of the saints or images, for denying the doctrine of transubstantiation, or for distributing Lollard tracts. In 1418, for example, a man from Bath was imprisoned at Salisbury and his books containing extracts from the Bible in English were publicly burnt; John Puttock, a dyer from Frome, was tried in 1431 for distributing Lollard pamphlets; William Wakeham of Devizes was accused in 1434 of reading the Bible in English and of spreading Lollard teaching. There were many other similar examples, and it is clear from the evidence given at these and other trials that Bristol was a main source of heretical views. Further east in the region Lollard groups were sufficiently strong and determined to join in the widespread revolts of 1431. In Wiltshire a group of Lollards under the leadership of John Kymrygge or Ketridge made an unsuccessful attack upon the cathedral at Salisbury in May 1431. Later in the same month another group of Lollards assembled at the village of East Hendred under the leadership of William Perkins and marched to Abingdon to attack the abbey. Both these attacks ended in complete failure and the leaders were executed, but it is an indication of the strength of Lollard feeling and of the determination of the critics of the Church that they should have been made at all, against such apparently overwhelming odds. In 1434 there was a Lollard rising at Wokingham, and in 1440 Cardinal Beaufort, Bishop of Winchester, felt sufficiently concerned about the spread of Lollard beliefs in his diocese to make a detailed enquiry about the spread of heretical and erroneous views and doctrines among simple men (Thompson 1965).

The dominating presence of large and wealthy monastic houses in so many towns inevitably gave rise on occasion to bitter quarrels between the monks and the townsfolk. An example of this occurred at Sherborne in 1437 when, after a long period of ill-feeling between the monks and the townsmen over access to the parish church of All Hallows which was attached to the monastic church, and over baptismal dues, bell-ringing, religious processions and a host of other minor matters, the townsmen actually set fire to the abbey church and did an immense amount of damage. The fierce heat of the fire left a red stain upon the stone-work of the church which is still clearly visible, 'the fossilised remains of a quarrel', and it was following the fire that so much rebuilding work was done upon Sherborne Abbey, including the fine fan vaulting of the choir, the first major fan vault in England.

A powerful mixture of economic grievance, anti-clerical feeling and political opposition to government policy gave rise to the widespread riots and disturbances of 1450. Much of the protest was focused upon the Church and upon Church leaders because of the prominent part played in political affairs by the bishops. In 1449 ships and men were gathered at Portsmouth for a last revival by Henry VI of the long war with France. The soldiers and sailors were soon in a mutinous mood through lack of adequate provisions and the royal failure to settle their long-overdue arrears of pay. In January 1450 Bishop Adam Moleyns of Chichester, one of the most prominent and also most unpopular of the king's advisers, was sent to Portsmouth to appease the troops. When it was discovered that he had not brought the arrears of pay, the soldiers and sailors burst into the *Domus Dei* where he was conducting a service, dragged him out of the church, and murdered him. The scandal and implications of their action lasted for many years; the whole town was placed under excommunication, and it was not until more than fifty years later in 1508, and then only after an elaborate ceremony of penance, that all the ecclesiastical restrictions and censures were lifted.

In June 1450 also, during the course of the widespread disturbances known as Cade's rebellion, popular anger was directed against William Ayscough, Bishop of Salisbury (1438–50), who was the King's chaplain and one of a small group dominating royal policy. While the Bishop was saying mass in the priory church of the order of Bonhommes at Edington on the northern edge of Salisbury Plain, a group of men, allegedly led by a butcher from Salisbury, entered the church, proclaimed the Bishop to be a traitor, dragged him out of the church, and on the hillside robbed and murdered him; they then proceeded to plunder the priory. Seventy-four men were later indicted for the crime.

A contemporary chronicler, obviously horrified by the story, described the dramatic events as follows:

> William Ascoghe, bisshop of Salisbury, was slayn of his owen parisshens and people . . . after that he hadde saide Masse, and was drawn from the auter and led up to an hill ther beside, in his awbe and his stole aboute his necke; and there they slew him horribly, their fader and their bisshope, and spoillid him unto the nakid skyn, and rente his blody shirte in to pecis. (Davis 1855: 64)

On the same day, 29 June 1450, 300 men were said to have attacked the Cathedral at Salisbury and the bishop's palace there, and other risings took place at Tilshead, Devizes, Wilton, Biddestone and elsewhere in Wiltshire (Thompson 1965; Watts 1983).

Lollard beliefs continued to form an important undercurrent to orthodox religious life in the region during the later fifteenth century, and occasional heresy trials continued right up to the eve of the Reformation. From the evidence of these trials it is clear that strong Lollard groups existed in the Chilterns, the Thames valley and in Bristol and its surrounding district. One example, typical of numerous others, was Thomas Taylor, a fuller of Newbury, who was charged in 1490 with possessing Lollard books, of denying the doctrine of transubstantiation, condemning images and of saying that it was better to give a penny to a poor man than to go as a pilgrim to Santiago. At his trial he renounced his heresy and was sentenced to perform public penance at Newbury, Reading and Wokingham. In north Berkshire an heretical priest, John Whithorn, rector of Letcombe Basset, drew a group of Lollards around him from Faringdon, Buscot, Coxwell and other places in the district, and they were charged in 1499 with possessing the gospels and other books in English. In 1508 Whithorn was again before the court charged with heresy, and this time he was sentenced to execution. Other cases which came before the Ecclesiastical Courts reveal a whole group of Lollard sympathisers in the industrial suburbs of Redcliffe and St Thomas on the southern edge of Bristol in 1511. Among them were John Bouway of Redcliffe Street who seems to have been their leader, Robert Quick a carpet-maker of St Thomas, Henry Tuck a wire-drawer, who knew the whole of the Apocalypse by heart, and several others. In 1514 the Ecclesiastical Court at Salisbury tried Lollards from a whole series of Wiltshire villages and towns including Devizes, Marlborough, Salisbury, Pewsey, Wilsford, Chirton and Marden. John Bent from Chirton and John Tropnel, a weaver from Bradford-on-Avon were executed in 1517–18. There is no doubt that there were many people throughout the whole region who were ready and eager to accept the changes in doctrine and Church organisation which came with the Reformation.

Farming during the Later Middle Ages

The changing economic circumstances following the catastrophe of the Black Death, with declining population, lower demand for corn leading to reduced corn prices and making arable farming less profitable, together with an expanding cloth industry and higher prices for wool, led to numerous changes in farming practice and land tenure throughout the whole of the Wessex region. These changes included a marked decrease in the extent of arable land and a retreat from the margins of cultivation which had been reached during the population peak of the thirteenth century, a great increase in large-scale sheep farming, a decline in the direct cultivation of their demesne lands by the major landowners and the widespread leasing of lands to tenants, coupled with a movement away from labour services and towards money wages. Lands which had been brought into cultivation during the high prices of the thirteenth century were allowed to revert to grass, and in many places were not to be ploughed again until the period of the Napoleonic Wars. The process of contraction and abandonment of arable land can be seen all over the region. At Whiteparish on the borders of Wiltshire and Hampshire, for example, the twelfth and thirteenth centuries had seen the appearance of seven new hamlets and an increase in the agricultural land of some 1,800 acres. During the fourteenth century several of these hamlets were abandoned or shrank to single farmsteads, former open fields were enclosed and turned to pasture, while the manorial system broke down as the demesne lands were leased out to small landowners (Taylor 1967; Hatcher 1977: 22–39).

At Inkpen on the Hampshire/Berkshire border, belonging to the Premonstratensian Abbey of Titchfield, the production of cereals declined from 362 quarters of grain in 1301 to 180 quarters in 1347. Likewise at Durrington on the Wiltshire chalklands the poorer lands which had been brought into cultivation during the thirteenth century were gradually allowed to revert to grass during the early decades of the fourteenth century, and the total area of demesne arable fell from 300 acres in 1324 to 213 acres in 1359 (Watts 1983: Hare 1981a).

Meanwhile the sheep flocks, especially those kept by the great landowners of the region, increased substantially. Large demesne flocks were to be found on many manors, often numbering 1,000 or more sheep (*VCH Wilts* IV: 19–22). At Heytesbury in 1411 the Hungerford estate had a flock of 1,479 sheep and 30 lambs, while in 1466 there were 1,526 sheep in the demesne flock there. By 1330 Glastonbury Abbey had 1,504 sheep on its Mendip manors of Doulting, Wrington, Marksbury, Mells, Batcombe and Pilton; while St Swithin's priory in Winchester had an enormous flock of more than 20,000 sheep on its scattered manors. Throughout the chalklands of Hampshire, Berkshire, Wiltshire and Dorset the great estates pursued a vigorous policy of flock management, with centralised control of all their flocks. The survival of the stock book of St Swithin's Priory for the years 1390–93 provides an unusually complete picture of a large-scale, closely controlled sheep-farming operation. In 1390 the priory had 20 flocks with a total of 20,357 sheep. Sheep were regularly transferred between manors, and the wool from all the flocks was brought to Winchester for sorting and sale. A similar integration of scattered flocks and centralised wool sales was pursued on the estates of the Bishops of Winchester and Salisbury, and on the Hungerford estates the central control over the flocks was even closer, with breeding flocks being maintained on the Somerset manors of Farleigh, Holt and Wellow sending sheep to the Wiltshire chalkland manors for grazing, and with the wool from the flocks being sent to the central wool store at Heytesbury (Hare 1981b).

By the end of the fourteenth century most lay landlords had ceased to use the labour services of their tenants to cultivate their demesne land and had instead begun to let the lands for regular cash rents. Many of the demesne lands on the great ecclesiastical estates continued to be directly cultivated, but by the end of the fifteenth century most Church land was also let to tenants. For example on the manor of Crawley near Winchester belonging to the Bishopric of Winchester, the lands were gradually leased to tenants, starting with the pigs in 1370, followed by the rabbit warren; in 1407 a tentative arrangement for leasing the demesne farm was made, followed by a permanent policy of leasing in 1448. The change in the policy of the great landowners from direct farming to leasing was not confined to the chalklands, but occurred throughout the region. For example, at Lopen near Crewkerne in south Somerset the amount of demesne arable was substantially reduced during the 1370s with a consequent reduction in the number of labourers required, and in the early fifteenth century the whole demesne was divided up and let to tenants in small parcels (Gras 1930; VCH Somerset IV: 166).

On the manor of Muchelney in the claylands of central Somerset the Benedictine abbey gradually substituted money rents for labour services during the fifteenth century in order to raise money to rebuild the monastery in the most up-to-date architectural style (Dunning 1978: 15). For the landlords this policy had the advantage of providing a guaranteed money income free from the necessity of imposing labour services and free from the unwilling labour and other services of tenants, and from the constant battles between the estate auditors and the manorial reeves. It also provided bishops and religious houses with urgently needed cash for lavish church and cathedral building projects and the foundation of expensive colleges, almshouses and chantries. Even the Cistercians were obliged to abandon their resistance to the leasing of their lands to laymen, since with the decline of their original enthusiasm they faced increasing difficulties in recruiting sufficient lay-brothers who actually worked the lands on their granges and scattered farms. For example the Cistercian abbey of Quarr on the Isle of Wight gradually leased more and more of its lands during the fifteenth century until by the early sixteenth century it was almost entirely dependent for its income upon money rents, a great contrast with its previous situation (Hockey 1970).

For the more enterprising tenants the chance to lease demesne lands provided a remarkable opportunity for enrichment and enabled numerous families to rise to wealth and gentry status. One such family who became wealthy and influential along the Wiltshire/Berkshire border were the Goddards of Aldbourne who during the fourteenth century had been tenants and manorial reeves on the estates of the Duchy of Lancaster. During the fifteenth century they seized the opportunity to lease the demesne lands at Aldbourne and Ogbourne and amassed substantial wealth so that by the early sixteenth century members of the family were being referred to as gentlemen (Hare 1981b).

The retreat of the great landowners from the direct farming of their demesne lands, and the increase in the leasing of lands for money rents in place of the labour services which had formerly been exacted, led to a greatly increased volume of transactions over land. Lands were exchanged and enclosed, often to be laid down to grass for sheep-farming, and as large demesne farms were fragmented and enterprising tenants seized the opportunities to build up farms and small estates, and as lands became vacant during the Black Death and other plagues, so some families rose from the position of bondmen in the fourteenth century to that of husbandmen or even yeomen by the sixteenth century. The increase in land transactions can be seen clearly on the estates of Titchfield Abbey as the figures (Table 8) for transactions over twenty-five-year periods, with a marked concentration during the five years following the Black Death, show:

Table 8 Peasant land transactions on the Titchfield Abbey Estates, 1272–1377.

	Period	Transactions
1272–1297	25 years	283
1297–1322	25 years	492
1322–1347	25 years	749
1347–1352	5 years	355
1352–1377	25 years	555

(Watts 1967)

Deserted and Shrunken Villages

As a result of plagues, falling population, decline in arable acreage, low corn prices, retreat from marginal lands and other farming changes of the late fourteenth and fifteenth centuries the desertion and partial desertion of villages occurred in many parts of the region. For example at Whiteparish where scattered settlements had proliferated during the twelfth and thirteenth centuries, the settlement at Cowsfield was almost completely deserted during the later Middle Ages, and the hamlets of Cowsfield Louveras, Whelpley and More were partially deserted; in part this was due to the effect of the Black Death which had a devastating impact on the area, in part it was the result of a slow, gradual decline during the fourteenth and fifteenth centuries (Taylor 1967).

Along the chalkland valleys of Hampshire, Wiltshire, Berkshire and Dorset whole villages were abandoned or were reduced to single farms. The Iwerne valley in the Dorset chalklands had a string of medieval settlements stretching from Iwerne Minster through Preston, Iwerne Courtney, Shroton, Ranston, Steepleton, Lazerton and Ash to Stourpaine where the Iwerne brook joins the Stour. During the later Middle Ages and early sixteenth century all these settlements except Iwerne Minster, Iwerne Courtney and Stourpaine disappeared or were reduced to single farmsteads. Similarly in the Piddle valley of Dorset the settlements and former villages at Little Piddle, Muston, Waterston, Druce, Burleston and Bardolfston disappeared or shrank to a single farm. Many of the sites still retain clearly recognisable earthworks, and at Bardolfston the grass-covered hollow way of the former village street with the former house-sites on either side and the yards and paddocks behind them give an admirable indication of what this small medieval village looked like (Taylor 1970).

Such desertions are not only to be found on the thin soils of the chalk-lands. At Eaton Hastings in the Thames valley north-west of Faringdon twenty-nine households were recorded in 1086, and a manorial survey of 1333 listed thirty-nine households, so that it was obviously a sizeable village. Decline set in during the later fourteenth century, probably following the Black Death, and by the early sixteenth century all the inhabitants had gone. Today only the tiny church with architecture dating from the twelfth and thirteenth centuries survives as a reminder of the village which once flourished there; the field beside the church is covered by the mounds of the former house sites on either side of the hollow which marks the line of the village street (Brooks 1969; Biddle 1961–62).

The village of Abbotstone two miles from New Alresford was a flourishing village until the early fourteenth century, and eighteen househol-ders were listed in the Lay Subsidy of 1327. By 1428, eighty years after the Black Death, fewer than ten households remained in the village, and a century later all the lands were in the hands of one landowner, John Pawlett. In 1589 the Bishop of Winchester agreed to amalgamate the two parishes of Abbot-stone and Itchen Stoke because the church at Abbotstone was utterly decayed and collapsed (Sanderson 1971).

At Mudford on the heavy clay soils north-east of Yeovil seven hamlets flourished during the twelfth and thirteenth centuries, but two were completely deserted during the later Middle Ages and three others declined to little more than single farmsteads. The site of Nether Adber, one of the former hamlets, remains as one of the most impressive and clearly defined deserted settlement sites in Somerset. The former house sites are clearly visible as grass-covered platforms, and the former village street and lanes remain as hollow ways; air photographs reveal the site of the moated manor house with its adjacent fish-pond, while beyond the houses large areas of ridge and furrow can be seen, showing the extent of the former common arable fields. At Nether Adber, as at many other places in the region, the evidence suggests that a change from arable farming to large-scale sheep-farming during the later Middle Ages is the probable explanation for the abandonment of this low-lying clayland site which must always have been a very damp and muddy place in which to live (Aston 1977).

The declining profitability of arable farming and the pressure from landlords and from those who had leased demesne land to establish ever-larger sheep flocks and large areas of unimpeded grazing land was responsible for the desertion of villages and hamlets in many other places. The process can be seen at work during the early sixteenth century in a group of parishes in south Dorset belonging to Sir William Fyllol. In 1521 his tenants at Bincombe complained that he was trying to evict them in order to keep sheep, while his tenants at nearby Winterborne Came complained that their lands were overrun by his sheep. They stated that 'because of the greate oppressions and injuries' they would not be able to pay their rent 'nor be able to Abide in their countrey by cause of the saide great oppressions'. It is clear that their complaints were in vain, for all along the south Winterborne valley there is a string of deserted village sites – Winterborne Herringston, Farringdon, Germayne, Came and Whitcombe. It was of these places and particularly of Winterborne Farringdon that the Dorset topographer, Thomas Gerard, wrote in 1630 'a lone Church, for there is hardlie any house left in the Parish, such of late hath beene the Covetousness of some private Men, that to increase their Demesnes have depopulated whole parishes'.

Likewise the whole village of Hardington in the wooded claylands near Frome, part of the former royal forest of Selwood, was turned into pasture during the fifteenth and sixteenth centuries by the Bamfylde family, the major landowners in the area, and in 1583 an observer commented upon the land-lord's action:

> Hardington, the which village is wholly enclosed and made pasture;
> and so no house left but his owne, and he pulleth downe the churche,
> and it is scarse knowne where the parsonage house stode, to which
> there is knowne to be glebe belonging but where it lyeth will hardly be
> founde; therefore some spedy care woulde be had to loke to it.

Other late medieval desertions came about because of the creation of deer parks. For example, just south of Salisbury along the Avon valley the road to Downton makes two long and apparently needless detours. Both detours take the road around late medieval parks, Standlynch and Barford, and the creation of both of these parks involved the destruction of a village and the eviction of the inhabitants. Today only Standlynch Farm and Barford Park Farm bear witness to the former existence of these settlements. At Wilton the

Herberts destroyed a large part of the common arable fields of Washerne to enlarge their park around their house, provoking violent but useless riots there in 1549; and in north Wiltshire during the sixteenth century the Dukes of Somerset created a great new park at Savernake, leading to fruitless complaints from their tenants that they 'should have no manner of common for their beasts which would be to their utter undoing'.

As well as economic decline, pestilence and social unrest during the later Middle Ages, the coastal areas also suffered badly from foreign raids during the long period of wars with France. The French frequently attacked the Isle of Wight, as in the invasion of 1377 when they landed at Yarmouth and advanced across the Island, creating great havoc and destruction in their path; Yarmouth and Newport were sacked, and Newtown never really recovered from the attack; although after a siege the French finally failed to capture Carisbrooke castle. There were further French invasions in 1402 and 1417 as well as many minor incursions and attacks upon shipping by pirates, so that in 1489 the Island was described as

> desolate and not inhabited, but occupied with beasts and cattle, so that if hasty remedy be not provided, the Isle cannot long be kept and defended, but open and ready to the hands of the King's enemies, which God forbid.
> (Hockey 1982: 81–102)

Likewise the Dorset ports suffered severely from French raids upon the coast. Melcombe Regis was burnt in 1377 and again in 1380, and Bridport and Lyme Regis and Poole suffered similar attacks. In 1401 the Patent Rolls of Henry IV record that Lyme Regis 'is so wasted and burned by attacks of the sea and assaults of the King's enemies and frequent pestilences that scarcely a twentieth part of it is now inhabited'. In 1469 a list and valuation of the possessions of the monastery at Abbotsbury explained that the low value of the manor of Portesham was 'because few tenants dare dwell there for fear of the enemies of the King and the whole kingdom of England frequently arriving and coming by sea there'. Bexington was burnt by the French in 1440 and the inhabitants were carried off as prisoners; the village never recovered and in 1451 the benefice was united with Puncknowle 'because of the poverty caused by the attacks of the enemy'.

Portsmouth was burnt by the French in 1338, for in spite of its importance as a naval port, it was undefended by walls, and although the town recovered sufficiently to be the base from which the English army sailed to the great victory at Crecy in 1346, it was again raided by the French in 1369, and 1377–80 (Temple Patterson 1976: 24–7).

Nonetheless in spite of the economic and other difficulties of the later Middle Ages, it was possible for energetic men to prosper and to acquire wealth and land. The number and quality of the surviving castles, houses, churches and monastic buildings in the region bear striking witness to the wealth that was available, and show that some families and individuals profited greatly from the conditions of the times. One of the most spectacular examples of rapid rise to power, fortune and influence was that of the Hungerford family whose wealth came from service to the Crown and especially to the Duchy of Lancaster. During the fourteenth century this family acquired a vast estate stretching over Somerset, Wiltshire and Berkshire, and used their lands for intensive and highly profitable sheep-farming on a large scale. Sir Thomas Hungerford, who was Speaker of the House of Commons in 1377 and chief steward and surveyor of all the lands of the Duchy of Lancaster in Wales and southern England, built the great castle at Farleigh Hungerford on the borders of Somerset and Wiltshire, while his son Walter, Speaker of the House of Commons in 1414, High Treasurer of England under Henry VI, and Baron Hungerford, greatly extended the castle, incorporating within it the parish church of Farleigh which became the family chapel.

The Martyns, an ancient Dorset family, acquired great wealth through trade and commerce in London. Sir William Martyn was lord mayor of London in 1493, and as well as his commercial interests he also enjoyed the lucrative office of Collector of Tonnage and Poundage in the City. Sir William's wealth enabled him to build the great house at Athelhampton Hall,

Plate 3.6 Lytes Cary, near Ilchester, Somerset. The late-medieval manor house of the Lyte family, and a good example of the sort of comfortable, elegant house which wealthy gentry families were building at that time. The photograph shows the solar wing, with the parlour below and the great chamber above, both lit by the fine oriel window which bears the date 1533. The building on the right is the medieval chapel of *c.* 1340. The house was occupied by successive generations of the Lyte family from the late thirteenth century until 1755.

as well as to rebuild the parish church at Puddletown nearby, complete with a fine private chapel now full of the family monuments. Other families amassed great wealth through the profits of the woollen cloth trade, among them Sir John Fastolf of Castle Combe and the families of Long and Lucas, both clothiers of Steeple Ashton, who were jointly responsible for the opulent rebuilding of the parish church there during the late fifteenth century.

Other late medieval houses in the region also provide abundant evidence of the available wealth. These include Ockwells Manor in the Thames valley near Maidenhead, a notable house of unusual plan, described by Sir Nikolaus Pevsner as 'the most refined and the most sophisticated timber-framed mansion in England', which was built by Sir John Norris between 1446 and 1466 out of the fortune he made in the royal service, and Great Chalfield in Wiltshire, a fine manor house built during the 1480s by Thomas Tropenell, also a royal servant and a steward to the Hungerford family on their Wiltshire estates.

Other notable late medieval buildings include fortified strongholds like Donnington, Nunney, Woodsford or the bishop's palace at Wells; and comfortable manor houses such as those at Barnston, Bingham's Melcombe or Moigne Court in Dorset, Lytes Cary in Somerset, Westwood and South Wraxall in Wiltshire, and many more.

Industries

The fourteenth and fifteenth centuries saw a massive development in clothmaking as the old trade centred on towns such as Bristol, Marlborough, Reading and Winchester declined in importance and was replaced by a new, thriving rural industry. One reason for this change was the guild restrictions encountered in the towns, but much more important was the increasing use of the water-powered fulling mill, which became more and more widespread during the fourteenth century. The industry moved into the countryside as mills were built along the fast-flowing streams and especially along the Wiltshire/Somerset border; previously small villages and hamlets sprang into prominence in the industry, and new thriving towns emerged such as Frome, Shepton Mallet, Bruton, Beckington, Pensford, Warminster, Westbury, Trowbridge and Bradford-on-Avon.

The most important product of this new, rural industry was undyed broadcloth, which was exported to the Low Countries for dyeing and finishing. This was a high-quality, heavily fulled cloth, and the weaving followed the fulling mills in moving to the countryside, since the fulling mills were by far the most capital-intensive part of the industry and were built and controlled by the wealthy clothiers. These men bought the raw wool and sent it out to cottagers to spin; from the fulling mills they distributed the yarn to weavers who worked in their own homes and who sent the cloth back to the mill for fulling and tentering or stretching. Some cloth was also dyed and finished by the clothiers, as is witnessed by the imports of dyestuffs – such as woad and madder and great quantities of the essential mordant, alum – through the ports of Bristol and Southampton during the fifteenth century, by the fame of the red cloth of Stroud and Castle Combe and the striped cloth of Salisbury, and by the late medieval carvings which survive in several parish churches such as Seend in Wiltshire and Spaxton in Somerset illustrating finishing tools and processes. The phenomenal growth of the cloth industry in the region during the later Middle Ages meant that many of the clothiers who supplied the capital and organised the whole process of production became very wealthy and famous especially during the sixteenth century, like William Stumpe of Malmesbury who bought the abbey there at the Dissolution of the monasteries, John Smallwood of Newbury, the 'Jack of Newbury' who paid for the rebuilding of Newbury parish church on the grandest scale, Thomas Dolman the Berkshire clothier who built Shaw House near Newbury, the grandest Elizabethan mansion in Berkshire, the Horton family of Bradford-on-Avon and Westwood, and families like the Baileys, Flowers, Longs, Yerburys, Lucases and others who for several generations were of crucial importance in the cloth trade and who through it acquired great wealth.

A good example of a village which was revolutionised by the spread of the cloth industry into rural areas is Castle Combe in Wiltshire. Castle Combe is unusually well-documented for the later Middle Ages so that it is possible to trace the rapid growth of the cloth industry there. During the early fourteenth century a fulling mill was established in the narrow valley north-east of Bath where the fast-flowing stream provided power for the mill wheel. The cloth trade flourished, and by the early fifteenth century three fulling mills were sited along the stream. In 1435 a gig-mill was being used to raise the nap on the cloth before shearing to produce a fine finish, the earliest reference in England to the mechanisation of this part of the cloth-making process. Castle Combe developed rapidly as an industrial centre, encouraged by the lord of the manor, Sir John Fastolf; by 1458 fifty additional houses had been built or rebuilt in the attractive local stone, and a new tower was added to the parish church, appropriately decorated with cloth working implements (Beresford and St Joseph 1958: 267–9).

Although the importance of many older towns which had traditionally dominated the cloth trade declined in face of the rapid rise of the rural industry based on the fulling mills, one town which did retain a substantial share of the trade was Salisbury. There were already fulling mills just outside the city by the late thirteenth century; there was a mill at Stratford-sub-Castle by 1277, and at West Harnham the fulling mill, which still survives there, was already in operation by 1299. During the fourteenth century cloth-making was well-established in Salisbury and the city was also an important centre for the marketing of cloth brought from the mills spread along the chalkland river valleys of Salisbury Plain and south Wiltshire. Wool and yarn were also sold in the markets, and throughout the fifteenth century London merchants and drapers regularly attended the Lady Day cloth fair held in the city. The Salisbury speciality was a fine striped cloth known as 'rays' (*VCH Wilts* IV: 115–47; Chandler 1983: 73–91). Reading, Newbury, Abingdon, Basingstoke and Romsey, which was an important cloth finishing and dyeing centre, also remained important in the cloth trade and prospered as manufacturing, marketing and distribution centres.

Other industries also developed during the fourteenth and fifteenth centuries. Lead mining on Mendip was important throughout the later Middle Ages, much of it under the control of the Bishops of Bath and Wells or of the Abbot of Glastonbury. The main centres of production were at Priddy, Charterhouse, East Harptree and at Chewton Mendip where the superb late medieval church tower is a reminder of the wealth which was derived from the lead mines (Gough 1967). Coal was mined in north Somerset and in the Kingswood area north-east of Bristol. Most of this medieval mining was small-scale production in shallow pits, but by 1437 a 'colepytte' at Kilmersdon near Midsomer Norton was deep enough to have underground passages and an adit or drainage channel, and the spoil mounds from these pits remain in the form of mounds, some large enough to be covered with trees. Small-scale working of iron ore was also to be found in several parts of the region, notably on the Brendon Hills, although the greatest supplies of iron ore came from the Forest of Dean, being brought down the Severn by barge and into the port of Bristol. Other locally important late-medieval industries included the manufacture of gloves and other leather goods, especially around Yeovil, Ilchester, and throughout the villages of south Somerset; pottery-making, notably at Bridgwater, Ham Green near Bristol, Donyatt near Ilminster, Crockerton near Warminster, Minety near Malmesbury, and on the heathland around Poole Harbour in Dorset. The amount of building work both secular and ecclesiastical meant that quarries throughout Wessex were kept busy producing stone, and that very large numbers of quarrymen, masons, carpenters, and a host of other building workers and associated craftsmen were provided with employment.

The two chief ports of the region, Bristol and Southampton, also prospered during the later Middle Ages. Bristol had an extensive trade with Ireland and with Spain, and benefited from the great increase in cloth production in east Somerset and west Wiltshire and in Gloucestershire and the Severn valley. Unlike Southampton, Bristol had the advantage of a secure harbour, safe from pirates and from foreign attack, while easy communications made Bristol the focal point of a rapidly expanding industrial region. By the mid-fourteenth century the customs returns for the export of cloth reveal that in spite of being badly affected by the Black Death, Bristol was the predominant English port for the export of woollen cloth, averaging 750 cloths annually or some 60 per cent of all the English trade; by 1460 the number of cloths exported had risen to 2,550 and by 1470 to over 5,000 annually. It was a mark of Bristol's prosperity that by a charter of 1373 the town was created a county, separate from both Gloucestershire and Somerset, while the merchants had sufficient wealth to rebuild many of the numerous parish churches, and to reconstruct Bristol Bridge over the Avon, with shops and houses on either side and the chapel of the Assumption built over the road across the middle of the bridge. In spite of the long wars with France, Bristol merchants during the fifteenth century established trading links with Iceland and penetrated into the Mediterranean, while they also built up a thriving import trade in wine from Bordeaux, woad from Toulouse, iron from northern Spain, alum and dye-stuffs, oil for soapmakers and cloth workers, figs, raisins, dates and oranges. The continuing prosperity was reflected in the fine new merchants' houses, in the chapels and halls of the craft guilds, in the church towers such as that of St Stephen's erected at the cost of the merchant John Shipward in the mid-fifteenth century, and above all in the church of St Mary Redcliffe on which the greatest of all the late medieval merchants and shipowners of Bristol, William Canynges, spent so much of his fortune, creating what is arguably the finest parish church in England. By the end of the fifteenth century it was Bristol merchants who financed and fostered interest in the early voyages of discovery to the New World (Carus-Wilson 1954, 2nd edn 1967: 1–41; Lobel and Carus-Wilson 1975: 10–14).

During the fourteenth and fifteenth centuries Southampton was well-situated to benefit from the thriving trade in the export of wool and hides from the Hampshire chalklands and from large parts of Dorset and from Salisbury Plain. Merchants from both Spain and Flanders were engaged in this trade and several foreign merchants took up residence in Southampton. Imports through Southampton included Gascon wine, woad from Toulouse, iron and fruit from Spain. But the prosperity of the port was badly affected by the outbreak of the Hundred Years War in 1336 which interrupted the trade in wool with the great market at Bruges, and by the continuing disruption of European trade through-out the mid-fourteenth century; in particular Southampton suffered a destruc-tive raid by the French in October 1338 when the raiders burnt the town, destroying three churches and many houses together with much wool, wine and other goods. Southampton's fortunes recovered during the later four-teenth century with the growth of the Italian trade which was to be its mainstay during the fifteenth century, the 'golden age' of Southampton's medieval trade. This trade was much more narrowly based than that of Bristol, for it depended very heavily upon annual visits of fleets of carracks and galleys from Genoa, Florence and Venice, and upon the import and distribution of wines, alum, dyestuffs, spices and luxury goods from the Mediterranean. In return the Italian ships took English woollen cloth, hides, wool, and tin which came to Southampton by sea from Cornwall. More is known about the distribution trade from Southampton than about any other English port during the fifteenth century, for a unique series of toll or 'brokage' books records the tolls levied on all goods going through the gates of Southampton and the places to which the goods were being sent. The Brokage Books show that regular consignments of woad and other dyestuffs such as weld and madder were sent by cart from Southampton to the clothiers of Romsey, Winchester and Salisbury, and beyond to Taunton, Bridgwater, Devizes, Shepton Mallet, and even to Bristol, while other cartloads were sent as far as Gloucester, Coventry, Leicester and the Midlands, even reaching Chesterfield, and as far north as Kendal. Large quantities of wine were also regularly sent to Winchester, Salisbury, Reading, Newbury, Andover and Oxford, and during the fifteenth century Southampton became the third largest importer of wine into England, outstripped only by London and Bristol. Italian merchants also found it convenient to ship goods for London such as wine, spices, silk, fruit and alum through the port of Southampton and thence by road on the relatively safe and easy route to the capital. The carts and packhorses returning to Southampton from this far-flung inland distribution trade brought wool and cloth for export. This was just the sort of steady, reliable trade needed by a port, and Dr Olive Coleman, who made a detailed study of the Brokage Books, observed that

> The pattern of journeys between Southampton and Coventry recorded in the Brokage Books is almost monotonous: carts go out loaded with woad and lesser quantities of alum, madder and wine, and a week or ten days later they are back with wool or cloth, or both, and start all over again.

She also pointed out the noticeably detailed nature of the information contained in these remarkable records of Southampton's trade:

> Inland distribution from Southampton can thus be minutely described. The name of every carter and every merchant is known; commodities such as woad, wine, fish and garlic, can be counted to the last balet, the last pipe, the last herring, the last clove . . . .
> (Coleman 1960–61; Ruddock 1951)

Through the Italian trade and because of its remarkable position as a distribution centre for southern England and beyond, the fortunes of the port of Southampton reached their zenith during the fifteenth century, and the wealth of the merchants, traders and carters is still evident from the impressive medieval walls and defences, the great fourteenth-century Wool House, and the fine collection of merchants' houses with their vaulted underground storage chambers.

The smaller ports of the region such as Poole, Weymouth, Lyme Regis, Minehead and Bridgwater also shared in the busy trade in woollen cloth and in the import of wines, salt, iron, oil, dyestuffs, alum and fish during the fifteenth century. Bridgwater, for example, ranked as the twelfth port in the country during the early fifteenth century, with a flourishing trade in the export of cloth and hides and imports of all sorts including wine, paper, salt, and iron as well as a thriving coastal trade, especially to the ports of south Wales.

The late medieval development of inland trade can be seen in the growing importance of markets and fairs such as those of Winchester, Bristol, Weyhill near Andover, Woodbury Hill near Bere Regis in Dorset, East Ilsley on the Berkshire downland, Whitedown on the bleak hill-top between Chard and Crewkerne in south Somerset and Priddy on the top of Mendip. The growth of economic activity and of road traffic can also be seen in the increased importance of road bridges, and in the many fine late medieval bridges. For example, in Wiltshire medieval bridges survive at Castle Combe, Combe Bisset, Harnham, Milford, and elsewhere and there are medieval causeways at Chippenham and Lacock. Maud Heath's Causeway runs from Wick Hill to Chippenham, a distance of $4\frac{1}{2}$ miles over the easily flooded marshy lands of the Avon valley. The lands to pay for its construction and maintenance were left by Maud Heath, a pedlar woman who was born nearby at Langley Burrell and who died in 1474. The building of bridges benefited the trade of some towns but led to the desertion and decline of other markets. For example, Harnham Bridge at Salisbury built to take traffic over the Avon and southwards from the new town of Salisbury by Bishop Bingham in *c*. 1230 meant that, although the market at Salisbury prospered, the much older market centre at Wilton was effectively by-passed and rapidly lost trade to the new rival. There were no bridges across the Thames between Wallingford and Oxford until the bridge at Abingdon was built in 1416; the new bridge caused a dramatic decline in the trade and importance of Wallingford.

Chapter 4

The Early Modern Period: Economic Development, Towns and Trade, 1500–1660

Rapid industrial expansion during this period made Wessex the most industrialised region in England; the production of woollen cloth increased dramatically, numerous other crafts, trades and industries flourished, and notable advances were made in agriculture. Population increased, trade developed, towns and ports grew rapidly and there were considerable changes in the structure of society. A new gentry class emerged whose fine houses and estates, parks and gardens are still a major feature of the landscape of the whole region. A much greater number and variety of documentary records exist for this period, so that it is possible to be much more precise about the industrial and farming practices and about social life. The wills, inventories and even account books of landowners, clothiers and farmers survive, as well as an abundance of manorial surveys, maps, court rolls, accounts and legal documents which have been preserved among estate records, royal and college archives or ecclesiastical muniments, giving a detailed picture of farming, land tenure, industrial growth and social change.

The Farming Districts

The chalklands of Wiltshire, Dorset, Hampshire and Berkshire

The chalklands make up the largest part of the region, the heartland of Wessex with the wide expanse of Salisbury Plain at its core, an area of bleak, windswept downland and sheltered valleys, where the characteristic nucleated villages were situated along the chalk streams, where great estates predominated and manorial control remained strong throughout this period.

Most of the arable land remained in open fields and although there was some enclosure, it had little effect overall until the eighteenth century. The production of corn, particularly of wheat and barley, was the main object of farming, and until the advent of cheap and easily obtainable artificial fertilisers in the later nineteenth century, the fertility of the thin chalkland soils could only be maintained by the intensive folding of the flocks of sheep which were pastured by day on the chalk downlands and close-folded at night on the arable lands on the lower slopes. Large sheep-flocks were therefore the most characteristic feature of chalkland farming and an essential factor in the successful production of corn. The importance of corn-growing in the farming of the chalkland was emphasised by Robert Seymer of Hanford near Blandford Forum in a report on the husbandry of the chalk region which he prepared for the newly founded Royal Society in 1665. Seymer concentrated almost entirely upon arable farming, and he clearly regarded livestock as of secondary importance although he was at pains to emphasise the importance of the sheep-fold. He reported that wheat was the most widely grown and valuable cereal crop, and that the two crops of wheat and barley between them accounted for most of the acreage of corn grown. The same emphasis is shown in the account book of Robert Loder who farmed on the Berkshire chalkland at Harwell and whose account book survives, covering the years 1610–20. Loder calculated that wheat and barley were the most profitable crops, and since he was conveniently near the highway of the river Thames his produce, including large quantities of barley for malting, could be sent by barge to Reading and on to London. Loder kept dairy cattle only to supply the needs of his household, not to produce milk or cheese for sale (Fussell 1936). The same farming pattern is shown in the notebook of Robert Wansborough, who farmed at Shrewton on Salisbury Plain during the 1630s. Like Robert Loder, Wansborough's main concern was to make a profit from his farming, and it was from corn-growing that his main profit came. Wansborough went to great trouble with cultivation and methods of sowing and in obtaining the best seed-corn, and experimenting with various dressings for his seed. He also took great care of his large sheep flock which he valued as an essential element in the production of corn on his thin chalk soil (Kerridge 1951–52).

The wool, lambs and mutton produced by the sheep were of course a valuable though secondary addition to the profits of chalkland farmers. It was above all for the dung which they deposited while folded on the arable land, and for their ability to act as walking dung-carts carrying the goodness of the chalkland pastures down to the cornlands that the sheep were kept. Edward Lisle, who farmed at Crux Easton on the Hampshire downland from 1693 until his death in 1722, and whose book *Observations in Husbandry* was an important farming manual of the eighteenth century, stressed the vital connection between the sheep-fold and corn production, and wrote that

> if a bane fell on sheep, corn would be dear, because there could not be a
> fifth part of the folding that otherwise there would be, and
> consequently a deficiency of the crop.

For an efficient sheep-fold it was essential to have a large number of sheep, so that on most chalkland manors the sheep of all the tenants were kept in a single, common flock with a shepherd who was employed by the whole manor. The seventeenth-century Wiltshire antiquarian, John Aubrey, described the familiar sight of the shepherds all over Salisbury Plain with their long white woollen cloaks with deep capes which came half-way down their backs. Defoe, travelling across the Plain early in the eighteenth century, found that the many shepherds were an invaluable assistance. He wrote:

> There is neither house nor town in view all the way, and the road which often lyes very broad and branches off insensibly, might easily cause a traveller to loose his way, but there is a certain never-failing assistance upon all these downs for telling a stranger his way, and that is the number of shepherds, feeding or keeping their vast flocks of sheep, which are every where in the way and who with very little pains, a traveller may always speak with.
>
> (Defoe 1927, I: 218)

On the Berkshire Downs and on the chalklands of Hampshire during the sixteenth and seventeenth centuries, as well as on the hilly parts of the Isle of Wight, large sheep-flocks were common. The Isle of Wight was noted for its sheep which were kept in common flocks on the downland and folded on the arable, where the main crops were wheat, barley, oats and peas. The downland of the Island, like other parts of the chalklands, also had numerous rabbit warrens, and there was a profitable trade in rabbits for the London market.

Since the sheep were such an essential part of chalkland farming, and since they were kept in common manorial flocks, it is not surprising that manorial records are full of references to sheep and to the management of the flocks. Typical of many others are the regulations for the conduct of the shepherd on the Wiltshire manor of Heale near Salisbury which were drawn up in 1629. The shepherd was to 'diligently attend and keepe his flocke' at all times, and he was not to leave the task to deputies or to children. He was to see that the sheep did not stray, and that they did no damage to the growing corn. He was to inform the owners at once if any sheep were sick or died; and

> if any sheepe be killed with stones or dogges or otherwise through the defaulte of the Shepherd, the Shepherd shall pay the owner for the same as two Tenants shall value it, otherwise to be deducted out of his wages.

The shepherd had to move the fold each day and pen the sheep in the fold each evening. He was also

> to keepe his sheepe from the scabb or other breakinge out as much as possibly he may, and forthwith treat and cure them yf any happen to be scabby.

123

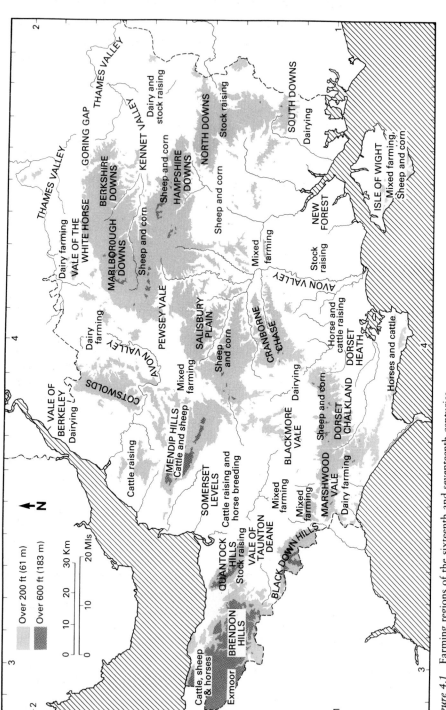

Figure 4.1 Farming regions of the sixteenth and seventeenth centuries

Finally he was to see that only those who had the right to do so brought sheep to the flock, or had the benefit of the dung of the fold. The tenants for their part were to contribute to the shepherd's wages in proportion to the number of their sheep, and they were each to provide every year a stipulated number of hurdles for the fold and an agreed quantity of hay for feeding the whole flock during the winter. Any tenant who failed to keep his part of the agreement would lose the benefit of the fold on his arable land. This last point was not an idle threat for at Heale during 1629–30 it was ordered by the manorial court that John Harford was immediately to deliver his quota of hurdles to the shepherd and

> . . . the foulde shall skypp over the said John Harford's land yf he shall faile in the doing thereof.

Another tenant at Heale was deprived of the sheep-fold

> for his insolencye to the Lord of this Mannor now in open Courte, and for refusing to obey the orders of this Courte, he shall not from henceforth have the benefitt of the Flocke to come upon his Land.
>
> (WRO 649/1)

The need for the common sheep-flock to manure the ground was one of the main reasons why the communal organisation of agriculture and the common arable fields survived longest on the chalklands. The compact villages grouped around the chalkland streams which were the only source of water, the shape of the manors, long and narrow, stretching from the river valleys up on to the high downland, often two or three miles long, and the dominance of the great estates, all helped to preserve the powers of the manor and of the manorial court, and made the communal organisation of agriculture at once much easier and more important than it was in the scattered farmsteads and broken countryside of the clayland areas where there was a much higher proportion of freeholders and small family farms, and manorial control was weak. Moreover, because the sheep-fold started at a different end of each large open field every year, and was moved day by day slowly across the field, the fact that the tenants' strips of arable land were scattered meant that each one had an equal share in the benefits of the fold and the whole of one man's land was not folded before that of another. The light chalkland soils required a fallow every second or third year. Some of the poorest soils therefore were cropped only in alternate years and were used for common grazing at other times; more common was a three year rotation as at Winterbourne Stoke (Wilts) when in 1574 it was recorded that

> Our custom is to divide the arable into three feilds; to sow two feilds and Leave one Sommer fallow . . . the Tennants Fould goeth all over two of the tennants feilds every year . . .
>
> (*VCH Wilts* IV, 1959: 43–64)

The chalklands provided fewer materials and arable farming gave less time for secondary employments than did the clay vales and the forest areas. John Aubrey was conscious of the marked contrast between the 'chalk' and the 'cheese' districts of Wiltshire, and even suggested that there were other consequences of these differences.

> In North Wiltshire and like the Vale of Gloucestershire (a dirty clayey country) the Indigenae or Aborgines, speake drawling; they are phlegmatique, skins pale and livid, slow and dull, heavy of spirit: hereabout is but little tillage or hard labour, they only milk the cowes and make cheese; they feed chiefly on milke meates, which cooles their braines too much, and hurts their inventions. These circumstances make them melancholy, contemplative, and malicious; by consequence whereof come more law suites out of North Wilts, at least double to the Southern parts. And by the same reason they are generally more apt to be fanatiques . . .
>
> On the downes, the south part, where 'tis all upon tillage, and where the shepherds labour hard, their flesh is hard, their bodies strong: being weary after hard labour, they have not leisure to read and contemplate of religion, but goe to bed to their rest, to rise betime the next morning to their labour.
>
> (Aubrey 1969: 11)

The clay vales of north and west Wiltshire, the Vale of the White Horse, north and west Dorset, south Somerset and the vale of Taunton Deane

The pattern of farming in these areas was quite different from that of the chalklands. Much of the clay area had already been enclosed into small family farms before 1500, or was enclosed by piecemeal agreements between tenants during the sixteenth and seventeenth centuries. There were many compact, nucleated villages – some of them quite large – but settlement was not by any means confined to these villages and many of the people lived in scattered and isolated farmsteads and hamlets; and although in some places the common arable fields did survive in the claylands, these were far less usual than on the chalk. The main aim of most clayland farmers was the production of milk to be turned into butter and cheese, and the rearing of cattle and pigs. Cattle were also brought into the region for fattening, many of them coming from Wales and Ireland. Arable farming was far less important, and although some farmers grew corn for their own use and to provide winter feed for their livestock, there were many 'all-grass' farms with little or no arable land. Sheep played a much less crucial role in the farming of these areas, though some farmers on the higher ground bred sheep for sale to chalkland farmers or in order to produce fat sheep and lambs for the market. Manorial control was far less strong and rigid in the clayland areas since there was much less communal organisation of agriculture.

Although cattle formed the backbone of clayland farming, it was not until the nineteenth century that there was much specialisation in the breeds or varieties which were kept. It is probable that the red Devon cattle predominated in the western part of the region, while the Longhorn and Old Gloucester breeds were more common in Wiltshire, but there is little definite evidence about this, and there was certainly a great deal of movement of cattle and intermixing of varieties, while many black cattle from Wales were also brought into the region for fattening before being driven on to market in London and other towns. The result was that most districts had a mixture of types, and few farmers confined themselves to any one particular variety. John Aubrey wrote that all types and colours of cattle were to be found in Wiltshire, and that most were a mixture of colours:

> The country hereabout is much inclined to pied cattle, but commonly the colour is black, or brown, or deep red.

As late as 1812 William Stevenson could write of Dorset that:

> There is no select breed of cattle in this county; the dairy cows of the chalky district, and the south-eastern parts of the county, are a long horned kind, rather short in the leg, with white backs and bellies, and dark spotted or brindled sides. They are a mixture of various breeds from Hampshire and other neighbouring counties, and more regard is paid to the quality of milk they are likely to produce, than to any other quality . . . In the western part of the county as well as in the vale of Blackmoor, the cows are mostly of the Devonshire kind.
>
> (Stevenson 1812: 374)

During much of the period from 1500 to 1900 it was a widespread practice throughout large parts of Somerset, Wiltshire and Dorset for landlords to rent out their dairy cows to a dairyman by the year. Under this system the farmer provided the cows, together with the necessary pasture and winter fodder, as well as a house for the dairyman and a dairy in return for an annual rent per cow, while the dairyman made his profit from the sale of milk, butter and cheese.

Much of the milk produced in the region was used for the production of cheese, and several different kinds were made. North Wiltshire produced a full-milk cheese, known variously as 'Gloucester' cheese from its resemblance to the cheese of the nearby vale of Berkeley, or as 'Marlborough' or 'North Wilts'. In Dorset, where large quantities of butter were also produced, several skim-milk cheeses were made, among them the famous 'Blue Vinny' or 'Vinney' cheese. The cheese of the Somerset levels was destined to become the best-known of all cheeses, the Cheddar. Defoe described in some detail the co-operative effort by which the cheese was made in Cheddar itself during the early eighteenth century.

> The milk of all the town cows is brought together every day into a common room, where the persons appointed, or trusted for the management, measure every man's quantity, and set it down in a book; when the quantities are adjusted, the milk is all put together, and every meal's milk makes one cheese, and no more; so the cheese is bigger, or less as the cows yield more, or less, milk. By this method, the goodness of the cheese is preserved, and, without all dispute, it is the best cheese that England affords if not, that the whole world affords.
>
> (Defoe 1927, I: 278)

Some butter and cheese was exported by sea, especially from the Dorset ports and from Bristol, but most was sold through the many west-country markets and fairs, and was bought by factors for dispatch to various towns especially to London. The markets at Marlborough, Tetbury, Wincanton, Frome and Yeovil were all famous for butter and cheese. Thomas Gerard who lived nearby wrote in 1630 of the quantity of cheese sold weekly in the market at Yeovil, 'which being made in great abundance in the adjoyninge country is weekly transported hence into Wiltshire and Hampshire'; and John Aubrey described Marlborough as 'one of the greatest markets for cheese in the west of England. Here doe reside factors for the cheesemongers of London'. Most of the sheep and cattle which were fattened in the region were also driven to London, Bristol and other towns for slaughter. Lean cattle for fattening on the grasslands of Somerset were imported from Ireland and from the ports of south Wales, especially through Minehead. Welsh drovers also brought cattle overland to sell at fairs such as Taunton and Whitedown near Chard. The dealers and drovers who engaged in this trade were not generally the sort of people who kept records of their transactions, and details of marketing and droving are therefore rare, but the occasional references which do survive leave no doubt of the importance of this trade in the economic life of the region (Bettey 1984).

In the Somerset Levels and the low-lying coastal plain of north-west Somerset many farmers relied on the raising of fat cattle for their livelihood, and Defoe was later to write of the area between Bridgwater and Bristol that farmers were 'wholly imployed in breeding and feeding of cattle'. Many farmers in the waterlogged Levels also made a substantial part of their income from wildfowl and eels, and from the rearing of huge flocks of geese which were kept for their down and feathers and were annually plucked. Thomas Gerard wrote in 1633 that the market at Langport was well furnished with fowle in the winter time, and full of pect eeles as they call them, because they take them in those waters by pecking an eele speare on them where they lye in their beds, but I cannot commend the goodness of them; marry, the fowle is fetched hence far and neere, but the waters being abroad such as are sent for it many times missing the Cawsway goe a-fishing instead of getting fowle.

(Bates 1900)

In the east of the region, along the Thames valley in Berkshire, where the river provided easy access to the London market, there was a good deal of arable land as well as riverside pastures where fat cattle were raised. William Camden at the end of the sixteenth century described the Thames valley as 'chequered with cornfields and green meadows, clothed on each side with groves'. Much of the corn was barley, grown to produce malt for the London brewers, and the towns of Abingdon, Wallingford and Reading grew wealthy on the profits of this river-borne traffic in malt. Other towns and villages in the area shared in this trade, and Robert Loder of Harwell sold barley for malting during the early seventeenth century at Abingdon, Henley, Newbury, Oxford, Wantage and Reading. The richest and most fertile of all the clayland areas was the vale of Taunton Deane where the mixed farming and the excellent crops of wheat, barley, oats and beans as well as apple orchards and fat cattle excited the admiration of travellers from Leland to Defoe, and was described by John Norden early in the seventeenth century as 'the Paradise of England' (Thirsk 1967).

The forests and heaths of Hampshire, Wiltshire and Dorset and the uplands of Somerset

The great royal forests continued as a dominant feature of the landscape until the mid-seventeenth century, and forests such as Selwood, Kingswood, Chippenham or Pewsham, Savernake, Gillingham, the New Forest, Alice Holt and several others continued to cover many thousands of acres. John Leland noted the thick woodland of Melksham and Brayden and wrote that 'Al the quarters of the foreste of Braden be welle woodid even along from Malmesbury to Chippenham', and in the mid-seventeenth century John Aubrey wrote that Melksham forest was 'so full of goodly oakes, and so neer together that they say a squirrel might have leaped from tree to tree'. He added that a deer might run in woodland all the way from Melksham to the Dorset coast. On the Isle of Wight the Forest of Parkhurst extended from the west bank of the Medina to the muddy shores of Newtown Creek. Scattered through the forest areas were numerous small settlements and farms, mostly devoted to dairy farming and the raising of pigs. The pigs fattened on the pannage of the New Forest were especially famous, and Thomas Fuller described how they

> feed in the forest on plenty of acorns . . . which going out lean, return home fat, without care or cost to their owners.

Even before disafforestation of the royal forests early in the reign of Charles I, they were subject to a great deal of encroachment by farmers and squatters as well as on a larger scale by local gentry. Sir Henry Baynton enclosed Spye Park between Lacock and Calne during the early seventeenth century at the expense of the royal forest of Pewsham. He was said to have killed the royal deer, felled the trees and built cottages in the forest which he let to his own tenants. His example encouraged the royal keepers to neglect their duties and to kill the deer for their own use, for they were said to have

> mayntayned their whole houses and families on venison, and made it their ordinarie Meate, and gave theire servants noe other foode.
>
> (PRO, Star Chamber, 8/47/19)

Likewise in Selwood forest, Sir John Thynne carved out his park at Longleat from the surrounding thick woodland; and the Duke of Somerset created a large new park at Savernake in spite of the protests of the tenants who had traditionally enjoyed right of pasture in the forest. The final disafforestation of the royal forests was very unpopular with tenants who possessed customary rights of pasture and other privileges within the forest, since the lands which they were allocated in lieu of their former rights were often insufficient or inconveniently situated. The riots in Wiltshire, Dorset and Gloucestershire – riots which were given a spurious but effective unity by the supposed leadership of 'Lady Skimmington' – were the largest single popular uprising in the region during the years before the Civil War and expressed a number of social and political discontents as well as protesting over the enclosure of the royal forests and the loss of their traditional rights there (Allen 1952; Kerridge 1958–59; Bettey 1975–76).

On the poor acid soils of the heaths and on the bleak upland moors such as Exmoor, the Quantock, Brendon, Blackdown and Mendip hills, there was little arable farming and most farmers concentrated on the breeding of cattle, pigs and horses, the latter generally being the small hardy 'heathcroppers' of Dorset and Hampshire or the almost self-sufficient ponies of Exmoor.

John Leland described his journey across the great open expanse of Exmoor as

> all by forest, barren, and moorish ground, where is store and breeding of young cattle, but little or no corn or habitation.
>
> (Leland 1907)

In a few parts of the Hampshire and Dorset heath where the soil was favourable some crops of oats were grown, and around Corfe Castle many farmers had small plots of hemp. Most heathland farmers derived much of their income from other employments. The most important of these was stone-quarrying, especially in the Isle of Purbeck. In addition, wild-fowling provided a substantial part of their livelihood for others, while deer-stealing was rife, and other employments came from peat, turf and furze cutting, much of which was sold for fuel in the adjacent chalkland areas. The digging of clay on the heath for bricks, tiles and pots also developed considerably during this period, especially around the shores of Poole Harbour where an export trade in clay products was added to the already important fishing trade with Newfoundland (Thirsk 1967).

Agricultural Improvements and Innovation

The sixteenth and seventeenth centuries saw a number of important advances in agricultural techniques and crops in the region. Among these were numerous enclosures by agreement amongst manorial tenants, the extension of the cultivated area by many small projects of enclosure, drainage and reclamation, and increasingly intensive land use by the practice of sowing 'hitch' crops such as vetches, peas, or oats on the fallows, thus gathering an extra crop. Robert Loder of Harwell in Berkshire, a very profit-conscious farmer, 'hitched' about a quarter of his fallow land every year during the period 1610–20; during the same period Robert Wansborough was growing occasional crops of vetches or oats on his fallows at Shrewton on the Wiltshire chalkland (Fussell 1936; Kerridge 1951–52). The growth of this practice was to lead to the abandonment of the old idea of a bare fallow every second or third year to rest the land. New field crops which were introduced or widely grown during this period included carrots which were extensively grown on the rich soils of the Vale of Taunton Deane and on the belt of sandy loam between Yeovil and Crewkerne. Turnips for cattle food were being grown in the Bristol region and in parts of the Somerset lowlands by the mid-seventeenth century; cabbages, clover, rape, rye-grass, vetches and sainfoin were all being grown as fodder crops and the seed was on sale in markets throughout the region. In addition, several 'industrial' crops were cultivated. Hemp and flax were the basis of the widespread rope, twine, net and sailcloth industries and were much grown on the rich clays of west Dorset and south Somerset as well as in parts of Hampshire; teazles which were used for raising the nap on woollen cloth before it was finished by the shearmen were extensively grown in north Somerset around Wrington, Blagdon, Ubley, Compton Martin and in the Chew valley. Woad, from which a rich blue dye was extracted and which was used by dyers as the basis for all the dark or 'sad' colours, was imported in great quantities through the ports of Southampton and Bristol during the fifteenth and sixteenth centuries. During the later sixteenth century, when the demand for dyestuffs such as woad, weld and madder, and of mordants such as alum increased rapidly as west-country clothiers turned from the production of undyed broadcloth to the lighter, coloured cloths, the cultivation of woad was introduced into the chalklands, especially around Salisbury, Cranborne, Lymington and Romsey, where it proved very profitable. Woad is a hungry plant and was much used as a first crop on newly broken downland or old grassland, which was often too rich and too much infested with soil pests for the immediate sowing of corn. Two men who were much involved in the production of woad during the early seventeenth century were the Salisbury lawyer, Henry Sherfield, and his stepson, George Bedford, who was a clothier in Salisbury. Both men leased lands in Hampshire, Dorset and Wiltshire for growing woad, including much newly broken grassland on Cranborne Chase; they sold their crops to dyers throughout the west country. The cultivation of woad required a great deal of labour, not only in the preparation of the ground and tending the crop, but also in picking and processing the leaves, since these had to be crushed in a mill, allowed to ferment and then be rolled into balls and dried before the product could be sold to dyers. In his will made shortly before his death in February 1607, George Bedford made bequests to the poor of the parishes of Damerham, Martin, Pentridge and Cranborne 'in remembrance of my good will for theire labours and worke bestowed on my business'. An inventory of his possessions made soon after his death shows the scale of his enterprise, for he owned 18 tons of woad ready for sale, many leases of land for woad-growing, woad stores and four woad mills, while money was owed to him for woad by dyers from Somerset, Wiltshire and Dorset (HRO 44M69/XLIV/16–18).

By the early seventeenth century hops were being grown in several places which were later to become famous for the quality of their beer, including Salisbury, Alton, Romsey and Dorchester. Notwithstanding the profitability, usefulness and spread of the cultivation of new varieties of fodder and other new plants, throughout the chalklands of the region it was wheat and barley which were by far the most important crops. An analysis of the surviving Dorset probate inventories for the first half of the seventeenth century shows that farmers on the heath had less than 15 per cent of their total wealth in crops, while farmers on the claylands had about 17 per cent, but in the chalklands farmers had on average 28 per cent of their wealth in their crops. It was from their corn that chalkland farmers derived the major part of their income, and the whole pattern of chalkland farming was geared to the production of corn crops and to the maintenance of the fertility of the thin chalk soils. Robert Wansborough from Shrewton was typical of chalkland farmers in the overriding concern which he showed for his corn crop and his arable land. Edward Lisle, who farmed at Crux Easton near Andover at the end of the seventeenth century and who wrote an important farming manual entitled *Observations in Husbandry*, also regarded his corn crops as by far his most important source of profit. The fertility of the chalk soils could only be maintained by folding the sheep flocks on them, and this was the main reason why the sheep were kept. Corn yields could only be increased by keeping ever-larger sheep flocks, and the number of sheep which could be kept was limited by the amount of winter and early spring feed which could be provided for them. It was here that the most important and dramatic advance in agricultural technique was made with the invention and rapid spread of artificially watered meadows. These meadows were carefully constructed with a network of channels and drains to cover the surface of the meadow during the winter with a shallow, rapidly moving sheet of water. This protected the grass from frost and stimulated a much earlier growth than would have occurred naturally, providing early feed for ewes and lambs during the early spring, the most difficult period of the year for livestock. The fast-flowing Wessex chalk-land streams were ideal for watering meadows and the idea spread very rapidly during the early decades of the seventeenth century along the valleys of the Avon and Wylye in Wiltshire, the Frome and the Piddle in Dorset, the Test and the Itchen in Hampshire and along many of the smaller chalkland streams so that they were a commonplace of farming technique by the later seventeenth century. There are references to a water meadow at Affpuddle on the river Piddle in Dorset in 1608, and from there the idea spread quickly into the valleys of the Frome, the Cerne, the Sydling, the Tarrant and the Gussage streams so that by 1650 there were water meadows all along these valleys. A similar rapid spread was experienced elsewhere on the chalklands. In 1669 John Worlidge of Petersfield in Hampshire could describe the watering of meadows as 'one of the most universal and advantageous improvements in England within these few years' (Worlidge 1669; Bettey 1977a: 25–29; Kerridge 1953 and 1954).

The early development of water meadows owed much to the encourage-ment by energetic landlords. When the tenants at Wylye agreed to water their meadows in 1632 the Earl of Pembroke's steward presided over the meeting of the manorial court at which the decision was taken; the introduction of water meadows at Affpuddle and the surrounding area was firmly supported by the lord of the manor, Sir Edward Lawrence, who was keenly interested in agri-cultural improvement. At Puddletown in October 1629 when the tenants met to decide about watering their meadows the manorial court book records that

> The honorable Henrie Hastings esquire Lord of the same Manor, being present with the tenants of the same and a great debate beinge theare had and questions moved by some of the tenants about wateringe and Improvinge theire groundes and theare heard att large, And thereuppon by Full Consent it was ordered in Courte and agreed unto by the tenants in Court . . .
> (DRO D39/H2)

Plate 4.1 Henry Hastings, 1551–1650, Lord of the Manor of Woodland, Dorset. Henry Hastings was a younger son of the Earl of Huntingdon, and as well as Woodland he also possessed lands at Mappowder and Puddletown. Although his life-style was eccentric, he was a leading figure in Dorset society and an active justice of the peace. His neighbour Lord Shaftesbury described Hastings in the great hall of his house which was '... strewed with marrow bones, full of hawks perches, hounds, spaniels and terriers, the upper sides of the hall hung with foxskins of this and the last year's skinning, here and there a polecat intermixed, guns and keepers' and huntsmen's poles in abundance. The parlour was a large long room as properly furnished; on a great hearth paved with brick lay some terriers and the choicest hounds and spaniels; seldom but two of the great chairs had litters of young cats in them, which were not to be disturbed, he (Henry Hastings) having always three or four attending him at dinner, and a little white round stick of fourteen inches long lying by his trencher, that he might defend such meat as he had no mind to part with to them...' The illustration shows him at the age of eighty-seven in 1638; he died in 1650 aged ninety-nine. (Reproduced in J. Hutchins, *History of Dorset*, 3rd edn, 1861–73.)

At Warmwell on a little tributary of the Dorset Frome a water meadow was constructed during the 1630s at the instigation of the lord of the manor, John Trenchard, an active land speculator and money lender in Dorset and elsewhere during the years before the Civil War. On several other manors along the Frome valley the driving force behind the creation of water meadows was Theophilus, Earl of Suffolk whose Dorset estate was centred on Lulworth Castle.

The water meadows continued in use throughout the eighteenth and nineteenth centuries, and were of incalculable importance in the agriculture of the chalkland districts. Their principal advantage was that they provided early feed for the sheep flocks, and so made it possible to keep much larger numbers of sheep than would otherwise have been possible. This in turn meant that more sheep were available for folding on the arable land, thus greatly increasing its productivity, so that the real profit from the water meadows emerged in the improved corn crops. The meadows also provided an abundant crop of hay, and thereafter they could also be used by cattle in late summer and autumn before being prepared for the next winter's watering. In those manors where water meadows were established the sheep flocks followed a regular calendar of grazing and folding throughout the year. The meadows were generally flooded or 'drowned' for varying periods from early October to Christmas, depending on the weather, and often also on complicated agreements with other manors in the same valley and with local millers about the use of the water. Meanwhile the sheep were pastured on the downland by day and folded on the wheat or the fallows at night. The meadows would be given further periods of watering after Christmas, especially during times of frost, so that by Lady Day, or even earlier in mild winters, there would be a sufficient growth of grass for the sheep to feed on them for short periods each day. This was the period when the water meadows really proved their value, when the downland grazing was exhausted, last year's hay had been eaten and before the natural growth of grass had started. The sheep were folded straight from the meadows on to the land destined for barley, since the dung and urine of the flock was particularly valuable at that time. Often the fold was continued after the barley was sown, providing both top-dressing and consolidation of the land, and even after the corn had appeared a further folding would encourage stronger growth. The water meadows were unsuitable for the sheep after the beginning of May, since then they were likely to contract liver-fluke and foot-rot from the damp pasture. By this time the meadows would in any case have been eaten bare, and the natural downland grazing would be available for the flock. The water meadows could be flooded for a few days and thereafter left for a hay crop. A floated meadow could produce up to four times as much hay as unwatered land. The meadows were generally used for cattle grazing during July, August and September before having the channels and drains cleared and the hatches repaired in readiness for the next winter.

Several factors led to the decline of the water meadows during the later nineteenth century – the slump in farming, new grasses, artificial fertilisers, and, above all, the heavy cost of maintenance. But for more than two centuries the water meadows were 'the crowning glory of agricultural achievement', and were an indispensable factor in the farming pattern of the chalklands.

Increasing quantities of lime, marl, ashes, soot and tanning waste were also used to improve the fertility of the soil in an effort to secure greater productivity. The laborious process of land drainage and reclamation also went on throughout the sixteenth and seventeenth centuries. Drainage schemes were carried out in the Somerset levels, especially in the area around Long Sutton, along the coast and in the tidal estuaries of the Yeo, Axe and Parrett rivers. Not all drainage schemes were successful. For example, during the 1630s a group of Dorset gentlemen, led by the Horseys and Frekes, began work on an ambitious but remarkably ill-conceived project to drain the Fleet, the large expanse of land between the Chesil beach and the mainland which is covered by salt water at high tide. The whole expensive project was a total failure and the participants lost heavily by it. Sir George Horsey was ruined, the family mansion at Clifton Maybank was sold and most of it was demolished; during the eighteenth century the front part of the house was purchased by the Phelips family and is now incorporated into their Elizabethan house at Montacute.

Another curious example of totally misplaced enthusiasm comes from West Parley and West Moors in the barren, acid, ill-drained heathland around Poole Harbour. In 1619 the tenants of the heathland there agreed to enclose their lands, claiming with super-abundant optimism that 'a great part of the wastes with good husbandry may be improved and made good arable and good pasture'. The enclosure duly took place, but in spite of all the optimism, the value of the land lay almost entirely in its use for cutting peat and, in order to ensure that all had an equal share of good and bad peat land, the enclosures were made in narrow strips right across the heath, each 22 yards wide and nearly 2 miles long. These long narrow strips can be seen today stretching across the heath. They were never worth enclosure, and the names of some of them such as 'Folly' and 'Troublefield' tell their own story.

By the later seventeenth century the farming changes in Wessex, including the introduction, rapid spread and widespread use of water meadows providing early grass and greatly increased crops of hay, the new fodder crops, very large sheep flocks, and new varieties of wheat and barley, had greatly raised the standards of farming practice and the yields of crops. They had also produced a new sort of profit-conscious farmer, intent upon improvement and increased productivity.

Industry

Throughout the sixteenth and seventeenth centuries the cloth industry continued to be by far the most important industry in the region, and the sixteenth century in particular was the 'golden age' of high-quality, undyed broadcloth production. As in the fifteenth century, the chief centres of this trade were in west Wiltshire at Bradford-on-Avon, Trowbridge, Westbury, Steeple Ashton and Warminster, across the Somerset border at Frome, Norton St Philip, Bath, Keynsham and Shepton Mallet, in south and west Somerset at Taunton, Dunster, Wellington, Milverton and Wiveliscombe, and in the vales of west Dorset from Sherborne through Beaminster, and Broadwindsor to Lyme Regis. These were all areas of pastoral farming with comparatively little arable land, and were composed mainly of small dairy farms, making butter and cheese, a type of farming which allowed time to engage in secondary employments – spinning, weaving, fulling and dyeing.

In the chalkland areas the cloth industry was of minor importance, for arable farming gave much less opportunity for engaging in by-employments. The Somerset JP's during the early seventeenth century evidently well understood the sort of countryside in which handicraft industries could flourish, when they reported to the Privy Council upon the eastern part of Somerset that

> a great part of it being forest and woodlands and the rest very barren for corn ... the people of the country (for the most part) being occupied about the trade of clothmaking, spinning, weaving and tucking.
>
> (PRO SP 16/187/51)

John Leland had been greatly impressed by the scale and importance of the woollen industry in the 1540s and wrote for example of Bradford-on-Avon that 'Al the toune of Bradeford stondith by clooth making', and of Trowbridge that it was 'very welle buildid of stone, and florishith by drapery'. Leland made similar comments on most of the towns of west Wiltshire and also on many of the little towns and villages of the eastern and north-eastern parts of Somerset, as for example of Pensford on the river Chew where he wrote that 'It is a praty market townlet occupied with clothing' and 'The towne stondith much by clothing', or at Chew Magna 'There hath beene good makyng of cloth yn the towne.' The most famous of all the sixteenth-century clothiers of Wiltshire was William Stumpe of Malmesbury whom Leland described as 'an exceding riche clothiar'. At the dissolution of the monasteries, Stumpe had purchased from the Crown the whole site of Malmesbury Abbey with the abbey buildings. Inside the abbey he built a mansion for himself and filled 'every corner of the vaste house of office that belonged to the abbay ... (with) ... lumbes to weve clooth yn'. Most of the cloth made in the region during the early sixteenth century was the heavy broadcloth, and much of the production was exported, generally undyed, to be finished on the continent. The Dorset ports – Poole, Weymouth and Lyme Regis – had a flourishing trade in cloth exports, shipping to the continent not only cloth produced in Dorset but also cloth from south Somerset, Chard, Crewkerne and district and from Taunton, Minehead and as far as Barnstaple. Lyme Regis had a considerable export trade during the seventeenth century in poorer quality woollen fabrics known as 'Kerseys' and 'dozens'. Many of these cloths were exported to France – especially to Brittany and Normandy where, it was said, they were purchased by poor people 'of a base disposition who would not go to the price of a good clothe'. Much of the cloth produced in Wiltshire and in the Frome area was, however, sent by packhorse to London to be sold at Blackwell Hall either to be dyed and finished by London merchants for the home market, or to be sent abroad (Ponting 1957; Bettey 1977: 40–2).

A good deal of cloth, already dyed and finished, was exported to Ireland, France and Spain from Bristol, and the surviving ledger book of the prosperous Bristol merchant John Smythe covering the years 1538 to 1550 shows that cloth was his most important export. Most of it came from the villages on the Somerset–Wiltshire border and was sent to Gascony and Spain. Smythe's principal supplier was John Yerbury of Bruton in Somerset from whom he bought an average of about seventy cloths a year. Besides wine and fruits Smythe also imported alum, woad, madder and other essential dyestuffs as well as large quantities of oil which was used to dress the raw wool before carding (Vanes 1975: 4–6).

The trade was organised by clothiers like Stumpe and Yerbury who bought the wool, had it cleaned, carded, and spun, employing in the process a large number of domestic workers, then sent the yarn out to weavers, arranged for fulling, finishing and dyeing of the cloth, and finally for its sale. The expansion of the trade during the sixteenth century brought great prosperity to many clothiers, especially in west Wiltshire and east Somerset, and established the fortunes of numerous wealthy families, among them those of Horton, Baily, Langford, Ash, Methuen, Whitaker and many others.

Many of the towns and villages of Hampshire and Berkshire also played a part in the cloth industry during the 'boom' years of the sixteenth century making mainly Kerseys and other coloured cloths. Market towns like Andover, Basingstoke, Alton, Whitchurch, Petersfield, Newbury, Abingdon and Reading were all centres of cloth production, as was Salisbury where the trade continued during the sixteenth century, although it had decayed at older centres such as Winchester and Romsey. Newbury achieved great prosperity during the early decades of the sixteenth century through the enterprise of the great clothier John Smallwood, who was known as Jack of Newbury. A century later Deloney's, no doubt greatly exaggerated, *Pleasant History* described in verse Smallwood's 200 looms, 200 men and 200 pretty boys, and

200 maidens all working together producing cloth in great harmony. More definite evidence for Smallwood's enterprise and prosperity survives in Newbury parish church, the nave of which was rebuilt at his expense. The whole church with its fine tower is an impressive memorial to the success of the cloth industry in Newbury at that time. Later in the sixteenth century another wealthy clothier of Newbury, Thomas Dolman, built Shaw House, one of the finest Elizabethan houses in Berkshire, completed in 1581. Another monument to the cloth trade in Newbury is the Cloth Hall, now a museum, which was built with money left by the Reading clothier, John Kendrick, in 1626 as a workshop to be run by the town where the poor might be set to work on cloth production. The sixteenth-century prosperity of Reading was also based upon the cloth trade, as well as upon its important market and agricultural trades such as malting, tanning and milling. The greatest of the Reading clothiers, John Kendrick, left money for a workshop at Reading, as well as at Newbury, where the poor could be set to work on spinning, weaving and cloth-making. The premises in Minster Street became known as the Oracle and after 1633 all cloth made in the town had to be brought there to be checked.

During the later sixteenth century, the production of lighter cloths, the 'new draperies', began to expand in the region, as well as 'medley cloth' for which the wool was dyed before spinning. For this cloth fine-quality Spanish wool was used, and by the early seventeenth century the manufacture of 'Spanish cloth' was well established. It was not only the business of weaving and tucking or fulling which provided employment in the region, but each weaver had to be supplied with yarn by the work of many spinners, and throughout much of the period spinning was the most important and universal (secondary) employment in the whole region. John Hooker's description of the situation in Devon in 1600 would have applied with equal force to most of the region, that 'wheresoever any man doth travel you shall fynde at the hall dore as they do name the foredore of the house, he shall I saye fynde the wiffe, theire children and theire servants at the turne spynninge or at theire cardes cardinge and by which commoditie the common people doe lyve'.

Besides the woollen industry, some other textiles provided employment in various parts of the region. Among these were silk-weaving, introduced into the area around Sherborne and Yeovil in the middle of the seventeenth century, and at the same time into various parts of Wiltshire, including Salisbury, Warminster and Malmesbury, and the manufacture of lace which provided work for many people from the sixteenth to the nineteenth century, notably around Lyme Regis and at Blandford Forum in Dorset, and at Salisbury and Marlborough in Wiltshire. Lace-making was ideal as a by-employment for women and girls and could easily be combined with other jobs; John Aubrey wrote in 1680 that 'our shepherdesses of late years do begin to work point whereas before they did only knit coarse stockings'; and Defoe noted that Blandford Forum was a handsome well-built town, but chiefly famous for making the finest bonelace in England, and where they shew'd me some so exquisitely fine, as I think I never saw better in Flanders, France or Italy . . .

This industry was killed by the competition of machine-made lace in the nineteenth century.

In parts of south Somerset and west Dorset the production of linen and sail-cloth was an important industry throughout the whole period. It depended very largely on locally grown flax which flourished in the rich soils of that area, though during the nineteenth century both flax and hemp were imported. The industry was centred around Crewkerne, East and West Coker and Chard in Somerset, and Beaminster, Broadwindsor and Bridport in Dorset. Originally dependent upon locally grown hemp was the rope, net, thread and webbing industry of the Bridport area. The rich soils of the Marshwood vale were highly suitable for growing hemp, and the industry was established at Bridport early in the Middle Ages. During the sixteenth and seventeenth centuries the town supplied ropes and nets to the Newfoundland fishing fleets which operated from the Dorset ports, as well as fulfilling the needs of the Royal Navy and of other merchant shipping. Thomas Fuller, author of *The Worthies of England* who was rector of Broadwindsor in west Dorset from 1634 to 1641, commented on the widespread cultivation of hemp in the area, and wrote that 'England hath no better than what groweth here betwixt Beaminster and Bridport, our land affording so much strong and deep ground proper for the same . . .'. His evidence is supported by the field-names of west Dorset, where in almost every parish there are closes bearing names such as Hemphay, Hemp Close, Hemp Lands as well as Flax Close, Flaxlands and Flecklands. Hemp and flax both required a great deal of care in their cultivation, and both demanded laborious preparation before they could be spun. These tasks as well as the work of weaving, net and rope-making, etc. all provided a great deal of employment in the scattered farms and cottages of west Dorset and south Somerset.

Although the cloth industry was by far the most important and widespread in the region, several other industries were also prosperous and expanding during the sixteenth and seventeenth centuries. Iron-smelting was an important trade in Hampshire, using charcoal from the New Forest, as was shipbuilding along the Hampshire coast, also dependent upon the oaks of the Hampshire forests. Glass-making became an important industry in Bristol, at Kimmeridge on the Isle of Purbeck in Dorset and in the New Forest. Coal-mining continued to expand in Kingswood, and in north Somerset where by the seventeenth century the mines had spread across the Mendip plateau to Mells, Kilmersdon, Babington, Walton, Timsbury and Clutton. Lead mining on Mendip reached the height of its prosperity during the sixteenth and seventeenth centuries, and metal mining was also extended to include calamine from Wrington, Shipham and Rowberrow, which was used to combine with

Cornish copper to make brass and provided the basis for the important Bristol brass industry. The brass was used mainly for pins and wire, but one of the products of this industry can still be seen in the many brass chandeliers and lecterns dating from the late seventeenth and early eighteenth century which survive in the parish churches of Bristol and Somerset. Bristol was also a centre of pewter manufacture using Cornish tin and Mendip lead (Gough 1967; Day 1973).

Along the Hampshire coast and especially in the coastal marshlands around Lymington, salt production continued to be an important occupation. The Southampton customs accounts list duties charged on Lymington salt during the sixteenth century, and in 1625 there were said to be five saltworks at Milford and Keyhaven, thirteen at Pennington, eight at Woodside, all in the shallow tidal marshes south-west of Lymington, and three others at 'Oxeye' and two in 'the Rows' which remain unidentified. At the end of the seventeenth century the processes by which the salt was manufactured were described in detail by Celia Fiennes (Lloyd 1969: 86–90).

In Bristol the refining of sugar which was to become such an important industry in the city was already established by the early seventeenth century, as was the tobacco trade which was to have an even greater impact on the city's fortunes. The manufacture of soap, using olive oil imported from Spain, also expanded rapidly in Bristol during the sixteenth century, and it was a soap-boiler, John Carr, who in 1586 left lands and money to found Queen Elizabeth's Hospital school in the city.

Early in the seventeenth century Sir Thomas Neale set up a paper mill at Warnford in the Meon valley and began the long story of paper-making in Hampshire, where the clear chalk streams are ideally suited for making paper, being strong enough to provide the necessary power and having pure, clear water for the production process. Moreover the ports of Southampton and Portsmouth provided a source of rags, old rope, sails and canvas which could be converted into paper. By 1700 there were ten mills in operation in the county (Shorter 1951–53: 1–11; Thomas 1969–70: 137–48). Paper was also made during the seventeenth century at several places in Somerset including Watchet, Banwell and Wookey.

Other industries included tanning and glove-making which was especially important in the Yeovil area of Somerset and in west Dorset, pottery-making, brick and tile manufacture using local clays, and there was a growing trade in tobacco pipes, notably around Amesbury, as smoking became more and more popular. In 1662 Thomas Fuller wrote of tobacco-pipe manufacture in Wiltshire that

> The best for shape and colour . . . are made at Amesbury in this county. They may be called chimneys portable in pockets, the one end being the hearth and the other the tunnel thereof . . .
>
> (*VCH Wilts* IV: 240–4)

The great increase in building work, ranging from large country houses and manor houses to farms and cottages which was such a marked feature of the late Tudor and the Stuart period, created an enormous demand for stone, timber, glass and plaster, and for building craftsmen. Good quality stone was transported long distances; for example, much of the stone for Longleat came from the quarries at Haselbury near Box, twenty-five miles from the site; stone from Ham Hill was carried nearly twenty miles to Sir John Strode's new house at Chantmarle in Dorset during the early seventeenth century. Some quarries developed a busy trade in ready-made fittings. For example, Richard Boyle, Earl of Cork, sent an order to Bristol in 1637 'to supplie me with Free stone chymnies, doores, and lightes readie made at the Free stone quarries at Donderry (Dundry) hill near Bristol' for his new house at Gill Abbey near Cork (Grosart 1886: 37). Traditional industries and employments such as malting, brewing, cheese-making, fishing and wildfowling continued to provide full-time work for some men and a secondary or by-employment for even larger numbers. It was the dual economy pursued by many farmers and their families, particularly in the pastoral and forest districts, combining their farming with spinning, weaving, fulling, or making use of divers natural resources – clay, peat, timber or fish – which enabled them to survive and even prosper in the economic changes of the period.

Towns and Trade

Increasing trade and the expansion of population during the period led to a great growth in the size of some towns. In Reading, for example, the town spread far beyond its medieval boundaries and the increasing population led to overcrowding and to the sub-division of houses into tenements (Slade 1969: 5–6). Likewise the flourishing cloth industry led to the growth of towns such as Taunton, Devizes, Newbury, Frome, Bradford-on-Avon and Trowbridge. In Frome a whole new suburb of houses for workers in the cloth industry was built during the seventeenth century in what has become known as the Trinity area. Bath grew as the fashion for taking the waters there became more popular during the seventeenth century, especially after Charles II and his court went there in 1663. Other towns like Basingstoke, Abingdon, Wantage, Shaftesbury, Warminster, Marlborough and Andover prospered from the expanding trade in cattle, sheep, corn and cheese and became important market centres serving not only their local areas but attracting dealers, drovers and cheese-mongers from London and elsewhere. Bristol was well-placed to benefit from the thriving export trade in cloth, attracting cargoes not only from the cloth-making areas of Somerset, Wiltshire and Gloucestershire but also cloths coming down the Severn by barge from the Midlands and traffic from south Wales. Already by the last decades of the fifteenth century Bristol merchants were looking beyond Europe, and beginning the long involvement of the port with overseas exploration to Newfoundland and the North American mainland. Adventurers from Bristol were already involved in exploration before John Cabot's first voyage of 1497, and continued with the voyages of Sebastian Cabot. Later Bristol was to play a leading role in the establishment of colonies in Newfoundland and New England. The population of Bristol was about 10,000 in 1500 and by the end of the sixteenth century it had grown to some 12,000 and the city had expanded far beyond its medieval walls.

The changes of the early modern period brought a sharp decline in the fortunes of a few towns. The most spectacular decline was that of Southampton which from being one of the most important centres of English foreign commerce had lost most of its trade by the end of the sixteenth century and was reduced to a very poor condition.

One factor in this rapid decline was the fact that during the sixteenth century the Italian galleys and carracks which had been so important in the trade of Southampton no longer came; even more crucial was the growth of the overseas trade of London. Much of Southampton's import trade in luxury goods, silks, spices, carpets, fruits and Oriental products was under the control of London merchants and had been sent by road straight to London, and Southampton had acted as an outport for the capital. During the sixteenth century the merchants began to import directly to the port of London; their ships passed Southampton and sailed on to the Thames estuary, as improved rigging, more manoeuvrable ships and better navigational aids made it easier to bring large ships up the Thames and into the port of London. The traffic in cloth, wine, tin and dyestuffs was also increasingly dominated by London, and the trade of Southampton decayed rapidly.

As early as 1530 the burgesses complained to Henry VIII that

> many Persons that wer lyke to have growne to greate substance have departed and forsakyn your said Towne, and moo (more) be in purpose and mynde shortly too departe from the same.

Although John Leland in *c.* 1540 could still wax enthusiastic about the excellence of the High Street and the 'many very fair marchauntes houses in Hampton', the main trade and wealth of the town had already departed. During the later sixteenth century the moat was dry, the walls in ruin and overgrown with ivy, the streets, houses and public buildings were neglected, and there were swarms of beggars in the town. Streams of paupers, vagabonds and wanderers drifted into Southampton from the Isle of Wight, the Channel Islands and from the villages of Hampshire, swelling the number of unemployed persons already seeking poor relief in the town, and, as the Court Leet complained, 'so poore as dayly they lye at mens dores for ther relyeffe'. In

1588 the port could not provide one ship to join the English fleet assembled against the Armada. The coastal trade continued, though on a reduced scale, and there was some traffic between Southampton and the Channel Islands, as well as a good deal of smuggling and privateering, but not until the coming of the railways in the nineteenth century were the fortunes of the port restored (Ruddock 1951: 255–72; 1949–50: 137–51).

Portsmouth also declined as a naval port during the sixteenth century as the new naval base and dockyard at Chatham supplanted it. The dockyard at Portsmouth was damaged and the storehouses destroyed by a serious fire in 1557, and there was another destructive fire in 1576. Moreover the sanitary arrangements in Portsmouth were extremely rudimentary, and in 1563 the town was attacked by a virulent plague in which more than 300 people died. The population declined to less than 1,000, and the town played only a small part in the defence against the Armada in 1588. Not until the seventeenth century did the fortunes of Portsmouth begin to revive when it developed as a military base and when the dockyard was once more expanded. Likewise its population increased; between 1603 and 1676 the number of communicants in Portsmouth rose from 469 to 2,560 – a staggering increase of 445 per cent, and Portsmouth became by far the largest and most populous town in Hampshire. In 1662 it was ranked in twenty-second place among English towns (Temple Patterson 1976: 28–37; Rosen 1981: 173–5).

The fortunes of some other towns suffered badly because of the dissolution of the wealthy monasteries which had brought employment, wealth and pilgrims: notable among these towns were Abingdon, Glastonbury, Malmesbury, Cerne Abbas, Abbotsbury, Bruton and Keynsham. The cloth-finishing trade, which had been the economic mainstay of Winchester, declined in the sixteenth century, especially following the collapse of Southampton's position as a major port. By the 1520s the population of Winchester had fallen to its lowest level with less than 3,000 people in the city and its suburbs. During the late sixteenth and early seventeenth centuries Winchester suffered a series of disastrous plagues and epidemics; and at the same time the influx of migrants into the town from the surrounding villages seeking for work, charity and poor relief created great social tensions and food shortages, and led to a number of experiments in poor relief and in setting the poor to work, although in spite of these efforts and of the number of ancient charities in the city, the growth of the problem always outstripped the efforts to cope with it. During the late seventeenth century the city recovered as a marketing centre and as the social focus for the gentry and professional classes of Hampshire, a revival which, like that of Bath, was fostered by a visit of Charles II who came with his court to Winchester for the races in 1682, and liked the city so much that he made several other long visits during the remaining three years of his reign (Rosen 1981: 176–84).

The trade of Salisbury, like that of Winchester, Romsey and the whole of southern Hampshire was depressed by the rapid decline of Southampton during the sixteenth century. The direct trade with the continent in 'Salisbury rays' came to an end, as did the importance of the merchants who had organised this commerce. Some manufacture of white broadcloth and flannels continued but Salisbury was never again to be so important in the cloth trade as it had been in the fifteenth century. The manufacture of the 'new draperies', the serges and medleys which brought a new trade to other textile towns in Somerset and Wiltshire, never made much headway in Salisbury. The city lost its industrial base and came to depend, like Winchester, on its position as a social and administrative centre. Salisbury remained the cathedral city at the head of a far-spread diocese, and was the chief market and the administrative, legal and social focus for much of southern Wiltshire. Trade-depression, lack of employment, plague and poor harvests combined to produce great distress in Salisbury, and in 1623 the city was described as

> so much overcharged with poore, as having in three Parishes neere
> 3,000 besides decayed men in a great many, . . . the poore being like
> Pharaoh's leane Kine, even ready to eat up the fat ones.

The number of paupers demanding relief in Salisbury led to a remarkable experiment initiated by some of the Puritan councillors who were determined to get the poor to work. They set up a workhouse and a municipal brewery, and organised a scheme to provide employment and training for children. Their ambitious schemes were never a complete success and had collapsed by the outbreak of the Civil War in 1642, but they were an interesting attempt by the town authorities to solve an apparently intractable problem (Slack 1972; 1975: 1–16).

The increase in population and the growing problem of poverty, unemployment and vagrancy presented a major problem for many other towns and villages, and in 1624 led Richard Eburne, the vicar of Henstridge in south Somerset, to suggest various remedies to 'reduce the excessive numbers of people'. His ideas included the urgent need to establish colonies in the New World to absorb the ever-increasing number of people. This suggestion was followed by several people, among them Sir Ferdinando Gorges in Bristol who was active during the 1620s and 1630s in promoting the colonisation of New England and who became the first Governor of New England and Lord Proprietor of Maine. In 1623 John White, the puritan rector of Holy Trinity, Dorchester, set up the Dorchester Company to promote colonisation and was instrumental in founding New Dorchester, Massachusetts in 1630.

The trade with Newfoundland and the establishment of fishing fleets specialising in cod from the Newfoundland grounds brought prosperity to the Dorset ports, especially to Poole whose good and safe anchorage became the base for a large Newfoundland fleet. Poole developed an extensive trade in the export of cloth, clothing, farming equipment, nets, ropes, cordage, and household goods to Newfoundland, and the rapid growth in the size and prosperity of the port was recognised by a charter of 1568 which gave it the status of a county with full jurisdiction over its internal affairs. Newfoundland fish from Poole, Weymouth, Bridport and Lyme Regis was sold all over southern England. John Aubrey wrote *c.* 1675 of the fish market in Devizes

> the best market for fish . . . they bring fish from Poole hither, which is sent hence to Oxford.

The Newfoundland trade continued until the nineteenth century to be of the greatest importance for the Dorset ports. It brought great wealth to the merchants engaged in it, and also fostered ship-building, cloth-production, and the rope, net and sailcloth trades of Bridport and west Dorset.

The weekly markets held in the towns, together with the annual fairs, were of vital importance in the trade of the region. Most of the weekly markets served only the surrounding villages, and had no more than a local significance, but a few markets attracted custom from long distances and specialised in particular commodities. For example, several of the towns in that area where the corn-growing chalkland region and the dairy-farming, cloth-producing claylands meet, had important corn markets; Shaftesbury, Salisbury, Wilton, Warminster, Wincanton and Bruton, for instance, all had busy markets for corn. During the 1630s an enquiry by the Privy Council found that the two markets at Bruton and Wincanton supplied corn to nearly 7,000 people in the surrounding cloth-making districts, and that most of this corn came from the Dorset and Wiltshire chalklands (PRO SP 16/187/51).

Grain sold in the markets at Shaftesbury and Warminster regularly supplied people living as far away as Bristol, and John Aubrey wrote of Warminster that 'It is held to be the greatest corn-market by much in the west of England' (PRO E 134/18 Jas I E 1; E 134/21 Jas I M29; and Aubrey 1969: 114).

Marlborough, Devizes, Yeovil and Wincanton also had important cheese markets, while large weekly cattle markets attracting more than local custom were held at Alton, Blandford Forum, Bridgwater, Crewkerne, Devizes, Dunster, Newbury, Reading, Highworth, Market Lavington, Sherborne, Swindon and Taunton. Notable sheep markets were held at Alresford, Basingstoke, Blandford Forum and Hindon, although most sheep were sold at the great seasonal sheep fairs. Glastonbury, Langport and Somerton in the Somerset Levels were famous markets for wildfowl, Bridport and Yeovil for hemp, flax and rope, while Winchester, Ilminster and Shaftesbury were noted for leather.

Horse-breeding was a speciality of the Somerset Levels and of the New Forest, and large numbers of horses were sold to dealers who came to the markets at Bridgwater, Glastonbury and Somerton and to Ringwood. The vale of Taunton Deane was noted for its breed of heavy horses which were sold in the market at Taunton (Edwards 1983).

Much detail about the trade at Yeovil market during the early seventeenth century emerges from a long and involved dispute over the profits of the market, the right to erect stalls and standings in the streets, and over the regulation of the market. The mass of evidence produced shows that besides butter, cheese, hemp, linen and leather, large numbers of sheep, cattle and horses were sold at the market each week, as well as corn, vegetables, hops, a variety of wooden and iron ware, and trinkets sold by itinerant pedlars and chapmen. The market evidently formed the major focal point for the large and fertile agricultural district surrounding it (PRO E. 134/9 Jas I, M 31; E 134/13 Jas I, E 19).

Similar evidence survives for the market at Shaftesbury, one of the most frequented of all the markets in the region during the sixteenth and seventeenth centuries; it attracted customers from all over north Dorset, east Somerset and south-west Wiltshire. The town contained 24 licensed inns and alehouses and each market day the streets were packed with stalls, standings, sheep-pens and carts bringing corn to the market, while cattle, pigs and horses were also displayed for sale in the streets. For a traveller from London, hurrying on to the west, the bustle, obstructions and confusion of the crowded streets of Shaftesbury on market days must have meant considerable hindrance and delay; but to the farmers of a wide area it represented the major outlet for their produce. A similar situation would have confronted the traveller through a score of other towns on market days – Abingdon, Wantage, Newbury, Andover, Basingstoke, Alton, Ringwood, Devizes, Marlborough, Taunton and numerous others; each also fulfilled the same crucial role in the economic as well as in the social life of its surrounding area (Bettey 1977a: 73–9).

Much business was also conducted at the numerous annual fairs of the region. Some of these were held within towns, like the eight fairs regularly held in each year in Bristol. Others were annually set up on isolated hill-tops where today it is difficult to imagine the stalls, pens, cattle, sheep, horses and merchandise, or to visualise the crowds that thronged to them. Important three- and four-day fairs were held at Whitedown Hill in south Somerset, Tan Hill and Yarnbury Castle in Wiltshire, Woodbury Hill near Bere Regis in Dorset, Weyhill near Andover, Magdalen Hill outside Winchester and at East Ilsley on the Berkshire Downs. Like the markets, many of the fairs were of little more than local significance, but some, such as those listed above, attracted custom from very long distances. John Aubrey commented on the celebrated sheep-fair held at Castle Combe on St George's Day each year, and called it 'the most celebrated faire in north Wiltshire . . . wither sheep-masters doe come as far as from Northamptonshire'. The partial record which survives of the dealings at Whitedown Hill Fair between Crewkerne and Chard for the 1630s shows that people came to it from all over west Dorset and south Somerset, and a few traders and dealers came from much further afield including drovers from Wales who brought cattle to sell there. Nothing now survives in the landscape to illustrate how popular the fair on this windswept hill-top once was. Likewise on the bare hill-top at Woodbury Hill nothing now indicates the former importance of the fair which attracted dealers from all over southern England.

A notebook kept by Sir Francis Ashley, the Recorder of Dorchester, concerning the people who were brought to him for trial or examination during the years 1614–35 provides some indication of the crowds, the atmosphere and the conditions of Woodbury Hill Fair. Many of those brought before Ashley at fair time had travelled long distances to attend the fair. For example, Margaret Hill, an arras-weaver of Aldersgate in London, was accused of stealing purses at the fair in 1617, and evidence was given by William Kent of Salisbury, 'hardwareman', and Michael Farringdon of Coventry, 'linendraper'. In 1620 Robert Watkins, a cook and baker from London, who had a stall at the fair selling refreshments was accused of 'having made such a fire at 12 o'clock at night that he (the nightwatchman) was in feare that he would set the booths afire'. Watkins was also accused of fortune-telling and illegal gaming. Evidence was given by Robert How, a chapman or pedlar of St Albans who stated that he had come to the fair by way of other fairs at Newbury, Winchester and Salisbury. Mention was also made of the temporary booths, shelters, standings and tents which were erected on the hill-top, as well as of 'a bower for people to lodge in for the night, lying upon hides of tanned leather that were in the Bower'. Notes on other cases include references to the crowded conditions at the fair, to cut-purses and tricksters, to the pens for cattle and sheep, and to the sale of horses, butter, cheese, cloth, canvas, haberdashery, lace, leather goods and trinkets, while traders mentioned included a mercer from Honiton, chapmen from Coventry, a shoemaker and packsaddle-maker from Wells, bonelace sellers from Berkshire and Oxfordshire, as well as stall-holders from all the neighbouring counties. Ashley also records an example of the sort of trickery which the rogues who travelled from fair to fair could perpetrate upon unsuspecting country people. David Morgan of Stony Stratford who described himself as a cutler had come to Woodbury Hill Fair in 1634 via London and fairs at Bristol, Salisbury, Southampton and Farnham. He had brought some knives to sell, but evidently depended for his livelihood mainly upon trickery, unlawful gaming and petty crimes. Morgan was said to have encountered a group of people on the hill-top at Woodbury Hill Fair who were eating tripe

> and begged of them some of their Tripes, which they willingly gave him; then he, to requite their kindness, told them that he would sell them a good bargaine, and showed them forth a piece of Cambricke, telling them that they should have itt for five shillings, itt being of greater valew; which bargaine the said company well liking of, they delivered him 5s for the same, but he stepped aside and folded up the Tripe which they had given him in cleane paper in the same manner that the

Cambricke was before folded, and delivered itt to the said company in stead of the Cambricke; And soe made them pay five shillings for their own Tripe.

(Bettey 1981)

The influence of Woodbury Hill fair is also shown in the way in which the date of the fair was used in manorial documents and Quarter Sessions records instead of a calendar date; also in 1648 a public thanksgiving in Dorchester was postponed because 'it falls out to be on Woodbury Fair Eve, at which time most of the town will be from home'. Two of the greatest of all the many sheep-fairs were at Weyhill near Andover at the junction of several ancient roads and trackways, and at East Ilsey high up on the Berkshire Downs where the sheep were bought by graziers for fattening in Hertfordshire and Buckinghamshire for the London market. John Aubrey described Castle Combe Fair as 'the most celebrated faire in north Wiltshire for sheep . . . wither sheep masters doe come as far as from Northamptonshire'. Aubrey's comment is confirmed by the list of sales included in the Castle Combe manorial accounts. In 1663 and 1664, for example, these show that farmers were bringing sheep for sale from all over north Somerset as well as from Wiltshire, and that buyers came from as far away as Buckinghamshire, Warwickshire and Northamptonshire (BL, Add MS 28,211). Two fairs were held on the hills outside Winchester: St Giles' Fair which during the later Middle Ages had attracted clothiers and woollen merchants from all over England and from Europe, declined greatly with the collapse of the trade of Southampton, but Magdalen Hill fair, held during July on open downland east of the city, continued to flourish, and great quantities of cheese, hops, cattle and horses were sold there each year. During the early seventeenth century more than half the horse sellers came from Somerset where horse-breeding was a speciality of the Levels; purchasers came from Wiltshire, Hampshire, Dorset, Berkshire, Hertfordshire, Sussex, Surrey and Middlesex (Rosen 1981: 151–5).

Many cattle and sheep for fattening in Wessex were shipped into the Somerset ports from south Wales and from Ireland, or were brought from Wales by drovers. References to the purchase of Welsh cattle occur in several estate and family accounts, and there were occasional legal suits over the trade. For example, in an action before the Court of Star Chamber in 1623 William Brounker, a yeoman of Whaddon in the Avon valley near Bradford-on-Avon, stated that he was a grazier and that for the previous thirty years he had been accustomed to 'repayre to certain fayres in Shropshire and the county of Radnor to buye Rother beasts there to stock his grounds as the Grasiers dwellinge neare your Subjecte in the said county of Wiltes use to doe'. In May 1622 he had purchased fifty beasts at Knighton fair in Radnorshire and had driven them back to Whaddon; the dispute arose because of an allegation that one of the cattle, a black cow, had been stolen. The record of trading at Taunton Fair during the 1620s and 1630s includes numerous entries concerning cattle sold to Somerset farmers by Welsh drovers; and the trading book of Whitedown Fair between Crewkerne and Chard, covering the years 1637–49, also records cattle from south Wales being sold to buyers from Somerset and Dorset. Further evidence of the activities of Welsh drovers occurs in the records of the dispute over the disafforestation of the royal forest of Gillingham during the 1620s, for one of the objections to its enclosure was that the roads and tracks through the forest were much used by Welsh drovers taking cattle to Southampton and to the Royal Navy at Portsmouth, and that enclosure would interfere with this traffic. But the most remarkable piece of evidence for the activities of the Welsh drovers comes, not from a documentary source, but from an inscription on a seventeenth-century cottage at Stock-bridge, at the point where the high road across the downland drops down to the valley of the Test. Here there is a small cottage by the river, with a paddock in front of it; it is still known as the Drover's Inn, and still bears the inscription in Welsh 'Gwair tymherus porfa flasus cwrw da a gwal cysurus' (Fine hay, sweet pasture, good ale and a comfortable bed).

A great fair for wool and yarn was held in Somerset each year at Norton St Philip. Like many other west-country fairs this one coincided with the patronal festival of the parish church and was held for several days around the feast of SS Philip and James (1 May). The 'great house or inn called the George' was emptied of much of its furniture and filled instead with the packs and bales of the merchants. Inns like the George at Norton St Philip played an important part in the marketing process, providing meeting-places, exchanges, banking and storage facilities as well as food, drink and lodging (Bettey 1977a: 79–82).

London was already receiving considerable amounts of grain down-river from Oxfordshire and Berkshire by the mid-sixteenth century, and the prosperity of the Berkshire markets – Reading, Wallingford, Abingdon, Newbury, Wantage and Faringdon – depended heavily upon the supply of agricultural products for the London market. The trade increased steadily in the reign of Elizabeth and during the early seventeenth century, so that when the flow of grain and other produce was cut off by the royalist seizure of Reading during the Civil War there was concern in both London and Reading, and some inhabitants of Reading claimed that the stoppage of trade was costing the town £2,000 per week. When the trade was restored with the parliamentary recapture of Reading in 1644 there was great rejoicing in the town (Fisher 1935; Durston 1981: 40).

Chapter 5

Religious Reform, Local Society, Government and the Civil War

The Reformation and Church Life

When the Reformation Parliament was summoned by Henry VIII and began its meetings on 3 November 1529, few in the region could have dreamed of the sweeping changes in religion and in religious institutions which the next few decades were to witness. No one would have been rash enough to forecast that within little more than a decade the wealthy and powerful religious houses, whose buildings dominated the towns and whose vast estates extended throughout all parts of the region, would have ceased to exist, and that the familiar figures of monks, friars and nuns would no longer be seen; that soon all the chantries would be dissolved, the Latin mass brought to an end, new services in English introduced, and radical changes made to the interior appearance of the multitude of parish churches throughout the region. There was little indication of the scale of the upheavals to come, for in spite of criticisms of its doctrine and organisation, and the unpopularity of some sections of its hierarchy, the strength of the Church throughout the whole of southern England in 1529 must have seemed overwhelming. The wealth, antiquity and splendour of the great monastic houses, including the richest of all at Glastonbury and the wealthiest English nunnery at Shaftesbury, as well as ancient, opulent foundations at Abingdon, Sherborne, Reading, Salisbury, Winchester, Wilton, Malmesbury, Lacock, Stanley, and a host of others, together with the many smaller houses, hospitals and other institutions seemed secure against all disasters and likely to last for ever. Nowhere in the region was more than a few miles from a major monastery or nunnery, and the Church estates and influence extended everywhere. Likewise money had been lavished upon the parish churches by their congregations during the previous century. The splendour of their architecture, towering over town and countryside, bore witness both to the wealth and to the piety of the people of Wessex, and apparently also to their attachment to the Catholic Church.

In Bristol the dominant position of the Church was clearly to be seen on all sides. The religious houses and parish churches were the principal landmarks on the Bristol skyline; the town was surrounded by monastic establish-ments – the priory of St James, the four houses of the Friars, and the opulent monastery of the Augustinian canons. Eighteen parish churches were clustered in and around the town to serve the spiritual needs of its 10,000 or so inhabi-tants. There were hospitals and almshouses in various parts of the town, as well as numerous chantry and other chapels. In Bristol, as in other towns and villages throughout the country, the parish churches were at the heart of com-munity life, and were the social, educational, charitable and cultural, as well as the religious, centres of the communities which they served (Bettey 1983).

We cannot here pursue all the many twists and changes in national policy towards the Church which together created the English Reformation; rather we shall concentrate upon the effects which all these manifold decisions had upon the ecclesiastical institutions of the region and upon Church life. For most places the multitude of personal doubts and indecisions, and all the manifold arguments which preceded the eventual acquiescence of most people in the religious changes have left little evidence in contemporary documents. Occasionally however we are able to catch a glimpse of the conflict between the arguments of the enthusiasts for reform and the doubts of those who preferred to adhere to the old ways. In Bristol, for example, the early Reformation changes were heralded and accompanied by a violent pulpit debate and by vociferous public exchanges between advocates of the new ideas and supporters of the established traditions. This 'battle of the pulpits' began in Bristol with three Lenten sermons preached during 1533 in the churches of St Nicholas, St Thomas and the Black Friars by Hugh Latimer, who at that time was rector of West Kington in Wiltshire but who was soon to achieve fame as one of the leading reformers, becoming Bishop of Worcester in 1535. In his Bristol sermons of 1533, Latimer attacked what he regarded as abuses in the Church, including pilgrimages, the veneration of the Virgin and the saints, the emphasis upon images and ritual. Of Latimer's fierce sincerity, genuine horror at superstitions and misleading teaching, and of his effectiveness as a popular preacher there can be no doubt. He was deeply disturbed at the sight of the multitude of pilgrims who were drawn to visit and make offerings at the shrine at Hailes Abbey in Gloucestershire which supposedly contained the blood of Christ.

> I dwell within half a mile of the Fossway [he wrote in 1533]. And you would wonder to see how they come by flocks out of the west country to many images, but chiefly to the blood of Hailes. And they believe verily that it was in Christ's body, shed upon the mount of Calvary for our salvation.
>
> (Corrie 1845: 364)

Latimer's Bristol sermons roused a storm of protest, and several preachers immediately sprang to the defence of the established order, notably John Hilsey, prior of the Dominicans, Edward Powell, a well-known preacher at

Court and at Oxford, who had already spoken out against the King's divorce, and William Hubberdyne, who was almost as popular a preacher as Latimer. The clash of rival pulpit orators created enough uproar and controversy for the matter to be brought to the attention of Thomas Cromwell who ordered that the 'infamy, discord, strife and debate' in Bristol should forthwith cease. How far it all affected the opinion of the majority of people in Bristol it is impossible to say, probably very little, for during the next few years through all the changes in religion there were few in the town who were prepared to defy the royal authority by actively or publicly supporting either cause (Elton 1972: 112–20; Powell 1971: 141–57; Bettey 1983).

For most people the perils of open defiance of government policy were sufficient to ensure their obedience, for under the efficient eye of Thomas Cromwell the government acted swiftly and ruthlessly against opponents or critics. For example, Gabriel Pecock, warden of Southampton Friary, attacked the doctrine of the royal supremacy over the Church in a sermon in Winchester Cathedral on Passion Sunday 1534; he was immediately arrested, and in spite of local testimony to his good life and character, and to the high reputation of his house, he was carried to imprisonment at Lincoln. In Somerset George Croft, rector of Shepton Mallet, was executed in 1538 for maintaining that 'the King was not, but the Pope was, head of the Church' (Dunning 1976: 29). The gradual, piecemeal nature of the religious changes also helped to secure acquiescence.

The number of monks and nuns in each house was much smaller than it had been two centuries earlier. Glastonbury was unusual in still having over 50 monks at the time of the dissolution; most other houses for men had far fewer, although the numbers of nuns generally remained high. In Hampshire, St Swithin's Priory at Winchester was the largest community with 37 monks and an annual income of over £1,500; Wherwell, Romsey, Christchurch and Beaulieu each had between 20 and 30 inmates, while the ten other monastic houses in the county had an average of between 10 and 12 monks or nuns (Kennedy 1970: 65; Dunning 1976: 25–7). In Berkshire neither of the two large, wealthy houses of Abingdon and Reading had more than 25 monks.

The visitation of the monastic houses carried out by Thomas Cromwell's commissioners in the years before the dissolution revealed few scandals but a good deal of laxity, although the fact that the commissioners were looking for evidence to use against the monks and were not above 'improving' on their findings must always be kept in mind when assessing their evidence. The most amusing, though probably the least trustworthy of the commissioners was Richard Layton. Typical of his findings was his report to Cromwell written from Bristol in August 1535 in which he listed with evident cynicism the great number of relics he had found in the local monasteries, and ended with a note of despair that he had not been able to find anything wrong at either the Augustinian house at Bruton or at the great Benedictine monastery of Glastonbury:

At Bruton and Glasenburie ther is nothyng notable; the brethren be so
straite keppide that they cannot offende, but faine they wolde if they
myght, as they confesse, and so the faute is not in them.

(Wright 1843: 7–10, 58–9)

Less colourful, but more credible, is the account of the visitation of the
Augustinian nunnery at Lacock in Wiltshire by another of Cromwell's
commissioners, John ap Rice, who found nothing wrong, but reveals
incidentally that the nuns continued to use the Norman-French language for
their services and other ceremonies, just as had been the custom at the time of
the foundation of their house in *c.* 1229.

Lacock, 20 August 1535

at Lacock as yet I can finde no excesses. And as for the house, it is in
good state and well ordered.

(Wright 1843)

Edington, 23 August 1535

So it is that we founde no notable *compertes* [*i.e. information or things
to report*] at Lacock; the house is very clene, well repaired and well
ordered. And one thing I observed worthy th' advertisement here: The
Ladies have their Rule, th' institutes of their religion and ceremonies of
the same written in the frenche tongue which they understand well and
are very perfitt in the same, albeit that it varieth from the vulgare
frenche that is now used, and is much like the frenche that the common
Lawe is written in.

(Wright 1843)

At the wealthy monastery of Reading, whose buildings dominated the whole
town, the commissioners likewise found all in good order, and discovered
£131 9s. 8d. in ready money as well as a great quantity of plate and silver. They
also found many relics, including two pieces of the Holy Cross, the hand of St
James, the stole of St Philip and a bone of St Mary Magdalene.

In only a few places did the commissioners find things seriously amiss,
and in these places it is difficult to disentangle the truth of their stories or to
judge how much it is the embroidered tale of someone with a grudge, or of a
monk or nun concerned to blacken the reputation of their superior or of their
fellows. At Romsey, for example, the Abbess and some of the nuns were
accused of scandalous relations with townsmen and with the chaplain; at
Cerne Abbas one of the monks, William Christchurch, wrote directly to
Cromwell making a number of accusations about the Abbot, Thomas Corton.
Christchurch alleged that the Abbot was guilty of gross immorality, that he had
let the abbey and its lands go to ruin, and that he and other monks had
numerous mistresses in the town and bestowed the goods of the abbey on their

children. He claimed that the Abbot

> openly solicits honest women in the town and elsewhere to have his will
> of them . . . The farms belongynge to the monastery be in . . . ruyne and
> decay by the abbot's wylfulness.
> (*Letters and Papers of Henry VIII*, viii, 148; ix, 256; xiii (2) 1090)

It is difficult to believe that these and other similarly extravagant claims
are any other than the feverish imaginings of a discontented and unhappy
monk. More usual, and certainly more credible, are the sort of faults and
general slackness revealed in a visitation of Glastonbury in 1538, when it was
alleged that works of charity were neglected and that although £15 yearly was
given to the monastic officials to distribute among the poor and to wayfaring
men, what happened to the money 'noo man can tell'. The services were said to
be so long and tedious that the brethren had no time to study, that in any case
they lacked books of scripture, there was no instructor to teach grammar to the
boys although 'ever agauynst every visitation then they have an Instructor,
when the visitation is done then he is taken away . . .' (Dunning 1976).

Many of the monasteries of the region surrendered without much open
protest or evidence of reluctance. The nunneries were much more anxious to
continue, and some attempted by gifts to Cromwell to avoid their fate. For
example, in December 1538 Thomas Arundel wrote to Cromwell on behalf of
the nuns at Shaftesbury:

> they have most heartily desired me to write unto your good Lordship to
> move their petition . . . that they may remain here, by some other name
> and apparel, his Highness' poor and true Bedeswomen, for the which
> they would gladly give unto his said Majesty five hundred marks, and
> unto your Lordship for your pains one hundred pounds.

Elizabeth Shelley, the last Abbess of St Mary's, Winchester, continued to
live in Winchester after the dissolution together with a small group of her
former nuns, supporting themselves in their communal life on the pensions
they received.

The dilemma facing the heads of religious houses in face of the King's
demand for the surrender of their houses is nowhere more tellingly expressed
than by Prior Edward Hord of Hinton Charterhouse. No irregularities had
been alleged against this Carthusian house near Bath, and as in other
Carthusiasn houses, strict adherence to their austere rule of life had been
maintained. Early in 1539 the Prior's brother, Alan Hord, who was a lawyer in
London, had written to the Prior urging him to surrender the house
voluntarily, thus ensuring good treatment and adequate pensions for himself
and for his monks. The Prior's reply to his brother with his anguished and
patently sincere defence of his priory, shows plainly the difficulty of a man torn

between expediency and conscience, and is an eloquent summary of the conflicting pressures which confronted the monks and nuns. Prior Hord wrote that he could not surrender the priory

> which is not ours to give, but dedicate to Almighty God for service to be done to his honour continually, with other many good deeds of charity which daily be done in this House to our Christian neighbours. And considering that there is no cause given by us why the House should be put down, but that the service of God, religious conversation of the brethren, hospitality, alms deeds, with all other our duties be as well observed in this poor House as in any religious house in this realm or in France; which we have trusted that the King's Grace would consider . . . Thus our Lord Jesus Christ preserve you in grace.
>
> (Wright 1843)

Later in 1539 Alan Hord's worldly-wise counsel prevailed and the priory at Hinton Charterhouse, consisting of the Prior and sixteen monks, was surrendered to the King.

In several monastic houses of the region the Crown avoided any resistance to the surrender of the house by securing the appointment of a complaisant abbot or abbess well before the final dissolution. Thus at the Benedictine nunnery of Wherwell, set deep in the meadows of the Test valley near Andover, Anne Colte (Abbess 1529–35) was induced by threats, allegations of scandalous behaviour and by promises of a large pension of £20 per annum, to resign her position. In her stead Morphita Kingsmill, a member of a Hampshire gentry family, was appointed; she was a ready tool in the hands of Cromwell and his commissioners, and put no obstacles in the path of surrendering the abbey in November 1539. In return she received an annual pension of £40; and the 24 nuns received pensions ranging from £6 to £2 13s. 4d. per annum. Payments were also made to 48 other persons comprising the chaplains, officials and servants of the nunnery (*VCH Hampshire* II, 1903: 135–7).

Likewise Henry Broke, Prior of St Swithin's at Winchester, was so harried and pressed by Cromwell's commissioners that he resigned with a pension in 1536; he was succeeded by William Kingsmill, a nephew of the new Abbess of Wherwell. Kingsmill owed his election entirely to Cromwell, and raised no objection to the surrender of the priory in 1539. One abbot, Thomas Stevens, had the unusual distinction of surrendering two abbeys for he was Abbot of Netley at its suppression in 1536 and then became Abbot of Beaulieu which he surrendered in 1538 (Kennedy 1970: 71–2).

Although there were no protests or risings in the region against the dissolution of the monasteries nor any influential voice raised in their support, it would be wrong to suppose that all were unpopular or that they served no purpose in the life of the community. St Mary's Nunnery at Winchester, the ancient Nunnaminster, was commended by Cromwell's commissioners in 1535 for the 'great relief daily ministered unto the poor inhabitants of the said city'. Netley Abbey on the eastern shore of Southampton Water was described as 'a large building situate upon the ryvage of the seas. To the King's subjects and strangers travelling the same seas, great relief and comfort.' Quarr Abbey, the Cistercian house on the Isle of Wight, was said to be a place of refuge for the inhabitants of the Isle of Wight and for strangers travelling the seas. Lacock Nunnery was reported in 1536 to provide great relief to the town and all the adjoining countryside. John Draper, the last Prior of Christchurch (in Dorset), appealed to Henry VIII to allow the house to continue on the grounds that it not only supported 'poor religious men' but also was used for worship by 1,500 people from the town and the surrounding hamlets. He wrote:

> the poor not only of the parish and town but also of the country, were daily relieved and sustained with bread and ale, purposely baked and brewed for them weekly to no small quantities, according to their foundation, and a house ordained purposely for them, and officers duly given attendance to serve them to their great comfort and relief.

The appeal availed nothing, for the house was dissolved in December 1539. Draper was awarded a pension of £133 6s. 8d., but by Letters Patent of October 1540 the church was granted to the parishioners (Cook 1954: 275).

Table 9 Wiltshire monastic houses in 1535

	Inmates	Annual income £ s. d.
Malmesbury	24	803 – 17 – 7
Monkton Farley	6	214 – 0 – 4
*Amesbury	34	553 – 10 – 2
*Wilton	12	652 – 11 – 5
*Kington S. Michael	3	38 – 3 – 10
Kingswood	15	254 – 5 – 10
Stanley	10	222 – 19 – 4
Bradenstoke	14	270 – 10 – 8
Maiden Bradley	8	197 – 18 – 8
Ivychurch	5	133 – 0 – 7
*Lacock	17	203 – 12 – 3
Edington	13	521 – 12 – 5
Easton	2	55 – 14 – 4
Poulton	3	20 – 3 – 2
Marlborough	5	38 – 19 – 2
15 Monastic houses	171 inmates	£4,183 – 19 – 9 annual income

* = Nunneries

The size of the monastic houses, their spread across the county, the number of monks and nuns, and the scale of their annual income can be seen from the figures for Wiltshire taken from the *Valor Ecclesiasticus* of 1535 (Table 9).

In addition to the monks and nuns, each house also had a large number of servants. At Lacock, for example, the 17 Augustinian canonesses had no less than 42 officials and servants in the house – 4 chaplains, 3 waiting servants, 9 officers of the household, a clerk, a sexton, 9 women servants and 15 hinds or farm labourers. When the house was surrendered in January 1539 Joan Temmes, the Abbess, received an annual pension of £40, and the other inmates had pensions ranging from £5 to £2 a year.

By 1540 all the monasteries had gone. Two major houses, Reading and Glastonbury, held out to the end. The last Abbot of Reading, Hugh Faringdon, together with two of his monks, refused to surrender the revenues and treasures of the abbey, but their protest was of no avail, and in November 1539 all three were hanged, drawn and quartered at Reading. Similarly at Glastonbury, the last abbot, the elderly Richard Whiting, and two of his monks were imprisoned at Wells for their refusal to cooperate in the dissolution of the monastery or to hand over the goods, plate, ornaments and valuables which they had hidden. In November 1539 they were dragged on hurdles to the top of Glastonbury Tor and brutally executed. The manner in which Cromwell's commissioners made repeated visits to Glastonbury, ransacked this rich and ancient foundation, and pressed the abbot and his monks to surrender the house and its great store of valuables to the Crown, is evident from the numerous letters of the commissioners to Cromwell. In September 1539 three commissioners (Richard Pollard, Thomas Moyle and Richard Layton) wrote to Cromwell from Glastonbury:

> Please it your lordship to be advertised, that we came to Glastonbury on Friday last past, about ten of the clock in the forenoon; and for that the abbot was then at Sharpham, a place of his, a mile and somewhat more from the abbey, we, without any delay, went unto the same place; and there, after communication declaring unto him the effect of our coming, examined him upon certain articles. And for that his answer was not then to our purpose, we advised him to call to his remembrance that which he had as then forgotten, and so declare the truth, and then came with him the same day to the abbey; and there of new proceeded that night to search his study for letters and books; and found in his study secretly laid, as well a written book of arguments against the divorce of the King's majesty and the lady dowager, which we take to be a great matter, as also divers pardons, copies of bulls, and the counterfeit life of Thomas Becket in print; but we could not find any letter that was material, and so we proceeded again to his examination concerning the articles we received from your lordship, in the answers whereof, as we

take it, shall appear his cankered and traitorous heart and mind against
the King's majesty and his succession; as by the same answers, signed
with his hand, and sent to your lordship by this bearer, more plainly
shall appear. And so, with as fair words as we could, we have conveyed
him hence into the Tower, being but a very weak man and a sickly. And
as yet we have neither discharged servant nor monk; but now the abbot
being done, we will, with as much celerity as we may, proceed to the
dispatching of them. We have in money £300 and above, but the
uncertainty of plate and other stuff there as yet we know not, for we
have not had opportunity for the same, but shortly we intend, God
willing, to proceed to the same; whereof we shall ascertain your
lordship so shortly as we may. This is also to advertise your lordship,
that we have found a fair chalice of gold, and divers other parcels of
plate, which the abbot had hid secretly from all such commissioners as
have been there in times past; and as yet he knoweth not that we have
found the same; whereby we think, that he thought to make his hand,
by his untruth to his King's majesty. It may please your lordship to
advertise us of the King's pleasure by this bearer, to whom we shall
deliver the custody and keeping of the house, with such stuff as we
intend to leave there to the King's use. We assure your lordship it is the
goodliest house of that sort that ever we have seen. We would that your
lordship did know it as we do; then we doubt not but your lordship
would judge it a house meet for the King's majesty, and for no man else;
which is to our great comfort; and we trust verily that there shall never
come any double hood within that house again. Also this is to advertise
your lordship that there is never a one doctor within that house, but
there be three bachelors of divinity, which be but meanly learned, as we
can perceive. And thus our Lord preserve your good lordship.

(Wright 1843)

The unworldly abbot and his monks were no match for such experienced and
ruthless men as the commissioners, most of whom had already spent three
years in receiving monastic surrenders, and on 16 November 1539 another of
the commissioners, Lord Russell, wrote to Cromwell:

My lord, this shall be to ascertain you that on Thursday the 14th day of
this present month the abbot of Glastonbury was arraigned, and the
next day put to execution, with two other of his monks, for robbing of
Glastonbury church, on Tor Hill, next unto the town of Glastonbury,
the said abbot's body being divided into four parts, and the head
stricken off; whereof one quarter standeth at Wells, another at Bath,
and at Ilchester and Bridgwater the rest, and his head upon the abbey
gate at Glastonbury . . .

(Wright 1843)

The dissolution was followed by a scramble among the local gentry, royal servants and wealthy merchants to secure the former monastic sites, buildings and widespread lands. The prosperous Bristol merchant, John Smythe, was able to buy some of the estates of Bath Abbey for himself, and acting as Mayor of Bristol also bought monastic lands for the town, lands which were later to make the Corporation one of the richest in England. The Horners of Mells had been tenants of Glastonbury Abbey for more than a century before the dissolution and had acted for the abbey as stewards and in various other capacities; in 1543 John Horner, 'little Jack Horner' of the nursery rhyme, paid the very large sum of £1,831 19s. 11¼d. for the neighbouring manors of Mells, Leigh-on-Mendip and Nunney, certainly a 'plum' but not dishonestly acquired as the rhyme suggests.

Men who had served Thomas Cromwell in all the complex administrative procedures connected with the long process of the dissolution were rewarded with west-country monastic lands. Sir Ralph Hopton, a Suffolk man, was granted Witham and the Glastonbury manor of Ditcheat; Maurice Berkeley, a lawyer and member of the Gloucestershire family, who had rendered loyal service to Cromwell, obtained Bruton abbey; Sir Edward Rogers acquired the nunnery at Cannington in west Somerset. Even those who did not approve of all the changes in religion nonetheless suppressed their feelings in the struggle to acquire land. For example, Thomas West, Earl de la Warr, who had openly declared himself against the policy of closing the monasteries, swallowed his reservations and acquired the site and lands of Wherwell Priory. The Winchcombe family of Newbury who were wealthy clothiers remained faithful to the Catholic religion for many years after the Reformation, but nonetheless acquired the valuable manors of Thatcham and Bucklebury from the spoils of Reading Abbey. Perhaps most interesting of all is Sir John Tregonwell who played a very prominent part in the dissolution of the monasteries as one of the Commissioners acting for Thomas Cromwell, and in 1540 acquired the site and most of the possessions of Milton Abbey in Dorset; but in spite of this he remained essentially conservative and Catholic in his religious views. He was knighted by Queen Mary at her coronation and was a prominent member of Parliament during her reign, but with the Elizabethan changes in religion Tregonwell retired to his Dorset estates and died there in 1565. He is buried in the former monastery church at Milton Abbas under a fine altar tomb in the old Catholic style (Bettey 1968–69: 295–302).

Most of the gentry bowed to the royal policy and accepted the fate of the monasteries as inevitable, while at the same time welcoming the new opportunities to acquire land. Few were as candid as Sir William Paulet who obtained a great estate in Hampshire including Basing House, becoming the first Marquess of Winchester, and who openly stated that he took the willow not the oak for his emblem, bowing to the prevailing winds. Lord Sandys, who had built the great house The Vyne at Sherborne St John during the 1520s, was a conservative in religious matters, but nonetheless acquired Mottisfont Priory

Plate 5.1 Mottisfont Abbey, near Romsey, Hampshire. An Augustinian priory was established here in an idyllic situation beside the river Test in 1201. After the Dissolution the property was acquired by Lord Sandys of The Vyne, whose support and sympathy for the old religion did not prevent him from obtaining monastic property. The cloisters which were in the foreground of this illustration were demolished, and the nave of the priory church was turned into a house. Further alterations took place in the eighteenth century, so that today only scant remains of the former church can be seen buried beneath the domestic architecture of the house.

and converted it into a secondary residence. The scale and rate of the dispersal of the former monastic lands can be seen in Somerset where by the time of the accession of Queen Elizabeth in November 1558, the Crown had already disposed of 63 per cent of such lands, while by the early 1570s as much as 85 per cent of former monastic lands and property had been disposed of to private individuals (Wyndham 1979: 65–74; 1980: 18–34).

Many of the purchasers of monastic land were royal servants or courtiers like Edward Seymour, Duke of Somerset, a leading privy councillor who, amongst other properties, acquired the lands of Maiden Bradley Priory in Wiltshire and the Benedictine abbey of Muchelney in Somerset; or Sir William Herbert (created Earl of Pembroke 1551) who obtained the site and lands of the nunnery at Wilton where he built a great house. Others were royal officials and administrators, most notably Thomas Wriothesley, Principal Secretary to the King, who obtained widespread lands in Somerset and Hampshire including Beaulieu and Titchfield Abbeys. George Owen, a Bristolian who became physician to Henry VIII, purchased the lands and property of St John's Hospital, Bristol. Several other families who had acted as Crown officials, local administrators and monastic stewards acquired estates on which their families

161

were to continue for many years. Among them were the Thynnes of Longleat, the Paulet family of Basing House near Basingstoke, and a near-neighbour, William Sandys of the Vyne who acquired the site and possessions of Mottisfont Priory, and William Sharington who had been master of the Bristol mint and who obtained Lacock Abbey (Wyndham 1979 and 1980; Kennedy 1970).

Another prominent group who acquired monastic lands were clothiers, merchants, and townsmen. Among these were the clothier, William Stumpe, who bought the monastic church, cloisters and extensive buildings of Malmesbury Abbey. John Smythe the Bristol merchant bought lands in north Somerset which had previously belonged to Bath Priory (Vanes 1975). The Southampton merchants and burgesses John and George Mille (father and son) bought lands of Quarr Abbey on the Isle of Wight and other monastic lands in south Hampshire, so that by the reign of Elizabeth the family was among the leading landowners of Hampshire (Platt 1973).

Not only did the dissolution of the Wessex monasteries result in a massive redistribution of lands and the appearance of a host of new families who had risen to wealth and prominence through the timely purchase of monastic spoils, but the changes were also accompanied by the destruction of many of the former monastic buildings. Churches, cloisters, domestic buildings and other structures were rapidly demolished by their new owners, either in order to sell the valuable lead from the roofs and thus recoup some of the purchase money, or to use the stone, timber and tiles for other purposes. Stone from the suppressed monasteries was used to erect forts along the coast against the threat of French invasion during the 1540s; material from Beaulieu was used at Hurst Castle, and stone from Quarr Abbey was used on forts at East and West Cowes. Stone, lead and timber from Reading Abbey were taken by barge down the Thames to Windsor to build lodgings, and the site continued to be used as a quarry for stone until the eighteenth century, leaving only fragments of capitals and other carving to show the exceptionally high quality of the workmanship there. Stone from Stanley Abbey was used by Sir Edward Baynton for his house at Bromham; stone and tiles from Bath Abbey were used on repairs to churches and houses in Bath; and for many decades after the dissolution stone from monastic sites was being used to repair roads. Much material from Glastonbury was used on the construction and maintenance of the causeway across the marshes to Wells, and as late as 1754 stone from Reading Abbey was used to build a bridge on the road between Henley and Wargrave (Hockey 1970; Slade 1969).

The scale of the destruction and the quality of the buildings which were destroyed are still apparent from the surviving ruins at Glastonbury, Abingdon, Sherborne, Malmesbury, Cleeve and many other monastic sites. A few monastic churches survive as parish churches. The nunnery church at Romsey was purchased by the parishioners for £100; Sherborne Abbey with all its demesnes and the great abbey church was sold by the Crown to Sir John

Horsey of Clifton Maybank for £1,250, and the parishioners purchased the abbey church from Horsey for £250 and made it into their parish church in place of the much smaller church of All Hallows which had previously served their needs. Other monastic churches which were converted to parochial use included Malmesbury, Milton Abbas, and Christchurch, Portsmouth and Cranborne. The refectory of the Cistercian abbey at Beaulieu became the parish church there. At Reading the nave of the Grey Friars church was granted by the king to the town for use as a town hall on the grounds that the existing hall was small and inconvenient because of the noise made by washerwomen as they washed their clothes in the adjoining river Kennet. The monastic cathedral at Winchester was reconstituted and a secular chapter installed to replace the monks; the great medieval diocese of Worcester was divided, and new dioceses created based on Gloucester and Bristol in 1542. At Bristol the former church of the Augustinian canons became the new cathedral, and the oddly constituted Bristol diocese comprised Bristol itself together with the county of Dorset which was transferred from the large diocese of Salisbury.

Several monastic buildings were converted into private residences. At Lacock and Milton Abbas the cloisters were made into dwelling houses; at Titchfield in south Hampshire Thomas Wriothesley turned the refectory into his mansion and made a gatehouse out of the nave of the church, using for his alterations some of the stone from Hyde Abbey at Winchester which he had also acquired. Sir William Paulet made his hall and kitchen at Netley out of the church itself. Both these houses preserved the layout of the cloisters as their courtyards. At Bisham on the Thames between Reading and Maidenhead, the former Augustinian priory was turned into a house by the Hoby family whose monuments are such a striking feature of the nearby parish church.

Reform in the Parish Churches

The early changes of the Reformation – the break with Rome, the elevation of the monarchy to the position of Supreme Head of the Church, the dissolution of the monasteries – had little effect upon the parish churches or their parishioners. The first major change came in 1538 with the Royal Injunctions which ordered that an English bible should be set up in each church, and that registers of baptisms, marriages and burials should be kept. Throughout the region surviving churchwardens' accounts reveal that this and subsequent orders of the government were immediately obeyed in the parish churches; for example, at All Saints', Bristol in 1538 the churchwardens purchased an English bible for 16s. 0d. and 'a boke for wrytt yn al christenynge, weddyng and beryng' for 1s. 8d. The Injunctions of 1538 also began the process of removing objects, images or paintings which could be regarded as idolatrous, but the interior appearance of most parish churches remained little changed until the sweeping reforms of the reign of Edward VI (1547–53). These started in 1547 with the dissolution of the chantries which brought great changes to the parish churches and abolished the religious guilds which had played such an important part in Church life. The next few years saw a great wave of destruction which transformed the interior appearance of the churches. At St Ewen's, Bristol, during 1548 the tabernacles, images, and the great rood or crucifix were all taken down, while a mason was paid 1s. 6d. for 'dressing upp the walls by the hye Altar', in other words for repairing the scars left by the removal of the statues.

There is little evidence of any objections from churchwardens or parishioners to the changes ordered by successive government edicts, nor to the provision of the English prayer books in 1549 and again in 1552. Nor is there evidence of resentment at the confiscation of the valuables of the parish churches during the later years of Edward's reign, but a careful study of churchwardens' accounts does reveal that a few, sensing what was afoot, disposed of their valuables or hid chalices and vestments before the King's commissioners arrived. Thus at St Lawrence, Reading, the bulk of the church plate was sold by the churchwardens in 1547 for £47 18s. 0d. and some of the money was used for paving streets; at Yatton on the low-lying coastal plain of north Somerset the silver cross from the high altar was sold by the churchwardens in 1547 and the money used to make a barrier against tidal floods, 'a sirten sklusse (sluice) or yere (weir) agenste the rage of ye salte water'.

Nor is there much evidence of hostile reaction to the restoration of Catholic worship during Queen Mary's reign (1553–58), even though it cost parishes a great deal of money to replace items which had been destroyed only a few months earlier. All the changes were of course ordered with the authority of both Church and State and the penalties for opposition were harsh. The story of the martyrs who were punished for their refusal to conform to the successive changes is well-known and need not be repeated here. Most in Wessex were drawn from the lower orders of society who had little power to influence the course of events. A few in more exalted positions did not escape persecution, however, like Stephen Gardiner, Bishop of Winchester 1531–55, who was suspended from his office and imprisoned in the Tower under Edward VI, although he was reinstated under Mary and conducted the marriage service of Mary with Philip II of Spain in Winchester Cathedral in July 1554. In 1555 the Archdeacon of Winchester, John Philpot of Compton, was burnt at Smithfield for his refusal to accept the restoration of Catholicism. Only occasionally is there an indication that conservatively minded churchwardens welcomed the restoration of the old order under Mary, as at Stanford in the Vale in Berkshire where the old stone altar was rebuilt and the wooden communion table 'which served in ye church for ye communion in the wycked tyme of sysme (schism)' was sold for 5s. 0d.

Queen Elizabeth's accession in November 1558 led to a further orgy of destruction in the parish churches, and the effects of all these changes upon the appearance and furnishings of the churches were profound, but little evidence survives to bear witness to the inner feelings of parishioners. Whatever their true convictions, few doubted that God was intimately involved in the minutest detail of their daily lives. Thus a hard-headed and highly successful Bristol merchant like John Smythe, when sending cargoes abroad, was careful to note against each entry in his ledger 'God send hit saff'; while the Berkshire farmer, Robert Loder, making up his accounts for the year 1616 wrote:

> This year sowing too early I lost (the Lord being the cause thereof, but that the instrument wherewith it pleased him to work) . . . the sum of £10 at least, so exceeding full was my barley with charlock, in all likelihood by means of that instrumental cause, the Lord my God . . . being without doubt the efficient cause thereof.
>
> (Vanes 1975; Fussell 1936)

The changes did however mean that many parish churches were neglected and had been allowed to get into a bad state by the later sixteenth century. Bishop Jewell of Salisbury wrote in 1562 that

> it is a sin and shame to see so many churches so ruinous and so foully decayed in almost every corner.

At Cothelstone in Somerset the chancel was said to be 'in decay insomuch that when it raineth the curate may not abide at the altar'. There were many other churches in similar or worse condition. Inevitably some of the most enthusiastic and sincere of the parish clergy had resigned or had been ousted from their benefices during the changes of the Reformation. A few however remained in their parishes throughout all the changes. The best-known of all such men is Vicar Aleyn of Bray in Berkshire who retained his benefice in spite of all the different religious opinions imposed by four monarchs. In Thomas Fuller's famous account the Vicar of Bray is said to have silenced a critic who complained that he was prepared to accept any theological change, 'being taxed by one for being a turncoat and an unconstant changeling, "Not so", said he, "for I always kept my principle, which is this, to live and die the vicar of Bray" '.

Another, perhaps more admirable example of a parish priest who remained in his parish throughout all the changes is John Chetmill of Sherborne. Chetmill was ordained as a priest early in the 1520s. In 1538 he became Vicar of All Hallows, Sherborne, in the parish church which was actually built up against the west wall of the great Benedictine abbey church of St Mary's. Here he must have been quite overshadowed in every sense by the wealthy, ancient abbey; but in 1539 the abbey was suppressed, and a year later the parishioners of Sherborne acquired St Mary's as their parish church. It must have been almost overwhelming for John Chetmill to find himself in charge of this enormous church with its outstanding architectural features; but he apparently accepted this change as he adopted the new services and theology of Edward VI's reign, the restoration of Catholicism and the Latin mass under Mary, and the return to Protestantism under Elizabeth. John Chetmill remained as Vicar of Sherborne until 1566. It would be quite wrong to think of a man like John Chetmill as a cynic or a time-server. He was obviously concerned for the well-being of his parishioners and there is evidence of his devoted work among them, not least in the fact that his signature appears upon so many of the surviving wills and probate inventories; Chetmill clearly visited the sick and dying, it is difficult to believe that he would have served their interests better by the resignation of his cure (Fowler 1951: 277, 286, 322–3).

The parish churches continued after the Reformation to be closely involved in many aspects of parish life. The Churchwardens had a host of secular duties imposed on them during the sixteenth century from oversight of morals and of recusants to the responsibility for the destruction of vermin; and the church courts continued to exercise jurisdiction over many matters ranging from slander or immorality to testamentary matters, non-attendance at church and unacceptable theological opinions. Processions around the parish bounds at Rogationtide continued in order to impress the boundaries upon parishioners' minds, although in many areas the growth of enclosures and hedgerows made the task unnecessary or impossible. On the open chalk downlands of much of the region where there were few obvious boundaries, such processions continued to be important, although even regular perambulations did not always avoid disputes between neighbouring parishes. For example the two neighbouring parishes of Stratton and Charminster on the chalk downlands of Dorset, engaged in a long and expensive legal dispute over their boundaries before the Exchequer Court during the early seventeenth century. In depositions to the Court in 1616 all the witnesses agreed that the bounds had regularly been walked each year, but it was alleged that

> the inhabitants of Charminster within this eight and thirty years have altered their course of procession . . . and at the first cominge of the now Curatt . . . in his first perambulation in procession dyd forsake their old and wonted way and course . . . and did appoynt the said Curatt to goe farther in upon Stratton by fifty acres or thereabouts than they did before . . .
> (PRO E134/13 Jas I Mich. 1)

Throughout Wessex the churchyards continued to be used for recreations, games, dancing and maypoles. In many parts the game of fives was popular and was played against the wall or tower of parish churches. At Martock and other places in Somerset and Dorset the evidence of the former fives court is still apparent by the wall of the church, and at Fordington in 1631 eight people were reported by the churchwardens:

for that they have played at a game with a Ball called Fives in the churchyard and thereby have broken the glasse of one of the windowes of the church, the reparacion whereof is unto the value of 5s. 0d.

(WRO Churchwardens' Presentments)

There are numerous similar examples. At Dundry, which overlooks the port of Bristol, there are references during the early seventeenth century to a fair being held annually in the churchyard and to all sorts of sports and games there – wrestling, dancing, maypoles, cudgels, fives and other sports. Schools were also commonly held in churches, and at North Cadbury in Somerset two alphabets can still be seen painted on a wall of the church vestry, a reminder of its former use as a schoolroom.

A central figure in the life of the parish was, of course, the parson. It is impossible to generalise about the standards and conduct of such a diverse body of men, and there is a great danger of highlighting the foolish, criminal or eccentric and of ignoring the majority who ministered quietly and faithfully in their parishes. Some indication of the variety among the clergy during the early seventeenth century can be seen in Dorset. Some of the clergy in the county were wealthy country gentlemen like Richard Russell who was lord of the manor of West Stafford as well as rector there, and who rebuilt the church where his vast monument dominates the chancel. Gilbert Ironside, incumbent of Winterborne Steepleton and Winterbourne Abbas, was also very wealthy and was appointed Bishop of Bristol in 1661 largely on the grounds that his wealth enabled him to undertake such an ill-paid bishopric. A few were scholars of distinction, notably Thomas Fuller, author of *The Worthies of England*, who was incumbent of Broadwindsor from 1634 to 1641. The poet Thomas Bastard was vicar of Bere Regis from 1592 to 1618; he was plagued by poverty and finally was imprisoned for debt at Dorchester where he died. Perhaps the most notable was John White, rector of Holy Trinity, Dorchester, from 1605 to 1648 whose influence extended far beyond the town, and whose powerful preaching and personal piety led Thomas Fuller to write of him, 'he stains all other men's lives with the clearness of his own'. One of John White's most remarkable achievements was his part in sending a group of puritan colonists from Dorset to settle in New Dorchester, Massachusetts in 1630. Most of the clergy had little to distinguish them either in education or in life-style from the working farmers among whom they lived. A few were rogues or misfits in their profession. The incumbent of Upwey frequented a local alehouse, and

was many times so drunk that he had to be carried home and could not read divine service on the Sabboth day.

(WRO Churchwardens' Presentments)

The vicar of Alton Pancras was said in 1609 to neglect the services in order to go to nearby Cheselborne 'to footeball upon the Sabothe daye'. But such men were exceptional and the majority of the clergy, in Dorset as elsewhere in the region, lived quietly in their parishes without incurring any comment at all, either good or bad. Notable for his piety and for his devotion to his parishioners was George Herbert (1593–1633) who was rector of Bemerton between Wilton and Salisbury from 1630 until his death in 1633. George Herbert's brief ministry as a country parson at Bemerton expressed a holiness that his poems and hymns have kept bright for succeeding generations, while his short book *The Country Parson* which he wrote at Bemerton still provides an ideal or 'a Mark to aim at' for parish clergymen.

The revival of Church life and the renewed concern for decency in church furnishings and decoration during the early seventeenth century, and especially during the Laudian period of the 1630s, is apparent from the very large number of pulpits, screens and pews, and from the quantity of church plate dating from this time.

The regular round of services, Sunday after Sunday, in the parish churches has left few memorials. In large parishes many parishioners were obliged to travel long distances to reach their parish churches. The evidence for these long journeys remains in the multitude of hat pegs which still adorn the walls of many churches and in the stone benches on either side of the porches where women left their pattens after walking across the muddy fields. In 1627 Ellis Pawley of Martock petitioned the Somerset Quarter Sessions for a renewal of his licence to sell beer at his house near the church, and his petition was supported by numerous parishioners who stated that

> he hath a convenient clenly house for the parishioners sometimes to refresh themselves in, (they) being so far from the parish church that often times on the Sabbath day and other hollydaies they cannot go home and come again to church the same day; and for that the women of the parish when they bring their young children to be christened do often stay there to warm their babes, coming sometimes a mile, sometimes two, from home in the cold.
>
> (Bates Harbin 1908: 34)

Local Society and Government

From the early sixteenth century the number of gentry families increased rapidly, aided by the opportunities for enrichment offered by the upheavals of the times, notably by the sale of monastic and chantry lands. The gracious houses of the newly rich, surrounded by their elegant parklands, became one of the most characteristic features of the Wessex landscape. Thomas Gerard, writing of Somerset and Dorset during the early seventeenth century, noted this upward movement in society and the increased prosperity of many yeomen and rich farmers who 'now beginne to encroach upon the Gentrie'; while of the 211 leading landowning families of Dorset at the beginning of the seventeenth century, 103 or nearly half the total number had appeared for the first time in the ranks of the gentry during the previous century (Ferris 1965). In Berkshire where the proximity of London meant that there were always successful merchants, courtiers, lawyers and others anxious to buy lands and establish themselves among the gentry, only half of the leading families of the county in 1640 had been in that position in 1600, and only four of those families were established in Berkshire in 1500 (Durston 1981: 38–53). Among the many fine houses dating from this period are The Vyne north of Basingstoke built for Lord Sandys between 1518 and 1527, Longleat, Montacute, Longford Castle south of Salisbury built by Sir Thomas Gorges in *c.* 1590 on a curious triangular plan, or Bramshill House in the north-east corner of Hampshire built by Lord Zouche in 1605–12, one of the largest and most impressive of all Jacobean houses. Others are more modest but nonetheless distinguished, such as the Elizabethan Shaw House near Newbury, built by the clothier Thomas Dolman; Chantmarle near Maiden Newton in Dorset, constructed of Ham stone by the puritan Strode family; Barrington near Ilminster; Avebury manor in Wiltshire; or Winterborne Anderson, the attractive house of soft-coloured red brick built near Bere Regis by the Tregonwell family in 1622 (Brown 1981).

Not all of the older families disappeared and numerous ancient names, among them Arundell, Luttrell, Sydenham, Gorges, Turberville, Rogers, Morton, Strangways, Trenchard and several others, continued to figure amongst the important landowners of the region, but beside them many new families rose rapidly to great wealth and status. Alexander Popham of Huntworth in Somerset became rich through his legal practice; his son, Sir John Popham, was also a lawyer and became Recorder of Bristol, member of Parliament, and finally Lord Chief Justice, presiding over the trials of Essex, Raleigh and Guy Fawkes. He purchased large estates and mansions at Wellington and Marksbury in Somerset and Littlecote in Wiltshire, and at his death in 1607 was buried under a huge tomb in Wellington church. The Phelips family also acquired great wealth during the sixteenth century through the legal profession, and by the end of the century could build their lovely house at Montacute. The twelfth-century castle and large estates of the Bishops of Salisbury at Sherborne were acquired first by Sir Walter Raleigh who built a new house there, and following his execution they passed to Sir John Digby, James I's ambassador to Spain. The Smyth family of Ashton Court just outside Bristol amassed great wealth as Bristol merchants during the sixteenth century, and bought the house and estate at Long Ashton in 1545. Thereafter they continued to add to their lands in south Gloucestershire and north Somerset, and successive members of the family devoted themselves to extending the house, enlarging the park and stocking it with deer, planting trees and laying out formal gardens, ceasing to be merchants and becoming instead country gentlemen. The house, its contents and surroundings were clearly intended to be a visible reminder to all of the wealth of the family and the new status to which they had risen. There are many similar examples from all over the region (Bettey 1982).

The rise of the new families is marked by their ornate tombs, memorials and family pews in the parish churches. Tombs such as those of the St Johns and Mompessons at Lydiard Tregoze, the Hobys at Bisham, the Oglanders at Brading, the Wriothesleys at Titchfield, the Paulets at Old Basing, and many others, or family pews such as those of the Carews at Crowcombe, the Pouletts at Hinton St George, the Frekes at Iwerne Courtney or the Lisles at Ellingham show the pride and wealth of the families and leave no doubt of their aggressive assertion of leadership in the local community.

Much detail about the possessions and life-style of the working farmers of the region can be reconstructed from their probate inventories or lists of goods which were made at their death in order that their wills might be proved in the Church courts. Most farmers had comparatively few possessions in their

---

Plate 5.2 Montacute House, near Yeovil, Somerset. The lands of the former Cluniac priory at Montacute were acquired at the Dissolution by the Phelips family, and the wealthy lawyer, Sir Edward Phelips, Speaker of the House of Commons and Master of the Rolls, built his great mansion nearby during the 1590s. Built of the local honey-coloured Ham stone, it was probably designed by a local architect-mason, William Arnold, and is one of the finest and most attractive of all Elizabethan houses. The illustration shows the west front of the house, with the central section which was inserted during the eighteenth century, and came from a nearby house at Clifton Maybank.

houses, their wealth was tied up in their farm stock, crops and equipment and their houses were sparsely furnished compared with the mass of furniture to be found in Victorian farmhouses. Because of the way in which farming varied so greatly over the region, it is difficult to choose 'typical' examples to illustrate the goods and possessions of the 'average' farmer. William Graynger who farmed at Calne in Wiltshire and who died in April 1597 left a total wealth of £13 6s. 0d., most of which was accounted for by his three cows and his butter and cheese-making equipment. He also made part of his living from weaving and possessed a spinning-wheel and a loom. His house consisted of two rooms, and in the hall he had a table, a form, a chair, and a cupboard; before the open fire was a pair of pothooks, a frying pan, a pottinger and a skillet. He also possessed 'three brass potts, fyve pewter platters, 5 pottingers, 8 sawcers, five salte cellars, 2 pewter cups, 2 pewter candelsticks and one brazen chaffing dish'. In the bedchamber he had one bedstead, with a mattress, canvas sheets, blankets and a coverlet, as well as a rack for storing his cheese, a lantern and a basket. This, together with his few clothes, made up his entire personal wealth.

Rather higher up the social scale was John Elford of Chetnole in north Dorset, who was described as 'yeoman', and who died in March 1637 worth £101 13s. 8d., an above-average figure for a working farmer at this time. He evidently depended for his income mainly on his cows and on the sale of butter and cheese, but he also had a by-employment as a candlemaker. His house consisted of a hall, kitchen, buttery and shop on the ground floor, with two chambers above. Most of his wealth was in his eight cows, eight calves and three bullocks, and in the candles in his workshop; but in his hall he had a long table with a form, five stools and a chair, one cupboard containing various pewter cups and plates, two brass candlesticks and 'one playning iron and a pair of bellowes'. In the buttery he kept his cheese- and butter-making equipment and two hundredweight of cheese, while in the shop he had tallow and candles and wicks and moulds. The two bedrooms contained three beds with their coverings and this, with his clothing, completed the possessions of this man who was among the richer of his fellow farmers at this time.

The different pattern and aims of farming on the chalklands are clearly reflected in the probate inventories of yeomen and husbandmen there. Arable land was far more important and wheat and barley provided the chief source of income, while sheep were more valuable than other livestock. George Sherwin of Forston near Charminster in Dorset who died in June 1626 worth £73 15s. 0d., had 14 acres of corn valued at £18, together with seventy sheep worth £22; he had three kine worth £8 and two horses valued at £4.

In a region so dominated by great estates, most farmers were tenants, holding their farms by copyhold tenure, generally for three named lives. The precise terms of this tenure varied according to the custom of each manor, and manorial control remained strong, especially on the chalklands, where common-field farming, the common flocks of sheep and cows, and the communal operation of the water-meadows, all tended to preserve the power of the manorial courts. The body of detailed, customary law, enforced in the manorial court, was the essential framework for the lives of farmers, and in many places it continued to be important well into the nineteenth century. The differences in the customs to be found in various manors was referred to by the surveyor of the manor of Iwerne Courtney in Dorset in 1553:

> Their customs are not so universall as if a man have experyence of the customs and services of any mannor he shall thereby have perfect knowledge of all the rest, or if he be experte of the customes of any one mannor in any one countie, that he shall nede of no further enstruccions for all the residewe of mannors within that countie.
>
> (BL Harleian MSS, 71)

At the bottom of the social scale were the squatters' hovels, erected on waste or common grazing land or on roadside verges. Increasing population and economic changes during the sixteenth century created a growing number of landless labourers with nowhere to live, who were especially attracted to those parishes where the waste or forest lands provided raw materials for various crafts. For example, at Kingston Lacy on the heathland of east Dorset there was clay for bricks, tiles and pottery, furze and peat for fuel, and poor-quality grazing for cattle and ponies; a survey of the manor in 1582 lists no less than thirty-five unauthorised and newly erected cottages on the heath, and there were many others which, having been erected earlier, had already become an accepted feature of the heathland. Such settlements could rapidly develop into a whole hamlet of squatters, regarded with great suspicion by established residents. At Netherbury in 1626 the parishioners complained to the Quarter Sessions that

> there are nowe Latelie erected eight or ten poore Cottages on which divers poore people dwell and . . . they take liberty to themselves to keep unlicensed alehouses and have diverse disorderlie meetings where (it is feared) manie stollen goods are consumed to the great griefe and losse of there honest neighbours.

Such 'cottages' were often no more than flimsy hovels, erected overnight in the belief that this would give the occupants squatters' rights to remain there. This was obviously intended at Cranborne in 1625 where the tenants complained to the lord of the manor, the Earl of Salisbury, that they were being deprived of grazing for their sheep and cattle by the number of squatters on their common lands, and that

> Richard Cooke intends either this night or the next to set up a house (which he hath already framed) upon the common of Alderholt, and hath placed straw upon the common in the place he hath made choice of to erect his house in . . .

Another example comes from a survey of Kingston Lacy (Dorset) in 1582, where clay for bricks, tiles and pottery attracted squatters to the large area of heath:

> There are within the said mannor certaine cottages newly erected and incroached on her Majesties waste, as namely Edward Dicke hath builte one cottage and maketh of her Majesties waste and soile there bricke and Tiles but by what right appeareth not and yeldeth no rent for the same. Giles Stagge has inclosed a plott of ground containing one acre. Richard Painter and Thomas Bennett have of late erected two tenements on the waste. Richard Dewe has erected a house and enclosed 2 acres out of the common. Margaret Earlethe hath inclosed 20 acres of land from the common adjoining the park pale to the hindrance not onlie of her majesties deare therin but also to her tenants for theire common therin.
>
> (PRO DL 42/116)

The social problems caused by the rapid development of such cottage industries were also evident at Holnest (Dorset) where in 1630 the inhabitants complained to the Quarter Sessions that

> divers boyes, young men and unmarried persons have by the Tilemakers and Brickmakers, Potters and others within the parish of Holnest ... been brought in to the said parish to worke at dayes labour ... who do live loosely, frequenting Alehouses and committing many disorders.
>
> (DRO Quarter Sessions 7–8 April 1630)

It is clear from the above accounts that such cottages or hovels were extremely flimsy, quick to erect and presumably not intended to last very long. Throughout the heaths and commons of the region numerous hamlets came into existence through the erecting of such hovels, and many gradually became established as villages, often still recognisable from the absence of an ancient church, by the presence of one or more nonconformist chapels, by their unplanned, haphazard appearance, or by the ironic names they were sometimes given such as Scotland, Ireland, Little London, World's End or Bineham City.

Newcomers, sub-tenants and squatters were generally unpopular with established residents who resented the depletion of the natural resources, and they were regarded with the greatest suspicion by the overseers of the poor, who naturally feared that they would become a charge upon the parish rates. Nevertheless the problem of squatters' settlements and of unauthorised cottages continued throughout the seventeenth and eighteenth centuries, and the increase in population served to exacerbate the problems of both employment and housing. The noted surveyor, John Norden, found a situation at Cerne Abbas in 1617 which illustrates the problem faced by many villages and market towns. He wrote that

> they that injoy the principall howses of the towne dwell from them and
> lett them to a masse of base people, meer mendicantes. As namelie one
> Mr John Nobley hath a fayer howse but noe competent under-tenant.
> Mr Lovelace also hath a fayre howse full of poore people. One Mr
> Fowell, Mr Devenishe and one John Williams, which laste hath a fayer
> howse and hath put neer a dozen lowsy people in it . . .

Shortage of housing in some parts of the region, coupled with the unwillingness
of many parishes to accept newcomers, meant that some unfortunate people
were reduced to desperate circumstances, and were either compelled to seek
shelter in the parish poor house or some hovel, or alternatively to risk the very
severe laws against unlicensed wanderers and beggars and take to the road.

In 1610 Lacock in Wiltshire was said to be 'surcharged by the multitude
of inmates and those of the poorest sort to the number of sixtie persons like to
lye in the Streete for want of houses'; and in 1647 John Bevan and his wife of
Brokenborough near Malmesbury, who had been evicted from the house
which they had rented, were 'constrained to dwell in a hollow tree in the streete
. . . to the great hazard of their lives they being anncient people' (Bettey 1977:
57–9).

Such problems were not confined to the countryside, for in a Charter
granted to the town of Reading by Charles I in 1638 it was stated that cottages
were being erected and houses subdivided by 'certain covetous persons
preferring their own private benefit before the public good', and that these
small dwellings were turned into

> obscure receptacles of poor people, not only natives and burgesses of
> the same borough but also of foreigners resorting thither from other
> places and creeping and intruding into that borough . . .
> (Slade 1969)

For the poverty-stricken or vagrant the ale-house offered some
temporary alleviation of their lot, and there was an amazing amount of
drunkenness. By far the commonest entries in the records of both Quarter
Sessions and of individual justices are concerned with unlicensed tippling,
excessive drinking, unlawful gaming in alehouses and similar related offences.
In 1612 the inhabitants of Calne, Wiltshire, petitioned the justices to reduce the
number of ale-houses in the town because of the excessive number and the
rivalry which existed between them over which could brew the strongest ale:

> thither do resorte all the greate drinkers both of the Town and Countrie
> to spend theyr tyme in idleness and theyr money in excessive drinkinge,
> being partly drunke and halfe mad no officer can well judge whether
> they be drunk, yea or no, and therefore cannot punish them according
> to the law, and all men for the most part love these Cupp companions
> so well that no man will take upon him to be sworne witness against
> any drunkard.

In 1646 a petition was presented to the Wiltshire justices signed by two ministers, three churchwardens and twenty-three others alleging that there were too many alehouses in Pewsey and that

> our children, servants and pore labourers are often by them drawne into these houses to spend theyr moneys and time to our great prejudice in neglectinge our husbandry and other occasions.

Earlier, in 1610 an alehouse-keeper from Lacock had been reported

> who for his owne gayne and advantage did keep, maintayne and suffer to be used in his house unlawful games, that is to saye tables, cards, and shuffleboard, and also drunkeness and other misdemeanors, to the great disturbance of his neighbours against the peace. . . .

Any outside source of entertainment was regarded with suspicion, as is seen in the chorus of shocked protest which greeted a company of puppet-players who travelled through the strongly puritan area of west Dorset in the autumn of 1630. They were turned out of Dorchester, then under the powerful influence of John White, the saintly but strictly puritan vicar of Holy Trinity, and in September 1630 they reached Beaminster, another highly moral town, which was to be strongly parliamentarian in the Civil War and was burnt by Royalist troops in 1644. The townsfolk of Beaminster were genuinely shocked by the puppet-players which they described as 'certain Blasphemous shewes and sights which they exercise by way of puppet-playing'. In a statement which reveals much about contemporary parental discipline, the townsmen of Beaminster complained to the Quarter Sessions that the players

> doe exercise their feats not only in the day time, but also late in the night to the great disturbance of the Townsmen there, and the grievance of divers of the Inhabitants who cannot keepe their Children and Servants in their houses by reason that they frequent the said shewes and sights late in the night in a disorderly manner.
>
> (DRO Quarter Sessions Accounts 1625–37)

The puppet-players were duly ordered by the justices to leave the county and not to return. It says a great deal for the dullness of everyday life in a small town like Beaminster during the seventeenth century as well as for the moral attitudes of the inhabitants, that a company of puppet-players could cause such havoc in the discipline of servants and children.

In the small, tightly knit rural communities of the region superstitious beliefs and practices were common, and the surviving records, especially those of the Quarter Sessions, contain numerous references to superstitions, magic, witches and accusations of witchcraft. The sort of difficulty which could face an old woman who had some skill in treating sick people or cattle can be seen in the case of Joan Guppy of South Perrott in west Dorset; she was accused of witchcraft and was obliged to obtain a certificate signed by her neighbours stating that she was not a witch but that 'she hath donne good to many people, as well in Curinge of dyvers people of wounds and such like things, and in the drenching of cattell and such like Exercises, and hath always lived of good name and fame without any spott or touch of Sorcerye or witchcraft'. Many old women in a similar predicament were not so fortunate in their neighbours (PRO E163/17/5; Star Chamber 8/149/24). At Rode on the borders of Somerset and Wiltshire a large party of men assembled in July 1694 and proceeded to throw several old women into the river, in the belief that witches would not sink. The sort of power which could be exercised in a rural community by a person with a reputation for supernatural power is seen in the case of Thomas Tyher of Charminster in 1616. He was accused by the churchwardens before the bishop's court of

> using witchcraft and performing publiclie physicke by unlawful meanes contrarie unto authoritie. Wee presente the said Tyher for giving purgations to those that be with child and unmarried and harlots and such like. Wee present him also for saying that Joanne Blick of Charminster had seven devilles in her and for undertaking to cast them out of her.
>
> (WRO, Churchwardens' Presentments for Dean's Peculiars, 1616)

It was not only the unlearned who were affected by superstitious beliefs. William Locke, the rector of Askerswell in Dorset from 1674 to 1686, cast the horoscopes of his two children and copied the details into the parish register. For the principal decoration of his hall at Montacute House Sir Edward Phelips chose to have a plaster-work frieze depicting the unaimiable rural custom of the 'Skimmington ride'. This was common throughout the region, and was the public ridicule and humiliation of anyone who had offended against the traditional standards of the community. At Quemerford near Calne in Wiltshire in 1618 Thomas Wells who had allowed himself to be nagged by his wife found a large company assembled at his door, with a band consisting of drums, pots, pans, pipes, cow-horns and sheep-bells. He and his wife were attacked, effigies were paraded, and only with difficulty were the mob restrained from ducking the wife in the river. Such processions and public expressions of popular disapproval continued through the eighteenth and nineteenth centuries in many villages, and were not unknown in the early twentieth century (Ingram 1984).

Local ceremonies and festivities marking feasts such as Christmas, Easter, Whitsun or Midsummer were also common. The texts of mummers' plays have survived from Marshfield in south Gloucestershire, Longparish, Hampshire, and from west Dorset. There were Shrove Tuesday games at Corfe Castle, Dorset, and Rode, Somerset, May-day processions at Wishford,

Wiltshire, Midsummer watches in Bristol, Robin Hood ceremonies at Lyme Regis, Dorset, distribution of bread and beer in the church at Marnhull, Dorset, on Easter Sunday, and many others.

In a case before the Court of Star Chamber in 1570 concerning alleged disturbances in the town of Weymouth, a witness stated that it had been the custom 'time out of mind', not only in Weymouth but in all the towns and villages of Dorset, that the inhabitants

> have used at the Springe tyme of the yere only of purpose to make
> sporte and pastime amonge themselves on Sundaies and other holydaies
> as also to continue honest company and mutual society with others the
> neighbours of the Townes and villages nexte adjoyninge, to electe and
> chuse one of the said Inhabitants to be Robin Hoode and another
> Lyttell John, which persons have bin appointed for the Trayninge and
> Enstructinge of the youth with divers kinds of activity and vertuous
> exercises, and especiallye of shottinge, whereby the youth is made the
> more prompt and ready to do the Prince service if neede should require.
> (PRO Star Chamber Eliz. J/19/6)

Finally, one other aspect of life in the region before easy and frequent contact with other areas, was the strength of local dialect and speech patterns, so that it was difficult even for persons from one part of the region to understand easily the speech of those from another district. For travellers from elsewhere it was often impossible. Early in the eighteenth century Daniel Defoe wrote that the dialect of the Yeovil region of Somerset was more difficult to comprehend than that of any other part of England:

> tis certain that tho' the tongue be all meer natural English, yet those that
> are but little acquainted with them, cannot understand one half of what
> they say.
> (Defoe 1927)

The Tudor reforms in local government, and especially the increased importance of the justices of the peace, meant that it was principally the gentry families who governed and administered each county. To be chosen to assume the heavy burden of a justice of the peace meant a valued addition to the political power and social status of a rising gentleman, and the position was eagerly sought after. The concentration of power and local authority within each county, particularly in the meetings of the justices in Quarter Sessions, gave an increased importance to the concept of the county as the principal unit of local government, and as the focus of local pride and patriotism. In Quarter Sessions the justices dealt with all aspects of daily life from crime and its punishment through the endless disputes over poor relief, bastardy, unlawful gaming and drunkenness, to the licensing of alehouses and concern for roads, bridges, charities and taxation. For example the Somerset justices meeting at the Quarter Sessions at Wells in January 1627 dealt among other things with various illegitimate and orphan children, a dispute between parishes about the responsibility for maintaining a beacon, the licensing of alehouses, complaints over rates, the maintenance of roads and bridges, and the provision of relief for Grace Mogridge of Porlock who had lost all her possessions 'by reason of a greate and terrible innundation of water'. The Dorset justices meeting in Quarter Sessions in 1635 dealt with matters as diverse as the increase in the number of poor and homeless people, the effects of a disastrous fire at the town of Bere Regis, a dispute over the right to glean corn after harvest in the common fields of Sherborne, measures to prevent the spread of plague in Blandford Forum, and a complaint that many of the inhabitants of Beaminster kept 'great fierce and dangerous doggs by meanes whereof the Constables and other Inhabitants there are fearful to goe abroad in the night tyme to execute theire office and negotiate theire businesse'. The justices also ordered the alehouse keepers in Sherborne to sell their wares by certain specified measures and not by the cup or jug, and also that they should not 'brew their owne beere of extraordinary strength of purpose to vent the greater quantity'.

Individual justices also had considerable powers to try minor cases, and to supervise the administration of the parish officers, for local government also depended heavily upon the unpaid work of other officials, churchwardens, overseers of the poor, waywardens and parish constables. Visible reminders of the authority of the constables survive in the many local prisons or lock-ups which remain throughout the region, such as those at Wells, Castle Cary, Pensford, Steeple Ashton, Bromham or Shrewton.

The responsibility for the defence of each county, for arms, beacons and for local musters of armed men, rested with the lords lieutenant, and their task was of particular importance along the coastlines of Somerset, and of Hampshire and Dorset. The threats of foreign invasion during the sixteenth century, first from the French and later from the Spanish, led to some notable additions to coastal defences. During the reign of Henry VIII a string of castles was built along the south coast, including the castles at Calshot, Hurst, Netley and Southsea on the Hampshire coast facing the Solent, and Sandown, Yarmouth and Cowes on the Isle of Wight; along the Dorset coast castles were built at Brownsea Island in Poole Harbour, and at Sandsfoot and Portland. Portland Castle is an excellent and well-preserved example of the military architecture of the time; it was built *c.* 1540 at a cost of £4,964, and an inscription within the castle reads:

> God save King Henri the VIII of that name, and Prins Edward, begotten of Quene Jane, my Ladi Mari that goodli virgin, and the Ladi Elizabeth so towardli, with the Kinges honorable counslers.

The threat from Spain during the 1580s led to further strongholds, lookouts and beacons being built, and along the Somerset coast circular towers equipped with cannons were erected at Woodspring, Knightstone, Uphill, Hurlstone and Porlock Bay; guns were also installed to guard the entrance to Bridgwater, while ships were stationed to prevent enemy access to the Severn estuary and to the port of Bristol (Dunning 1978: 43–4).

Growing discontents during the early decades of the seventeenth century over inflation, unemployment and vagrancy, enclosures and disafforestation, and over the royal policy on religious matters, taxation, foreign policy and Parliament, all served to create divisions among the ruling gentry. During the 1630s the King's actions and advisers were as unpopular in Wessex as elsewhere in England, and the region was suffering under impositions, wardships, the billeting of soldiers and other grievances. Archbishop Laud's orders about church ceremonies, ornaments and vestments were fiercely resented in many places, especially in the cloth-working towns which were predominantly Puritan in sympathy. The churchwardens of Beckington near Frome were prepared to go to prison in 1635 rather than obey the bishop's order to move their communion table from the middle of the chancel, where it had stood since the Reformation, to the east end of the church and to ensure that it was decently railed. It was also the opposition of the Puritans to what they regarded as the unseemly excesses of church ales and other parish recreations that brought these ancient festivities to an end. As early as 1596 the Puritan gentleman Sir Francis Hastings of North Cadbury in Somerset bequeathed various sums of money to several local churches

> upon condition that they never use againe theyr churchales, to the prophaning of the Lorde's Saboathe, the abusing of his creatures in dronkennes and ryott, and the corrupting of their youthe by trayning them up in gaminge and lascvious wantonnes, and sundry other disorders.
> (Cross 1969: 117–18)

Royal taxation was bitterly hated, and the ship money tax became increasingly difficult to collect. Even in Hampshire which, like Dorset, was vulnerable to attacks by sea, and had ample evidence of naval problems such as the strength and growing depredations of the Dutch and French navies, and was also able to see the annual gathering of the Fleet in Portsmouth Harbour, nonetheless the ship-money tax was paid with reluctance. Sir John Oglander of Nunwell in the Isle of Wight who was sheriff and collector of ship money in 1637 found that the tax could only be collected with great difficulty, that the boroughs, and especially Winchester, Andover and Southampton, were very reluctant to pay, and that many in the country districts pleaded poverty. Part of the reason for the difficulties of collection in Hampshire was that the inhabitants were already forced to pay heavy county taxes for the carriage of timber to the naval dockyards at Portsmouth and Chatham from the New Forest and the forests of Bere, Pamber and Alice Holt. The county had also suffered badly from the

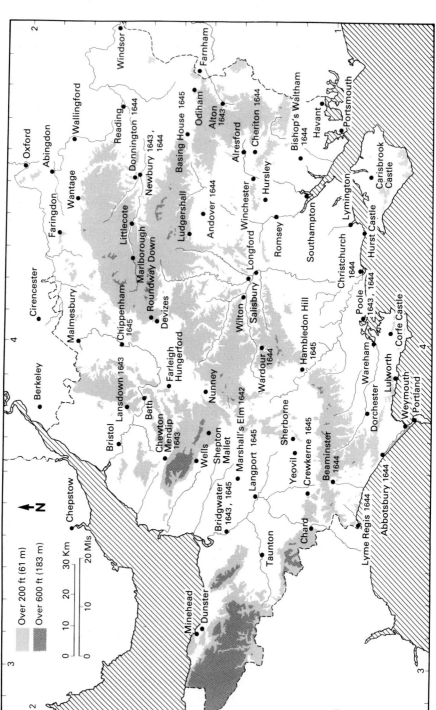

Figure 5.1 Battles and bases of the Civil War

sharp depression in the cloth trade and from the decline of Southampton. Oglander wrote of the poverty of the coastal region, 'from Emswoorth to Christchurch all alonge the sea Coasts being 30 miles in length the inhabitants (most fischermen) ar so poore as they ar not able to paye, and most of them not whereon to distrayne' (Haskell 1981).

In 1636 the sheriff of Dorset, Sir John Freke, wrote that the tax was paid 'like drops of blood', and when a third demand for ship money was issued in October 1636 the volume of protest became even stronger. William Basset, the sheriff of Somerset, found it impossible to collect the tax in some districts, and wrote to the Privy Council to complain of 'factious spirits' who stirred up the volume of objections. Even those who were later to fight fiercely for the Crown were greatly troubled at the royal policy. The wealthy young landowner Thomas Smyth, whose estates stretched across north Somerset and south Gloucestershire and who was later to die while fighting in the royal army, wrote in 1637 to ask for a reduction of the tax in his district:

> Divers of the inhabitants have repayred unto mee, and I finde them much discontented . . . I desier you will allowe (an abatement of tax) . . . Otherwise I feare you will finde the people rude and addicted unto opposicon.

Thomas Smyth, like his father-in-law Lord Poulett of Hinton St George, was eventually and with some misgivings to support the royal cause. His friend and neighbour Alexander Popham who was heir to vast estates in Wiltshire and Somerset, strongly supported the parliamentary cause and became a colonel in the parliamentary army. Similar divisions of friends and families were to occur throughout the region, and many of the gentry families were uncertain and divided in their loyalties, even though support for the King revived among many as soon as actual fighting began. The Earl of Pembroke who, like the King, was a great collector and patron of the arts, and who together with several other members of his family, the Herberts of Wilton, had been closely associated with the Court and had entertained the King and Queen at Wilton, became disaffected on the eve of the war and thereafter skilfully divided his loyalties between King and Parliament. As Clarendon scornfully expressed it in his *History of the Rebellion*, the prime concern of the Herberts was to avoid danger for themselves:

> that though they wished they (the parliamentarians) might rather be destroyed than the King, they had rather the King and his posterity be destroyed than that Wilton should be taken . . .

John Paulet, Marquess of Winchester, who was a Catholic, retired to his great mansion at Basing vainly 'hoping integrity and privacy might preserve his quiet'.

The Civil War

The Civil War had a devastating effect upon Wessex, for as well as the major battles which were fought in the region, the damage caused by the constant passage of the armies of both sides was immense. Many people who bore no arms and declared no support for either side in the conflict, nonetheless suffered the effects of war when their crops were destroyed, their goods confiscated or plundered and their trade interrupted. The region had great strategic significance for both sides, since it possessed important and well-fortified towns, ports and castles, provided a link between the strongly royalist south-west of England and the King's headquarters in Oxford, and gave access to the Channel ports which was crucial to both sides for maintaining communication with the continent.

The fighting took place against a background of indifference and neutralism, and of an equal hatred for the damage caused by the armies of both sides. Many friends, divided by a political and religious conflict they could neither understand or control, would have shared the elegantly expressed sentiments of Sir William Waller, the parliamentary general, who before the battle of Lansdown wrote to his old acquaintance Sir Ralph Hopton, the royalist commander

> That great God, which is the searcher of my heart, knows with what a sad sense I goe upon this service, and with what a perfect hatred I detest this warr without an Enemie . . . The God of peace in his good time send us peace, and in the meane time fitt us to receive it: Wee are both upon the stage and must act those parts that are assigned us in this Tragedy: Lett us do it in a way of honor, and without personall animosities . . .

Many merchants and tradesmen found themselves dragged reluctantly into a conflict which they did not want and in which they vainly struggled to remain neutral. In Bristol which was described by William Prynne as 'a place of the greatest consequence of any in England, next to London . . . the metropolis, key, magazine of the West', the Common Council which governed the city did not declare itself either for King or for Parliament in 1642, but strengthened the defences and tried unsuccessfully to keep out the forces of both sides. The cathedral cities of Wells, Salisbury and Winchester supported the Crown; Bath, Taunton, and the ports of Bridgwater, Poole and Lyme Regis were strongly parliamentarian. In the two strategically important naval ports of Southampton and Portsmouth there was strong support for Parliament; both places had suffered from the royal policy, both were influenced by the adherence of the Royal Navy to the parliamentary side. Soon after the outbreak of the war both towns were taken for Parliament and their loss was a vital factor in the eventual defeat of the royalist forces. The King's decision to establish his headquarters at Oxford in November 1642 was followed by strenuous royalist attempts to garrison Abingdon, Wallingford and Reading as a first line of defence against the parliamentary forces in London. Reading suffered badly in the war; it was captured and pillaged by the parliamentary forces under the Earl of Essex in April 1643, only to be abandoned to the royalists again; then in May 1644 it was once more taken by the parliamentarians. By the end of the war the once-thriving cloth and malting trades were in ruins, the merchants impoverished and the Corporation heavily in debt because of the heavy taxation and impositions of both sides (Wanklyn 1981: 55–79).

Major battles in the region included that at Lansdown near Bath (5 July 1643) where the fiercely royalist Cornish infantry displayed incredible heroism against an apparently impregnable parliamentarian defence on the steep hill-top, 'they stood as upon the eaves of a house for steepness, but as unmoveable as a rock'. This was a courageous but foolhardy attack in which the Cornish army lost their beloved leader, Sir Bevil Grenville, and which sadly depleted the finest fighting force on the King's side. A week later the Cornish army under Sir Ralph Hopton completed the overthrow of Waller's parliamentary forces at Roundway Down outside Devizes (13 July 1643), and prepared the way for the capture of Bristol by Prince Rupert on 26 July 1643. On 20 September 1643 occurred the royalist victory at the first battle of Newbury, which led to the capture of Reading for the Crown. At Newbury the royalist cavalry triumphed over the parliamentary army, this time commanded by the Earl of Essex. The first battle of Newbury marked a high point in the royalist fortunes in the region, and gradually the tide began to turn in favour of Parliament. On 29 March 1644 a parliamentary force under Waller completely defeated Sir Ralph Hopton's army at Cheriton near Alresford, a 'great victory over our enemies beyond all expectation'. Later in 1644, after a further royalist defeat in the north at Marston Moor (2 July 1644) the royal fortunes revived in the west with a triumphant victory at Lostwithiel in Cornwall (21 August 1644), the skilful and daring relief of Basing House which had been under siege by the parliamentary forces throughout the whole summer, and the failure of Parliament to take full advantage of their superior strength at the second battle of Newbury (27 October 1644). Slowly, however, the royal forces were being weakened and the parliamentarians were growing stronger and more confident. In April 1645 Parliament formed the New Model Army from garrisons at Windsor, Reading and elsewhere, with a new organisation and discipline which was eventually to win the war, and in June 1645 came the decisive defeat of the royal forces at Naseby. In Somerset a parliamentary army under Sir Thomas Fairfax defeated a much stronger contingent of Goring's royalist forces at Langport (10 July 1645), perhaps the most impressive of all the achievements of the New Model Army. Langport was the last major battle to be fought during the Civil War in the region, but throughout the war there had been numerous skirmishes, minor engagements and sieges, and several towns, among them Bristol, Reading, Abingdon, Wallingford, Bridgwater, Taunton and Devizes, had changed hands, some of them several times. Castles at Winchester, Sherborne, Corfe, Donnington and Wardour had been besieged and taken, often with great destruction.

Corfe Castle had been acquired in 1635 by Sir John Bankes, attorney-general to Charles I; his wife, the indomitable Lady Bankes, held the castle for the Crown during three years of repeated attacks until the parliamentary forces at last gained access by treachery in March 1646. Thereafter the castle, like so many others, was systematically wrecked by undermining and explosives so that only the dramatic ruin remains of this great fortress which was once one of the most notable and strategically situated castles in England. Most spectacular of all was the final overthrow of the Marquess of Winchester's palatial stronghold at Basing House on 14 October 1645. Cromwell, fresh from the successful siege of Winchester which had fallen to Parliament on 6 October, arrived at Basing House on 8 October to supplement the forces of Colonel Dalbier who had besieged the house since August. With him Cromwell brought the heavy siege guns which had done so much damage at Winchester. By 14 October the defences of Basing House had been sufficiently battered for a full-scale assault to be mounted. Within an hour the defenders had been

Plate 5.3 Wardour Castle, near Tisbury, Wiltshire. Built by John Lord Lovell at the end of the fourteenth century; later it passed into the hands of the Arundell family who created an Elizabethan house within the castle. The Catholic Arundells strongly supported the King during the Civil War, and their castle was besieged and eventually taken by the parliamentary forces, after which the fortifications were 'slighted' and the castle ruined. During the eighteenth century a large Georgian mansion was built nearby for the eighth Lord Arundell.

overpowered. There followed the indiscriminate massacre of the unfortunate inhabitants of the house, the burning of the structure and the plunder of its rich contents. The soldiers were joined by local people in stripping the house of anything valuable, so that within a day only the bare walls remained. On 19 October Parliament ordered the demolition of Basing House, and so thoroughly was the work done that it left only the foundations and a few ruined fragments of what had been the largest private residence of any subject in England.

The great battles and the capture or loss of towns and castles were only part of the story of the Civil War in Wessex; for most of the inhabitants the ever-present threat during the war years was from the passing armies of both sides, and from lawless bands of soldiers roaming the countryside, plundering and stealing. The Thames valley and much of Hampshire suffered badly from the passage of armies, and in Wiltshire and south Somerset there were few villages without some scars of war. The royalist army under the dissolute Lord George Goring in particular left a trail of devastation, and 'Goring's Crew' became a by-word in the region. Estate accounts from many districts tell the same story of uncultivated land, destroyed crops, stolen cattle and horses, damage to property and the inability of tenants to pay their rents. John Curridge, a husbandman from Tarrant Rushton in east Dorset wrote to his landlord, the Earl of Salisbury, in 1647 explaining that he could not pay his rent because of the number of soldiers billeted upon him:

> I have had so manie souldiers that I am not able to pay the rent that is past. . . . I have paid contribution money ever since the warrs began, . . . besides there was never no gathering for otes, hay or anie thing whatsoever. . . . They eat up my corne that I was enforst to bye my seede. This is the truth. . . .

Likewise the lawyer John Turbervill of Tolland in west Somerset wrote in 1647 that his house

> is and hath been full of soldiers this fortnight, such uncivil drinkers and thirsty souls that a barrel of good beer trembles at the sight of them, and the whole house nothing but a rendezvous of tobacco and spitting.
> (Dunning 1978: 60)

It was the feeling of helpless outrage at indiscriminate destruction that led to the remarkable rising of the Clubmen in 1645. The Clubmen claimed to be neutral and to be concerned only to protect their property against the damage caused by both sides. They gained support throughout much of Somerset, Dorset, Wiltshire and Hampshire. Their simple aims were admirably summarised in the slogan on one of their banners:

> If you offer to plunder or take our cattle,
> Be assured we will give you battle.

During the summer of 1645 there were several minor clashes between the Clubmen and both royalist and parliamentary troops, and in August 1645 a large company of Clubmen were overwhelmingly defeated at Hambledon Hill in Dorset by parliamentary troops under Cromwell. Cromwell wrote to his commander, Sir Thomas Fairfax:

> they are poor silly creatures, whom if you please to let me send home, they promise to be very dutiful for time to come, and will be hanged before they come out again.

The whole episode of the Clubmen, while not materially affecting the course of the Civil War in the region, remains a remarkable example of protest by ordinary farmers, craftsmen, tradesmen and labourers, and illustrates the sufferings and difficulties which were caused by the war. Like the risings against the enclosures of the royal forests during the 1620s, and the agricultural labourers rising in 1830, the Clubmen were making an heroic gesture in the face of much stronger forces, and their protest reveals the deepest feelings and attachments of rural society (Underdown 1979).

In November 1647 Charles I became a prisoner at Carisbrooke Castle and was later moved to Hurst Castle before being taken to London for his trial. On his last journey through Hampshire much of the old loyalty to the Crown reasserted itself especially in Winchester where the King was welcomed by the Corporation. Loyalty to the Crown was also displayed by those gentry families, such as the Nortons of Abbots Leigh and the Wyndhams of Trent, who sheltered Charles II during his flight after the battle of Worcester in September 1651; and also by those who supported the ill-fated rising in Wiltshire in 1655 led by Colonel John Penruddock.

The restoration of the monarchy in 1660 was welcomed by many people in the region, and there were scenes of wild rejoicing in many towns and villages. At Sherborne, for example,

> Sir John Strangways read the Proclamation . . . after which followed shouts and acclamations and several volleys; the Conduit ran wine two daies together, the loyal Town being transported with the glorious triumph of that joyful day.
>
> (Bayley 1910)

At Hinton St George near Crewkerne, the home of the fiercely royalist Poulett family, there were likewise scenes of wild rejoicing, and Lord Poulett later described their feasting, drinking and huge bonfire:

this was our way, what others did I have not heard, but I am confident that they all did to their proportion; for soe many bonfires appeared about us farr and near that if we had not known the true cause of it, we should have apprehended a general risinge of the fanatiques. . . .

The Restoration came too late for some Royalist families such as the Oglanders of Nunwell in the Isle of Wight, the Paulets of Basing House, or the Tichbornes of Tichborne, who were greatly impoverished or even ruined by their steadfast support of the royal cause. Sir John Stawell, a leading Somerset royalist, was forced to pay such heavy fines to Parliament that he had to abandon the grandiose plans for his great mansion at Low Ham near Langport, but his son finished building the church there, a faithful copy of a medieval church in the Gothic style, with the prominent inscription across the chancel screen:

My sonne, feare God and the Kinge and meddle not with them that are given to change.

Chapter 6

Industrial Change and Urban Growth, 1660–1815

In 1660, despite all the changes which had occurred during the previous century and a half, many aspects of daily life were little different from what they had been when the Tudor dynasty had come to the throne in 1485; by 1815 few parts of Wessex had not been profoundly affected by turnpike roads, canals, improved harbours, new industries, agricultural advances, and a host of changes in population and social structure. Everywhere the impact of this period of change, prosperity and rapid growth is still very evident. Most town centres and market-places were rebuilt, or the houses were enlarged and re-fronted in the latest style, many villages and farms were completely reconstructed, while the wealth of many towns and of ports such as Bristol, Bridgwater, Weymouth, Lyme Regis and Poole is still apparent from the fine eighteenth-century mansions, warehouses, customs houses and the large, opulent, nonconformist chapels. Bath became the leading social centre of England and the arbiter of taste in dress, furnishings, architecture and social behaviour.

The region had been described and analysed as never before by travellers and observers as diverse in their interests as John Aubrey, Celia Fiennes, Daniel Defoe and Arthur Young, and by the reporters appointed at the end of the eighteenth century by the newly formed Board of Agriculture. By the early nineteenth century large-scale maps of the region were available, and William Smith, the so-called 'father of English geology' who lived near Bath, had revolutionised the study of geology and had already published in 1779 his first geological map covering the area around Bath. In 1801 the first Census showed the full extent and distribution of the population of the region, and the comparative sizes of the towns, ports and villages. All of these manifold developments, coupled with a rapid growth in population, could not fail to have a dramatic impact upon all aspects of life in the region.

Industry and Communications

The seventeenth century saw the introduction of new types of cloth known as 'medleys' because they were made by mixing wool dyed in two or more colours before spinning, or as 'Spanish cloths' because they were made partly or wholly of fine wool imported from Spain. The Tudor broadcloth produced in the region had been a thick, hard-wearing cloth, weighing more than 20 ounces per square yard, whereas the new coloured cloths were much lighter at about 16 ounces per square yard. It was the readiness of the industry in west Wiltshire, east Somerset and south Gloucestershire to change to the production of this new type of cloth which ensured the continued prosperity of the textile trade in these areas, whereas the woollen-cloth industry in many of the older centres such as Reading, Newbury, Andover, Dorchester, Marlborough and Malmesbury declined rapidly.

The textile trade also continued to prosper in west Somerset by turning to the production of serges or perpetuanas, a worsted cloth made from combed long fibres of coarse wool, much of which was imported from Ireland through the ports of west Somerset and north Devon. The serge trade was centred upon Exeter, and it was generally in Exeter that the finishing and marketing of the cloths took place, but much of the production was carried on in Wellington, Taunton, Milverton, Wiveliscombe and other towns and villages of west Somerset, as well as in Devon (Mann 1971; Ponting 1971: 30–4).

There can be no doubt of the fortunes which were made in the woollen-cloth industry during this period. Wealthy clothiers included John Ash of Freshford on the river Frome near Bath who lent large sums to the parliamentary cause during the Civil War, the Yerburys of Trowbridge and Bradford-on-Avon who, unusually for clothiers, were staunch supporters of the Crown, William Brewer, also from the Trowbridge–Bradford-on-Avon area who, according to Aubrey, 'driveth the greatest trade in medleys of any clothier in England' (Aubrey 1969: 113), and, the most successful family of all, the Methuens of Bradford-on-Avon. By the mid-eighteenth century the Methuens had become firmly established in the ranks of the gentry and were sufficiently wealthy to purchase the great mansion at Corsham. They were not alone in their rise from clothier to gentleman; Defoe, who was a well-informed and perceptive commentator on the woollen-cloth trade, wrote of the high quality of the cloth and of the fortunes made in the trade:

> the finest medley Spanish cloths, not in England only but in the whole world, are made in this part . . . many of the great families who now pass for gentry in those counties have been originally raised from, and built up by this truly noble manufacture.
>
> (Defoe 1927, I: 281)

The fine clothiers' houses of Bradford-on-Avon, Trowbridge, Chippenham, Warminster and Frome also bear witness to the prosperity of the trade and to the affluence of those who controlled it during the eighteenth century. It was of the Trowbridge clothiers' houses that Sir Nikolaus Pevsner wrote that they 'would make quite notable additions to the *palazzo* architecture of, say, Verona'.

As well as enriching the clothiers the industry provided employment for an whole army of spinners, weavers, dyers, fullers and finishers, and the trade continued to be the largest single employer of labour, apart from agriculture, until the early nineteenth century. The Napoleonic War years brought a boom to the trade, effectively removing foreign competition. An example of the fortunes to be made at that time is the firm established by John and Thomas Clark of Trowbridge, two brothers who started in business in 1801 with a capital of £500 lent to them by an uncle. By hard work and business enterprise they prospered greatly and by the end of the war in 1815 the firm was worth £10,929 (*VCH Wilts* IV, 1959: 169; Rogers 1976).

It was during the Napoleonic Wars that new machinery began to take the place of the old hand methods in the industry. The first spinning jenny, a machine which was to revolutionise this previously time-consuming process and deprive many people in the region of their traditional work, was introduced at Shepton Mallet as early as 1776. Its appearance provoked a riot in which many people from Wiltshire and the Frome valley participated. Consequently it was not for another ten years that spinning jennies and carding machines came to be common in the region, and even then there was still considerable opposition to them. There was a riot at Bradford-on-Avon in 1791 over the introduction of a carding machine, and the offending instrument was burnt by the mob. The flying shuttle which was to mechanise the weaving process also caused great disturbances when it appeared. There were serious riots at Trowbridge in 1792 which had to be quelled by the militia, and the use of the flying shuttle in the region came about very slowly and in the face of great opposition from the workers (Mann 1971; Rogers 1976: 17–45). An example of the way in which the introduction of machines caused distress among hand-workers far from the main centres of cloth production can be seen in a letter which was written by Charles Francis, rector of Collingbourne Ducis near Ludgershall in east Wiltshire, to Lord Ailesbury in 1792 complaining of the hardship caused in his parish by the introduction of machine-spinning:

> the women and children who used . . . in these parts of Wilts to be employed in spinning are now almost all totally out of work oweing to those execrable spinning-jennies, which have enabled clothiers, who do not consider the extent of the evil, to spin at home the wool they use. Picking stones in the field for the road has been for the last fortnight the

Plate 6.1 Hand-loom weaver at work. This photograph shows the traditional west-country method of cloth production by hand-loom, and illustrates the process which played such an important part in the economic life of the region throughout the whole period with which this book is concerned. The loom shown here was photographed in 1903 at Palmer and Mackay's factory in Trowbridge, a firm which continued producing cloth until 1963, and the loom is typical of the narrow hand-looms which were used to produce 'cassimeres' during the first half of the nineteenth century. Although weaving was the last of the processes in the manufacture of woollen cloth to which power was applied, power-looms had been in use since the 1840s and by the 1870s hand-loom weaving, which had traditionally been carried on in weavers' own homes, had given way to factory production using power-looms. (Photograph: M. J. Lansdown.)

employ of our spinners . . . Can no preventative of these cruel machines,
My Lord, be adopted?

(Rogers 1976: 19–20)

Like many other towns in the neighbourhood, Frome in east Somerset
developed very rapidly because of the prosperity and growth of the woollen-
cloth industry during this period. Between 1660 and 1700 the number of
rateable inhabitants increased four-fold, and Defoe compared the growth of
the town with that of Manchester. Much of the new housing development
during the late seventeenth and early eighteenth centuries was carried out by
the Yerbury family who were the leading clothiers in the town. They built
workers' houses on fields to the west of the town which has since become
known as Trinity after a church built there in 1837. A survey of 1785 shows
that a quarter of the inhabitants lived in the Trinity area, which remains as a
remarkable example of seventeenth-century artisans' housing, and a powerful
reminder of the former importance of the cloth trade in the town (Leech 1981).

Silk-weaving, which was introduced into the district around Yeovil and
Sherborne during the mid-seventeenth century, became increasingly important
during the eighteenth century and spread into various parts of Wiltshire
including Salisbury, Warminster and Malmesbury, where many people were
employed as out-workers. The manufacture of lace provided work around
Lyme Regis, Blandford Forum, Salisbury and Marlborough. Lace-making was
an ideal by-employment for women and girls since it could easily be combined
with other jobs; John Aubrey wrote in 1680 that

our shepherdesses of late years do begin to work point [i.e. lace]
whereas before they did only knit coarse stockings.

(Aubrey 1969: 109)

At Blandford Forum Defoe observed that it was

famous for making the finest bonelace in England, and where they
shew'd me some so exquisitely fine, as I think I never saw better in
Flanders, France or Italy.

(Defoe 1927, I: 217)

In south Somerset and west Dorset the production of linen and sailcloth
continued to be important throughout this period, based largely upon home-
grown flax and centred upon towns and villages such as Martock, Merriott,
East Coker, Crewkerne and Chard in Somerset and Beaminster,
Broadwindsor, Bridport and Lyme Regis in Dorset. Rope and net-making was
also a prosperous and busy industry in the same district, using locally grown
hemp and supplying both the Royal Navy and the Newfoundland fishing
fleets.

Coal-mining in the north Somerset area of Kilmersdon, Radstock, Midsomer Norton, Timsbury, Pensford, the Bedminster district south of Bristol and in Kingswood flourished during the eighteenth century as population expanded, as the demand for coal for steam engines and other industrial purposes increased and above all as improved roads and rivers and eventually canals and tramways made it easier to get the coal from the coal fields to the towns (Atthill 1976: 150–5; Down and Warrington 1971). The Mendip lead mines reached the peak of their production during the late seventeenth century, but gradually the more accessible seams were exhausted and continual flooding as well as cheap alternative supplies of lead made deeper mining uneconomic. The working of calamine ore which yielded zinc for the brass foundries of Bristol and district continued in the area of Shipham and Rowberrow on the western edge of Mendip (Gough 1967: 112–56). Iron was worked at various places in the region including Wick and Frenchay near Bristol, at Seend in Wiltshire and most notably in Hampshire at Gosport and at Fontley on the river Meon west of Fareham. At both Gosport and Fontley Henry Cort manufactured iron-work for Portsmouth dockyard and developed important new processes for producing and forging iron. Henry Cort also developed at Fontley a process for producing large quantities of malleable iron using coal, and established a rolling-mill to supply the ever-increasing demands of the naval dockyards. Fussells' iron-works were established at Mells in 1744 and soon became famous for the production of edge-tools such as sickles, scythes, bill-hooks, spades, shovels, hatchets and pick-axes (Hudson 1965: 62–4, 162–3).

Glass-making developed rapidly in Bristol during the seventeenth century, and early in the eighteenth century Defoe counted fifteen glass cones in the city. These made the high-quality 'Bristol blue' glass, as well as window glass and glass bottles for the export of wine, beer and cider to America and the West Indies. In 1788 one of the principal glass-makers, John Lucas, moved his business out of Bristol to establish a prosperous glass industry at Nailsea in north Somerset, using the cheap coal which was mined there, as well as local supplies of sand and limestone (Thomas 1984).

Many other industries were to be found across the region during the eighteenth century, including pottery, glove-making, leather-working, brewing, the production of bricks, tiles and drainage pipes, soap-making, tobacco and snuff-manufacture, and paper-making. In Hampshire a Huguenot refugee, Henri de Portal, had begun paper-making at Bere Mill in the Test valley near Whitchurch in 1712, while paper for the banknotes of many countries was made in mills at Whitchurch and Laverstoke, all using the pure water of the upper Test. In Berkshire by the end of the seventeenth century there were paper mills at Sutton Courtenay and Cookham on the Thames, and at East Hagbourne near Didcot. The mill at Sutton Courtenay had begun paper-making as early as 1631, and by the end of the century there were four corn mills and a paper mill under one roof there. Paper for Bank of England bank-notes was made at Sutton Courtenay from 1697 to 1724, a tribute to the quality of the Thames water at that time.

Until the later eighteenth century when improved means of transport became available, most quarries supplied purely local needs, for only exceptionally fine stone was worth the trouble and expense of carrying it very far. Two places on the Dorset coast enjoyed easy access to the sea so that stone from their quarries was widely used during the seventeenth century. These were at Purbeck and Portland. Although the use of Purbeck marble for church monuments had declined after the Reformation and in the face of the challenge from Derbyshire alabaster, a great deal of Purbeck stone was cut out in slabs and sent to London from Poole and Swanage for use in roofing and paving. Defoe commented on this trade in the early eighteenth century:

> the isle of Purbeck is eminent for vast quarrys of stone which is cut out flat and us'd in London in great quantities for paving court-yards, alleys . . . and the like; and is very profitable to the place, as also in the number of shipping employed in bringing it to London.
>
> (Defoe 1927, I: 208–9)

By the end of the eighteenth century some four hundred people were employed in the quarries, and 50,000 tons of stone were shipped from Swanage each year (Claridge 1793: 41). The stone from the island of Portland was little used during the Middle Ages, and extensive quarrying did not begin until the seventeenth century. The reason for this was that although the best Portland stone is of extremely high quality, the finest limestone in England, it lies under some thirty feet of rubble or 'over-burden', and it was not until the seventeenth century, when Inigo Jones popularised the stone by using it for the portico of the Banqueting Hall at Whitehall and for the restoration of Old St Paul's Cathedral, that there was sufficient demand or capital available to support the labour involved in large-scale quarrying. Leland who wrote at length about Portland in the 1540s, and who obviously found the wild landscape of the island with its isolated and suspicious inhabitants very interesting, does not mention stone-quarrying there at all. In 1593 a survey of the royal manor of Portland reported that there were quarries on the cliffs which were let for 5s. 0d. per annum, but the surveyor was much more impressed by the oil-bearing shale which he found along the shore, 'a kinde of blacke stone or ore earth of Minerall matter apte to burne'. By 1650, however, the quarries on the island were evidently important and were said to be worth £5 per annum. The really massive development of the Portland quarries occurred after 1666, when the stone was chosen by Wren for the construction of the new St Paul's Cathedral, and for the city churches after the Fire of London. Thereafter it rapidly became extremely popular and fashionable, and was used for buildings all over the country wherever it could conveniently be transported by sea (Bettey 1972: 176–85).

Bath stone was also extensively worked during the eighteenth century, largely owing to the enterprise of Ralph Allen who seized the opportunity presented by the completion of the Avon navigation between Bath and Bristol in 1727, which made it possible to take stone by barge down-river to Bristol, to expand the production of the quarries on Combe Down. Allen was also able to provide the stone from his quarries for the massive expansion of Bath. His house at Prior Park, overlooking Bath, was designed by the Bath architect John Wood who played such an important part in the architectural development of Bath.

The manufacture of malt and the brewing of beer were important trades in the Thames valley and right across the chalklands of Hampshire and Dorset where plentiful supplies of barley for malt were available, as well as unlimited pure, hard water from the chalk streams. Malt for the London breweries was a principal product of Abingdon, Wallingford and Newbury, and there were many small local breweries as well as a few towns where brewing was a major industry, notably Alton and Dorchester. Above all, Reading, with good water transport to London, became the chief malting town of the whole Thames valley, and by 1760 was the most important manufacturing centre for malt in Britain (Mathias 1959: 394). The most notable success story in the trade is that of the Simonds family. William Simonds, the second son of a yeoman farmer who owned lands in the Hurst–Arborfield–Wokingham area of Berkshire, used a legacy of £550 to set himself up as a maltster and brewer in Reading during the 1760s. By the time of his death in 1782 his business had prospered greatly and he had purchased four alehouses. His son, W. B. Simonds, who carried on the business, supplying malt and beer to the London market, had amassed a sufficient fortune by 1789 to engage the architect Sir John Soane to design a brewhouse and residence for him with his own wharf by the river Kennet in Seven Bridges Street, Reading, and to spend £6,400 on building work. In 1799 a Boulton and Watt steam engine was installed to provide power in the brewery, and by the early nineteenth century the firm had already become one of the major English brewers (Corley 1976: 77–87).

To those who have to travel on them most roads at times seem tedious, badly maintained and difficult, and there is no lack of criticism of the roads of Wessex by seventeenth- and early eighteenth-century travellers. The diarist, Samuel Pepys, then Secretary of the Admiralty, travelled from Oxford via Hungerford to Salisbury and thence to Bath and Bristol with his wife and servants in June 1668; his whole journey illustrates the difficulties which faced travellers – bad roads, expensive and inadequate inns, the absence of signposts and the difficulty of finding the way especially across open country like the Berkshire Downs or Salisbury Plain where the correct route was often uncertain and there were few landmarks. It was frequently necessary for Pepys to hire expensive guides to show the party the road; at Salisbury he was indignant at the exorbitant prices he was charged at the inn and for horse-hire, while at Bath the party found 'our beds good but we lousy'. Even with a guide the party got lost on the way across Salisbury Plain between Wilton and Bath, and only by great good fortune did they manage to arrive at Chitterne and find an hospitable inn just before darkness fell; otherwise they would have had to spend the night on the Plain. As it was, the only room in the inn was occupied by a pedlar, but the unfortunate fellow was immediately turned out of bed so that Pepys and his party could be accommodated. Likewise on their return journey from Bath to London they completely lost their way in the muddy roads of the Kennet valley between Newbury and Reading (Latham and Matthews 1976, ix: 224–36). In 1687 the intrepid traveller, Celia Fiennes, journeyed from Salisbury to Bath via Warminster and found the road so waterlogged that her coach stuck fast in the mud and 'severall men were forced to lift us out; its made only for Packhorses which is the way of carriage in those parts'. She noted also that the coal from Kingswood was all brought to Bristol on packhorses since carts would have stuck fast in the muddy, rutted tracks (Morris 1949: 237–40).

Early in the eighteenth century Daniel Defoe would have been unable to find his way across Salisbury Plain between Shaftesbury and Salisbury had it not been for the numerous shepherds tending their flocks whom he encountered on the way and who could direct him (Defoe 1927, I: 218). The coming of turnpike roads, which began with an Act of Parliament for the turnpiking and improvement of some miles of road around Bath in 1707, gradually revolutionised the road system and the standard of maintenance.

In Hampshire between 1750 and 1772 seventeen turnpike trusts were set up, covering more than 300 miles of road and including all the major routes in the county. By the early nineteenth century the Bristol Turnpike Trust was the largest single Trust in the country with 180 miles of road and with a high reputation for the quality of its maintenance, a reputation enhanced in 1818 by the appointment of John Loudon McAdam as Surveyor. Many of the turnpike roads in Wiltshire and Hampshire were also very good, and Arthur Young, who was often critical of turnpikes, described the road from Salisbury to Winchester via Romsey in 1768 as the best road he had ever seen, even though there was considerable wagon traffic on it (Young 1768: 249).

The improvement in the roads had an enormous effect upon economic activity and upon the development of towns, ports and watering-places, notably upon Bath and Southampton. Traffic increased substantially, especially stage coach, carrier and mail services; the speed of coach services on the London–Bath route increased from 7.4 mph in 1771 to 9.6 mph in 1836, or by nearly 30 per cent. Likewise the massive growth in traffic is shown by the sevenfold increase in the toll income of the Southampton Turnpike Trust between 1770 and 1830 (Freeman 1979: 411–34; Albert 1972). Improved communications led to the rapid growth of Reading and other Berkshire towns. In 1725 the Kennet between Reading and Newbury was made navigable by barges, thus enabling malt and other agricultural produce from the Newbury area to be carried direct to London.

River navigation was improved along the Parrett and the Tone between Bridgwater and Taunton by a company established in 1699, the Avon was made navigable between Bristol and Bath in 1727, and attempts were made to provide a navigable waterway along the Hampshire Avon as far as Salisbury. In 1772 the navigation of the Thames was improved and canals linked it to the Midlands, while the Thames and Severn canal opened in 1789. The Kennet and Avon canal providing a direct link between Bristol and London opened in 1810.

Increased trade and traffic led to a growth in the number of inns in market towns, catering for the entertainment and business transactions of travellers and dealers. Somerton with a population of about 1,000 in the mid-eighteenth century had sixteen inns around the market-place. Devizes with some 3,000 inhabitants had no less than 41 licensed premises. Marlborough which benefited greatly by the increased traffic between London and Bath had 25 inns, 2 victuallers and a lodging house by 1790, and much of the town's prosperity came from the coaching trade. Similarly the fine Georgian buildings on either side of the Bath road at Speen, which is now part of Newbury, were originally built as inns for the accommodation and entertainment of travellers along that busy road (Dunning 1978: 54–6; Stedman 1960: 295–8). Fine eighteenth-century inns such as the Star and Garter at Andover, the White Hart at Whitchurch, the White Hart at Stockbridge, the King's Head and Bell at Abingdon, the Catherine Wheel at Marshfield, the Dolphin at Southampton or the King's Arms and the Antelope at Dorchester, are eloquent reminders of greatly increasing traffic along the newly established turnpike roads. Growing trade and commercial prosperity are also apparent from the numerous market houses, town halls, guildhalls, and corn exchanges dating from the late seventeenth and the eighteenth centuries. Notable examples are the fine town halls at Abingdon, Faringdon, Windsor, Wootton Bassett, Wallingford and Stockbridge, the Guildhall at Winchester, the Exchange at Bristol and the market-places with their crosses at Somerton, Salisbury, Milborne Port, Malmesbury and elsewhere.

Farming and Agricultural Improvement

The period from the Restoration to the end of the Napoleonic Wars saw continuing advances in agriculture and in farming techniques and productivity. The adoption of improvements such as enclosures, water-meadows, convertible husbandry, greater use of fertilisers – marl, lime, chalk – new crops such as turnips, cabbages, clover, sainfoin, ryegrass, carrots, and new rotations, as well as 'industrial' crops such as woad, teazles, flax and hemp, all became much more common and widespread. There was a much greater interest among farmers in greater yields and higher profits. Some of the most eminent and enthusiastic advocates of improved farming lived and farmed in the Wessex region. Among them were John Worlidge of Petersfield whose influential treatise *Systema Agriculturae* was published in 1669 and recommended new crops and methods such as turnips, new strains of grass and water-meadows. Edward Lisle, whose work entitled *Observations in Husbandry* was published in 1757, farmed at Crux Easton on the chalklands of north Hampshire; he grew fodder crops of turnips, rape, grass, clover and sainfoin, and experimented with chalk, marl, malt dust and other fertilisers. Jethro Tull (1674–1741) farmed first at Howberry across the Thames from Wallingford, and later at Prosperous Farm in south-west Berkshire near Hungerford. Here he tried many of his experiments with horse-drawn drills and hoes, and different methods of cultivation and seed sowing. His book *Horse-Hoeing Husbandry* was published in 1733. Other influential writers who urged the adoption of new farming methods included the authors of the County Reports for the Board of Agriculture formed in 1793. Among the most competent and influential of these Reports were those by Thomas Davis who was steward on the Longleat estates in Wiltshire and Somerset, and whose Report on Wiltshire was published in 1794; and John Billingsley, an enthusiastic promoter of improved farming methods who farmed at Ashwick Grove near Shepton Mallet, and whose Report on Somerset was published in 1795. The new approach to farming can be seen in the growing popularity of cattle-shows, ploughing matches, sheep-shearings, wool exhibitions, agricultural improvement societies and experimental farms. The Odiham Agricultural Society 'for the encouragement of Agriculture and Industry' was in existence by 1785, and by the end of the eighteenth century there was also an Hampshire Agricultural Society and an annual wool exhibition at Magdalen Fair near Winchester. Most important of all, the Bath and West of England Agricultural Society was founded in 1777, and its influence was soon felt far and wide in its shows, meetings, lectures, practical demonstrations and publications. In 1780 the Society founded the first experimental farm in the country at Weston near Bath (Hudson 1972; 1976).

The most notable and obvious change in farming techniques was the enclosure of the open arable fields and the extension of arable over large areas of former chalk downland. Early in the eighteenth century Defoe noted that a good deal of Hampshire downland had been converted from sheep-walk to wheat land, especially the twenty-five miles between Winchester and Salisbury, while around Basingstoke he saw 'a pleasant, fertile country, enclosed like the best of England' (Defoe I: 187). Much of this enclosure was arranged by private agreements and exchanges among tenants anxious for a more convenient system of landholding; early agreements were often registered by a Decree in the Court of Chancery, later enclosures were carried through by Act of Parliament, the majority of Enclosure Acts being secured during the

Napoleonic War period (1793–1815) under the impetus of very high corn prices. Defoe also commented upon the vast flocks of sheep which were kept on the chalk downlands and folded on the arable land:

> by folding their sheep upon the plow'd lands, removing the fold every
> night to a fresh place . . . this, and this alone, has made these lands,
> which in themselves are poor, and where, in some places, the earth is
> not above six inches above the solid chalk rock, able to bear as good
> wheat, as any of the richer lands in the vales, though not quite so
> much . . .
>   (Defoe 1927, I: 285)

It was the extension of arable land, the use of water-meadows and new fodder crops to provide increased hay and feed for the larger sheep flocks, the folding of the sheep on the cornlands, and the pursuit of higher cereal output under the impetus of rising corn prices which were the hallmarks of chalkland farming in Wessex during this period (Jones 1960: 5–19; Bettey 1977: 24–39).

The process of enclosure and the extension of arable on the chalklands took long to complete, although it was given great impetus by the high corn prices of the Napoleonic War period. In 1793 John Claridge could write of Dorset that 'The most striking feature of the county is the open and unenclosed parts, covered by numerous flocks of sheep, scattered over the Downs.' At the same time William Marshall, writing of the area around Salisbury at the same period, recorded that as well as a good deal of recent enclosure there was still much open field surviving (Claridge 1793: 5; Marshall 1778: 308–10). Within the next few years many of these downs were enclosed and made into new compact farms. Such farms on the chalklands all over the Wessex region can often be distinguished by their architecture and by their names; for example, in Dorset farm names such as Botany Bay, Normandy, Canada, Quatre Bras, and in Wiltshire names such as Waterloo, Hougomont, Quebec and New Zealand reveal the date of their formation.

There is no doubt that enclosure, the extinction of common rights and the consolidation of farms had a great effect upon productivity, profits and upon the rents that could be charged to tenants, as well as upon the appearance of the countryside. In Wiltshire, for example, rentals rose sharply after the parliamentary enclosures of the Napoleonic War period:

> farm rentals which before enclosure might have been from £15 to £40,
> rose to from £100 to £400 after enclosure . . . This brought a wealthier
> class of tenant who could farm on capitalist lines instead of on a
> subsistence basis or with inadequate stock.
>   (*VCH Wilts* IV, 1959: 67).

The inconvenient scattering of lands in the unenclosed open fields was undoubtedly inefficient; for example, at Durrington in the Avon valley near

Amesbury in the 1790s one farm of 75 acres had 89 separate parcels of land scattered throughout the six great fields, and another farm of 146 acres had its land in 94 separate plots. Improvements in agricultural practice were inevitably difficult to achieve in such circumstances, apart from all the difficulties inherent in common field farming and the necessity for tenants to follow a similar farming calendar and cropping rotation. But the social consequences of enclosure and larger farms were a heavy price to pay for the undoubted gains in efficiency and productivity. Thomas Davis, steward of the Longleat estate 1779–1807, and the author of the *General View of the Agriculture of Wiltshire*, 1794, was an enthusiast for improved agriculture and pursued an active policy of improvement on the Longleat estates through enclosures, larger farms, drainage, better crop rotations, improved buildings, water-meadows and better stock, and during his stewardship the annual rental on the Longleat estate doubled, rising from £4,500 to £9,197 *per annum*. But Davis was also deeply aware of the social costs, and in 1805 he wrote that

> There are numberless villages which supported a substantial yeomanry of 20 or 30 copyhold or leasehold tenants living on their own estates, £20–£30 a piece, and attending for their own sakes to all the minutiae of a farmer's profits; now all are in the lord's hand and let to one, or at the utmost, to two farmers, and the houses turned into cottages for the habitation of a miserable, dispirited set of labourers, the descendants probably of the original owners. This is not the tale of fiction, nor the language of romance . . . it is a fact, staring in broad daylight in nearly half the villages throughout the west of England.
>
> (*Bath and West of England Agricultural Society Papers* X, 1805: 38–56)

Similarly David Davies, Rector of Barkham near Reading in Berkshire, writing in 1795, stressed the disastrous social consequences of enclosure:

> an amazing number of people have been reduced from a comfortable state of partial independence to the precarious condition of mere hirelings, who when out of work immediately come on the parish.
>
> (Davies 1795; Horn 1981: 80)

In Wiltshire an examination of the land-tax assessments for forty parishes during the period 1781–1831 reveals that there was an overall decline of one-eighth in the number of farmers, and that this decline was much more marked in the corn-growing chalklands (where it was as much as one-third), than it was in the dairy-farming claylands where smaller farms continued to provide economic units (*VCH Wilts* IV, 1959: 68–9). In some parishes the decline in the number of farms after enclosure was dramatic, for example at Durweston in Dorset where thirty small farms were amalgamated to form two very large holdings (Bettey 1974: 136). The fate of the small farmers of Bere Regis was typical of many hundreds of others right across the chalklands. In 1776 there were 46 tenant farmers in the manor of Bere Regis of whom 26 had copyhold tenements of less than 30 acres each. Corn prices were rising, but on thin chalkland soils such as those of Bere Regis production could only be increased by keeping more sheep for folding, and no additional downland grazing was available where extra sheep could be kept by the copyholders; they had no land to spare for fodder crops even if the rotation of the common fields could be adapted to accommodate such crops; new methods such as water-meadows demanded more capital investment than they could raise. By 1796 many of their strips in the common arable fields had been thrown together, while gradually, as tenements became vacant, they were amalgamated into larger holdings. Long before the final and formal end of the open fields of Bere Regis by an Enclosure Act of 1846 the 26 smaller holdings had been swallowed up by the larger farms (Kerr 1968: 123–31, 268–71). Even in the fertile dairy-farming parish of Trent near Sherborne the number of farms declined from 68 in 1740 to 41 in 1783, while by 1839 the number of farms had sunk to 12 (Sandison 1969: 71–2, 87).

The disappearance of the small farms with all its social consequences for rural life was commented upon by the Dorset dialect poet William Barnes, who was a perceptive observer of the nineteenth-century rural scene:

Then ten good dairies were a-ved,
Along that water's winden bed,
An, in the lewth (shelter) o' hills and wood,
A half a score farm-housen stood:
But now, – count all o'm how you would,
So many less do hold the land, –
You'd vind but vive that still do stand,
A-comen down vrom gramfer's.

Throughout the clayland and forest parts of the region during the eighteenth century, former waste, common, marsh and woodland were enclosed, drained, limed, marled, ploughed and brought into cultivation. Even at the end of the century however there were still large areas of unimproved common ground. In 1794 Abraham and William Driver in their *General View of the Agriculture of Hampshire* noted with astonishment 1,200 acres of rough common at East Woodhay near Newbury, 1,000 acres at Kingsclere, 1,000 acres at Froxfield Barnet, 7,000 acres at Botley near Southampton, more than 3,000 acres of Bagshot Heath within Hampshire, 5,675 acres of waste on the Isle of Wight, as well as vast areas within the royal forests – Alice Holt, Woolmer, Bere Forest and the New Forest. All advocates of improved husbandry methods, and especially the reporters appointed by the Board of Agriculture, were unanimous in condemning the bad effects of these areas of common and waste both upon the farming of the locality and upon the morals of the inhabitants. John Billingsley, writing of Somerset in 1798, drew a memorably unsympathetic picture of the under-employed cottager, dependent upon a piece of common land to keep his livestock:

> moral effects of an injurious tendency accrue to the cottager, from a reliance on the imaginery benefits of stocking a còmmon. The possession of a cow or two, with a hog, and a few geese, naturally exalts the peasant in his own conception above his brethren in the same rank of society. It inspires some degree of confidence in a property, inadequate to his support. In sauntering after his cattle, he acquires a habit of indolence. Quarter, half and occasionally whole days are imperceptibly lost. Day-labour becomes disgusting; the aversion increases by indulgence and, at length, the sale of a half-fed calf or hog, furnishes the means of adding intemperance to idleness. The sale of the cow frequently succeeds, and its wretched and disappointed possessor, unwilling to resume the daily and regular course of labour, from whence he drew his former subsistence . . . exacts from the poor's rate that relief to which he is in no degree entitled.
>
> (Billingsley 1798: 31)

Likewise in Berkshire, William Mavor, a leading farmer in the county, wrote of the dwellers near commons and forests as idle and shiftless:

> from the facility with which they obtain fuel and mere subsistence wherever there are large wastes and particularly near forests the lazy industry and beggarly independence of the lower orders of people who enjoy commons is a source of misery to themselves and of loss to the community.
>
> (Mavor 1813: 328–9)

An alternative view of common land and the society it produced is given by Gilbert White the naturalist parson who lived at Selborne for most of his life (1720–93), on the edge of Woolmer Forest. White's view is expressed in his celebrated *Natural History of Selborne* (1789); he wrote that forests and wastes

> are of considerable service to neighbourhoods that verge upon them, by furnishing them with peat and turf for their firing; with fuel for burning their lime; and with ashes for their grasses; and by maintaining their geese and their stock of young cattle at little or no expense.
>
> (White 1789: 22)

The change which enclosures, improved farming and the extension of arable wrought in the appearance of the landscape of many parts of the region can be illustrated from the transformation which occurred on the Mendip plateau. Under the impetus of ardent advocates of improvement, notably John Billingsley, some 27,500 acres of land were enclosed with dry-stone walls between 1771 and 1813, giving the plateau its characteristic modern appearance. After enclosure and allotment of the fields to individual owners, new farms were built which can be easily recognised by their architectural style and by their names such as Canada, Wellington, New House, Victoria or Tynings, the Somerset word for enclosure. The new landscape with its regular fields and straight roads gives every indication of careful surveying and deliberate planning.

As was shown in Chapter 4, pp. 133–5, the most distinctive and important of all farming improvements in the Wessex region was the widespread creation of water-meadows along the valleys of the chalkland streams. The artificial flooding or 'floating' of riverside meadows in order to encourage an early growth of grass was already being practised during the early seventeenth century. The early grass of the water-meadows and the abundant crops of hay which they produced rapidly became an essential feature of chalkland farming, enabling larger flocks of sheep to be kept; the flocks were folded at night on the arable lands, their rich dung greatly improving its fertility and productivity. As early as 1669 John Worlidge of Petersfield in Hampshire could write that the water-meadows were 'one of the most universal and advantageous improvements in England within these few years' (Worlidge 1669: 16–17). By the end of the eighteenth century the water-meadows had spread along almost all the chalkland valleys of the region, and were of incalculable value for arable farming. John Claridge writing in 1793 claimed that 'the early vegetation by flooding, is of such consequence to the Dorsetshire farmer, that without it, their present system of managing sheep would be about annihilated' (Claridge 1793: 34). Similarly, Thomas Davis, the steward of the Longleat estates, summed up their value in Wiltshire:

> none but they who have seen this kind of husbandry, can form a just idea of the value of the fold of a flock of ewes and lambs, coming immediately with bellies full of young quick grass from a good water-meadow, and particularly how much it will increase the quantity and quality of a crop of barley.
>
> (Davis 1794: 194)

In the Somerset Levels much drainage work, together with enclosure and improvement of the marshland or 'moors', was carried out by Acts of Parliament in the decades after *c.* 1770. An area of nearly 20,000 acres between the Polden Hills and Wedmore was drained between 1770 and 1800; the large expanse of Kings Sedgemoor south of the Poldens was drained by the construction of a great channel nearly ten miles long which took water into the Parrett estuary at Dunball and provided an entirely new outlet for the river

Cary. The effect of these and numerous other smaller drainage schemes and marshland enclosures, together with new channels for the rivers Axe, Brue and Huntspill, can still be clearly seen in the landscape where the deep drainage channels or 'rhynes', fringed by pollarded willows, divide the lush grasslands, creating one of the most distinctive of all farming regions (Williams 1970).

The period from the Restoration to Waterloo saw the introduction of much more widespread cultivation of numerous crops. These included hemp, flax, teazles and woad. Woad was much grown around Cranborne Chase along the Wiltshire–Dorset border, and in the Keynsham and Cheddar districts of Somerset; it also proved to be a useful crop to grow on newly broken chalkland, since it would feed hungrily on the superabundant fertility stored in the soil after many centuries of sheep grazing. Much attention was also paid to the cultivation of fodder crops, turnips, carrots, rape, clover, ryegrass and sainfoin. At the same time improved varieties of wheat, barley, oats, peas and beans, as well as new methods of cultivation and crop rotation, gradually increased the yields from traditional crops.

The agricultural prosperity of the region throughout the eighteenth century, and especially during the years of high corn prices of the Napoleonic Wars, is apparent from the many dated examples of comfortable farmhouses and well-built barns, stables and cattle-sheds, much larger and more substantially built than earlier farms, and with much more storage capacity and ample accommodation for the larger, improved breeds of horses, cattle and pigs. Notable examples of such farms and farm-buildings, including some of the brick and timber built barns raised on staddle-stones to prevent the entry of rats and mice, can be seen at Yetminster (Dorset), Hurstbourne Tarrant and Compton Manor farm near Michelmersh north of Romsey (Hants), Steeple Ashton and Urchfont (Wilts) and at Tintinhull (Somerset). Equally the many thousands of surviving probate inventories of farmers show the rising standard of domestic comfort and the well-furnished houses, in great contrast to the sparse furnishings of earlier farmhouses (Machin 1976; 1978).

The large-scale cultivation of the potato as a field crop was a fairly late development in the region, but from the late eighteenth century potatoes became an increasingly common crop and element in human diet, especially for the poor in the years of very high corn prices during the Napoleonic Wars. Thomas Davis (1794: 51) wrote of Wiltshire in 1794 that

> Potatoes have of late been very much cultivated in all parts of this district, but particularly on the sandy lands. The general introduction of this valuable root, has been exceedingly fortunate for the labouring poor, of whose sustenance they now make a very considerable part, especially in the season when wheat is dear.

John Billingsley (1795: 115) reported that in north Somerset thirty or forty years ago it was an extraordinary thing to see an acre of potatoes in one spot, and in one man's possession; now there are many parishes in this district which can produce fifty acres.

The potato rapidly became a vital element in the food of farm labourers, and during the early nineteenth century it was not only in Ireland that many were saved from starvation by the potato crop.

Other improvements whose widespread use was fostered particularly by the high corn prices of the Napoleonic Wars, included iron equipment in place of the old wooden ploughs or 'sulls', new drills, harrows, threshing and winnowing machines. Land-drainage was made much easier by the availability of cheap clay pipes, many of them made in Bridgwater. Increasing quantities of marl and lime were used to improve the fertility of the soil, as well as ashes, soot, rags, tanning waste, seaweed and even fish. New breeds of heavier horses gradually replaced oxen, and new breeds of sheep, more productive of wool and mutton such as the Southdowns and Hampshire Downs gradually replaced the old horned breeds of Wiltshire and Dorset.

Population Change and the Growth of Towns and Ports

During the seventeenth and eighteenth centuries the population of the region grew rapidly, although most people continued to live in villages or scattered hamlets and farmsteads; the majority of towns remained very small by twentieth-century standards, and population growth in all the towns of Wessex was far outstripped by the spectacular development of towns in the Midlands and north; nonetheless a few towns in the south expanded greatly so that they were soon much greater than all their neighbours.

Table 10   Estimated population and population changes in Wessex

(a) Estimated population of Wessex 1701–1831

	1701	1751	1781	1801	1831
Berkshire	76,790	85,977	104,309	112,701	147,008
Dorset	87,427	88,318	112,490	102,633	161,026
Hampshire	108,409	134,148	186,252	174,513	317,781
Somerset	214,096	222,526	240,880	252,834	408,702
Wiltshire	150,307	157,206	180,927	184,614	242,831
Bristol	27,000	50,000	55,000	68,088	142,825

Table 10   cont.

(b) Estimated population change 1600–1700		(c) Estimated population change 1700–1800	
	Increase %		Increase %
Berkshire	24	Berkshire	47
Dorset	12	Dorset	36
Hampshire	−3	Hampshire	109
Somerset	21	Somerset	32
Wiltshire	27	Wiltshire	27
Bristol	125	Bristol	152

Note: These figures are based on Deane and Cole 1967: 103; Census returns for 1801 and 1831; Little 1954: 329–32; Darby 1976a: 6–7

In 1660 there were no more than five towns in the region with populations above 5,000: these were Bristol, Salisbury, Portsmouth, Winchester and Southampton. On the basis of the uncertain evidence of the Hearth Tax Returns of 1662 it is plain that Bristol far exceeded all the other towns in size, having a population of some 25,000, more than three times larger than its nearest rival Salisbury whose population was probably not much more than 6,500; Portsmouth and Winchester each had populations of no more than 6,000; while Southampton probably numbered barely 5,000 people. Other towns were much smaller: Reading probably no more than 3,000; Bath, although growing in popularity as a spa, was still contained within its medieval walls and had a population of no more than 2,000. By the time of the first Census in 1801 the position had changed markedly. Three towns had raced ahead of the others in population – Bristol with 63,645, Bath with 32,000 and Portsmouth including Portsea with 32,166. All other towns of the region lagged far behind these three; for example Reading had fewer than 10,000 people, Southampton and Salisbury almost 8,000 each, Winchester fewer than 6,000; while towns such as Taunton, Poole, Trowbridge and Devizes had considerably fewer inhabitants. All were to grow rapidly during the early decades of the nineteenth century.

Increased economic activity and especially the growth of foreign trade brought expansion and improvement to several ports, notably to Bristol. This was the 'golden age' of Bristol which was the leading English port outside London, and the 'metropolis of the west', possessed of thriving industries and at the centre of a great commercial network. The population of Bristol grew from about 20,000 in 1700 to 68,000 in 1801, and the built-up area of the city expanded rapidly. The trade of the port increased as new markets and new sources of supply were opened up in America and the West Indies, as the demand for African slaves grew and Bristol's involvement in this notorious trade increased, and as imports of sugar, cocoa, wine, tobacco, iron and timber were brought in to provide the raw materials for Bristol's main industries. The position of the port at the centre of a web of communications by land and water brought regular barge services from the Severn and the Welsh coast, and by 1750 there were ninety-four carriers making regular journeys from Bristol to Coventry, Nottingham, Leicester, Leeds and other distant towns (Minchinton 1954: 69–89). The port of Bristol played a major part in the English colonisation of the New World, and between 1654 and 1686 more than 10,000 indentured servants, whose names are recorded in the city archives, sailed from Bristol for Virginia, Maryland, Newfoundland, New York, Boston, Pennsylvania and the West Indies, while some thirty settlements on the American continent came to be called 'Bristol'. Bristol's position facing the Atlantic meant that the city was admirably situated to attract trade from the New World during the eighteenth century, and to engage in the notorious triangular trade, taking slaves from Africa to America and the West Indies and returning with sugar, tobacco, timber, cotton and rum. Slave-trading from Bristol reached a peak in 1738–39 when 52 ships sailed from the port for the African coast; in the 1748–79 season 47 ships took part in the trade and carried a total of 16,640 slaves across the Atlantic (Carus-Wilson in Lobel, 1975: 15; Walker 1972: 189–92).

The slave trade of Bristol declined during the later eighteenth century in face of competition from London and Liverpool, so that by the time the public conscience was properly aroused to outrage at the appalling cruelty and inhumanity of the traffic, the number of Bristol slave ships had fallen to less than 20; but it was in Bristol that Thomas Clarkson and others working for the abolition of the trade in slaves concentrated much of their early efforts. Clarkson commenced his investigations in the city in 1787, and thereafter visited Bristol many times to collect evidence on the horrors and barbarities practised by the slave traders, and on the dreadful conditions in the slave ships (Clarkson 1808, I: 293–367). The Atlantic trade, especially with the West Indies, brought great prosperity to Bristol; between 1709 and 1771 the tonnage of shipping using the port increased from 15,365 tons to 33,462 tons per annum, and the affluence of the city during these years is still reflected in its buildings. Visitors came to participate in the flourishing trade and commerce and in the many Bristol industries, to take ship for foreign ports, to seek health and diversion at the increasingly fashionable Hotwells spa, or to visit the smart and rapidly expanding village of Clifton with its healthy downs and sublime gorge. But the facilities of the port of Bristol did not keep pace with the increase in its trade nor with the growth in the size of ships. Twice in every twenty-four hours ships in the port were ignominiously deposited on the mud as the tide went out, and the largest ships could not come up the narrow, twisting channel of the river Avon to the port at all. Many schemes for improvement were put forward, but not until 1802 was a start made on solving the problem when William Jessop was commissioned to construct the Floating Harbour. When this was completed in 1809 it transformed the port as well as the appearance of the city, creating a permanent pool of some 85 acres in which ships could float safely at all states of the tide.

Other ports along the Bristol Channel also shared in the great expansion of trade. Minehead had a trade in serges with the West Indies while Bridgwater produced glass, bricks and tiles which were exported through the port and brought a prosperity which is still apparent from its fine eighteenth-century houses, especially in Castle Street which Sir Nikolaus Pevsner called 'the most perfect Georgian street in Somerset'. The trade of the Dorset ports was based largely on the Newfoundland fisheries, exporting woollen cloth, Dorset ales and agricultural produce, Bridport ropes and nets, and importing cod, salmon, oil and furs. Poole also had a large trade in the export of pottery clay which was dispatched to the continent, to Bristol, London and to Liverpool for the Staffordshire potteries. By 1815 it was estimated that 20,000 tons of potter's clay were shipped from Poole each year, and by 1840 nearly a third of all English pottery was made from Poole clay (Stevenson 1812: 60; Hudson 1965: 77). The wars of the eighteenth century, and the great growth in the size and prestige of the Royal Navy, established Portsmouth as the centre of British sea-power. It was from Portsmouth that almost all of the great fleets and expeditions set out, and to Portsmouth that the victorious ships returned. The dockyard was greatly enlarged and increased in size from 26 to 82 acres, the defences of the port were strengthened, and the town grew rapidly in size so that by 1801 it had a population of 32,000, equal to that of Bath, and these two towns were, after Bristol, by far the largest and most populous in the region. Ships were built not only at the larger ports like Bristol, Portsmouth and Southampton, but at numerous creeks and inlets all along the Hampshire coast. The facilities required were rudimentary, and the proximity of the New Forest and the availability of timber more than compensated for a remote situation. During the period from 1690 to 1820 naval vessels were built at Portsmouth and Gosport, on the river Hamble at Bursledon and Hamble, in Southampton at Northam, at Redbridge and Eling on the river Test, at Bailey's Hard and Buckler's Hard on the Beaulieu river, and at Binstead, Cowes, Poole and Itchenor. In 1786 at Bursledon the small firm of Parsons launched the *Elephant* which was to be Nelson's flagship at the Battle of Copenhagen, and several frigates and merchant ships were also built there. Buckler's Hard became one of the most important of all the rural shipbuilding centres, and was especially notable for the firm of Henry Adams whose best-known ship, the *Agamemnon* of 64 guns and 1,376 tons was launched in 1781 (Holland 1971: 24–7, 107–9, 122–34).

One problem which continued to afflict towns and villages alike was that of fire. Several towns suffered repeated fires; Beaminster in west Dorset was almost destroyed in 1644, and there were further fires there in 1684, 1781, 1786 and 1842. The great fire which so severely damaged Blandford Forum in 1731 was only the most serious in a whole series of conflagrations there, including major fires in 1579 and 1677. The long street of Marlborough was burnt to the ground in the space of five hours in 1653, when a strong wind fanned the flames, and the town suffered several other fires during the following century. The speed with which a fire could take hold, and the amount of destruction it could cause in a short time, together with the in-efficiency of most contemporary fire-fighting equipment, made it one of the most dreaded features of life, especially in the chalkland villages where the houses were situated close together along the village streets and the roofs were thatched. The hooks which were used to pull the burning thatch from the roofs in an effort to stop a fire from spreading are still to be seen at Market Lavington (Wilts) and Bere Regis (Dorset), while manorial records are full of exhortations about the perils of fire. The parish records throughout the region are also full of the pathetic stories of those who had 'lost all by fire'.

Ironically, it was in the thatched-roofed, tightly packed villages of the chalklands, where the risk from fire was greatest, that fuel for cooking and heating was most difficult to obtain. Most of the villages were far from any coalfield, and the tree-less downlands provided little fuel for poor families. In many places, therefore, it was the practice to use cow-dung dried in the sun as fuel. The Cornish traveller and writer, Peter Mundy, who travelled through Dorset and Wiltshire in 1635 wrote that

> For Fewell they use Cowdung, kneaded and tempered with short strawe or strawe dust, which they make into flatt cakes, and clapping them on the side of their stoney walls, they become dry and hard, and soe they use them when they have occasion.

This custom continued until well into the nineteenth century, and the Dorset dialect poet, William Barnes, could write during the 1840s of one of the benefits that a village could derive from a piece of common land:

> An when the children be too young to earn
> A penny, they can g'out in sunny weather,
> And run about, an' get together
> A bag o' cow-dung vor to burn.

The Gentry

The seventeenth and eighteenth centuries saw the gentry and aristocracy of the region greatly increase their power, influence and prestige. As the owners of great estates, landlords, employers of labour and dispensers of patronage, and as members of Parliament, justices of the peace, royal agents, lords lieutenant, sheriffs, commissioners for musters, coastal defences, sewers, and countless other governmental duties, even the lesser gentry dominated the political and social life of their neighbourhoods. Above all through the Commission of the Peace, the fulcrum of local administration, the gentry exercised complete power over local government. The numerous houses, gardens, lakes, parks and woodlands surviving from this period, as well as the enormous, ornate family monuments in the parish churches and the memorial towers and obelisks on so many hill-tops, all bear witness to the power, wealth and self-confidence of the local gentry families. The lives of the fortunate inhabitants of such houses as Wimborne St Giles, Kingston Lacy, Hinton St George, Longleat, The Vyne, Ashdown Park, Mottisfont or a host of other country houses large and small were very far removed even from that of the farmers and tradesmen of the region, and were a whole world apart from the daily conditions of the craftsmen, small-holders and labourers.

During the eighteenth and nineteenth centuries new sources of wealth derived from military or naval service, political office, coal mines, trade, shipping, colonial plantations or investment, all contributed to the creation of ever-larger and more opulent houses and increasingly lavish expenditure on

---

Plate 6.2 Blaise Castle Hamlet, near Bristol. The hamlet consists of ten cottages, irregularly arranged around a small green; it was designed by John Nash in 1811 for the Quaker banker, J. S. Harford. It was intended as a model village for estate servants and retainers; all the houses are different and all are self-consciously romantic and picturesque. So skilfully has the design and composition been arranged, however, that the hamlet is the best and most attractive example of a model village in the region.

gardens, parks and landscapes. At Milton Abbas in Dorset a little market town was swept away from the vicinity of his house by Joseph Damer, Earl of Dorchester; at Erlestoke in Wiltshire, Dogmersfield in Hampshire and elsewhere whole villages were destroyed or were moved to new sites in order to lay out parks or to show off a mansion or parkland to best advantage (Taylor 1970: 160–2; Meirion-Jones 1969–70: 111–127). The work and influence of the great landscape designers such as William Kent (1685–1749), Lancelot (Capability) Brown (1715–83), Humphrey Repton (1752–1818), and others can be seen in gardens, parkland and landscapes throughout the whole region. Kent worked on the lavish lay-out of the grounds at Great Badminton and Wilton; Capability Brown was consulted by numerous estate owners and his ideas influenced the planning of landscapes at Dodington, Longleat, Benham Park at Speen near Newbury, the nearby park at Highclere, Broadlands, Cadland House near Fawley, and, perhaps best of all his work, at Bowood near Calne where the architecture of Robert Adam is complemented by the spectacular man-made landscape with lake, cascade, temple, mausoleum, grotto and vast plantations, all of which were started by Brown and completed by Repton. Other work by Repton included the parkland and gardens surrounding the Hippisleys' mansion at Ston Easton in north Somerset, the grounds of the Methuens' great mansion at Corsham Court and the surroundings of Blaise Castle and Leigh Court both near Bristol. At Blaise Castle the Quaker banker John Harford also employed John Nash to design an Orangery, a thatched dairy and, the ultimate essay in the *picturesque* style, the self-consciously romantic estate cottages of Blaise Castle hamlet, built in 1810–12 as a little model village around a green.

The south-west corner of Wiltshire saw the two most spectacular examples of total transformation of the landscape by wealthy landowners. At Stourhead the banker Henry Hoare began to lay out the grounds in the valley below his house in about 1741. During the following thirty years work continued in creating a great lake, the planting of innumerable trees and shrubs, the building of bridges, temples, grottoes, rustic cottages, a ruined convent and many other structures. The result is one of the most overwhelmingly beautiful pieces of artificial countryside ever created. Nearby at Fonthill near Tisbury William Beckford used his immense wealth derived from plantations in the West Indies to create a fantastic Gothic folly, designed by James Wyatt, a large cruciform building 350 ft by 290 ft with a great octagonal tower 225 feet high. Almost all of this has gone; the tower collapsed in 1825 and most of the rest has been demolished, but the equally extravagant landscape remains – the woodlands, laid out regardless of expense, with lakes, temples, grottoes, statues, elaborate gateways and lodges, the whole landscape created by Beckford's eccentric and wayward genius and made possible by his extraordinary wealth.

Many of the gentry families were passionately interested in gardening and in the planting of trees and the preservation of woodlands. Their motives ranged from a desire to beautify their surroundings to a scientific interest in botany, and from a prudent concern to provide timber and coppice wood for the estate to the provision of coverts for pheasants and foxes. A good example of a seventeenth-century garden survives at Ashdown House near Lambourn on the high Berkshire downland. The house was built by the Earl of Craven for Elizabeth, Queen of Bohemia, in *c.* 1660, and constructed of chalk blocks with stone dressings; the geometric garden was laid out at the same time with a box-hedged parterre flanked by avenues of trees. Slightly earlier, Sir John Oglander whose estate was at Nunwell on the Isle of Wight, became an expert on the cultivation of fruit trees. At Nunwell he planted with his own hands a hundred Portugal quinces as well as

> Pippins, pearmains, puttes, hornies and other good apples, and all sorts of pears ... cherries, damsons and plums. In the upper gardens, apricocks, mellecatoons and figs. In the Court, vines and apricocks: in the Bowling Green the vine and infinity of raspberries ... When my successors hereafter reap the fruits of my labours, let them remember the founder.
> (Bamford 1936: 84, 95)

Among other notable formal gardens were those at Goldney House near Bristol, at Eastbury Park the great mansion built by Bubb Doddington near Blandford Forum in Dorset, Appuldurcumbe on the Isle of Wight, the garden surrounding the Herberts' house at Wilton, and at Tintinhull near Yeovil in south Somerset. The fine garden at Goldney House with rare plants and shrubs, a fountain, water garden and one of the finest of all grottoes, was created during the years 1737–63 by the Bristol merchant Thomas Goldney around his house at Clifton overlooking Bristol and the river Avon. A survey of Broadlands near Romsey made in the 1730s just before the estate was purchased by the 1st Viscount Palmerston, described the 'fine gardens with fountains plentifully supplied with water by an Engine, and fine Fish Ponds and canals stocked with Fish, Wild Ducks and Barr Ganders', and also mentioned 'a Fair Avenue to the Front of the House having four rows of Horse Chestnut Trees above twenty years growth'.

To cater for the demand for garden plants and seeds a new profession of nurseryman and seedsman developed; for example, by 1782 John Kingston Galpine of Blandford Forum was able to supply a remarkably comprehensive range of plants and seed and was issuing 'A Catalogue of the most Useful and Ornamental Hardy Trees, Shrubs, Plants, etc., also of the Herbaceous Plants, Fruit-Trees, Garden Seeds, Flower Roots, Flowering Shrubs, etc.' At Merriott near Crewkerne on the rich and easily worked soil of south Somerset there was a long tradition of nursery gardening dating back to the Middle Ages, and during the eighteenth century the Whitley family, who were later lords of the manor, carried on an extensive nursery business there (*VCH Somerset* IV,

1978: 57). The firm of Suttons of Reading who were destined to become the most famous seedsmen in the region, was founded in 1806 by Martin Hope Sutton, a keen botanist and plant collector (Harvey 1983). It was the enthusiasm of the gentry families for tree-planting that introduced so many new varieties of trees and shrubs during the eighteenth century. The number of trees planted on the estates was prodigious. At Bowood during the late eighteenth century the Earl of Shelburne planted 150,000 trees every year (Young 1796: 76). At Stourhead during the 1790s Colt Hoare planted more than 2,000 acres of woodland; his account books show payments for beech, chestnut, ash, birch, elm, holly, oak, sycamore, maple and thorn. He also introduced the rhododendron bushes which now surround the lake. At Fonthill during the same period William Beckford was planting trees with the same abandon as he was building his house, using trees and shrubs of all kinds, but preferring indigenous species such as oak, birch, Scotch fir and larch.

It was not only extremely wealthy landowners who were interested in tree-planting. On a much more modest scale than those already mentioned, James Frampton of Moreton in Dorset and his son, also James, were greatly concerned with their woodlands, both as a commercial undertaking and as an adornment to their estate. During the Napoleonic War they planted many thousands of trees and completely transformed the appearance of that part of Dorset. Their detailed account books show that between 1791 and 1800 no less than 600,000 trees were planted on their estate, and work continued at a similar rate during the first decade of the nineteenth century. It is to men like the Framptons and many other similarly minded country gentlemen that we owe the present wooded appearance of so much of the Wessex landscape.

The wealth and dominance as well as the social concern of numerous gentry families is reflected in the many almshouses and schools which they founded and charities which they endowed. Notable almshouses include the elegant College of Matrons at Salisbury, founded by Bishop Seth Ward in 1682; Colston's almshouses in Bristol, established by the Bristol philanthropist Edward Colston in 1691; or the Brick Alley almshouses of 1718 at Abingdon; Somerset Hospital at Froxfield, endowed by the Duchess of Somerset in 1694, and many others including the numerous village almshouses and small charitable endowments. Likewise there are many schools founded by benevolent individuals such as the grammar school at Martock of 1661; the charming Free School at Newton St Loe near Bath, founded by Richard Jones in 1698; Lord Weymouth's Grammar School at Warminster of 1707; Boyles School at Yetminster founded in 1697; or Churcher's School at Petersfield, endowed by the East India merchant, Richard Churcher, in 1722.

The dominance of the gentry is also reflected in the many estate and 'model' villages, designed to make an attractive approach to the great house as well as to provide housing for servants. The best-known of such villages in Wessex is Milton Abbas built during the late eighteenth century by Joseph Damer, Earl of Dorchester, to accommodate a few of those displaced by his demolition of the market town which stood beside his house. Another fine example of the consciously 'picturesque' style is the Duke of Beaufort's estate village at Great Badminton, with its assorted lodges, almshouses and rustic dwellings, including several *cottages ornées*. Other similarly decorative villages and hamlets are to be seen at Blaise Castle near Bristol, Erlestoke, Sandy Lane and Tollard Royal in Wiltshire, Selworthy and Lympsham in Somerset, East and West Lockinge on the Loyd-Lindsay estate near Wantage, and East Tisted in eastern Hampshire.

Poverty and the Treatment of the Poor

The opulence and ostentation of life in the great country houses of the region contrasted starkly with the conditions of the poorly paid and badly housed labourers. The increase in population, coupled with the effects of enclosures, engrossment of holdings, changes in farming practice, and the decline of the cloth industry in the face of growing competition from the north of England, all played their part in creating problems of poverty and unemployment. Evidence is to be found in the way in which squatters' settlements and hovels proliferated on heaths and commons. One of many examples of such hovels and of their flimsy construction and rapid erection is found in the memorial accounts of Downton in Wiltshire in 1698:

> Munday 16 May 1698
> An account of those that in a riotous manner broke the Lady's waste within the Franchises of Downton by digging holes in the ground to putt in posts for erecting of a Cottage on the said waste ... and notwithstanding the workmen (whose names are hereunder) were forbidden by John Snow, servant to the Lady Ash, from proceeding any further in the said worke, yett in contempt thereof they have proceeded and finished the said cottage.
> Nicholas Lawes, senior, who is the owner of the Cottage
> Samuel Wheeler, carpenter
> Walter Sheppard, apprentice to Abr. Wheeler
> Joseph Chalke, junior, who thatched the said Cottage
> George Noble who breaded the walls of the said Cottage
> One other man who holpe digge the holes for erecting the said Cottage.
> (WRO 490/932)

A good example of a squatters' community grew up on the waste land at the edge of Warminster Common in Wiltshire, in an area of heath and woodland well away from the town. During the seventeenth century a few small cottages

214

were built there, and in spite of the half-hearted attempts by the Longleat estate to prevent the growth of the settlement, other squatters' hovels were erected during the eighteenth century. By 1781 there were more than 1,000 people living there in some 200 badly constructed shacks and hovels, lacking even the most rudimentary facilities. The water-supply came from the stream which was polluted with filth and rubbish, disease was rampant, and the place was notorious for violence, crime, drunkenness and poverty.

Already by the later seventeenth century appeals were being made to the Quarter Sessions by small towns such as Cerne Abbas and Milton Abbas in Dorset, complaining that they were overwhelmed with poor people because of the decay in trade; and there were further complaints from towns and villages throughout Dorset in 1695 over the great number of 'loose and idle persons' demanding poor relief. The numbers grew rapidly during the eighteenth century. For example, at Corsley between Frome and Warminster, on the edge of the elegant parkland surrounding the mansion at Longleat, some 30 persons were in regular receipt of poor relief during the 1720s and the annual cost to the parish rate-payers was about £200; by 1802 the number of paupers in the parish had risen to 236 and the annual cost was £1,640 (Davies 1909: 78, 302–4). At Trent on the border of Somerset and Dorset the annual expenditure on poor-relief rose from about £60 *per annum* during the 1740s to nearly £160 *per annum* by 1800 (Sandison 1969: 71–4). At Crawley on the chalkland near Winchester the annual cost of maintaining the parish poor rose from £79 in 1776 to £290 in 1809, and by 1819 it had rocketed to £440 (Gras 1930: 577–84). The poor-rate on the island of Portland rose from £32 in 1776 to £327 in 1803 (Bettey 1970: 65–7). The records of poor-relief from towns and villages throughout Wessex show a similar picture of the growing burden of poor-rates and of increasing poverty and distress.

A workhouse or poorhouse to accommodate the poor and destitute was established in Bristol as early as 1698, and other towns rapidly followed suit; by 1750 few large villages were without a poorhouse, and many were rebuilt and extended during the following decades. In 1787 the rector of Barkham near Wokingham, David Davies, who had an intimate knowledge of the life and conditions of the labourers in his parish, found that when rent, fuel, clothing and other necessary items had been taken into account as well as food, there was a deficit in the income of most of the labourers' households in his parish, and this could only be made up by charity or poor-relief (Horn 1981). Bread with a little bacon or cheese and vegetables had become the staple diet of labouring families, and it was under the pressure of bad harvests and high corn prices during the French Wars that the hostility to the potato finally broke down among the labourers of southern England.

A crisis came in 1795 when an exceptionally severe winter was followed by a cold, wet summer and a very poor harvest. In May 1795 the Berkshire magistrates, meeting at the Pelican Inn at Speenhamland on the outskirts of Newbury, decided that it was necessary both for humanitarian reasons and in order to prevent riotous disorders to supplement labourers' wages from the poor rates. They therefore agreed to link minimum wages to the price of bread on a sliding scale, so that

> When the Gallon loaf . . . shall cost 1s–0d . . . every poor and industrious man shall have for his own support 3s–0d weekly . . . and for the support of his wife and every other of his family 1s–6d.

As the price of bread increased so the wages supplement was increased *pro rata*. This scheme was never made official, but it was widely adopted, especially in Berkshire, Dorset and Wiltshire. In some areas the system was varied and relief was given in bread or flour, or in subsidised foodstuffs, as at Newton Valence in Hampshire where cheap flour was sold to the labourers. The method of supplementing wages from parish funds adopted at Speenhamland and copied in so many other places was a sensible expedient to meet the acute distress caused by a temporary dearth of corn, and it did prevent utter destitution or starvation among the labourers and their families during the years of scarcity and hardship, a period which probably witnessed more acute distress and helplessness in the region than any time since the Black Death of the fourteenth century. But in 1795 it could hardly have been foreseen that prices would continue at a staggeringly high level for twenty years, and that the wage supplement would come to be adopted as a long-term attempt to cope with the pressing problem of inadequate wages and chronic unemployment (Bettey 1977: 63–7). Throughout the period of the French Wars there was a persistent undercurrent of unrest in many rural communities. As well as food shortages and actual hunger, wages were failing constantly to keep pace with food prices. In Wiltshire, winter wages only advanced from 6s. 0d. per week in 1794 to 7s. 0d. or 8s. 0d. by 1805, although they then jumped to 12s. 0d. by 1814. But in 1814 the weekly wage would only buy the equivalent of nine loaves of bread, whereas in 1785 the average weekly wage would have bought fourteen loaves (*VCH Wilts* IV, 1959: 81). The contrast between the opulence of the gentry, the wealth and extravagance of their mansions, parks and gardens, their varied diet, elegant clothes and armies of servants, together with the prosperity of the larger farmers, with their well-built, comfortable houses, and the wretched conditions of the poorly paid, ill-housed and inadequately fed labourers throughout southern England was a striking feature of the region which forced itself upon the attention of observers. One of the most perceptive commentators upon the conditions of the poor was Sir Frederick Morton Eden whose detailed enquiries were published under the title *The State of the Poor* in 1797. Eden recorded the ordinary diet and conditions of labourers and also the food provided in the parish poorhouses which, unlike the later workhouses, did not set out to provide an inferior diet or conditions which would deter only the most desperate from applying for admission. He found that bread was by far the most important single item of diet for the working class, followed by cheese, potatoes and beer, with very small quantities of meat, butter, vegetables, milk, tea and sugar. At Minehead, for example, the diet in the poorhouse consisted of:

Breakfast: Bread and Beer on Sundays.
         Broth on all other days
Dinner: Beef or mutton on Sundays and Thursdays.
         Fried greens, potatoes and bread on Mondays, Wednesdays and Saturdays.
         Oatmeal, boiled water and meat on Tuesdays and Fridays.
Supper: Bread and beer, or bread and cheese.

At Seend and many other parishes in Wiltshire Eden found that the families of labourers had been badly hit by the introduction of spinning machines which had deprived them of an important by-employment and subsidiary income

> since the introduction of machinery, hand-spinning has fallen into disuse. The Clothier no longer depends on the Poor for the yarn formerly spun at home . . . so that their maintenance must chiefly depend on the exertions of the men, whose wages have not increased in proportion.

At Petersfield in Hampshire Eden found that the labourers' wages were seven shillings a week in 1794 and had increased to nine shillings by 1796. He found the parish poorhouse particularly well-run and closely supervised by the overseer, and noted that 'to his good management the reduction of the (poor) rates is principally ascribable'. Again the diet in the poorhouse was no doubt similar to, if not better than, the ordinary diet of labourers outside, and consisted of the following:

Breakfast: Bread and milk.
Dinner: Pickled pork, pudding and vegetables on Sundays, Wednesdays and Fridays
         Cold meat etc. on Mondays
         Bread and cheese on Tuesdays, Thursdays and Saturdays
Supper: Bread and cheese.

In Dorset Eden commented upon the effects of 'engrossing' or amalgamation of farms and the effects of this upon the smallholders who were evicted from their farms. At Blandford Forum he wrote, 'The rapid rise of the Poors' Rates in this parish is generally attributed to the high price of provisions, the smallness of wages, and the consolidation of small farms, and the consequent depopulation of villages, which obliges small farmers to turn labourers or

217

servants . . .'. Eden also described the domestic economy of a labourer's family at Blandford. The family consisted of a labourer aged 52, one daughter aged 18 who kept house for him, another daughter of 8, and two sons aged 6 and 3; his wife had died shortly before Eden's visit. The man earned six shillings a week in winter, seven shillings a week in summer and slightly more during the harvest. The children earned nothing, and the family were dependent upon the parish to pay their house-rent and for occasional sums in poor relief. For clothing they relied upon gifts from neighbours. Their food consisted of:

Breakfast:	Tea or Bread and cheese.
Dinner and Supper:	Bread and cheese, or potatoes, sometimes mashed with fat from broth, and sometimes with salt alone.

Bullock's cheek is generally bought every week to make broth. Treacle is used to sweeten tea instead of sugar. Very little milk or beer is used.

This family was chosen by Eden as typical of the rural labouring poor, and was not selected as being especially badly off.

A few years later, in 1826, William Cobbett observed the extreme poverty of the labourers in Wiltshire existing alongside the fine farms, well-filled rickyards and well-cared-for livestock. During his journey between Salisbury and Warminster, for example, he was filled with shame at the extreme poverty and appalling wretchedness of the labourers and their families, and wrote:

Plate 6.3   Farm Buildings at Parsonage Farm, Hurstbourne Tarrant near Andover. These timber-framed, thatched barns are typical of the late seventeenth- and eighteenth-century farmsteads of the chalkland valleys throughout Wessex. Other local building materials shown in the illustration include brick and flint. The farmyard also includes a small timber-framed granary with brick infill which is lifted up on staddle-stones to prevent rats and mice from getting at the stored corn. Such granaries are to be found all over the region, and are especially common in the corn-growing chalklands.

It is impossible for the eyes of man to be fixed on a finer country than that between the village of Codford and the town of Warminster; and it is not very easy for the eyes of man to discover a labouring people more miserable.

    (Cobbett, 1912, II: 67)

The results of these long years of misery and abject poverty were to be witnessed in the Swing Riots of 1830.

Plate 6.4   Ashdown House, near Lambourn. Built for William, first Earl of Craven during the 1660s, the house was intended for Elizabeth, Queen of Bohemia, the daughter of James I, in whose service Craven had spent many years. It is an excellent example of the neat, formal style of the period, and the contemporary garden around the house also survives; the roof is crowned by a balustrade and a lofty timber and copper-covered cupola from which wide views across the Berkshire Downs and the Vale of the White Horse can be obtained. The house remained in the Craven family until 1956.

The Monmouth Rebellion

By far the most notable popular uprising to occur in the region during this period was the Monmouth Rebellion of 1685, and this was provoked not by poverty or hunger but by fervent loyalty to the Protestant religion. The enthusiastic support which the Duke of Monmouth received from the craftsmen and labourers of Dorset and Somerset during his ill-fated attempt to take the throne in 1685 is one of the most tragic and pathetic incidents in west-country history, and the harsh punishment of Monmouth's misguided and betrayed followers has left a deep mark in popular memory. The young, handsome though ineffectual, Duke of Monmouth had made a triumphal progress through the west country in 1680, encouraged by the Dorset landowner and leading politician, Anthony Ashley Cooper, Earl of Shaftesbury; Monmouth was received by many of the gentry families with great deference and enthusiasm and was entertained by the Thynnes at Longleat, by George Speke at Whitelackington, Edmund Prideaux at Forde Abbey, William Strode at Barrington, and by the Pouletts and Sydenhams at Hinton St George and Brympton D'Evercy. Monmouth chose Lyme Regis, with its strong Puritan tradition and memories of heroic resistance to the royal forces during the Civil War, for his landing with 82 men on 11 June 1685, and he was welcomed in west Dorset with great rejoicing as the Protestant saviour who would depose the Catholic James II and ensure the survival of the Protestant religion. Monmouth stayed at Lyme Regis for a week, while recruits from west Dorset and south Somerset came in to join his army. In Dorset, and later in Somerset, however, Monmouth's recruits were almost all from the lower classes, serious, upright and god-fearing nonconformist and puritan smallholders, mariners, artisans, cloth-workers and craftsmen, while most of the gentry and the wealthier farmers stood aside. On 18 June Monmouth marched his motley and untrained army away from Lyme Regis to Taunton where more recruits swelled his following to between 3,000 and 4,000 men. At Taunton Monmouth received a rapturous welcome and was proclaimed King; he then began the march which, he hoped, would take him to Bristol and thence to London to claim the throne. At Bridgwater he was joined by more recruits, farmers from the Somerset Levels and from the Quantock Hills and Exmoor, cloth-workers and tradesmen, bringing his numbers to some 6,000. Meanwhile his progress was being watched and followed by the royal army under Lord Feversham and John Churchill, later Duke of Marlborough; the King's army blocked the road to Bristol and prevented Monmouth from crossing the Avon or from entering Bath. The decision not to go on and attack Bristol was the turning-point in Monmouth's ill-fated attempt to gain the English throne. At Keynsham he turned back and after an inconclusive skirmish with the royal troops at Norton St Philip, Monmouth's army retreated through Frome, Shepton Mallet and Wells to Bridgwater and to the crushing defeat which awaited them at Sedgemoor on the night of 5–6 July 1685. Monmouth himself fled from the battlefield and was later captured on Horton Heath in east Dorset while attempting to reach the coast. His foolhardy enterprise had been ill-conceived and badly-planned, and Monmouth had totally failed to provide energetic leadership for his untrained followers or to appreciate the tactical problems he faced; above all his slow progress through Dorset and Somerset had frittered away any advantage he might have gained from speed and surprise.

After the Rebellion came the terrible retribution. More than 300 of Monmouth's followers died on the battlefield or were killed while attempting to flee, and some 500 others were taken prisoner and locked up in the church at Westonzoyland. Merciless summary execution was inflicted upon many of the rebels, while others were imprisoned to await the arrival of a commission headed by Lord Chief Justice Jeffreys. Jeffreys sat at Winchester, Salisbury, Dorchester, Exeter, Taunton and Wells, and in this 'Bloody Assize' the prisoners were tried, sentenced and executed with the greatest possible speed. In Dorchester nearly 350 men appeared before the court, of whom 74 were hanged and 175 were transported for their part in the rising; in Somerset some 500 were tried and 144 executed. The executions took place almost immediately, while the Assizes were still in progress, and were carried out in various places throughout the west country so that the impact would be as harsh and widespread as possible. Equally designed as an awful warning, was the display of the heads and quarters of the unfortunate victims, and the accounts of many parishes throughout Somerset and Dorset contain references to expenditure on this grisly business. Even those not directly involved in the fighting did not escape, like Alice Lisle, an octogenarian widow, of Moyles Court between Fordingbridge and Ringwood on the outskirts of the New Forest, who was accused of harbouring rebels who had escaped from Sedgemoor, and who was tried by Jeffreys and executed in the square at Winchester; or Charles Speke from Whitelackington near Ilminster, who was executed for having greeted Monmouth and because his family had been prominent among those who had welcomed Monmouth during his progress through the west country in 1680.

The men who had followed Monmouth were for the most part pious, simple countrymen from the farms of the Marshwood Vale, from Taunton Deane and the Somerset lowlands, or cloth-workers and craftsmen from Puritan towns like Lyme Regis, Beaminster, Dorchester, Bridport, Crewkerne, Taunton and Bridgwater, who had been moved by religious zeal and concern for the Protestant religion, and by a deep hatred of Popery and arbitrary government. Their idealism was misplaced and ill-considered, but it hardly deserved the dreadful fate which it so quickly incurred (*VCH Hants* II, 1903: 97; Earle 1977: 169–70; Dunning 1978: 65; Wigfield 1980).

Many of those who escaped execution were transported to the West

Indies. During the autumn of 1685 several shiploads of rebels left from Weymouth, Bristol, Bridgwater and other ports. Eighty men left Weymouth on the *Betty* of London, sixty-seven went by the *Jamaica Merchant*, ninety-one on the ironically named *Happy Return*, all bound for Barbados. Among those who were transported from Dorset was Azariah Pinney, one of the few wealthy persons of good family who had joined Monmouth. He was a member of a long-established west Dorset family, his father, John Pinney, had been the minister of Broadwindsor during the Commonwealth. The family possessed land in Bettiscombe, and also had a considerable lace-making and textile business. When Azariah was sentenced at Dorchester for his part in the Monmouth affair, his family were able to use their wealth and influence to secure better treatment for him, and he was transported as a free emigrant. His sister, Hester, used her entire savings of £65 as a ransom for her brother, while Azariah's elder brother, Nathaniel, spent more than £100 on equipping him for the journey to the West Indies on the *Rose*. Once in the West Indies he was free to act as agent for other members of the family, selling lace and a variety of other goods, and building up a substantial business. Eventually he became a plantation-owner on a large scale and established a secure fortune; in 1696 he became a member of the House of Assembly and later was Treasurer of the islands. Like so many others, a few days under Monmouth's standard dramatically changed Azariah Pinney's whole life, though, unlike him, few of his fellow rebels derived any profit from their involvement in the rising (Pares 1950).

Churches, Chapels and Parish Life

The central role which the parish churches and church officials continued to play in village life during the seventeenth and eighteenth centuries can be reconstructed in detail from the many surviving churchwardens' accounts and from the voluminous records of the church courts. In addition to their original function of maintaining the fabric of the parish church and providing the things necessary for the conduct of the services, the churchwardens had heaped upon them by Tudor and Stuart governments a mass of secular duties ranging from the care of the poor to the payment of bounties for the destruction of vermin. An indication of the range and variety of their duties can be seen in the churchwardens' accounts for Cerne Abbas (Dorset) in 1686. The churchwardens paid for repairs to the church, for a new Book of Common Prayer, for bread and wine for the Holy Communion, for washing the parson's surplice and the altar cloth, and for repairing the instruments of the village musicians who accompanied the services. But in addition to these church duties, they also paid the ringers for peals on the King's birthday and to commemorate the Gunpowder Plot and the Restoration of the Monarchy; they contributed money to help English sailors who had been captured by Turkish pirates in the Mediterranean, for the relief of 'Mary Francis and Benjamin Cimber and their children beggeing who had lost all their goods by fire'; they gave small sums of money to 14 men who claimed that they had been shipwrecked on the Dorset coast; they sent money to help the French protestants who were being persecuted for their religion; they paid for the repair of the church clock and for work on the maintenance of the local roads. Finally they rewarded those who brought birds and animals – sparrows, hedgehogs, stoats and foxes – which were regarded as vermin. During the eighteenth century additional expenditure was required for the maintenance of the fire-engine and its pipes, and for payments to the ringers who celebrated the various triumphs of the British forces, the news of which reached Cerne Abbas very quickly. For example, in 1759, the 'year of victories', the churchwardens' accounts record:

Gave the Ringers when Prince Ferdinand defeated the French in Jarmony	6s–0d
Gave the Ringers when Quebec was taken.	5s–0d

(DRO, Cerne Abbas Churchwardens' Accounts)

Among the clergy of Wessex there was a great gulf between the rich bishoprics, well-endowed cathedral canonries and wealthy benefices, and the incumbents and curates in the many poorly paid parishes. The region included the Bishopric of Winchester which was one of the most lucrative, and Bristol which was among the poorest. During the eighteenth century the income and status of the more fortunate clergy increased substantially as rising land values, improved agricultural production and higher prices for farm produce raised the value of their tithes. The opulent life-style of the clergy in the wealthier parishes is still apparent from the fine Georgian rectories and vicarages which are such a prominent feature of many villages, and also from the numerous expensive and elaborate monuments and memorials to the clergy in churches and cathedrals. Non-residence and pluralism were as common in Wessex as elsewhere. A survey of Wiltshire in 1783 showed that out of 262 parishes, the incumbents of 124 were non-resident (Ransome 1971). Hannah More, who did so much to relieve poverty and ignorance in north Somerset among the lead and calamine workers of Mendip, the colliers and glass-workers of Nailsea and the poor of Bristol, reported in 1796 that 'We have in this neighbourhood thirteen adjoining parishes without so much as a resident curate.' She also lamented the fact that of the children of the area 'hardly any had ever seen the inside of a church since they were christened' (More 1834, I: 451).

An episcopal visitation of the diocese of Bristol in 1735 revealed both the reasons for so much of the non-residence and also its consequences. The Bristol diocese included the county of Dorset and there the bishop found that pluralism and non-residence were widespread. The rector of Chilfrome 'has not resided since his institution and lives at Westbourn in Sussex. Mr Osborn, the vicar of Bradpole is his curate.' The incumbent of Tarrant Hinton lived at Breamore in Hampshire; his nephew acted as his curate, but was himself the rector of Hammoon and also curate of Tarrant Monkton. The rector of Langton Herring was a fellow of King's College, Cambridge, but actually resided at Eton where he was tutor to Lord Milton's sons. The incumbent of Wyke Regis also lived at Eton, 'on account of his wife's illness and for the education of his boys'. At Weston Buckhorn the bishop noted wryly that the rector 'does not reside and complains much of ill-health, tho' he looks the picture of health itself' (Bettey 1973–4: 74–5).

There are few descriptions of the atmosphere and character of ordinary parish-church services in the region during the Georgian period, when congregational responses were led by the parish clerk and singing was accompanied by village musicians. The general impression is of dullness, of long sermons which went above the heads of the congregation, and a general somnolence. It is not without significance that 'wakers' were employed in some churches; for example at Wiveliscombe in west Somerset a bell 'to wake the people in church' was bought in 1712, and a man was paid 5s. 0d. a year to ring it. The sexton of Henstridge used a whip to ensure that the congregation stayed awake and that the boys were well-behaved (Dunning 1975: 57). The atmosphere is perhaps best recaptured in Thomas Hardy's lines on services in Dorset during the nineteenth century:

> On afternoons of drowsy calm,
> We stood in the panelled pew,
> Singing one-voiced a Tate and Brady psalm,
> To the tune of Cambridge New.

Protestant nonconformity grew rapidly in the Wessex region after the Restoration, and groups of Baptists, Quakers, Presbyterians and Independents were to be found in most towns and in many country parishes. At Devizes an Anabaptist conventicle was established during the religious ferment of the Civil War and Commonwealth, and this was followed by congregations of Baptists, Presbyterians and Independents in the town. Similar meetings were to be found throughout Wiltshire, especially in the cloth-working towns and villages of west Wiltshire and along the Somerset border, where they were described in 1670 as meeting 'in by-corners and in woods and edges of counties or hundreds' (*VCH Wilts* III, 1956: 109). Dr Joseph Priestley resided at Bowood from 1773 to 1790 and often preached to the Unitarian congregation at Calne. The Bishop of Salisbury complained of the number of dissenters in the Warminster district in the 1670s, and about 'divers great and outrageous meetings', while at Southwick near Trowbridge there were said to be 340 dissenters in the parish in 1676 and only 100 who conformed to the Church of England. (*VCH Wilts* III, 1956: 109–10). A similar picture can be seen in the towns of Hampshire, and especially in Southampton and Portsmouth, and by the end of the seventeenth century there were few towns or large villages in the county without one or more dissenting meeting houses.

This growth of nonconformity continued during the eighteenth century, especially after the preaching of John Wesley and the early Methodists. George Whitefield, together with John and Charles Wesley, made Bristol the base for their early preaching, and it was in Bristol in April 1739 that John Wesley took the momentous step, following George Whitefield's example, of preaching in the open air:

> I submitted to be more vile, and proclaimed in the highways the glad tidings of salvation, speaking from a little eminence in a ground adjoining to the city to about three thousand people . . .
> (Curnock ed., II, 1884–85: 167–73)

Within a year of his arrival in Bristol in 1739, John Wesley had taken a piece of land in the Horsefair and had begun building the New Room, the first Methodist church, marking the real beginning of Methodism with all its tremendous implications for the religious and social life of the country. Bristol remained the principal centre of John Wesley's work, and his brother, Charles, lived in Bristol from 1749 to 1771, and it was there that he wrote many of his best-loved hymns.

The diversity of eighteenth-century religious life in the region, the formal and respectable services of the Church of England, carefully avoiding 'enthusiasm' or fanaticism on the one hand, or 'Popery' on the other, and the wealth of different nonconformist chapels, can best be appreciated in the surviving buildings and their furnishings. Eighteenth-century churches such as those at Blandford Forum built after the fire of 1731, St George's Portsmouth (1754), St George's Portland (1766), Babington near Frome (1750), and the superb classical church attached to the mansion of the Duke of Beaufort at Great Badminton (1785), all with their careful arrangement of pews for the wealthy and galleries above for the poor, and their emphasis upon the pulpit rather than the altar, are eloquent of the cold formality of the services. The family pews, graded seating arrangements and crowded galleries of churches such as Cameley south of Bristol, Minstead in the New Forest, Stoke Charity north of Winchester, or Mildenhall and Old Dilton in Wiltshire are a reminder of the social distinctions, pew rents and 'respectability' of the Church of England. Likewise the multitude of nonconformist chapels with names such as Salem, Ebenezer, Bethel, Sion and Bethesda, and the multiplicity of the different sects and denominations bear witness to the fervour and fierce rivalry of the many different sects. The large town chapels show that the nonconformists were not lacking in wealth, and that they were supported by many leading merchants and tradesmen. A small minority of Catholics survived in spite of all persecution, especially where they had the protection and encouragement of wealthy Catholic gentry. They were comparatively numerous in Hampshire and Berkshire, and along the fringes of Wiltshire and Dorset. Leading Catholic families included the Arundells at Wardour, the Paulets at Basing House, the Tichbornes at Tichborne, and in Berkshire the Englefields and the Blounts (Bossy 1975: 100–3). At Ufton Court in the parish of Ufton Nervet near Reading the house was held by the Catholic Perkins family from its construction in 1570 until the last John Perkins died without issue in 1769. During all this time their practice of Catholicism remained unbroken, their chaplains served the neighbourhood, and during the eighteenth century the congregation in the attic chapel numbered more than ninety people. A priest remained in the deserted building until 1803; and the house contains three cunningly contrived hiding places for priests.

Another remarkable Catholic family were the Welds of East Lulworth on the Dorset coast. Having made a fortune as London grocers, the family acquired the castle and estates at East Lulworth and the surrounding district in 1642. In the grounds of the castle, which is now a ruin, are two churches, one is the parish church, the other is a Catholic chapel built by the Weld family in 1786–87, the first building to be erected especially for Catholic worship in England since the Reformation.

Spas, Watering-Places and Sea-Bathing

During the later seventeenth century the use of mineral springs and sea-bathing became increasingly fashionable and was to bring prosperity to several towns and resorts in the region. By far the most remarkable growth occurred in Bath which was to be transformed into the principal English spa town, a leading centre of fashion and high society, with the finest Georgian architecture in the country. Until the mid-seventeenth century Bath had remained a small, unimportant town, dependent upon the cloth trade, confined within its walls, and with only a dim memory of its ancient Roman splendour. In 1622 the Mayor of Bath complained that 'we are a very poor City, our Clothmen much decayed, and many of their workmen amongst us relieved by the City'. The town also suffered during the Civil War, especially in the aftermath of the battle of Lansdown (1643), and subsequently from the repeated demands for money and provisions from the armies of both sides (McIntyre 1981: 197–8). The popularity of the spa grew rapidly during the later seventeenth century, attracting increasing numbers to take the waters, including Charles II and his Court in 1663, followed by other fashionable and aristocratic families, including the Duke of York, and Samuel Pepys who left a notable description of Bath and the bathing facilities in his Diary (Latham and Matthews 1976, IX: 224–36).

By the end of the century there were gravel walks, bowling greens, tennis courts and coffee houses, and Celia Fiennes could describe Bath as 'the town and all its accommodation is adapted to bathing and drinking of the waters and nothing else'; while a few years later Defoe wrote sourly that

> in former times this was a resort hither for cripples . . . but now we may say it is the resort of the sound, rather than the sick; the bathing is made more a sport and a diversion, than a physical prescription for health; and the town is taken up in raffling, gameing, visiting, and in a word, all sorts of gallantry and levity
>
> (Defoe 1927, II: 34)

Under the strict rule of the arbiter of fashion and behaviour, Richard (Beau) Nash, who became Master of Ceremonies in 1704, Bath developed into the leading centre of fashionable society in the country; the recommendation of the efficacy of the Bath waters by the physician, Dr William Oliver, author of the influential treatise entitled *A Practical Dissertation on the Bath Waters* (1707), also helped to make Bath the leading health resort. The influx of the nobility and gentry led to a massive expansion of the town and created the opportunity for Ralph Allen to develop the building stone of Combe Down, and for architects such as John Wood the Elder and his son John Wood the Younger and others to design fashionable houses; the result was the creation of the most architecturally distinguished and elegant of English cities, and the most beautiful of English spas. The elder Wood's most notable designs were Queen's Square and the Circus; the first was completed in 1736, and the Circus was begun in the year of Wood's death in 1754 and finished in 1758. He also designed Prior Park, Ralph Allen's mansion at Combe Down on the hillside overlooking Bath. John Wood the Younger designed Gay Street, Milsom Street and, his greatest triumph, the Royal Crescent built during 1767–75.

The success of Bath in attracting the wealthy and notable in English society during the eighteenth century is apparent from the multitude of memorial tablets on the walls of the Abbey, recording in elegant prose and verse the incredibly numerous virtues of those who had failed to benefit from the Bath waters and who are buried there. The rapid rise in the popularity of Bath is also apparent from the population figures. The Hearth Tax of 1664 shows a town of fewer than 2,000 people; by 1700 the number had risen to about 2,500, and by 1750 there were 10,000 residents and many more visitors at the height of the season. The 1801 Census recorded 32,200 inhabitants, making Bath the ninth largest town in England (McIntyre 1981: 197–249).

Another spa which became fashionable during the early eighteenth century was at Hotwells down the Avon from Bristol, where warm waters rose through the tidal mud of the Avon and were said to provide beneficial treatment for all kinds of ailments. Throughout the eighteenth century visitors flocked to take the waters and to enjoy the dramatic views of the Avon Gorge and the bracing air and healthful walks on the Clifton Downs. Hotwells and the village of Clifton both grew rapidly, with Georgian squares and crescents, and with churches and chapels to cater for the visitors. Southampton also emerged from its long period of decline and enjoyed a remarkable revival of its fortunes during the eighteenth century, both as a spa for taking medicinal waters and as a healthy resort increasingly popular for sea-bathing. Both the medicinal springs and the sea-bathing were patronised by Frederick Prince of Wales in 1750, and later by his three sons the Dukes of York, Gloucester and Cumberland. Their visits brought a renewed prosperity to the town, and baths, assembly rooms, lodging houses and a theatre were built, coffee houses and a circulating library opened, coaching inns developed, and a start was made on building a Polygon, which was to be the centre of the town's new-found social activity, although that project was never completed. The population increased from about 3,500 during the 1750s to 4,500 by 1774 and to nearly 8,000 by 1801; there were daily coach services to London, Bath, Bristol, Salisbury and Oxford, and by the end of the century Southampton was one of the foremost resorts and watering places, frequented by the leaders of fashionable society (Temple Patterson 1966, I: 39–60).

Along the Hampshire coast, Christchurch and Lymington as well as Southampton had developed as resorts by the end of the eighteenth century. Charles Vancouver in the *General View of the Agriculture of Hampshire*, published in 1810, described all three places as 'much frequented in the summer for sea-bathing', and went on to observe that at Southampton the company was 'much more select than usual at such places', and that the town had 'a high reputation as a watering-place of elegant and fashionable resort'. He also remarked that although the accommodation at Southampton was expensive, it was 'generally of the best sort and truly elegant'.

Lyme Regis and Melcombe Regis on the Dorset coast also became popular resorts for those who sought sea-bathing. Jane Austen described Lyme Regis in her novel *Persuasion* (1818):

> As there is nothing to admire in the buildings themselves, the
> remarkable situation of the town, the principal street hurrying into the
> water, the walk to the Cobb, skirting round the pleasant little bay,
> which in the season is animated with bathing machines and
> company . . . are what the stranger's eye will seek.

In 1780 the Duke of Gloucester spent the winter at Melcombe Regis, and soon afterwards built a grand residence, Gloucester Lodge, on empty land to the north of the town. From 1789 George III regularly visited the town, staying at Gloucester Lodge, and the new popularity and rapid growth of the resort is reflected in its architecture and names. The Esplanade along the shore was started in 1785, and the spread of the resort can be traced through Gloucester Row, Royal Crescent, Chesterfield Place, Charlotte Row, Brunswick Terrace, Frederick Place, Waterloo Place and Victoria Terrace. In 1809 the crucial debt which the place owed to the patronage of George III for setting the royal seal of approval upon its qualities as a resort, was recognised by an enormous statue of the King, erected by 'The grateful Inhabitants' and so positioned that it faces up the Esplanade, presiding now over the packed masses of modern holiday-makers on the crowded beach.

Chapter 7

Expansion and Development during the Nineteenth Century

During the nineteenth century the population of Wessex increased more rapidly and dramatically than ever before; the number of people more than doubled between 1801 and 1901, and this explosion had profound effects upon all aspects of life and work. Moreover, the population expansion was very uneven: a few towns developed at a tremendous rate, while the population of many rural communities scarcely grew at all, or after initial growth declined sharply during the later part of the century. The overall pattern of growth can be seen from Table 11.

Table 11 Population growth, 1801–1901

County	*1801*	*1851*	*1901*	*% Increase during the century*
Berkshire	111,000	170,000	256,000	131%
Dorset	114,000	184,000	200,000	75%
Hampshire	219,000	405,000	798,000	264%
Somerset	274,000	444,000	433,000	58%
Wiltshire	184,000	254,000	271,000	47%
Bristol	68,000	159,000	337,000	395%
Total	970,000	1,616,000	2,295,000	137%

Some towns and a few villages increased massively in size during the course of the century. As shown in Table 12 in 1801 only four towns in the region had populations of more than 10,000; these were Bristol, Bath, Portsmouth, and Reading. The next largest town, Southampton, had a population of only 8,000 in 1801, and most other towns were much smaller. By 1901 all these major towns had experienced great population growth and had spread far beyond their early-nineteenth-century boundaries.

Table 12   Population of the principal towns, 1801–1901

Town	1801	1851	1901	% Increase
Bristol	68,000	159,000	337,000	395
Bath	33,000	54,000	50,000	51
Portsmouth	33,000	72,000	188,000	470
Reading	10,000	21,000	72,000	620
Southampton	8,000	35,000	105,000	1,212

The development of industries, communications, ports, military establishments and seaside resorts had by 1901 created more than a dozen large new conurbations in the region, many of them having developed during the nineteenth century from villages or even hamlets. Among the numerous examples of spectacular growth are those detailed in Table 13.

Table 13   Examples of rapid population growth, 1801–1901

Town	1801	1851	1901
Swindon	1,198	4,879	45,000
Bournemouth	—	695	47,003
Aldershot	494	875	30,974
Christchurch	3,773	4,379	32,941
Sonning	436	487	10,196
Sandhurst	222	815	5,571
Weston-super-Mare	487	4,594	19,448
Portland	1,619	5,195	15,199

But those places which experienced such a massive increase in population were exceptional, and for most of the small towns and villages the normal trend was for a steady increase in population during the first half of the nineteenth century, followed by an appreciable decline thereafter. Even in places which did experience substantial population increase, the rate of growth fell far behind the spectacular expansion of the manufacturing towns of the Midlands and the north, and taken overall, this was a period of relative decline in the Wessex region when its industries, especially the cloth industry, were overtaken by competition from the north, and when the port of Bristol failed to match the growth and prosperity of Liverpool as the major Atlantic port. The decline is particularly evident in the towns and villages of the chalklands where arable farming was very badly affected by the farming depression of the late nineteenth century. This can be seen in Table 14 which gives examples of towns from Wiltshire and Dorset:

Table 14   Population decline in chalkland towns,
1801–1901

	1801	1851	1901
Dorset			
Beaminster	2,140	2,832	1,702
Bere Regis	936	1,242	1,014
Corfe Castle	1,344	1,966	1,440
Cerne Abbas	847	1,343	643
Sturminster Newton	1,406	1,916	1,877
Blandford Forum	2,326	3,948	3,850
Shaftesbury	3,047	3,992	3,403
Cranborne	1,801	2,737	2,464
Wiltshire			
Amesbury	721	1,172	1,143
Great Bedwyn	1,632	2,193	877
Market Lavington	2,156	2,910	978
Ludgershall	471	580	576
Marlborough	2,367	3,908	3,046
Mere	2,091	2,991	1,919
Pewsey	1,179	1,921	1,722
Warminster	4,932	6,285	5,547
Ramsbury	1,963	2,696	1,779
Downton	2,426	3,898	3,065

A few of the smaller towns did maintain their growth during the century. For example, Chippenham prospered because of the development of its engineering industry and its population rose dramatically:
    1801–3,366;   1851–4,999;   1901–12,677.

Likewise at Calne the food-processing industry, especially Harris's Bacon, meant that population growth continued throughout the century:
    1801–3,767;   1851–5,117;   1901–5,518.

Wellington in Somerset managed to retain its textile industry and alone among the cloth-producing towns of the region did not decline:
    1801–4,033;   1851–6,415;   1901–7,283.

Taunton, as the county town and administrative centre of Somerset, with easy access to canal and railway transport, grew rapidly:
    1801–5,794;   1851–13,119;   1901–19,525.

Yeovil prospered as a principal market for the fertile lands of south Somerset and as a manufacturing centre for the important glove and leather-working industry of the district:
    1801–2,774;   1851–7,744;   1901–11,704.

Plate 7.1   Market Day at Yeovil, *c.* 1900. Yeovil is a good example of that multitude of west-country market towns which were so important in the economic and social life of the surrounding communities during the period 1500–1900. Notice the stalls set up along the street as they had been during the whole of the previous four centuries and more; the agricultural implements and the tools stacked up for sale, the cow being driven through the street, and the gas street-light in the foreground.

Reading with its diversity of small industry and manufacturing, notably malting, brewing and the manufacture of biscuits, drew unemployed labourers from all over Berkshire. Between 1831 and 1861 in the parishes of St Giles and St Mary in Reading the population increased by 99 per cent and 60 per cent respectively, while during the same period the population of the county as a whole only rose by 17 per cent. At Alton where the brewing industry grew rapidly, the population more than doubled during the century from 2,026 to 5,479. A few local administrative and market centres also increased in size, for example Basingstoke rose from 2,589 to 9,510; Fareham increased from 3,030 to 8,246; Andover from 3,304 to 6,509; Abingdon from 4,356 to 6,689; and Newbury from 4,275 to 6,983. Other towns which grew substantially as ports, military establishments, holiday resorts or dormitory towns will be discussed later in this chapter.

   In most towns and villages, however, the population declined during the last decades of the century. Widespread migration from the villages to the expanding towns of the north or the Midlands, or overseas, especially to the United States, was the background to village life throughout the region during the later nineteenth century (Saville 1957: 2 and 3). The notes attached to the

233

various *Census Reports* which explain or comment upon marked changes in the population of particular towns and villages show clearly the importance of migration and emigration in reducing the number of inhabitants. For example, in the Wiltshire Census of 1861 there are constant references to migration to the towns in search of work, to the depression in the woollen industry and to emigration as reasons for decreases in population. In 1871 decreases all over the county were attributed to the scarcity of agricultural employment because of the increased use of machinery or steam power, and to 'the preference of young women for domestic service in the towns'. At Malmesbury it was stated that part of the labouring population had emigrated to the oilfields of Ohio, and at Warminster the decrease in population was attributed to the coming of the railway which had

> diverted the traffic connected with the corn market, caused many of the inns to be closed, and induced a large number of sack-carriers and others to seek employment elsewhere.
>
> (*VCH Wilts* IV, 1959: 318–26)

A witness before the Royal Commission on Labour in 1893 reported that in Wiltshire, owing to the 'perfection' of machinery, the harvest could be secured in as many days as it used to take weeks, given good weather; and that harvest earnings, instead of being from £6 to £8 as in former times, were considered good at £3. Many families responded to the advertisements in the local newspapers offering assisted passages to Canada, Australia or New Zealand, or took up the offers of the Canadian Pacific Railway of free land for settlers in Manitoba (Havinden 1966: 97, 100). At Corsley near Warminster as early as 1852 about two hundred persons were said to have emigrated during the previous three years, and there was a similar exodus of labourers from Halstock and the neighbouring parishes in north Dorset, bound for the United States in 1851 (Davies 1909: 80–1; Kerr 1968: 24).

Many of the clergy and gentry assisted labourers and their families to emigrate in the belief that this was the only means by which the vicious problems of unemployment, poverty and dependence upon the poor rates could be alleviated. Overseers of the Poor also saw emigration as a possible solution to their problems; at Corsley in 1830 the parish paid for sixty-six of the least desirable residents, poachers and 'men suspected of bad habits', to sail from Bristol to Quebec; while during the 1840s the Overseers at Buckland Newton (Dorset) assisted young men to emigrate to Australia. In 1836 a group of thirty people emigrated from Childrey on the Berkshire Downs near Wantage, and in 1854 there was a large exodus from Thatcham when a group of Mormons left to join fellow-believers in Salt Lake City (Satre 1978: 322).

In brief therefore the general pattern of population movement in the region during the nineteenth century was of a general increase during the early decades, and of the massive expansion of a few towns, ports, seaside resorts and military establishments, while during the later decades these expanding towns were surrounded by numerous others whose population was declining and by many villages which were much smaller than they had been during the 1840s and 1850s. The following sections of this chapter will explore some of the causes and consequences of these movements of population.

Canals

It is an indication of the comparative industrial and business zeal of the two regions that the period of optimistic enthusiasm for canal-building came much earlier to the north of England than it did to the south. The Duke of Bridgewater's famous canal from Worsley to Manchester was opened in 1761, and many others quickly followed where the Duke had led, but, although the Thames and Severn Canal which linked the Severn waterway via the Stroudwater Navigation to the Thames at Inglesham near Lechlade was completed in 1789, the building of a canal linking Bristol and London did not start until 1792 and the Kennet and Avon Canal was not opened for through traffic until 1810. The Wilts and Berks Canal which provided a link from the Kennet and Avon at Semington near Melksham to the Thames at Abingdon also opened in 1810. Earlier, under the impetus of high war-time corn prices, two canals had been built in Hampshire, the Andover Canal from Redbridge on Southampton Water came up the valleys of the Test and Anton to Andover, and was opened in 1796, while the Basingstoke Canal, which ran from Basingstoke via Odiham to join the river Wey above Weybridge, began operating in the same year. The low-lying lands of Somerset around Bridgwater, Taunton and Langport, which were drained by the rivers Brue, Tone, Yeo and Parrett, were also affected by canals and waterways. From the 1790s the ancient watercourses of the area, which had been used by barges since the Roman period, were greatly improved and extended, so that barges from the Bridgwater estuary could reach as far inland as Glastonbury, Langport, Taunton, Ilminster and Chard. It was, however, the Kennet and Avon canal, joining the port of Bristol and the rapidly growing resort of Bath to London, and serving numerous towns including Bradford-on-Avon, Trowbridge, Devizes, Pewsey, Hungerford, Newbury and Reading on its route, which was the most important and heavily used waterway in the region. It was also a remarkable achievement in canal-building and design, a broad canal 57 miles long and incorporating 106 locks along its length, with fine bridges and aqueducts, elegantly built of Bath stone in the best Georgian tradition, with the spectacular flight of locks at Caen Hill near Devizes, part of a series of twenty-nine locks in a two-mile stretch of the canal, by which barges were taken up the rise of 237 feet into the Vale of Pewsey, and with great pumping stations at Claverton and Crofton. The Somerset Coal canal which was opened in 1805 and ran from the mines at Radstock and Timsbury, joined the Kennet and Avon at Limpley Stoke; this enabled coal from the Somerset coalfield to be carried easily and cheaply to Bath and Bristol, as well as eastwards to the towns and villages within reach of the canal through Wiltshire and Berkshire, as far east as Reading. The Kingswood coalfield was also linked with the Kennet and Avon via a horse-drawn tramway from Mangotsfield to the river Avon near Bitton. The Wilts and Berks canal linked Bristol and the north Somerset coalfield to the Vale of the White Horse, Oxford and the upper Thames valley.

Although they were to be so totally eclipsed by the railways, for a few decades the effect of the canals was enormous, and the quantity of goods which they carried far outstripped the wagons and pack-horses which they replaced. The barges on the Andover canal carried away tremendous loads of corn from the Hampshire chalklands and returned with coal, and the canal had an important influence upon the siting and trade of Tasker's Waterloo Iron works at Clatford near Andover, one of the most important iron-founders and manufacturers of agricultural implements in the region. At the peak of its activity during the 1830s and 1840s the Bridgwater and Taunton canal was carrying annual loads of more than 70,000 tons, mostly of Welsh coal; while in 1837, the last year of operation unaffected by railway construction, the Wilts and Berks canal carried 66,751 tons of goods, made up as follows (Hadfield 1955):

Somerset coal (tons)	43,642
Other coal (tons)	965
Corn, stone, etc. (tons)	14,884
Manure (tons)	1,578
Salt (tons)	1,550
Sundries (tons)	4,132

It was coal which was the major component of cargoes along the Kennet and Avon Canal, most of it Somerset coal, but also coal from the Kingswood coalfield where, as the result of the increased demand which followed the building of a tramway to the Avon, production greatly increased, reaching 524,000 tons annually at its maximum in the 1870s. Production in the Somerset coalfield was also greatly stimulated by the Coal Canal, and by the late 1830s the canal was carrying some 120,000 tons a year. Other cargoes on the Kennet and Avon included Bath stone from the mines at Box and Corsham, timber and other imported goods and luxury items from Bristol, among them products from Birmingham and the Midlands which had come down the Severn by 'trows' or barges. From Bristol also came West Indian sugar, French wines, Irish timber and leather and other goods from the Forest of Dean, slates from Wales, hardware and pottery from the Midlands, salt from Droitwich, and imported fruits, spices and luxuries. Some indication of the effect of the Kennet and Avon canal can be seen from the rapidity with which traffic and toll receipts along it increased during the early years of its operation, as shown in Table 15.

Table 15   Traffic and toll receipts on the Kennet and Avon Canal, 1812–23

Year	Toll receipts (£)	Goods		
		Coal and stone from Somerset Coal Canal (tons)	Other goods (tons)	Total (tons)
1812–13	20,126	66,741	59,558	126,299
1813–14	31,287	77,737	62,258	139,990
1814–15	25,849	81,751	70,529	152,280
1816	27,141	76,079	60,757	136,836
1817	32,201	74,115	67,768	141,883
1818	35,911	89,173	84,627	173,800
1819	33,031	92,802	95,953	188,755
1820	30,611	100,739	84,922	185,661
1821	32,920	103,171	77,833	181,004
1822	37,874	103,152	75,393	178,545
1823	37,725	106,569	82,134	188,704

(Clew 1968; *VCH Wilts* IV: 272–9)

By the 1830s, just before the arrival of the railways, the Kennet and Avon canal was carrying more than 340,000 tons of goods each year, and the Wilts and Berks nearly 63,000 tons. In spite of their importance and the amount of traffic which they carried, however, the canals of the region failed to provide their shareholders with any substantial profits. The costs of construction were very high, and none of the canals was in a position to provide the shareholders with reasonable dividends before the railways arrived and gradually took away most of the traffic. For example, the Westport Canal along the Parrett valley, which opened in 1840, was closed in 1878, by which time its receipts had dwindled to almost nothing. The dramatic effect of railway competition upon its income can be seen from the figures in Table 16.

By 1870–71 the revenue from tolls was down to £347 (Hadfield 1955). Neither the Kennet and Avon nor the Wilts and Berks paid any dividends of more than 3 per cent, and the average was a good deal lower. On 30 June 1841 the Great Western Railway line between London and Bristol was opened to traffic, and the effect upon the canals was dramatic and disastrous, in spite of all the efforts of the canal companies to cut costs, remain competitive and keep their business. The Kennet and Avon lost all through traffic, and receipts fell from £51,173 in 1840–41 to £39,936 in 1841–42, and to £32,045 in 1842–

Table 16   Toll receipts of the Westport Canal, 1848–57

Year	£	Year	£
1848–49	1,484	1853–54	1,440
1849–50	1,420	1854–55	919
1850–51	1,428	1855–56	832
1851–52	1,469	1856–57	868
1852–53	1,685	1857–58	672

43. In 1852 the canal was bought by the Great Western Railway company, and although it continued to operate until early in the twentieth century, the traffic was allowed to decline until by 1910 it had virtually ceased altogether (Clew 1968; *VCH Wilts* IV, 1959: 272–9).

Railways

The coming of the railways had a profound effect both upon the landscape and upon the social and economic life of the region, and the impact was much more widespread than that of the canals, affecting all areas and all aspects of life and work. The complex story of the various schemes, the rival companies, and the many projected routes has already been recounted in numerous books and need not be told again here; but the consequences of the railways, and their influence which penetrated to the remotest villages and farms cannot be ignored. The expansion of the railway network throughout the region during the mid-nineteenth century proceeded rapidly; indeed, in view of the amount of earth-moving, bridge-building, tunnelling and engineering work involved, as well as the capital accumulation and legal work necessary, the progress is staggering. The railway from London reached Southampton in 1840; in 1841 Brunel's broad-gauge line from London to Bristol opened; Taunton was reached in 1842; a branch of the London and Southampton railway reached Gosport in 1842 and Portsmouth and Salisbury both had railways by 1847, Westbury by 1848 and Frome in 1850. The Southampton and Dorchester railway, 60 miles long, was promoted under the leadership of an energetic Wimborne solicitor, A. L. Castleman. The line became known as 'Castleman's Corkscrew' or 'Castleman's Snake' because of its circuitous route, running from Southampton by way of Ringwood, Wimborne, Poole Junction, Wareham, Wool and Moreton, it reached Dorchester in 1847. In 1857 the Wiltshire, Somerset and Weymouth line from Westbury through Yeovil and thence via Yetminster, Maiden Newton and Dorchester to Weymouth was finally completed, having been under construction through difficult country for several years. The London to Exeter line via Salisbury, Gillingham, Sherborne, Crewkerne and Chard was opened to Exeter in 1860. The famous Somerset and Dorset railway, which ran through beautiful countryside and was to inspire great affection in its passengers and even greater nostalgia among students of railway history and lovers of steam trains, began operating in 1862, at first from Burnham-on-Sea to Poole, thus linking the Bristol channel and the English channel. In 1874 the Somerset and Dorset line from Bath to Bournemouth was established and provided a through route from the Midlands to the Dorset coast. Meanwhile the West Somerset railway reached Watchet from Taunton in 1862 and was extended to Minehead in 1874. The Bristol and North Somerset railway, linking the Somerset coalfield to Bristol and running through Pensford and Paulton to Radstock across difficult country, crossing the river Chew at Pensford by a spectacular viaduct, was opened for traffic in 1873 (Thomas 1960; White 1961; Atthill 1967). In addition to these major lines, the network was completed by a complex pattern of branch-lines serving individual towns and districts which had been by-passed by the main routes.

The effect of the railways upon the canals of the region has already been discussed; agriculture was also greatly affected, for the railways made it possible for farmers, even in the most remote parts of the region, to obtain new equipment, new and improved breeds of cattle and sheep, artificial fertilisers, tile drains and drainage pipes, and materials such as barbed wire and corrugated iron sheets. Most important of all, the railways opened up a vast new market for liquid milk which could now be sent to the towns. The demand from the growing population of London increased greatly after the cattle plague of 1868 had destroyed many of the dairies in and around the metropolis, and as tighter controls on health, cleanliness and sanitation made town cow-keeping more difficult. Dairy farmers throughout the region from the claylands of north and west Wiltshire and the Vale of the White Horse in Berkshire to the Marshwood Vale in Dorset, and from the Somerset levels to the former forest areas of east Hampshire, ceased converting the bulk of their milk into cheese and butter and began to send it to the towns by rail. The railways thus virtually killed the local small-scale production of the great variety of different west-country cheeses in favour of the liquid milk trade. They also encouraged the development of wholesale milk companies; the earliest wholesale depot for milk destined for the London market was opened at Semley in the Vale of Wardour on the London and South Western railway line between Sherborne and Salisbury in 1871, and the Anglo-Swiss Condensed Milk Company (later the Nestlé Company) opened a factory at Chippenham in 1873. By 1879 the North Wiltshire Dairy had new buildings at Stratton near Swindon where milk for the London market was cooled before dispatch. In 1881 the Surrey Farm Dairy Company opened a depot at Tisbury; and in 1882 the Semley Dairy which collected milk from farms all over south

Plate 7.2 Wiltshire Creameries, Chippenham. The coming of the railways revolutionised dairy farming in the region, since it enabled liquid milk to be dispatched to the towns instead of having first to be turned into butter and cheese. The nineteenth century also saw the development of a number of wholesale dairy companies for processing liquid milk. This photograph shows the Chippenham depot of Wiltshire Creameries in 1924; note the horse-wagons for collecting milk from the farms and the De Dion Bouton lorry used for the same purpose.

Wiltshire and north Dorset was advertising the twice-daily dispatch of cooled milk for the London market. The railways thus rapidly became the essential life-line of the dairy farmers of the whole region (Whetham 1964–65; *VCH Wilts* IV, 1959: 65–91, 224–8).

One consequence of the vastly increased possibilities for the sale of liquid milk was that dairy farming became much more important, and the number of cattle kept increased greatly. Table 17, compiled from the Agricultural Returns made to Parliament, shows very clearly the general trend.

The railways also had a marked effect upon the fortunes of arable farmers, for they made possible the distribution of cheap imported foodstuffs and especially wheat from the prairies of Canada and the United States, and thus played a crucial part in the great depression in English agriculture during the last quarter of the nineteenth century, in which arable farming was particularly badly hit.

Market gardening was greatly stimulated by the coming of the railways, and there was an increasing demand for flowers, fruit and vegetables to supply the markets of London and other growing towns. A notable development was strawberry-growing for the London market which became very important in

Table 17   Number of cattle kept in the region,
1875–1913

County	1875	1898	1913
Berkshire	37,147	43,564	49,990
Dorset	77,372	86,380	93,947
Hampshire	62,658	84,344	91,730
Somerset	210,960	229,722	237,032
Wiltshire	92,052	111,568	123,001
Total	480,189	555,578	595,700

(Sources: *Parliamentary Papers* 1875, lxxix,
C1303; 1899, C9304; 1914, xcviii Cd 7271)

the area of light, warm soils to the east of Southampton Water in the triangle between Botley, Swanwick and Fareham, and also in Somerset around Cheddar along the southern slopes of Mendip. In 1913 no less than 2,584 acres were devoted to strawberries in Hampshire and 278 acres in Somerset (Parliamentary Papers 1914: xcviii). Similarly market-gardening developed on the rich soils of the Bromham area of Wiltshire between Devizes and Chippenham, also within easy reach of the railways. An impetus was also given to various firms of seedsmen and nurserymen by the improved transport facilities. Firms such as Suttons of Reading, Dunns of Gillingham, Hilliers of Winchester, Scotts of Merriot near Crewkerne and Kelways of Langport all found that they had a regional and even national market rather than a purely local one. Suttons' grandly named Royal Berkshire Seed Establishment at Reading was founded in 1806; by the 1860s it was offering carriage-free delivery of 'Every Kind of Seed required for the Farm and Garden', and was 'under the distinguished patronage of her Most Gracious Majesty the Queen and H.R.H. the Prince of Wales'. At Gillingham in north Dorset Shadrach Dunn began his seed business in 1832, selling grass, clover, sainfoin and lucerne seed in the local markets, and establishing a reputation for his locally grown Dorset marlgrass clover-seed. The railways provided the means of expansion into markets throughout the region. It was also through the railways that nurserymen such as Hilliers of Winchester and Scotts of Merriott began to build up a national reputation for the quality of their products and the comprehensiveness of their stocks of trees, shrubs, fruit-bushes, roses and other plants.

On industries such as cloth-production, coal mining, stone-quarrying, brewing, brick and clay tile manufacture, and the making of agricultural implements and steam engines the railways had equally profound effects, creating a national rather than a purely local market and transforming previously small firms into large undertakings. To some market towns the railways brought new prosperity and greatly increased trade, while others which were not on a railway line rapidly declined. In Dorset, for example, the railways changed Sherborne, Gillingham, Bridport and, above all, Dorchester, into bustling centres of population and enterprise, while Cerne Abbas, Beaminster, Cranborne, or Bere Regis, avoided by the railways, declined rapidly, their markets died, stage coaches ceased to run through them and they virtually ceased to be towns at all. A similar pattern and distinction can be observed all over the region. One effect of this was a drastic decline in the number of markets and fairs which had once been so important in the economy. The extent of the decline can be seen from the figures in Table 18.

Table 18 The number of markets and
fairs in each county in 1792 and 1888

County	1792	1888
Berkshire	26	14
Dorset	43	25
Hampshire	56	24
Somerset	97	52
Wiltshire	43	28
Total	265	143

(Source: *Parliamentary Papers* 1888, liii)

Among the weekly markets and annual fairs which were discontinued by 1888 were many which were very ancient and had formerly been of great importance. For example, in Hampshire and the Isle of Wight places such as Titchfield, Tangley, Waltham, West Cowes, Yarmouth, Christchurch, Boughton, Kingsclere, Liss, Beaulieu and elsewhere had all ceased to be held by 1888, while the two ancient fairs which had formerly been held on the outskirts of Winchester – at St Giles Hill on 12 September and Magdalen Hill on 2 August – and which had once attracted buyers and sellers from all over the region and beyond, had also come to an end.

The little market town of Swindon was transformed by the coming of the Great Western Railway. In 1839 it was decided that the chief locomotive depot and repair shop should be built near Swindon at a convenient half-way point, and where, ironically, the Wilts and Berks canal could provide ample supplies of water for the engines. The first workshops were opened in 1843. Almost immediately the company began to build houses for its workers nearby; these were followed by a church, St Marks, designed by Gilbert Scott for the use of the railway employees and completed in 1845 at a cost to the company of £5,500, its fine spire rising above the workshops and the railway line. In 1845 also a school for railwaymen's children was opened, and by 1853 when the Mechanics' Institute was completed nearly 250 houses had already been built, many constructed of Bath stone brought by rail from the excavation of the Box tunnel. As with all the early projects of the GWR, Swindon railway village was designed with flair and imagination, and is a fine example of mid-nineteenth-

242

century planning. The modest but well-designed and attractive cottages were laid out in orderly rows, close to the workshops and near the school, church, hospital and other services provided by the company. As the railway prospered, so New Swindon grew, rapidly overshadowing the market town beside it. The growth of the population was as follows (Table 19):

Table 19 The population of Swindon, 1831–1911

1831	1,742	1881	19,904
1841	2,459	1891	33,001
1851	4,879	1901	45,006
1861	6,856	1911	50,751
1871	11,720		

The town continued to be dominated by the Great Western Railway, and at the end of the nineteenth century four-fifths of the working population were employed by the company, on the railway or in the workshops. Another place revolutionised by the arrival of the railway was Eastleigh, south of Winchester on the London and South Western line to Southampton and Portsmouth. A railway junction was opened in 1842 where the branch line which at first went only to Gosport left the main line to Southampton. A railway village housing workers on the line grew up and developed into a town when the L & SWR carriage and wagon works were moved there from Nine Elms in 1891, followed a few years later by the locomotive repair workshops.

Resorts

It was the railways which brought the massive growth in the seaside-holiday trade. In Somerset the first hotel at Weston-super-Mare was opened in 1810 and a coach service from Bristol began in 1814, but holiday-makers only began to arrive in large numbers after the coming of the railway early in 1841. Likewise at Clevedon, although there are houses along the sea-front with names such as Adelaide, Brunswick and Clarence which obviously date from the early part of the century, it was the opening of the branch railway line from Yatton in 1847 which led to the expansion of the resort as well as to the growth of nearby Portishead. The same is true of Burnham-on-Sea to which a branch line was extended from Highbridge in 1858. After the arrival of the railway, the growth of these resorts was extraordinarily rapid, and Weston-super-Mare in particular leapt from being a tiny fishing hamlet of less than five hundred people at the beginning of the century to being the largest town in

Somerset, except for Bath, in the early twentieth century. The population figures are as follows (Table 20):

Table 20   The population of the Somerset resorts, 1801–1901

	1801	1851	1901
Burnham-on-Sea	653	1,701	4,922
Clevedon	334	1,905	5,900
Weston-super-Mare	487	4,594	19,448

Minehead, which had for centuries been a small port taking coastal traffic, occasional ships from Ireland and cargoes of coal and cattle from south Wales, was reached by the railway extended through Watchet from Taunton in 1874. It remained a small, select resort until the coming of Butlin's Holiday Camp in the mid-twentieth century, but nonetheless the population rose by some 80 per cent between 1851 and 1901 as the following details show: 1801–1,168; 1851–1,542;   1901–2,782.

The architecture of these Somerset resorts reflects their nineteenth-century growth and rapid development. For example, at Clevedon the early-nineteenth-century houses are along the sea-front; these are in the classical style of the 1820s; spreading up the hillside are roads dating from the mid-Victorian development of the resort, with names such as Victoria Road, and Albert Road; the houses are detached villas in a solid neo-classical style. Higher still come the late-nineteenth-century semi-detached houses in Gothic or Italianate style, occasionally interrupted by a few mock-Tudor or Jacobean houses. The pier, which is now a sad ruin awaiting restoration, was built during the 1860s, and the Royal Pier Hotel with its embattled tower commanding the beach is c.1870. By 1880 the population of the town had already more than doubled; it had libraries, coffee houses, entertainments, a hospital, the largest swimming bath in the west of England and the largest skating rink outside London (Dunning 1980; 1983).

An equally dramatic explosion of population following the coming of the railways can be observed in the resorts along the south coast. At Southsea the marshy common along the sea-front was gradually drained and reclaimed during the early nineteenth century, thus preparing the way for the development of the resort. Most of the early work was done during the 1840s by Thomas Ellis Owen, a local architect and speculator who began to build terraces of villas on waste land to the east of Portsmouth facing on to Southsea Common. His houses were let on short leases at high rents to naval and military officers who wished to make a temporary home for their families during a period of service duty in Portsmouth. Owen prospered greatly from his initiative; he was twice mayor of Portsmouth, and was the virtual creator of Southsea. Others soon followed his example, and with the coming of the

244

railway providing a direct link with London in 1847, Southsea began its rapid development as a holiday resort as well as a residential suburb of Portsmouth, with all the characteristic features which were demanded by Victorian holiday-makers – hotels and boarding houses, piers, ornamental gardens, and sea-front walks. In Dorset, the vital influence of a railway link in the development of the resorts is apparent at Weymouth, Melcombe Regis and Swanage, while Lyme Regis where the hills and valleys of the Dorset–Devon border would have made a railway grossly expensive to build, went into a slow decline. Again, the population figures (Table 21) tell their own story:

Table 21   The population of the Dorset resorts, 1801–1901

	1801	1851	1901
Lyme Regis	1,451	2,852	2,095
Weymouth	1,267	2,957	4,497
Melcombe Regis	2,350	5,273	7,473
Swanage	1,382	2,139	3,455

The coming of the railway to Southampton also provided a great boost for the resorts on the Isle of Wight. The improved access, and the great improvement in internal communications on the Island which followed the construction of a railway network, coupled with royal patronage by Queen Victoria and Prince Albert with their great private mansion, Osborne House, and the growing popularity of yachting among the rich and fashionable, led to the development of hotels and boarding houses at Ryde, Ventnor, Shanklin and Sandown.

The most striking example in the whole region of the massive and rapid growth of a resort was Bournemouth. The site of Bournemouth, on the coastal fringe of the great heathland area of the Hampshire–Dorset border, was uninhabited until 1810 when Lewis Tregonwell, a member of the wealthy Dorset landowning family, built a holiday home for himself, and then a few cottages for servants, friends and relations. After Tregonwell's death in 1834, a 'marine village' was planned by Sir George Tapps-Gervis who had acquired the land. He commissioned a fashionable architect from nearby Christchurch, Benjamin Ferrey, who was rising to prominence as a designer of churches, to lay out an estate of detached villas, set among the pine trees which Tregonwell had planted and which have remained such a characteristic feature of the area. Hotels and pleasure-gardens followed, and the resort began to attract wealthy patrons who sought a quiet retreat in the healthy climate. But growth was slow, and by 1851 there were still only 691 residents. The startling expansion of Bournemouth occurred after the opening of the railway link with London in 1870, and the Somerset and Dorset line from Bath and the Midlands in 1874. By 1881 the population of Bournemouth had already reached 16,859, and it grew to 78,674 by 1911, a growth which transformed Bournemouth from a quiet backwater into one of the major towns of the country.

Between the Napoleonic War and the War of 1914–1918 several parts of Wessex were transformed by the creation or massive extension of naval and military bases. Apart from numerous small military establishments, there were four places greatly changed by the construction of large-scale garrisons – Portsmouth and Portland were vastly expanded as major naval bases, and the army took over control of large areas of Salisbury Plain and of the heathland on the Hampshire–Surrey border around Aldershot. The growth of the royal dockyard and its crucial role during the Napoleonic War, as well as the great number of soldiers stationed in Portsmouth, had led to an expansion of its population from 33,226 in 1801 to 41,587 in 1811. During the war the dockyard employed more than 4,000 men, or 36 per cent of the established labour force in the town. After the war the number employed was drastically reduced, and by 1830 only 2,000 were employed in the royal dockyard. Nonetheless the population of Portsmouth continued to rise, reaching 46,743 in 1821, 50,389 in 1831, 53,032 in 1841 and 72,096 in 1851. Along with the growth of population went the continued spread of military establishments and naval depots, garrisons and barracks as well as hulks moored in the harbour, while the town developed more and more hotels and common lodging houses, inns, beer-houses, music halls and brothels. Large areas within and around the town walls were occupied by narrow streets full of the most appalling slums, and parts of the Landport area of the town and of Old Portsmouth consisted of badly built, grossly overcrowded courts and alleys, devoid of either sanitation or a supply of pure water. By the 1840s many parts of Portsmouth had become a by-word for insanitary conditions and for the prevalence of such diseases as typhoid, tuberculosis and cholera, with an annual death-rate of 25.37 per thousand inhabitants compared to a rate of considerably less than 20 in healthier rural areas of Hampshire. In 1846 a local physician and enthusiastic sanitary reformer, Dr W. C. Engledue, founder of the Royal Portsmouth Hospital, emphasised in an horrific calculation the urgent need for action to improve the sanitation of the town:

> At present the island of Portsea is one large cesspool, for there cannot be less than 16,000 cesspools daily permitting 30,000 gallons of urine to penetrate into the soil. Just reflect on the character of the well-water . . . which becomes mixed every year with 365 times 30,000 gallons of urine, to say nothing of other abominations.

Conditions of sanitation, hygiene and water supply were greatly improved during the 1850s with the establishment of Improvement Commissioners, a Board of Health and a Waterworks Company which by the 1860s was supplying piped water to most parts of Portsmouth.

In response to the increased range and penetrating power of naval guns, and because of fears of French naval power, the defences of Portsmouth were greatly strengthened during the 1860s and 1870s. Six heavily armed forts were built along the crest of Portdown Hill overlooking the town, the harbour and the dockyard; three forts guarding Spithead and the entrance to Portsmouth harbour were erected on the shoals between Portsmouth and the Isle of Wight. This massive scheme of defence, making Portsmouth the most heavily fortified town in Europe, was not completed until 1880, by which time the danger of attack from France was no longer regarded as a serious threat, and the forts became known, somewhat unjustly, as 'Palmerston's folly', since he was the Prime Minister when their construction had been ordered.

During the later decades of the century the population of Portsmouth with its suburbs of Southsea and Landport and with its crowded Service establishments, continued to grow very rapidly. The population figures are shown in Table 22.

Table 22   The population of
Portsmouth (Portsea Island), 1851–1911

1851	72,096	1891	159,251
1861	94,329	1901	188,133
1871	113,569	1911	231,141
1881	127,989		

Another expansion of the royal dockyard facilities occurred during the last quarter of the century, with the construction of shipbuilding, fitting and repair facilities for ever-larger warships, culminating in 1906 with the launch of HMS *Dreadnought* which began a new era in heavily armed and armoured battleship construction. Among the developments, Whale Island in Portsmouth harbour was greatly increased in size by the dumping of excavated soil from dry-dock construction, and became the Royal Naval Gunnery School, known from one of the hulks in which it had previously been accommodated as HMS *Excellent* (Temple Patterson 1976).

Further along the coast, the great naval base at Portland was built as a counter to the potential threat from the French naval stronghold at Cherbourg. The decision to establish a naval base at Portland was taken as the result of a Royal Commission which reported in 1844. The necessary Act of Parliament was passed in 1847, enabling the Admiralty to acquire land for the dockyard and also for the construction of a military fortification and citadel on the Verne, the highest point on the island of Portland, overlooking the proposed harbour. The foundation stone of the breakwater enclosing the anchorage was laid by Prince Albert in 1849 and in 1872 the main part of the project was formally declared to be complete by Albert Edward, Prince of Wales. The breakwater with its entrances is some $3\frac{1}{2}$ miles in length, and encloses a sheltered, deep-water anchorage of two square miles. The extremely arduous work of building the breakwater was done by convict labour, and the convicts were housed in a prison especially established on the island of Portland for that purpose. As a consequence of the construction of the breakwater, the dockyard and naval base, and the defensive citadel on the Verne guarding the whole harbour and its approaches, Portland became one of the most important and well-defended naval bases in the country (Bettey 1970).

During the Crimean War a large army barracks was built beside the village of Aldershot where the open heathland of the Hampshire–Surrey border provided space for rifle-ranges, artillery practice, and good training ground for cavalry and infantry. The garrison grew with phenomenal speed, and Aldershot was soon totally engulfed by the army and completely identified with it. This is evident from the population figures (Table 23):

Table 23   The population of Aldershot, 1801–1901

1801	494	1861	16,720
1811	498	1871	21,682
1821	525	1881	20,155
1831	665	1891	25,595
1841	685	1901	30,974
1851	875		

The expansion of the garrison continued during the twentieth century, and can be traced in the large military churches which were built to serve it – All Saints 1863, St George 1892, St Andrew 1927. The medieval church of St Michael was enlarged in 1865 and again in 1910. The previously remote and thinly populated village of Aldershot became the country's chief military centre, and famed throughout the British Empire. Likewise the development of army barracks and training establishments to the north of Aldershot at Farnborough led to a massive growth of population from 477 in 1851 to 11,500 in 1901. Also part of the great military area of the heathland is the Royal Military Academy at Sandhurst which is in the south-east corner of Berkshire, and which became the major training school for officers.

In 1895 the War Office purchased a large area of Salisbury Plain for army training and manoeuvres, and during the early years of the twentieth century large permanent establishments were set up, first at Tidworth where the barracks and other buildings were started in 1903, and later at Larkhill and at Bulford where a vast complex was built during the First World War and continued thereafter until it now covers more than a square mile of the Plain. The influx of very large numbers of men, together with barrack buildings, gunnery ranges, workshops, and later, tank training grounds, inevitably had an enormous impact on the remote and previously isolated settlements on the Plain, on the open landscape of the chalk downland and on the remarkably well-preserved archaeological monuments of the area.

Port Developments

The nineteenth century witnessed major developments in both of the two main commercial ports, Bristol and Southampton, as ships increased in size and draught, and as the canals and railways brought vastly improved internal communications. During the early nineteenth century Bristol declined rapidly from its eighteenth century 'golden age'; the West Indian trade diminished, very high harbour dues discouraged merchants, and the vigorous competition from Liverpool diverted trade. Although the port facilities at Bristol were greatly improved by the construction of the floating harbour between 1804 and 1809, the work failed to halt the port's decline. Ships still had the difficult eight-mile journey up the Avon, and the administration of the port by the Society of Merchant Venturers was inefficient and expensive. Not until 1848 after a long agitation were the docks finally taken over by the Corporation and harbour dues reduced. It is a telling commentary on the decline of the port of Bristol that although it led the way in ship design with large steam-driven vessels like Brunel's *Great Western* launched in 1837 and the *Great Britain* launched in 1843, neither ship was to use the port of Bristol regularly (Buchanan 1976). By 1850 Bristol had declined to sixth place among the principal English ports, having been overtaken not only by Liverpool, Newcastle and Hull, but also by the rapidly expanding port of Southampton which was already in fifth place among the English ports in 1850. The comparative figures for the trade of Bristol and Southampton in 1850 are as shown in Table 24.

Table 24 Vessels and tonnage using Southampton and Bristol, 1850

	Inwards		Outwards	
	Ships	Tons	Ships	Tons
Southampton	626	152,117	603	147,519
Bristol	730	137,812	276	79,448

(Source: *Parliamentary Papers* 1851, lii)

The growth of trade in the port of Southampton after the arrival of the railway from London in 1840 was spectacular. A Southampton Dock Company had been established by Act of Parliament in 1836, and a new dock which greatly improved the facilities of the port was opened in 1843 close to the new railway terminus. By 1851 a second dock had been built on reclaimed land to the east of the town. The convenience of the railway connection with London meant that Southampton began to be regularly used by the new steamship companies, the

Royal Mail, the P and O, and the Union and the Castle lines, and the seal was set upon its modern prosperity as the major passenger and liner port of the kingdom. As a result of its remarkable growth and prosperity as a liner port, the population of Southampton almost doubled from 60,051 in 1881 to 119,012 in 1911. Further developments at the port of Southampton included a succession of new docks and harbour facilities culminating in the Empress Dock on the river Itchen opened in 1890, and the intimate link between the port and the railway which was finally cemented in 1892 when the docks were acquired by the London and South Western Railway Company, which in 1923 became part of the Southern Railway system. Meanwhile, early in the twentieth century, the White Star and Cunard lines transferred their ships from Liverpool and made Southampton their chief terminal. Vast new passenger docks were constructed along the reclaimed waterfront of the river Test, most notably the King George V dock opened in 1933 which was designed to accommodate the largest liners, including the *Queen Mary*. The Ocean Terminal, the finest and most opulent in the world for the reception of passengers opened in 1953. In that year 650,000 passengers passed through the port.

Meanwhile, the port of Bristol had, belatedly, attempted to overcome the disadvantages which its site presented to large modern ships, first by various schemes of deepening and straightening the river Avon during the 1850s and then by the development of dock facilities at the mouth of the Avon with railway connections to Bristol and to the Great Western system. In 1868 a railway and pier was constructed at Portishead for a passenger service to Ireland, and during the 1870s a dock was built there, financed by Bristol Corporation. At the same time work was started on a new dock at Avonmouth to cater for the largest ships which could not reach Bristol. The first dock at Avonmouth was completed in 1877; in 1908 the Royal Edward Dock was opened, and the docks were extended again in 1922 and 1928. By the end of the nineteenth century therefore Bristol had regained a premier position for the handling of certain cargoes, especially the import of bulk grain, but even so, although in 1897 the tonnage of grain imported into Bristol amounted to 676,345 tons, yet this represented only 8 per cent of total United Kingdom imports, and Bristol's export trade remained small.

The smaller ports along the English Channel and the Somerset coast continued to have a substantial coastal traffic and links with France, Spain, the Low Countries and Ireland. Portsmouth remained an important commercial as well as a naval port, and Poole (with its fine natural harbour), Weymouth, Bridport and Lyme Regis all had busy coastal trade. Poole exported potters clay from the Dorset heathland and corn from the chalklands; building stone from Portland was exported from Weymouth, and Bridport continued to import hemp and flax and export ropes, nets and cord. The growth in the popularity of seaside holidays and of yachting stimulated the growth of harbours on the Isle of Wight, Southampton Water and the Beaulieu and

Lymington rivers. In Somerset Bridgwater and Watchet were the main ports for coastal traffic. Bridgwater's major product continued to be bricks, clay roofing-tiles and drainage pipes, and a new dock with warehouses and a railway connection was built there between 1837 and 1845. Watchet was transformed by the opening of the iron-ore mines on the Brendon Hills during the 1850s, since the ore was shipped from Watchet to South Wales for smelting.

Nineteenth-century Industries

A remarkable feature of the industrial scene in Wessex during the nineteenth century is the final disappearance of the woollen-cloth manufacture from most districts. The cloth trade had already declined greatly throughout Dorset, Hampshire and Berkshire by the beginning of the century, leaving only a few workers in towns such as Newbury and Reading which had once been important centres of cloth manufacture, and production was concentrated in the towns of West Wiltshire – Melksham, Bradford-on-Avon, Trowbridge, Westbury – and around Frome in east Somerset. During the Napoleonic War the industry in these towns was prosperous, for French competition had been removed, there were government orders for cloth, and order-books were full. With the end of the war in 1815 the trade entered a period of stagnation, interspersed with years of acute depression, distress, hardship and unemployment among the workers. A few firms continued to do well, for example, J. and T. Clark who had started in business in 1801 with a capital of £500 were worth £10,929 by 1815 and had increased their capital to £59,000 by 1824, having moved to a new factory in Trowbridge and installed a 10 hp steam-engine purchased from Boulton and Watt in 1814 at a cost of £1,000 (Rogers 1976).

Table 25   The population of Trowbridge and Frome, 1801–41

	1801	*1811*	*1821*	*1831*	*1841*
Trowbridge	5,799	6,075	9,545	10,863	11,148
Frome	8,748	9,493	12,411	12,240	11,849

As Table 25 shows Trowbridge and Frome in particular continued to prosper and grow, the population of both increasing rapidly. The trade in both towns had turned away from dependence upon the high-quality, expensive broadcloth which had been the traditional product of the west country, to the

251

manufacture and export of cassimeres, lighter-weight cloths with a twill effect which became very popular. Other towns such as Bradford-on-Avon, Chippenham, Warminster and Melksham which kept to the traditional product were much less successful.

From the 1830s the prosperous section of the industry became increasingly concentrated upon Trowbridge and the surrounding area. At Salisbury the flannel industry which had been prosperous in the early years of the century, could not meet the competition from cotton goods, while the serge industry of south and west Somerset also contracted, partly owing to the loss of a traditional export market in India with the expiry of the East India Company's monopoly. Towns such as Chard, Milverton, Wiveliscombe and Wincanton were badly affected by the collapse of this traditional industry which had brought great prosperity during the eighteenth century. Only in Wellington did serge-making remain prosperous, owing largely to the Fox family, bankers and manufacturers, who introduced worsted combing and spinning machinery to their factory and ensured that Wellington was the one Somerset town engaged in cloth production whose population continued to grow throughout the nineteenth century.

The reasons for the decline of the textile trade throughout the region are complex and still the subject of much argument. Difficulties with fuel supplies, competition from the new centres of production in Yorkshire, resistance to new methods and machinery, all played their part, but above all it was changes in demand and in fashion that were crucial. The demand from the rapidly growing mass market of industrial workers was for cheaper cloths of moderate quality, not for superfine, highly finished broadcloths and fancy cloths in which the western trade had specialised. It was the worsted and cheaper cloths which were to dominate the market and which catered for the ready-made garment industry centred upon Leeds, and the industry in the west of England was not well-placed or well-equipped to supply this market (Mann 1971; Ponting 1957).

The enormous human problems created by the contraction of the industry and the recurrent depressions which it experienced during the early decades of the nineteenth century can be illustrated by one moving letter, written by a weaver who had left Bradford-on-Avon in 1834 and travelled with a companion first to Gloucestershire and then on to Yorkshire vainly seeking for work. The unsigned letter is addressed to his wife Margaret Rudmer in Bradford-on-Avon, and is stamped 'Huddersfield July 7 1834'.

Junen the 6   1834

Dear wife   i have taken the liberty to write thes few lines to you hoping
to find you in good helth as it leaves me at present i and willham
alexander have trafeld throu glostershier and from their to yourkshier
and can gett no work for the weavers are all out for weages we was at a
meating in feldes of 5000 pepell standing for weadges we could go into
work as Black sheep as they caul that is working under prise and we are

afraid to go in to work bein in danger of our lives and so it is no youss
to walk a bout yourkshier no longer and it is no youss to com home so
we are goin a way to London
Dear wife i cannot rest a bout you and my dear child i want to see you
but i shall not yet —————————— willham remember is kind love to is
wife and fameley he want to see them and is in trobel a bout them but
he say it is no yous to com home to no work he oufen talks about his
ouldes child but cannot se her we thought it our dutty to lett you know
whar we was but we cannot tel where we shall be to morrow so pay for
the letter be tewen you 2 wifs ————— hop god well bles you all and us
to   good bey
(W.R.O. 77/101)

Industries which continued to be important in the economic life of
Wessex included the coal mining industry of Bristol and north Somerset, stone
quarrying and mining at Box, Corsham and elsewhere near Bath, the Portland
stone industry, brewing in Hampshire and Dorset, malting at Newbury,
Reading and along the Thames, glove-making in south Somerset around
Yeovil, silk production at Overton, Whitchurch and Winchester, and at
Sherborne, Gillingham, Chippenham, Devizes, Mere and Malmesbury. There
were also numerous other centres of specialised production. Sacks for hops
were made at Alton, ropes and nets at Bridport, cotton, glass, tobacco, cocoa
and chocolate were specialities in Bristol, biscuits were made at Reading,
blankets at Newbury, while Ringwood, Romsey, Basingstoke and Andover
were famous for hops. Paper was made at various places on Mendip, and along
the chalkland streams of Hampshire, notably at Whitchurch and at Laverstoke
where the paper for banknotes was made. Clay pipes were made at Amesbury
and Marlborough, corsets were made by sailors' wives around Portsmouth and
Southampton, sailcloth and linen were manufactured in west Dorset and south
Somerset around Beaminster, Broadwindsor, Crewkerne and East Coker.
Employment for women and girls in various parts of the region was provided
by straw-bonnet making and straw-plaiting, notably at Aldbourne in Wiltshire
and along the Kennet valley in Berkshire, stocking-knitting especially around
Christchurch and Ringwood, and 'buttony' or the making of elaborate fancy
buttons, a craft centred on Blandford Forum and Sturminster Newton.

Agriculture during the Nineteenth Century

The high prices of agricultural produce during the Napoleonic Wars brought
great prosperity to farmers throughout Wessex and encouraged many changes

in agricultural practice. The most obvious and far-reaching change was the enclosure of the former common arable fields into self-contained farms. High prices also encouraged the enclosure and conversion of commons and wastes such as the high ground of the Brendon, Quantock and Mendip Hills in Somerset and the chalk downs of Berkshire, Hampshire and Dorset. The importance of the war period in the process of parliamentary enclosure is apparent from the figures given in Table 26.

Table 26

(a) Percentage figures for enclosure by Act of Parliament at different periods

County	Pre 1793	1793–1815	1816–1829	Post 1829
Berkshire	21.4	57.4	5.7	15.5
Dorset	21.1	44.3	11.0	23.7
Hampshire	29.7	38.8	8.6	22.9
Isle of Wight	—	77.6	—	22.4
Somerset	35.0	46.1	4.6	14.3
Wiltshire	35.4	46.7	9.7	8.2

(Source: Turner 1980: 176–81)

(b) Total number of acres enclosed by Act of Parliament in each county, and number of Acts relating to each county

County	No. of acres enclosed by Act of Parliament	Proportion of County	Number of Acts
Berkshire	154,992	34%	133
Dorset	94,078	15%	105
Hampshire	156,522	17%	164
Isle of Wight	3,220	3%	5
Somerset	171,234	16%	172
Wiltshire	255,118	30%	179

(Source: Turner 1980: 176–9)

The most spectacular single example of land reclamation was on Exmoor, where the enclosure of some 22,000 acres was authorised by Act of Parliament in 1815. In 1818 this large tract of undeveloped moorland and bog was bought from the Crown by John Knight, whose fortune had been made from iron-works in Shropshire. It was the work of the Knight family which turned much of this waste land into farms and created the modern landscape of Exmoor (Orwin and Sellick 1970; Havinden 1981: 172–98). Between 1771 and 1813 some 24,000 acres of Mendip were enclosed by Parliamentary Act, and another 3,500 acres by private agreement. This involved the construction of about 1,650 miles of new fences and hedges, many of them the dry-stone walls which give the central Mendip plateau much of its distinctive modern appearance. Some fifty new farmsteads were also created (Williams 1971: 65–81; Buchanan 1982: 112–26).

Although the prosperity which high prices and greater productivity brought to farmers did not extend to the farm labourers, nonetheless there is no doubt of the excellence and high standards of much of the farming of the region during much of the nineteenth century, with intensive cultivation, high yields, mechanisation, new methods, new crops and feedstuffs and improved varieties of seed and livestock. This is witnessed by the surviving farm-houses, barns, stock-yards and cattle-housing, by the model farms, and also by the comments of contemporary observers. As early as the 1770s Arthur Young described the vale between Farnham and Alton as the finest ten miles in England; and during the 1820s William Cobbett, who was by no means uncritical, enthused over the excellence of the farming which he saw in many parts of Wessex during his *Rural Rides*. In Hampshire at Burghclere, Highclere, Hurstbourne Tarrant, and along the valley of the Itchen, and in Berkshire across the downlands, the Vale of the White Horse and at Shalbourne and Inkpen, Cobbett commented upon the high standard of farming and the fine crops, cattle and sheep which he saw. In Wiltshire, although he was appalled by the condition of the labourers, he found the agriculture of the Avon valley down to Salisbury and of the Wylye between Salisbury and Warminster as fine as anything he had ever seen. Thirty years later, another perceptive observer, L. H. Ruegg, the editor of a Dorset newspaper, in an essay on *The Farming of Dorsetshire*, published by the Royal Agricultural Society in 1854, wrote that the standard of farming throughout the county was as high as any in England: 'From Woodyates to six miles beyond Dorchester (nearly the entire length of the chalk district) there is no better farming in the kingdom.'

To this development of 'High Farming' with high capital investment in buildings, stock, implements, enclosures, drainage, water-meadows and other improvements, high input of fertilisers, and high yields of corn, milk and livestock, the gentry families and large landowners made an important contribution. In Wiltshire, for example, the Herbert family of Wilton with the largest estate in the county made notable contributions to agricultural improvement. Farmers on their estates were encouraged to adopt new methods and advanced systems of cultivation; help was given towards the costs of enclosures, drainage, the creation of water-meadows, the planting of wind-breaks; new farm-houses and buildings were provided, and the estate prided itself upon the excellence of its labourers' cottages. As a result of these improvements, higher rents were charged to tenants, which in turn had the effect of stimulating improved and more profitable farming methods (*VCH Wilts* IV, 1959: 90–1).

The Duke of Wellington, in spite of the abuse heaped on him for his political opinions by Cobbett and others, was a benevolent landlord and ran his estate at Stratfield Saye with great vigour and efficiency, spending large sums on drainage and land improvement, and building good farmhouses, cottages, barns and stock-housing. The estate at Buscot in the north-west corner of Berkshire which belonged to Edward Lovedon was also famed for the high standard of its farming, and especially for the excellence of its dairies, with a celebrated herd of dairy shorthorn cows, and much attention paid to the breeding and housing of cattle, horses and pigs. Prize-winning colts from the Buscot stables were much sought after and commanded high prices, while Edward Lovedon had a wharf built on the Thames with warehouses where cheese from his dairies could be stored before it was sent by barge to London. Already by 1813 it was said that between two and three thousand tons of Gloucester cheese were sent annually from the wharf (Mavor 1813: 375).

One aspect of the agricultural improvements, particularly on the chalklands, was that farm sizes increased substantially. On Salisbury Plain, for example, they ranged from 800 to as high as 5,000 acres, and large farms were also common on the downlands of Berkshire and Hampshire (Caird 1852: 85, 310; Little 1844: 62). Improved farming enabled a few farmers to make great profits. One example of this was the Stratton family who during the course of the nineteenth century rose from being small dairy farmers in the Vale of Pewsey to become one of the best-known farming families in the county. They were enthusiastic 'improvers'; became noted breeders of prize-winning Dairy Shorthorn cows, and are reputed to have introduced into Wiltshire the first mowing machine, the first steam threshing machine and the first steam plough (*VCH Wilts* IV, 1959: 86–7).

Wealthy enthusiasts for agricultural advances also exerted influence through the building of model or 'example' farms. The Norfolk Farm was established at Windsor during the late eighteenth century by the ardent agriculturalist George III. During the 1850s Prince Albert rebuilt the Norfolk Farm and added two more showpieces in Windsor Great Park, the royal dairy at Frogmore an elaborate building in the Renaissance style, beautifully tiled and equipped throughout, and the Flemish farm, completed in 1858, built of brick with extensive cattle-sheds to house the royal herd of champion Herefords, and provided with all the latest implements and labour-saving devices. Among numerous other model farms was that established at Sutton Waldron between Shaftesbury and Blandford Forum in Dorset, where the farming rector, the Rev. Archdeacon Anthony Huxtable, attempted during the 1840s to provide an example of the best and most modern practices for his parishioners. In north-west Berkshire a famous experimental farm was set up by the noted agricultural pioneer and member of Parliament Philip Pusey (1799–1855). Pusey inherited an estate of 5,000 acres at Pusey in 1830. He was one of the most influential advocates of improved farming, a founder-member of the Royal Agricultural Society in 1838 and editor of its journal, interested in all branches of scientific farming and farm mechanisation, and the

Plate 7.3   Threshing Scene on Salisbury Plain, *c.*1900. The introduction of steam-power revolutionised some of the traditional farming jobs; none more so than threshing. What had been the work of a whole winter could now be accomplished in a couple of days by the peripatetic gangs which followed the threshing-machine from farm to farm. The illustration shows threshing in progress on Salisbury plain about 1900; the sacks are printed with the words Bratton, Westbury. The figure in the foreground is the rat-catcher with his dog.

man responsible for the agricultural implement section of the Great Exhibition of 1851 (Caird 1852).

At Privett on the east Hampshire chalklands near Petersfield, W. W. Nicholson of nearby Basing Park built a number of new farms during the mid-nineteenth century, constructed of brick and flint, with Welsh slate roofs, and including barns, cattle-housing and cart-sheds. He also employed Sir Arthur Blomfield to build a new church for his tenants at a cost of £22,000.

An excellent example of a model farm survives intact at East Harptree in the Chew valley, south of Bristol. The farmstead contains 1¼ acres under a single roof, with wide-span cast-iron pillars and arches, and a glass and galvanised iron roof. Within, everything from cattle-housing to threshing equipment and grain storage was provided, and power was supplied throughout the building by a water-wheel. The stream which drove the water-wheel could also be diverted to sluice out the cattle pens and bullocks' yard; the lower floors provided cattle housing, a milking parlour and dairy, while the upper floor was adapted for grain and hay storage, and the preparation of animal feedstuff. This model farmstead was the centre of a 900 acre farm, and it is still used for most of its original purposes. It was built in 1859 at a cost of £15,000, and was designed for the owner, William Taylor, by Robert Smith who had previously worked on the design of model farms at Windsor for Prince Albert.

The new agricultural methods gave birth to a large number of firms manufacturing and supplying machinery and implements. Several of these firms started as blacksmiths or farriers, gradually developing into foundries, steam-engine works or implement makers. Notable among such firms was Taskers of Andover, which was started at Abbots Ann near Andover in 1809 by Robert Tasker, a working blacksmith, and developed into the massive Waterloo Iron Works, helped by the proximity of the Andover Canal and by the growing demand from farmers for new iron ploughs, harrows, gateposts, feeding troughs and barn-machinery. The firm rapidly developed its own iron foundry, and soon began to make all kinds of wagons, pumps, prefabricated iron bridges, farm machinery and mills, later adding seed drills, threshing machines and steam engines to the long list of high-quality products (Rolt 1969).

A similar rapid development from humble beginnings can be seen in several Wiltshire firms such as Reeves of Bratton near Westbury, Brown and May of Devizes, J. W. Titt and Henry Carson of Warminster and numerous others, who produced improved iron ploughs, threshing machines, elevators and all kinds of tools, as well as steam engines (*VCH Wilts* IV, 1959: 84–5; Reeves 1978). In Somerset, Fussells of Mells became nationally famous for their edge tools, scythes, sickles, bill-hooks, reaping-hooks and hedging tools, as well as all other kinds of cutting tools for farmers. The Fussell family began producing edge-tools and other farming equipment during the 1740s; their business expanded rapidly in the river valleys around Mells where water-power was available to drive the mills and grind-stones. The most notable evidence of the former prosperity of the industry is the church at Chantry which was built for their workers in 1846 by the Fussell family to serve a new parish created out of the old parishes of Whatley, Mells and Great Elm, whose populations had been swollen by the edge-tool workers. The outside of the Fussells church at Chantry is decorated by angels, each of which carries one of the company's products – a scythe, reap-hook, bill-hook, etc. Other implement manufacturers in Somerset which developed from blacksmiths and wheel-wrights included Maggs of Wincanton, John Smith of Chard, Parsons of Martock, James Wensley of Mark, Spink and Elsey of Bridgwater and many others. In 1870 Francis Eddison established his Steam Ploughing Works just outside Dorchester, and played an important part in the ploughing up of so much of the chalk downlands which for centuries had been sacred to sheep grazing (Kerr 1968: 238–44; Buchanan and Buchanan 1980).

The most spectacular nineteenth-century farming developments were concerned with arable farming. Apart from the major and far-reaching change which came with the opportunity to send liquid milk to the towns by the railways, and the consequent decline in farm-based cheese and butter-making, advances in dairy farming were less remarkable. They did however include the almost complete substitution of Dairy Shorthorn cows for the old Longhorn breed, and a development of great importance, the introduction of a standardised Cheddar cheese. The man responsible for the widespread adoption of a standard scientific method of cheese-making in place of the old haphazard practice which depended upon the dairymaid's skill, was Joseph Harding (1805–76) who farmed at Marksbury and Compton Dando near Bath during the mid-nineteenth century. He introduced scientific methods, insisting on absolute cleanliness in the dairy, the use of the thermometer and hydrometer instead of the dairymaid's thumb and judgement. He also designed improved equipment, and recommended careful training for dairymaids. By meticulous attention to detail he was able to produce a cheese which did not vary in quality and consistency as the older products had, and through his lecture tours and his descriptions of his methods in the *Journal* of the Bath and West Society, Joseph Harding's influence had, by the time of his death in 1876, spread far beyond Somerset or the West Country, and he deserves to be remembered as the father of modern Cheddar cheese.

The Agricultural Depression

Much of the agricultural prosperity and development in the region ended abruptly and dismally with the farming depression which began in the late 1870s. A period of cold, wet summers and poor grain yields coincided with the fall in prices of both corn and cheese as imports flooded into England from the United States, Canada, Australia and elsewhere. Hardest hit by the low corn prices and poor harvests were the farmers on the chalklands who were dependent upon corn-growing for the greater part of their livelihood. Between 1870 and 1890 the acreages of wheat and barley grown throughout the chalklands of Wiltshire, Dorset, Hampshire and Berkshire shrank by more than 25 per cent as more and more land was laid down to grass. The author, Rider Haggard, who visited Dorset in 1901 to collect material for his survey of *Rural England* wrote that 'From Yeovil to Dorchester, the capital of the county of Dorset . . . it is pasture, pasture all the way, scarcely relieved by the sight of a single piece of arable'. Chalkland farmers were also hit by a sharp fall in the price of wool during the last decades of the century, and by disease which ravaged the sheep flocks. The sheep population of Dorset declined by as much as 40 per cent between 1870 and 1900, and in Wiltshire by more than 20 per cent. The decline in numbers continued, and between 1880 and 1950 the number of sheep kept in Wiltshire dropped by 90 per cent; the folding flocks were abandoned, and the water-meadows were allowed to go out of use. Wheat which in 1847 had sold at 70 shillings per quarter had already fallen by 1870 to 46 shillings, and by 1894 was down to 24 shillings a quarter. Dairy farmers were also badly affected by the run of cold, wet summers, poor hay

259

Plate 7.4 Wessex Saddleback pig. Pig breeds were not standardised until the nineteenth century, when selective breeding and crosses with various foreign strains brought about a vast improvement in English pigs. The Wessex Saddleback, based on the hardy, black pig of the Hampshire forest area, became very popular throughout the Wessex region. It grew rapidly and fattened easily, and it was admirably suited to the needs of dairy-farmers engaged in cheese-making who could use the whey for pig-feeding.

crops, cattle disease, and above all by the influx of cheap American cheese to the English markets.

Landlords were also badly affected by the inability of their tenants to pay an economic rent during the slump and by the difficulty of finding tenants willing to take farms at all. In 1895 the Royal Commission enquiring into Agricultural Distress reported of Dorset that 'Ownership of agricultural land is rapidly becoming a luxury which only men possessing other sources of income can enjoy'. The effects can be seen in the rent-roll of the estates of the Earl of Pembroke in Wiltshire. In 1874 the net annual income was £11,138; by 1890 it was down to £4,907; and in 1896 there was a loss of £2,122 (*VCH Wilts* IV, 1959: 104). During the 1890s Lord Wantage who was the largest landowner in Berkshire, with an estate of 20,500 acres or about one-twentieth of the whole county, was obliged to take some 13,000 acres in hand to farm himself during the depression for want of suitable tenants (Havinden 1966). The scale and intensity of the depression and the farming changes which it brought can also

Table 27   The impact of the agricultural depression, 1875–1913

(a) Acreage under crops and temporary grass

County	1875	1898	1913
Berkshire	366,908	366,303	349,078
Dorset	471,068	482,417	477,413
Hampshire	696,768	715,406	676,731
Somerset	825,628	856,631	848,911
Wiltshire	739,381	736,430	706,240

(b) Acreage of permanent pasture

County	1875	1898	1913
Berkshire	111,096	165,653	172,739
Dorset	231,759	297,977	315,161
Hampshire	163,788	277,077	285,800
Somerset	536,654	651,070	684,587
Wiltshire	310,722	421,293	444,175

(c) Numbers of cattle, sheep and pigs

County		1875	1898	1913
Berks	Cattle	37,147	43,564	49,990
	Sheep	307,481	173,918	128,815
	Pigs	41,421	25,349	18,294
Dorset	Cattle	77,372	86,380	93,947
	Sheep	524,297	365,310	292,973
	Pigs	42,009	57,175	46,478
Hampshire	Cattle	62,658	84,344	91,730
	Sheep	612,889	388,706	293,143
	Pigs	71,882	68,118	56,260
Somerset	Cattle	210,960	229,722	237,032
	Sheep	743,813	538,225	400,929
	Pigs	91,894	124,277	98,981
Wiltshire	Cattle	92,052	111,568	123,001
	Sheep	765,265	513,729	392,155
	Pigs	65,476	66,257	48,993

(Sources: *Parliamentary Papers* 1875, lxxix; 1899, C9304; 1914, xcviii)

be seen from Table 27, which reveals the decline in arable, the increase in the acreage of permanent pasture, the growth in the number of milking cows and beef cattle, and the rapid fall in the size of the sheep flocks and in the number of pigs kept in each county. The tables also show that the changes were most marked between 1875 and 1898, and that by 1913 some slight recovery is already apparent.

The Conditions of the Agricultural Labourers and the 'Swing Riots'

The ending of the Napoleonic War in 1815 and the consequent recession in agriculture led to a sharp reduction in the wages of farm labourers and to appalling hardship, poverty and misery among their families. This was especially marked in the corn-growing regions where there was little alternative employment and labourers were completely dependent upon their employers. The counties of Berkshire, Dorset, Hampshire and Wiltshire became notorious for the low wages, poor housing and miserable conditions of farm labourers. Average weekly wage-rates on the chalklands of Wiltshire during the winter months in the period 1770–1830 were as follows:

1770	5s. 0d.
1794	6s. 0d.
1804	8s. 0d.
1814	12s. 0d.
1817	8s. 0d.
1823	7s. 0d.
1830	7s. 0d.

(*VCH Wilts* IV, 1959: 81)

One effect of wages which barely enabled families to exist was that increasingly farm labourers were compelled to rely on relief from the poor rates, a process which produced a degraded, helpless and hopeless workforce, and which in the words of the authors of the definitive study of the Labourers' Revolt of 1830, began 'the transformation of the poor into forelock-pulling charity receivers' (Hobsbawm and Rudé 1969: 293). The contrast between the excellence of the well-stocked, productive farms with comfortable farmhouses and substantial buildings, and the wretched conditions of the poorly paid, ill-housed and inadequately fed labourers impressed many contemporary observers, notably William Cobbett. In 1826 during his *Rural Rides* through Wiltshire Cobbett wrote scathingly of the conditions of the labourers; in the valley of the Avon from near Marlborough to Salisbury he observed:

> In taking my leave of this beautiful vale, I have to express my deep shame as an Englishman, at beholding the general *extreme poverty* of

those who cause this vale to produce such quantities of food and raiment. This is, I verily believe it, *the worst used labouring people upon the face of the earth.* Dogs and hogs and horses are treated with more civility; and as to food and lodging, how gladly would the labourers change with them!

(Cobbett 1912, II: 55, 67)

In 1813, before the worst of the distress had begun and while wages were still comparatively high, William Mavor wrote that the 'decent pride' of the labourers of Berkshire had been wholly lost, and that their cottages consisted of

ragged thatch, broken tiles, floor of earth, and walls brown from smoke, and only one bedchamber for his numerous family.

(Mavor 1813: 50; Satre 1978)

It was the combination of low wages, poor conditions, unemployment together with the bad winters and poor harvests of 1829 and 1830 that finally led to the great explosion of anger and frustration through the corn-lands of the region, the 'Captain Swing' riots of November 1830. The riots have been described and analysed in great detail which need not be repeated here (Hobsbawm and Rudé 1969). This is not to underestimate the scale or importance of the events, however, for although the period of actual rioting was so brief, lasting for less than a fortnight, the impact upon the whole Wessex region was dramatic, providing a rare glimpse of the feelings of that large but hidden section of rural society which seldom figures in official records, county directories, manorial surveys, landownership returns or taxation and voting lists, and of those whose names appear only in the parish registers of baptisms, marriages and burials or as recipients of poor relief. In several parts of the region the riots, machine-breaking or other forms of violence or intimidation were preceded by threatening letters allegedly from the mythical 'Captain Swing' whose name gave a unity to the whole movement, or were foreshadowed by arson and rick-burning. For example on 10 November 1830 Swing letters were received by farmers in the Portsmouth area and at Holyport near Maidenhead in Berkshire warning against the use of threshing machines and threatening arson and violence. A few days later similar letters were received by farmers at Exton in east Hampshire and at Bray and Windsor in Berkshire. Such letters with their threats of the awful vengeance to follow were very frightening to isolated landowners and farmers who were almost entirely reliant on their own resources for defence, and the letters were especially common in the traditionally unruly, lawless forest areas such as Windsor forest or Cranborne Chase. For example, a letter to the Wimborne (Dorset) landowner Edward Castleman uncompromisingly declared:

Sunday night your house shall come down to the Ground, for you are an inhuman monster and we will dash out your brains – Banks and your sett ought to be sent to Hell. The Hanley Torches have not forgot you.

The 'Hanley Torches' were presumably from Sixpenny Handley on the Dorset–Wiltshire border which was later to be described by one of the local justices as

a singular place [with] a wild dissolute population of poachers, smugglers and deer stealers . . . from whence our principal rioters have issued.
(Parry Okeden 1930)

The popular novelist, Mary Mitford, who lived at Three Mile Cross, a village on the turnpike road between Reading and Basingstoke, on the Hampshire/Berkshire border, recorded the terror she felt at the rick burnings, the fires

breaking forth night after night, sudden yet expected, always seeming nearer than they actually were . . .

She wrote also of her fear of the gangs of labourers roaming the countryside, their visits to lonely farms and the inadequacy of the forces of law and order to cope with the situation (Mitford 1832, Vol 5: 6–9). From mid-November 1830 outbreaks of arson, rioting and machine-breaking became increasingly common, and spread rapidly through the region. The Duke of Wellington's estate at Stratfield Saye was attacked by fire-raisers on 15 November, and on 16 November fires were started at St Nicholas Hurst and elsewhere in Berkshire so that farmers in the Windsor Forest area were led to offer rewards for the conviction of incendiaries and a *Forest Association* was formed at Wokingham to combat arson. On 15 November also the first serious riot in the region occurred. This was at the village of Thatcham east of Newbury where the labourers assembled and marched from farm to farm to demand higher wages and money for food and drink. The riots spread to neighbouring villages and several threshing machines were destroyed. The hatred and violence of the labourers was focused upon threshing machines which they saw as depriving them of their traditional winter work.

By 17–18 November there were riots, demands for higher wages, machine-breaking and intimidation in many parts of Berkshire and Hampshire, in the Thatcham area, around Aldermaston, at Wasing, Shalford, Brimpton and at Speen in Berkshire; around Petersfield, Havant, Overton, Micheldever, Basingstoke, Winchester and elsewhere in Hampshire; by 19 November disturbances had reached Andover, Alresford and Stockbridge and

Plate 7.5 Milking-gang, Bratton, Wiltshire. The laborious and time-consuming tasks of twice-daily milking continued unchanged until the coming of electricity and the modern milking-machine. This gang of milkers worked in the same way and at the same speed as their medieval predecessors. Note the traditional west-country smocks, the three-legged milking stools and the one-handled pails. Here some shelter is provided for cows and milkers but many cows continued to be milked in the fields in all weathers.

riots had begun in Wiltshire with a labourers' rising at Wilcot near Marlborough. Thereafter the movement spread rapidly across the Wiltshire corn-growing areas of the Marlborough Downs and Salisbury Plain. By 23 November when the riots in Wiltshire were at their most widespread, 25 towns and villages were affected in the county. On 25 November a pitched battle occurred at Pyt House near Tisbury between some 400 labourers and a troop of yeomanry which had been sent from Hindon to disperse them. Pyt House was the elegant home of John Bennett who had a large estate in the Wardour vale and who was one of the county members of Parliament. Bennett had taken a hard line over the labourers' grievances, and was alleged to have said that

> 8s 0d per week is sufficient to maintain a man, his wife and family on barley bread and potatoes, which is good enough for them.

Although he later denied this statement, he was clearly not thought of as a friend by the labourers, who set out armed with bludgeons and crowbars to destroy his threshing machines and to demand higher wages. Bennett summoned a troop of yeoman cavalry from Hindon some three miles away, and when they arrived a pitched battle occurred in the woods surrounding Pyt House. One labourer, John Hardy of Tisbury, was shot dead, several others were wounded, and twenty-five arrests were made. In Wiltshire, as elsewhere, the riots were in the arable, low-wage areas, where employment prospects during the winter were bleak, 'chalk was riotous, cheese was tranquil'.

The disturbances in Dorset occurred slightly later than those in Berkshire, Hampshire and Wiltshire, and the fact that the fiercest discontent of labourers was felt in the corn-growing, chalkland areas can be seen very clearly in the county, since the riots were almost entirely confined to the arable parts, while the pastoral vales of west Dorset, an area of small dairy farms largely worked by family farmers, was virtually untouched by the disturbances. Frenzied activity by the county magistrates in Dorset with great numbers of special constables sworn in, the yeomanry and coast-guards employed to help, as well as some concessions and agreements to raise wages, quietened the rioters and peace was restored by the end of November. Somerset was much less affected by the Swing riots. As in west Dorset, much of the land was given over to dairy farming or stock-rearing, while the textile industries provided some alternative work and by-employment. There were, however, some disturbances in the Frome area along the Wiltshire border, and at Banwell in north Somerset where there was a riot by the paupers in the village poor-house and prisoners were released from the lock-up. For the most part the Swing riots in Wessex consisted of arson, the breaking of threshing machines and demands for a moderate increase in wages. There were, however, a few spectacular confrontations such as the battle at Pyt House, and a few other major incidents. Notable among these were the attacks on foundries and agricultural implement-makers at Fordingbridge, Hungerford, Wantage and elsewhere, including most notably of all the attack on Tasker's Waterloo Works at Upper Clatford near Andover on 20 November 1830 (Rolt 1969: 41–54). The labourers' loathing of the Poor Law system was shown at Selborne and Headley in east Hampshire on 22 and 23 November when they systematically destroyed the Poor Houses of both parishes. Perhaps the most spectacular attack was on the very large sawmills belonging to Charles Baker near the centre of Southampton, the major part of which was set alight and went up in flames on the night of 23–4 November, destroying timber, saws and machinery estimated to be worth £7,000. In Berkshire on 22 and 23 November there were riots at Hungerford and the neighbouring villages, including major and well-organised outbreaks at Kintbury and at Inkpen, Hampstead Marshall and West Woodhay. Later there were riots at Lambourn and across the Berkshire Downs, accompanied by the breaking of threshing machines; so severe were the riots and so numerous were the rioters that at Hungerford the magistrates agreed to meet the labourers' delegates at the Town Hall and discuss their grievances, and were persuaded to agree to a weekly wage of 12*s*. 0*d*. and an immediate payment of £5 to send the rioters away.

By early December 1830 the Captain Swing riots, the last great revolt of the farm labourers of Wessex, had run their course, and the authorities regained control through special constables, the yeomanry and the militia. The seriousness of the outbreak of rioting and the relative scale in each county, with the destruction caused can be seen from Table 28.

Table 28   The Swing Riots

County	No. of incidents	Fires started	No. of threshing machines and other agricultural machines broken
Berkshire	165	13	78
Dorset	42	12	10
Hampshire	208	15	52
Somerset	15	2	3
Wiltshire	208	18	97

(Source: Hobsbawm and Rudé 1969: 304–5)

After the riots came the retribution. Special commissions to try the rioters sat in Berkshire, Dorset, Hampshire and Wiltshire, and in a conscious endeavour to deter others and to squash any future risings, very harsh sentences were imposed, especially by the first Special Commission which opened at Winchester on 18 December 1830. The number of prisoners and the sentences imposed are summarised in Table 29.

Table 29   Trials of the Swing Rioters

County	No. of prisoners tried	Acquitted	Fined	Whipped	Jailed	Sentenced to death	Executed	Sentenced to transportation
Berkshire	162	41	—	—	78	27	1	45
Dorset	62	33	—	1	15	6	—	13
Hampshire	298	108	2	—	68	101	3	117
Somerset	40	26	—	—	13	—	—	1
Wiltshire	339	139	—	—	47	52	1	152

(Source: Hobsbawm and Rudé 1969: 308–9)

Across the whole of the Wessex chalklands, from Wantage to Weymouth, there were few villages unaffected by the Swing riots or by the savage way in which they were suppressed, and the bitter memory of these events long remained in the minds of labourers and their families. W. H. Hudson in *A Shepherd's Life* has described how the details of the harsh repression and terrible punishment were still fresh in the villages of Salisbury

Plain at the end of the nineteenth century (Hudson 1936: 144–5). To the ruling classes of the region the ferocity of the labourers' protest and the strength of the demand for a living wage had come as a great shock, and the suppression of the revolt and the harsh punishments meted out to the prisoners were a great relief. Their attitude was well expressed by Mary Frampton, sister of James Frampton of Moreton in Dorset, one of the most active and unpopular of the county magistrates, whose house and property had on several occasions been threatened by the rioters. When a petition was presented to the King for a reduction in the sentences of the thirteen Dorset men sentenced to transportation, Mary Frampton wrote in her journal:

> Fortunately . . . as they were already on board the transports and the
> wind fair, the petition would be too late. Care was taken at the
> deportation of these men . . . to send them to those parts of New Zealand
> and New Holland where their agricultural knowledge and labour might
> be useful. Thus very probably at a future time rendering our
> disturbances here a blessing to our Antipodes.
>
> (Parry Okeden 1930)

It was the recent memory of the Swing riots that led James Frampton, the Dorset county magistrate principally concerned with the Piddle valley and a man now even more passionately devoted to maintaining law and order, to react so violently to the attempt of some labourers to set up a Friendly Society of Agricultural Labourers at Tolpuddle in 1833 and 1834. His reaction was to create the Tolpuddle Martyrs whose trial in Dorchester, transportation and the public outcry which it roused – a protest which was eventually successful in getting the six Tolpuddle labourers brought back to England – had the incidental effect of creating a group of folk heroes in a way which, oddly, had not happened to individual participants in the Swing riots in spite of the courage which many showed, the heroism of their futile protests and the harshness of the sentences which were imposed on them (Horn 1976: 126).

The Bristol Riots

The difficult political and economic conditions of the 1820s and early 1830s produced other riots and upheavals in the region although they were less widespread than the Swing riots. There were periodic violent protests among the weavers and clothworkers of west Wiltshire and east Somerset who were badly affected by the decline in trade after the ending of the Napoleonic War and because of the introduction of machinery, and it was only by chance that a rising of cloth-workers early in 1830 caused by depressed trade and a reduction in wages did not coincide with the Swing riots. The Bristol riots occurred in October 1831, a spectacular expression of political discontent and frustration about various local issues, including economic difficulties in the city and port of Bristol, the loss of commerce to London and Liverpool, the decay of the West India trade, low wages and unemployment. The actual riots were sparked off by the acrimonious debate over parliamentary reform during the autumn of 1831 and the rejection of the Reform Bill by the House of Lords; the Bishops of Bristol and of Bath and Wells had both voted against reform. The Recorder of Bristol, Sir Charles Wetherell, MP, had also been an active campaigner against parliamentary reform. When therefore Wetherell arrived in Bristol on 29 October 1831 to open the Assizes, he was greeted by an angry mob; without an effective police force, and with insufficient and badly led troops, the tumult was allowed to develop rapidly until it became a full-scale riot.

The Bristol Riots lasted from Saturday, 29 October until Monday, 31 October; the city gaol was stormed and the prisoners released, the Mansion House was invaded and its cellars looted, the Bishop of Bristol's palace was attacked, ransacked and destroyed. Ecclesiastical records were burnt, furniture and valuables were plundered; the Mansion House and the Custom House in Queen's Square were set on fire, and many rioters were too drunk on looted wine to escape from the flames. People poured into central Bristol from many miles around to join in the plunder and looting. Only on Monday, 31 October when troops arrived from Gloucester, Bath and Keynsham were the riots suppressed. The whole incident was unparalleled in the history of Bristol or of any other west-country town; it blew up so quickly and developed so rapidly that the authorities were quite unprepared to cope with the ferocity and number of the rioters. Eventually eighty-one rioters were convicted and four were hanged. Lieutenant-Colonel Brereton, an officer who had served in the Napoleonic War and who by 1831 had been given the apparently undemanding job of commanding the small number of troops in the Bristol district had failed to recognise the gravity of the situation in time, and had not employed his troops effectively against the rioters. He committed suicide before he could be sentenced by a court-martial.

Labourers, Rural Conditions and the Treatment of the Poor

The small increases in wages which were secured by the farm labourers in 1830 did not last for long, and for much of the rest of the nineteenth century many farm labourers, especially those on the large, corn-growing farms of the

Plate 7.6   Farm labourer and his wife, *c.* 1900. The photograph shows Ambrose Matthews and his wife from Bratton in Wiltshire. He is wearing a smock-frock, the traditional working dress of west-country farm labourers, together with corduroy trousers and billycock hat. His wife is wearing the typical working dress of sun-bonnet, a black bodice and skirt, covered by an apron. The smock shown here could be opened in front, which was useful for milking and other general farm work. Carters wore shorter smocks, while for tending sheep on the windswept downlands, shepherds had longer smocks closed in front. Many shepherds also wore a long woollen cloak. Aubrey describes the seventeenth-century Wiltshire shepherds wearing 'a long white cloake with a very deep cape, which comes half-way down their backs, made of the locks of the sheep'.

chalklands, remained ill-paid, badly fed and inadequately housed. There were of course many exceptions to this generalisation, and numerous model villages existed, as well as good estate and farm cottages, and benevolent employers, but the evidence of independent observers, royal commissions and parliamentary reports is overwhelming that low wages and bad housing remained commonplace throughout the whole of Wessex. The new Poor Law of 1834, with its system of grim union workhouses, failed to eliminate poverty, and the labourers and their families continued to exist on a tightrope between destitution and subsistence, especially in the arable areas where the demand for labour fluctuated with the seasons and was subject to the caprice of the weather. The old problem of seasonal unemployment remained unchanged. In 1833 the Select Committee on Agriculture in Berkshire and Wiltshire was told that

> It is the surplus labourers that are suffering, of which there are many in almost every parish, and these men are very badly off . . . . There are no surplus labourers generally speaking in the summer, (but unemployment) . . . commences very soon after harvest, and they remain in that state till the Spring work comes in . . . .
>
> (Quoted by Gash 1935: 90–3)

The evidence presented to the Commission appointed by Parliament to enquire into *The Employment of Women and Children in Agriculture* in 1843 (Parliamentary Papers 1843, xii), provides abundant evidence about rural conditions in all parts of Wessex. One witness was Rachel Hayward, wife of John Hayward, a farm labourer of Stourpaine in Dorset. She gave evidence about the appallingly crowded conditions in which the family lived, as well as about their meagre, monotonous diet:

> There are eleven of us in our family – myself, my husband, three daughters and six sons. We have two rooms, one down stairs and the other up stairs over it. We all sleep in the bedroom. My husband gets 8s or 7s a week; my two eldest daughters get about 3s 6d a week at buttoning, and three of my boys get 5s a week together; in all about 16s 6d a week. We have 16½ lugs of potato-ground on which we grow potatoes and a few vegetables; for that we pay 7s 7d a year rent. We pay 1s a week for the cottage, and coal and wood cost us 1s 8d a week at this time of year (December). We get ¾ cwt of coal a week. I buy besides, every week ¾lb soap, 1oz tea, ½lb bacon. I reckon we eat a pound of bread each day; that with the potatoes gives us enough. My three boys that are out at work went out at nine years old.

This family was evidently greatly helped by the daughters' by-employment of button-making which was very common in that part of Dorset, and by their

271

potato-ground. Some farmers allowed their labourers to have small plots of ground to grow potatoes without charging them any rent. This was very useful to the families, but it was not always total benevolence on the part of the farmers, since it meant that during the summer and autumn, while alternative employment was available elsewhere, the labourer and his family were unlikely to leave the farm, since they would then lose their potato crop. The poor-quality, monotonous diet inevitably affected the labourers' vigour and power of initiative. Richard Jefferies, who wrote with such intimate knowledge of Wiltshire farming and farm labourers in his classic work *Hodge and his Masters*, attributed the slowness and lack of energy of the labourers to their poor diet. In a letter to *The Times* in 1872 Jefferies wrote of the Wiltshire labourer that his diet was mainly bread and cheese, and that 'His food may, perhaps, have something to do with the deadened slowness which seems to pervade everything he does – there seems a lack of vitality about him.'

In 1867 a parliamentary commission was appointed to enquire into the 'Employment of Children and Young Persons and Women in Agriculture'. This also produced a mass of evidence about the domestic and daily life of working people, and on housing conditions, and one of the commissioners, the Hon. E. Stanhope, reported of Dorset that

> the cottages of this county are more ruinous and contain worse accommodation than those of any other county I have visited, except Shropshire; . . . The estates of Lord Rivers, . . . is notorious for its bad cottages. And such villages as Bere Regis, Fordington, Winfrith, Cranborne, or Charminster (in which there is an average of 7 persons to a house) . . . are a disgrace to the owners of the land, and contain many cottages unfit for human habitation.

Stanhope also commented upon the neglect in the villages of the most elementary sanitary precautions. 'In village after village the answer was "there is nothing like one privy to every cottage". I saw whole rows of cottages with none, and abounding with nuisances of all kinds. Remonstrance is generally disregarded, and the state of filth, in which many parishes are left, calls aloud for some active interference to relieve the present authorities of a responsibility they have grossly neglected.' The effect of this absence of even the most rudimentary sanitary arrangements for many labourers' cottages, coupled with the overcrowded conditions, lack of adequate ventilation and the dampness of many of the dwellings, inevitably led to rheumatism, tuberculosis, bronchitis and many other diseases. The mid-nineteenth-century Bristol surveyor and land-agent, William Sturge, who was as familiar with the slums of Bristol as with the villages of north Somerset, was in no doubt that conditions in the villages were often worse than those in the towns, and that because of the bad drainage, overcrowding and general filth, 'A country village is in consequence often far more unhealthy than the town.'

Some of the large estates had been active in improving the housing-conditions for their workers, and the new estate cottages of the mid-nineteenth century, with their typical architectural features, high gables, elaborate decoration and 'rustic' character, and all built to the same plan, are to be seen in many villages and hamlets throughout the region. William Cobbett had, for example, been struck by the appearance of Erlestoke in Wiltshire in 1826:

> I came to a hamlet called Earl's Stoke, the houses of which stand at a few yards from each other, on the two sides of the road; every house is white; and the front of every one is covered with some sort of clematis, or with rose-trees or jasmines. It was easy to guess that the whole belonged to one owner . . .

But the Parliamentary Report of 1867, which has already been quoted, makes it clear that the labourers' houses in a great many villages remained unaffected by any 'improvement', and that conditions in many of them were appalling, even though many no doubt looked 'picturesque' enough from the exterior and to the casual observer. At Cerne Abbas, for example, the parliamentary commissioners found that the cottages were

> Very poor: most of them are thatched. There is scarcely one with three bedrooms; most have two, but the separation is often very indifferent indeed. Rooms in most cases very low, hardly six feet, and the windows are very often not made to open. In these cottages the sanitary arrangements were very bad, one privy often serving five or six cottages.

Some improvements were noted by the commissioners, particularly in villages belonging to large estates. For example, at Wimborne St Giles the Earl of Shaftesbury had rebuilt the cottages which were said to be excellent, and at Cranborne Lord Salisbury had greatly improved some of the cottages though some which were let by copyhold tenure for life remained very bad. Generally the housing conditions for labourers throughout the chalkland region were found to be deplorable. The situation was somewhat better in Somerset, and throughout the claylands, where there were more small, family farms and where dairy-farming provided a very different kind of agricultural environment. Moreover in north Somerset and the Mendip area the proximity of Bristol and the existence of alternative forms of employment in coal and lead mining or in the cloth trade served to keep wages at a higher level. At Clevedon, for example, where work was available in the rapidly growing resort, Sir Arthur Elton of Clevedon Court had built several new, improved cottages on his estate, but his land-agent stated that this had done little to

Plate 7.7 Sheep-shearing, *c.* 1895. The very large flocks of sheep which were kept on the chalklands meant that the annual sheep-shearing on most farms was a long and arduous task. Often it was undertaken by contract gangs of highly skilled men who could work very rapidly. The illustration shows a shearing gang from Chitterne in Wiltshire. Note the large number of men employed, the variety of head-gear, and the supply of drink for refreshment. The women rolled and packed the shorn fleeces.

relieve overcrowding since 'people who have a good cottage with three bedrooms will often take in as many as eight lodgers, and herd with their families in the kitchen'.

Few labourers with families were able to save enough to maintain themselves in old age, and the grim prospect of the workhouse was a constant sombre threat in the background of their lives, a threat which is easily recoverable from the numerous stern, forbidding and solidly built workhouses which survive as abiding monuments to the nineteenth-century method of dealing with the problem of poverty. The efforts which were made to deter paupers from applying for relief by making the conditions in the workhouses unattractive were occasionally only too successful. In October 1841 William Adler of Donnington just outside Newbury, who had been ill all the previous summer and whose requests for relief for himself and his family had been refused unless they entered the workhouse, was found dead, and an enquiry found that he had died from starvation rather than submit to the indignities of the workhouse. In certain workhouses, like that at Andover during the 1830s and 1840s, the cruelty and unfeeling treatment of the paupers by the master and matron could make life unbearable for the inmates. At Andover the paupers were kept so short of food that some of them were reduced to gnawing the gristle from the old, decayed bones which they had been set to crush for fertiliser. Savage punishments, beatings and other ill-treatment of the paupers by the brutal master were commonplace. When the conditions were publicised by *The Times* in 1845 and 1846 public opinion was deeply shocked, and reforms were introduced, although once the publicity had subsided the conditions in the Andover workhouse deteriorated once more (Longmate 1974: 199–35).

Attempts to alleviate their lot by the labourers themselves ranged from Chartism to Trade Unionism, and from the Temperance Movement and the Friendly Societies to the many nonconformist sects, notably the Primitive Methodists. Robert Owen founded his *Harmony Hall* at West Tytherley between Salisbury and Winchester in 1841, where 100 adults and 40 children were to live a rational, ordered life together. Friendly Societies which provided money for members who were ill and paid for their funeral when they died, and whose annual feasts and processions were one of the major events in village life, became very popular and widespread. In 1801, for example, there were 123 Friendly Societies in Somerset and 30 in Wiltshire; by 1855 there were 565 in Somerset and 271 in Wiltshire (Fuller 1964). Increasingly the larger national societies such as the Oddfellows and the Foresters replaced the local societies, with great rivalry and competition for members, so that by the end of the century towns and larger villages often had several competing benefit clubs. Corsley near Warminster was not unusual in having seven societies – the Ancient Shepherds, Working Men's Benefit Society, Hearts of Oak, Oddfellows, Foresters, Corsley Gathering Club, and Corsley Mutual Provident Society or Baptists Club (Davies 1909: 250–5, 277).

Churches and Church Life during the Nineteenth Century

The central theme running through the history of all denominations in the region during this period is of expansion and development: new churches and chapels, the restoration of ancient parish churches and a massive growth in activity and concern which would have amazed most of the eighteenth-century clergy. At the beginning of the nineteenth century the Church of England was ill-equipped to cope with the rapidly growing population and the developing towns of the region. The organisation of the Church and its framework of dioceses and parishes was best suited to a predominantly rural society and only slowly was it adapted to cater for the new towns. Even where enough churches existed it was not always possible for newcomers to secure a seat, since many pews in both the established and the nonconformist churches were rented and were regarded as private property by those who had paid for the right to sit in them, and often had rebuilt, decorated and adorned them to their own taste. Joseph Leech, the editor of a Bristol newspaper, published a long series of articles on local churches during the 1840s under the name 'Churchgoer', and wrote in 1847 that

> every pew is like a preserve: you must not put your hand on the first door you meet, for if this green cloth lining, these soft cushions, these rich carpets, these mohair hassocks, these morocco-bound, gilt-edged Prayer Books and Bibles lying about, be not sufficient to protect the seat from rash intrusion, you must be very dull or very daring indeed . . .

When Leech visited Yatton church he could not find a vacant pew and was obliged to sit with the poor on a bench at the back of the church. It was so unusual to see a well-dressed man occupying such a seat that

> even the school children who, headed by the master carrying a music book in his hand, entered in a long file . . . and . . . came pat, pat, clatter in their wooden shoes up the aisles, immediately descried the stranger, and looked over their snub noses at me as if I had two heads.

Likewise in 1851 Blagdon parish church was described as

> full of great pews which it requires a person of considerable stature to peep over; and not content with this wooden defence from observation, the clergyman and some others have further enclosed themselves with thick curtains.
> (Dunning 1976: 78–9)

To rent a pew was a mark of gentility and affluence for which the 'respectable' were willing to pay dearly, and this provided a valuable source of income to the churches. A Southampton auctioneer told the Parish Vestry at All Saints in 1845 that he was obliged to pay a high rent for his house because a pew in the church went with it, but that as he was a dissenter he had been able to let the pew at a profit. At St Mary's, Southampton in 1845 one man was said to let his family pew for £10 a year, while he and his family sat in one of the free pews which had been provided when the church was enlarged in 1834. The problem of private pews continued throughout the century. A particularly fierce and protracted dispute occurred at Warminster over the pew maintained in the parish church since the seventeenth century by the Halliday family who, in spite of being dissenters, insisted that the right to the pew was their freehold property. At the restoration of the church during the 1880s the pew was removed, but J. E. Halliday began an action against the vicar which he finally won in the House of Lords in 1891, and the pew was replaced. This created great ill-feeling in the town and the pew was taken from the church at night and smashed; it was replaced under police escort and remained in its position in the south chancel aisle until Halliday died in 1913 when it was finally surrendered (*VCH Wilts* VIII, 1965: 120–1).

In 1836 the diocesan organisation of the region was changed. The dioceses of Bristol and Gloucester were united, and the county of Dorset which since the Reformation had been part of the Bristol diocese, was restored to the diocese of Salisbury. In 1897 the bishopric and diocese of Bristol was re-founded, now consisting of the Bristol itself with the southern part of Gloucestershire and a large area of north Wiltshire including Swindon.

Throughout the whole of Wessex the Church of England made valiant efforts to build new churches and restore the old so as to accommodate more people, and enormous sums of money were raised for this purpose. Even so, rapid increases in population and changes in its distribution meant that in many places only a small proportion of the population could be accommodated in the parish churches. The population of Frome in 1801 was 8,747 and by 1821 it had grown to 12,411, but there was still only one parish church, with seats for 800 people. Not until 1844 was a new church, Christchurch, built, and even then only a fifth of the town could find room in the two churches. In Southampton the population of St Mary's parish rose from 4,708 in 1821 to 14,885 by 1841, much of the increase coming from the growth of working-class suburbs, yet until St Mary's church was enlarged in 1834 it could accommodate only 650 people, and not until 1848 was the parish divided by the creation of Holy Trinity, with a new church. To make matters worse, the rector of St Mary's, the Reverend Earl of Guilford, was a notorious pluralist and absentee, who seldom appeared in Southampton and left the conduct of the parish to a curate; St Mary's was in the gift of the Bishop of Winchester, and in 1797 the Bishop bestowed it on his son, the Earl, who held it until 1850. For nearly the whole of that period he held the living together with several others in plurality and with the Mastership of the Hospital of St Cross in Winchester (Temple Patterson I, 1966: 113; II, 1971: 26–7, 65–7). Similar problems of pluralism and non-residence of the clergy affected many places during the early decades of the century. When Augustus Hare was rector of Alton Barnes in the vale of Pewsey during the 1830s he recorded that at the adjacent church of Alton Priors

> only once in three weeks did a clergyman from a distance come to perform service in the church, and in the intermediate time no notice was taken of the parishioners.
>
> (Hare 1872 I: 296)

W. H. Hudson in his classic account of life on the downlands of south Wiltshire gives a graphic illustration of the neglect of parish churches and the infrequency of services in his story of the little church at Tytherington in the Wylye valley. There was only one service a quarter, and a small terrier belonging to a farmer's wife, followed its mistress to one of the services and was locked in the church. Not until three months later was the door opened again, and the dog found, in a pitiful condition but still alive because it had been able to lick the moisture which streamed down the walls of the church (Hudson 1910: 110–11).

In all parts of the region the number of new churches built and of old churches restored was impressive. In Hampshire, for example, between 1832 and 1864 there were 82 new churches built; in Wiltshire between 1837 and 1887, 32 churches were enlarged, 98 were restored, 51 rebuilt and 45 completely new churches were erected. In Dorset during the period 1840–76 there were 233 parish churches of which 158 had more than £500 each spent on them, and many had several thousand pounds spent in lavish restorations and rebuilding. One example out of many of individual generosity and zeal for church building was Mary Caroline, Marchioness of Ailesbury, who lived at Tottenham House in Savernake Forest from 1837 to 1879 and was largely responsible for rebuilding or restoring nearly all the parish churches in that part of Wiltshire, as well as for the construction of four new churches, including the grandiose St Katherine's church, built for the Savernake estate workers in 1861 to a design by T. H. Wyatt. So thorough were many restorations that they involved the virtual demolition and rebuilding of the churches, regardless of the antiquity or architectural interest of the original structure. A contemporary illustration of the 'restoration' of Broadwindsor church in west Dorset in 1868 shows that only the tower was left standing and that the walls were almost entirely rebuilt. The notable Saxon church of Lady St Mary at Wareham was completely demolished and rebuilt in 1840. There were many other similar examples of unnecessary demolition or over-zealous restoration. Furnishings not in accord with the restorers' conception of 'correctness' were also ruthlessly removed. Only in the few churches which escaped the attention of the restorers, such as Cameley near Bristol, Old Dilton near Westbury in Wiltshire or Minstead in the New Forest, is it possible to see the sort of richness and interest which was a common feature of the pre-Victorian parish church.

Likewise, the influence of the Evangelical and Tractarian movements within the Church of England, although they had the effect of improving the services, singing, sermons and congregational participation, also destroyed one of the most attractive features of Wessex church life, the village bands or groups of church musicians and singers which had for long accompanied the services. They were gradually superseded, at first by barrel-organs and harmoniums, and later by the organ which appealed particularly to those who wanted 'seemliness' and 'decency' in the services. An example of the way in which the village musicians were replaced can be seen from the churchwardens' accounts of Crewkerne in Somerset. Throughout the eighteenth and early nineteenth centuries there are occasional references in the accounts to small sums being spent on the musical instruments, a violin, bass viol and bassoon. This continued until 1823 when the curate, Dr Robert Ashe, presented the church with a new London-made organ. The musicians' services were immediately dispensed with, and an organist was employed at a salary of £25 *per annum* together with an organ-blower at £2 *per annum*. At Purton in Wiltshire, where music for the services had been supplied by village musicians playing flutes and viols in the west gallery, an organ was acquired in 1851, whereupon all the musicians left the church.

The rapid growth in the number of nonconformist churches meant that even small rural communities possessed three or four different places of worship in addition to the parish church. In the provision of education, the encouragement of charities, friendly societies, temperance movements, social diversions and missionary activities, these many different churches had a profound effect upon the lives and attitudes of all classes of society. To take only one example, the north Somerset village of Chew Magna in 1851 had a population of 2,124 people, and for any one of these who wished to attend religious worship there was a choice of seven different establishments – two Church of England churches, a Wesleyan Methodist chapel, a Wesleyan Reform chapel, a meeting house of the Society of Friends, a Baptist chapel and a preaching room of the Brethren. All except the last of these churches ran a Sunday school and provided some general education in addition to their religious services and all were active in charitable and missionary work. Besides the churches and the Friendly Societies, some individuals were also active in charitable and educational work, most notably the two remarkable sisters Hannah and Martha More who devoted themselves to spreading Christianity and education among the lead miners of Mendip, the glass-workers and coal miners of Nailsea and other groups of neglected and impoverished workers.

The Great Estates

No account of Wessex during the nineteenth century would be complete without some discussion of the crucial role which the great landowners and great estates continued to play in the life of the region. The estates of private landowners as well as of institutions such as the Crown, the Duchy of Cornwall, Oxford and Cambridge colleges and the colleges of Eton and Winchester, continued throughout the century to dominate the landscape of Wessex and the economic and social life of many villages. The country house with its well-wooded parkland remained one of the most widespread and characteristic features of the whole region, and great houses like Ashdown Park, Stratfield Saye, Beaulieu, Dunster Castle, Hinton St George, Montacute, Melbury, Wimborne St Giles, Longleat, Wilton and scores of others, sustained by rents from their farms and manors, continued to emphasise the power, wealth and influence of their owners. The extent to which landownership in the region was concentrated into a few hands was demonstrated by the enquiry into the ownership of land in England made by order of Parliament in 1872–73 and published in 1874. For the first time since Domesday Book of 1086 precise figures were available concerning the possessions of the landowners and the size of their estates. For example, the enquiry revealed how much of Dorset and Wiltshire was dominated by great estates.

The enquiry also revealed publicly for the first time the vast possessions of individual landowners in the region. It showed that the Marquis of Bath, whose seat was at Longleat, owned 55,000 acres of which 20,000 were in Wiltshire and 8,000 in Somerset; the Earl of Pembroke, who lived at Wilton, owned 42,244 acres in Wiltshire or some 5 per cent of the whole county. The Marquis of Lansdowne owned 142,916 acres, although much of this was in Scotland and Ireland. George Wingfield-Digby of Sherborne Castle owned 21,000 acres in Dorset and 5,000 in Somerset; the Marquis of Ailesbury at Savernake had 55,000 acres which included 38,000 in Wiltshire; the Earl of Craven at Ashdown Park possessed 19,000 acres in Berkshire; Sir Robert James Loyd-Lindsay of Lockinge House near Wantage had an estate of 20,500 acres in Berkshire; the Earl of Portsmouth of Hurstborne Park near Whitchurch possessed 17,500 acres in Hampshire. There were numerous similar examples of very large estates in the region. The effect of the dominance of the region by gentry families and wealthy landowners can be seen in many features of the modern landscape, in estate cottages, schools, almshouses, hospitals and other public buildings, in the restored or rebuilt parish churches, and in the great country houses, many of which were enlarged, rebuilt or extensively altered during the nineteenth century. Notable among the many new houses of the century was Osborne House built near East Cowes on the Isle of Wight for Queen Victoria and Prince Albert by Thomas Cubitt in 1845.

Table 30

(a) Proportion of each county occupied by estates of more than 10,000 acres		(b) Proportion of each county occupied by estates of between 1,000 and 10,000 acres	
County	Per cent	County	Per cent
Berkshire	17	Berkshire	37
Dorset	36	Dorset	35
Hampshire	21	Hampshire	38
Somerset	20	Somerset	30
Wiltshire	36	Wiltshire	30
National average	24	National Average	29

(Bateman 1876, rev. edn 1971)

In 1825 Charles Brudenell-Bruce, 1st Marquis of Ailesbury, engaged the architect Thomas Cundy to extend Tottenham House in Savernake Forest on a grand scale with a series of splendid reception rooms and a marble ballroom which effectively converted the house into a palace, and permanently impoverished the family, but which demonstrated beyond doubt the power and prestige of the family and their political and economic dominance of the whole district including their tight control over the town of Marlborough and its parliamentary representation.

Highclere Castle, the largest mansion in Hampshire, was remodelled and virtually rebuilt by Sir Charles Barry for the Earl of Carnarvon in 1839–42; Bear Wood, an enormous mansion between Reading and Wokingham, was built for John Walter, owner of *The Times*, to the design of Robert Kerr in 1865–68. Perhaps the most aggressive use of wealth and the total assurance of aristocratic power can be seen in one of the last of the great country mansions to be built, Lord Portman's house at Bryanston near Blandford Forum. It was designed by Norman Shaw and built during the 1890s; its stark, uncompromising outline, emphasised by the bright red of its brickwork, dominates the town of Blandford Forum and all of the surrounding countryside.

By the time that Bryanston was built, however, the times had changed, landed wealth was no longer so great and the long agricultural depression had diminished rent-rolls, while lavish spending on buildings and on over-large establishments and a recklessly extravagant life-style had strained the resources of many landholding families. One example, admittedly an extreme one, of the sort of difficulties which could beset an estate and a landowner will serve to illustrate this. When the 3rd Marquis of Ailesbury died in 1875, his estate which was the second largest in Wiltshire was encumbered with the expense of maintaining several dowagers; moreover it was badly managed and poorly farmed; rents were low, the farms and the buildings had been allowed to deteriorate, and the estate was in no position to meet the slump in agricultural profits. Above all it was cursed by the longevity of Brudenell-Bruce wives, and

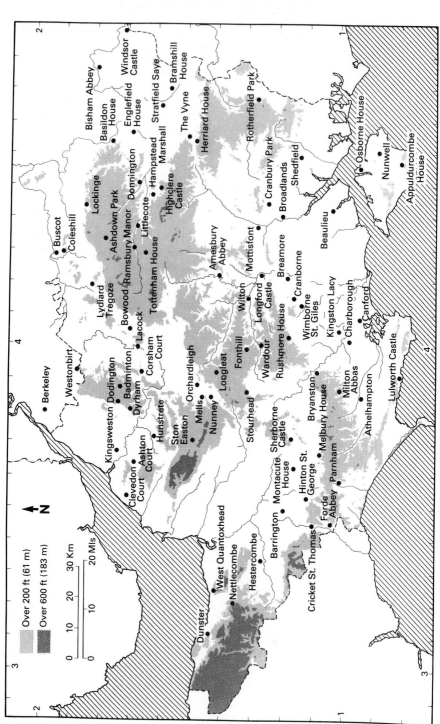

Over 200 ft (61 m)

Over 600 ft (183 m)

0   10   20   30 Km
0   10   20 MIs

N

Dunster

West Quantoxhead

Nettlecombe

Hestercombe

Cricket St. Thomas

Barrington

Montacute House

Hinton St. George

Forde Abbey

Parnham

Melbury House

Bryanston

Athelhampton

Milton Abbas

Canford

Charborough

Lulworth Castle

Sherborne Castle

Stourhead

Longleat

Fonthill

Wardour Castle

Rushmore House

Wimborne St. Giles

Kingston Lacy

Cranborne

Breamore

Beaulieu

Longford Castle

Wilton

Mottisfont

Amesbury Abbey

Orchardleigh

Mells

Nunney

Easton

Ston

Hunstrete

Dyrham

Badminton

Corsham Court

Lacock

Totterham House

Ashton Court

Clevedon Court

Kingsweston

Dodington

Westonbirt

Berkeley

Bowood

Lydiard Tregoze

Ramsbury Manor

Littlecote

Highclere Castle

Hampstead Marshall

Donnington

Ashdown Park

Lockinge

Coleshill

Buscot

Basildon House

Bisham Abbey

Englefield House

Stratfield Saye

Bramshill House

Windsor Castle

The Vyne

Herriard House

Rotherfield Park

Cranbury Park

Broadlands

Shedfield

Osborne House

Nunwell

Appuldurcombe House

Figure 7.1 Some major country houses and ...

was encumbered with an annual charge of £5,000 for jointures to dowagers. The final blow came in the form of the 4th Marquis who succeeded in 1883, at the age of 19, having acquired an insatiable appetite for spendthrift living and lavish expenditure on wine, women and horses, and having already amassed debts of £175,000. On succeeding to the estate he attempted to sell it to Sir Edward Guinness, later Earl Iveagh. The other members of the family strenuously opposed the sale, and contested it through the courts and eventually appealed to the House of Lords. Finally Lord Iveagh withdrew his offer, leaving the Savernake estate even more deeply in debt through legal charges. By the time the 4th Marquis died in 1894 at the age of 30, his debts were said to amount to £345,000 and all the 15,000 acres of the estate in Yorkshire had been sold. In spite of valiant efforts by the 5th and 6th Marquises, the estate never recovered; the woodlands including Savernake Forest had to be handed over to the Forestry Commission, and the great mansion at Tottenham House became a school (Stedman 1960: 258–64, 349–50).

Chapter 8

The Great War and Aftermath, 1914–1939

The changes which have occurred throughout Wessex since 1914 have been so rapid and so revolutionary that it is possible here to do no more than draw attention to some of the most important and far-reaching developments before the outbreak of the Second World War in 1939. In countless ways the Great War marked a more profound and abrupt break with the past than anything which had occurred before. The moment when the old, secure fabric of society was irretrievably split in one local community can be seen precisely in a photograph taken in August 1914 at Bratton near Westbury in Wiltshire. It shows the young men of Bratton, Edington, Tinhead and the neighbouring villages and hamlets along the escarpment of Salisbury Plain, being taken off to enlist as volunteers in the army at Devizes, in a cavalcade of the cars of local gentry families, amid scenes of great patriotic enthusiasm, flag-waving and fond farewells. In the background is the iron-foundry and agricultural implement works of R. and J. Reeves, the principal employers in the district, and the first car is being driven by one of the Reeves family. Many of these volunteers were never to return; the war memorials show that 20 men from Bratton died in the war, and 24 from Edington, and those men who did return came back to a new world of rapid change and upheaval very different from that which they had so gaily left on that sunny August afternoon in 1914. Even the implement works in which most of them had been employed and which supplied the farms throughout west Wiltshire and far beyond declined steadily after the war as large-scale production of tractors, balers and combine-harvesters, beyond the manufacturing capacity of a local family-run business, destroyed much of the trade (Bettey 1977: 61).

The human effect of the Great War of 1914–18 can everywhere be seen on war memorials in towns and villages alike, showing the appalling death-toll among young, active men of the communities. In Somerset alone, for example, more than 11,000 men were killed in the war out of a population of less than 450,000. Everywhere the casualty rate was grim; from Trent near Yeovil with a total population of less than 350, 35 young men went to the war and 12 of them never returned; from Imber, the little village on Salisbury Plain from

Plate 8.1 Leaving for the Great War, August 1914. This rather faded photograph nonetheless captures the end of the old rural England. It shows the young men of Bratton, Edington and Tinhead in Wiltshire, who have volunteered for service in the war, being taken off in the cars of the local gentry to enlist, amid scenes of great patriotic fervour and enthusiasm. Many of these volunteers were never to return, and those who did came back to a new world of rapid change and upheaval, very different from that which they had so gaily left in August 1914.

which the inhabitants were evicted in 1943 so that it could be used for military training, 25 men went to the Great War out of a total population of 200, and three of them gave their lives in the conflict; 350 men from the town of Frome were killed in the war, more than 300 from Trowbridge. Of the countless moving memorials of the gruesome death-toll of those four years, two in the church at Mells near Frome are outstanding: one is to Raymond Asquith, the brilliant eldest son of the Prime Minister, H. H. Asquith; the other is to Edward Horner who was killed in France in 1917, a remarkable equestrian monument designed by Sir Alfred Munnings and Sir Edwin Lutyens. Edward Horner was the last direct male heir to the estate which the Horner family had acquired after the dissolution of Glastonbury Abbey in 1539. Few families and scarcely any villages escaped totally from this slaughter of young men.

The Great War and its immediate aftermath accelerated the change from a world of horses, wagons, dusty lanes, oil lamps, thatched roofs, cob-walls, labour-intensive farming, locally made tools and home-made entertainments to the modern influx of cars, lorries, motor-buses, tractors, tarmacadam roads, council-houses, electricity, telephones, wireless, piped-water, mains-drainage, standardised household articles and mass entertainment. In the narrow streets of towns the rapid growth in the number of motor cars soon created traffic chaos and clouds of dust as well as causing numerous accidents. In Salisbury, for example, the dusty city streets began to receive treatment with tar as early as 1912; by 1925 there were 21 firms of motor engineers, and by 1930 motors outnumbered horse-drawn vehicles by ten to one. Dr John Chandler in his recent history of Salisbury has described the changes brought by motor vehicles during the 1930s as follows:

> Between 1932 and 1936 the motor car effected a profound change in what might be called the townscape of Salisbury. Much that is now taken for granted in any street scene originated in those five years, and has been only little modified since. The first car park was constructed – on the site of the present coach station – and the first car park charges levied. For the first time a decision was taken to demolish buildings – in Salt Lane – to make way for a car park. The first parking restrictions – in Castle Street – were imposed. The first one-way streets – Fish Row and Butcher Row – were designated. Traffic lights were placed at strategic junctions. Pedestrian crossings made their first appearance. Thirty mile per hour speed limit signs were erected at all the entrances to the city. And the first police patrol car was bought to ensure that they were observed.
> (Chandler 1983: 151)

The period following the Armistice in 1918 saw the distribution of population swing even more markedly in favour of a few large, prosperous towns such as Southampton, Portsmouth, Bournemouth, Reading, Swindon and Bristol, and a continuing drift away from the smaller villages and hamlets.

A few towns with particularly prosperous industries or a thriving tourist trade increased substantially in population, such as Yeovil which grew from 13,760 in 1911 to 19,000 by 1931 because of the employment provided by engineering, aircraft-production and glove-making, or Chippenham which grew from 5,300 to 8,500 during the same period as engineering replaced the former woollen-cloth trade of the town. Reading, with its varied industries and employments including malting, brewing, biscuits, seed production, county administration, local marketing, the University College and a good rail link to London, grew from 87,700 in 1911 to 97,150 by 1931. Poole, which had a fine natural harbour and a busy port exporting clay and agricultural produce, and a thriving pottery industry, grew from 38,900 in 1911 to 57,200 by 1931. The development of the oil-refining industry which was soon to be so important along the shores of Southampton Water was already leading to the growth of villages such as Fawley and Exbury during the 1920s and 30s. Weston-super-Mare continued its rapid growth as a holiday resort, increasing from 23,000 in 1911 to 32,000 by 1931, making it the largest town in Somerset after Bath;

Table 31

(a) County populations 1911, 1921, 1931

County	1911	1921	1931
Berkshire	281,000	295,000	311,000
Dorset	211,000	225,000	239,000
Hampshire including Isle of Wight	953,000	1,008,000	1,103,000
Somerset	455,000	462,000	470,000
Wiltshire	286,000	292,000	303,000
Bristol	357,000	377,000	397,000
Isle of Wight	88,000	95,000	88,000

(b) Population of major towns 1911, 1921, 1931

Town	1911	1921	1931
Bath	51,000	69,000	69,000
Bournemouth	79,000	92,000	117,000
Portsmouth	231,000	247,000	249,000
Reading	88,000	92,000	97,000
Southampton	119,000	161,000	176,000

likewise Burnham-on-Sea increased from 4,300 to 7,700 during the same period as its popularity as a holiday retirement resort grew. Bournemouth continued its spectacular development, and its population grew from 79,000 in 1911 to 117,000 by 1931.

But these places were exceptional. Most of the smaller market towns scarcely grew at all, or even declined in population between 1911 and 1931. Newbury, Dorchester, Sherborne, Taunton, Bridgwater, Salisbury, Basingstoke, Andover and Winchester had small increases in population, but the population of many of the smaller towns such as Hungerford, Lambourn, Wallingford, Faringdon, Bridport, Beaminster, Sturminster Newton, Bruton, Castle Cary, Devizes, Marlborough and many others declined during the same period. Many villages along the south coast grew rapidly as dormitories for Portsmouth, Southampton or Bournemouth, or as seaside and holiday resorts, but in most other villages throughout the region population was static or declined in face of the decreasing need for farm labour. The rapid increase in the population of Tilehurst on the western edge of Reading from 8,300 to 14,000 in the decade 1921–31 was entirely due to residential development, and many villages along the Thames valley within commuting distance of London had similar rapid growth. Likewise dormitory suburbs and villages dependent upon Bristol, such as Kingswood, Long Ashton, Nailsea, Thornbury and Yate, grew rapidly; Keynsham also developed after the

287

building of a large chocolate-factory there by the firm of J. S. Fry during the 1920s.

One other factor which led to population growth in a few places was the establishment of even more military bases. The army continued to occupy large parts of Salisbury Plain, and the overwhelming importance of the army in Aldershot is evident from the fact that of the population of 35,000 in 1911, 22,500 were males and only 12,500 females; at Bulford on Salisbury Plain which had 341 people in 1891 the development of the army barracks increased the population to 4,000 by 1931, and a large garden-village with tree-lined streets was created to accommodate the soldiers and their families. During the inter-war years several new military bases, aerodromes and flying schools were established. For example, Didcot with its good rail links became a military barracks and Ordnance depot and its population grew from 707 to 2,164 between 1911 and 1921. In Wiltshire new army camps and Royal Air Force bases were built at Figheldean, Rollestone, Upavon, Chiseldon, Tidworth and elsewhere; while in Hampshire aerodromes were constructed for the RAF at Abbots Ann, Calshot and Worthy Down.

Agriculture remained overwhelmingly the most important economic activity, but the return to arable farming during the war years 1914–18 was merely a brief interlude in the long story of decline which was not finally halted until the Second World War. Wherever possible farmers continued to concentrate upon liquid milk production with which foreign imports could not compete, and cereal acreages continued to fall, as did the number of labourers employed in farming. The proportion of land laid down to permanent pasture in Wiltshire rose from 42 per cent in 1870 to 75 per cent by the 1930s. In Somerset, which had always had a greater concentration upon dairy farming, the proportion of permanent pasture was even higher and rose from 63 per cent in 1870 to 83 per cent by the 1930s. Likewise sheep which for centuries had been the mainstay of chalkland farming continued to decline in profitability and their numbers dwindled rapidly. In Dorset, for example, where in 1850 there had been more than 500,000 sheep, the number had fallen to 300,000 by 1900, and had dwindled to fewer than 50,000 by 1939. In Wiltshire sheep numbers also showed a steady decline from 774,000 in 1870 to 448,000 in 1914, 217,000 in 1924 and by 1939 the number had fallen to 162,000. Even these figures do not reveal the full extent of the change which had come over farming, for whereas the nineteenth-century flocks had been mostly Hampshire Downs which were folded on the arable lands, they were replaced during the twentieth century by cross-bred sheep kept for mutton and wool, less labour-intensive grassland breeds, more suited as it was said to 'dog and stick farming', that is they could be easily managed by one man. The water-meadows were also allowed to fall into disuse as the value of their earlier and more vigorous growth was no longer thought to be worth the high labour costs involved in their maintenance, and as the great folding flocks of sheep which had once fed on them were no longer kept. The remains of the water-meadows which were once such a crucial feature of chalkland farming, and the sad ruins of weirs, hatches, channels and drains are still to be seen along almost every chalkland stream.

One important inter-war development in dairy farming originated in Wiltshire. This was the Hosier bail milking system, an easily transportable milking parlour which was used in the fields, and which meant that lands remote from farmsteads and on the chalk downlands could, in conjunction with a piped water supply, support herds of dairy cows. The system was invented by A. J. Hosier of Wexcombe near Collingbourne Ducis, where a factory was established to manufacture the prefabricated milking parlours which rapidly became popular in all parts of Wessex.

In a few favoured areas the growth of large nearby conurbations or easy access to the railway network provided an opportunity for the development of market-gardening or specialist fruit-production. Thus on the warm light soils around Bournemouth, Southampton and Portsmouth vegetable-growing be-came important, as also at Bromham on the belt of Greensand near Devizes and at Long Ashton close to Bristol. Even more specialised were the strawberry and other soft fruit districts in the Hamble valley around Swanwick and Botley where many hundreds of acres of strawberries and bush and soft fruits were grown for Southampton, Fareham and Portsmouth and for the London mar-ket, and the area of strawberry-growing around Cheddar in Somerset, along the southern slope of Mendip. Market gardens also developed around Bristol, Bath and Weston-super-Mare, and on the rich easily worked soils around South Petherton in south Somerset.

Another major development which occurred during the inter-war years was the continuing extension of the influence of local government into many spheres of daily life. Following the establishment of County Councils in 1889 and of Parish Councils and Urban and Rural Districts in 1894, local govern-ment became increasingly involved in and responsible for police and fire services, education, public works, roads, health, housing and welfare. Council houses became a familiar feature of towns and villages alike: for example, of the 36,000 new houses built in the Bristol area during the inter-war years, many of them to rehouse people harshly removed from the cosy and companionable though insanitary slums to new estates, 15,000 were council houses built by Bristol Corporation. Large new administrative offices for County and District Councils became an intrusive feature of many towns, dominating the central area in Winchester, Trowbridge, Dorchester, Bristol and elsewhere, but pro-viding a valuable source of employment throughout the region.

The other major and far-reaching change of the inter-war years was the rapid decline and break-up of the great estates and the great country houses which had for so long dominated the towns and villages of Wessex. The slaughter of the Great War brought grievous losses to many landed families, while higher taxes, death duties, and the rapid decline in the profits of farming meant that many owners had to sell their lands even though the price of land was so low. Before 1914 income tax took barely 4 per cent of the gross rental of estates such as Wilton or Savernake in Wiltshire; by 1919 it was taking over 25 per cent, while land tax and other charges made further inroads on profits. As early as 1915 when the only son of Sir Edward Antrobus was killed in action the whole Amesbury Abbey estate of some 10,000 acres came on to the market; and in 1917–18 outlying parts of the Wilton estate were sold. During the 1920s more and more estates were broken up and sold under the pressure of taxation, death duties and the low profits and rents from farming. The Marquis of Bath sold nearly 9,000 acres of the Longleat estate soon after the war; the Marquis of Ailesbury sold 25,000 acres of the Savernake estate in 1929. In these cases as elsewhere, the estate survived but with a greatly decreased acreage, and the same pattern was followed on the Earl of Carnarvon's estate in Berkshire, Earl Waldegrave's estate in Somerset or the Weld and Digby estates in Dorset and in many others. Other estates were more completely broken up. The Phelips family left their great Elizabethan house at Montacute, the St Johns left Lydiard Tregoze, the Pophams departed from Littlecote, the Guests' house at Canford became a school, as did Milton Abbey, Tottenham Park and Brympton D'Evercy, the Longs' mansion at Rood Ashton near Trowbridge was allowed to fall into ruin, many others were saved by the National Trust or by local authorities. The principal beneficiaries of the break-up of the great estates were the tenant farmers who were able to buy their farms. The scale of the revolution which occurred in landowning during the 1920s and 30s is apparent from the figures for Wiltshire where in 1914 less than 10 per cent of farms were owner-occupied, while by 1941 37 per cent of the farms and 36 per cent of the area farmed in the county were farmed by owner-occupiers (*VCH Wilts* IV, 1959: 105–14; Thompson 1963: 327–45).

Above all the years 1914–1939 were marked by the development of new industries and new commercial ventures and developments. There was a massive growth in the tourist and retirement industry, reflected in the continuing expansion of Southsea, Bournemouth, Weston-super-Mare, Burnham-on-Sea and Minehead. Biscuits, brewing and seed production at Reading, railway workshops at Swindon and Eastleigh, the Royal Navy dockyards at Portsmouth and Portland, meat processing at Calne and Trowbridge, dairy products at Chippenham and Melksham, rubber production at Bradford-on-Avon, engineering and glove-making at Yeovil, and the continuing military presence at Aldershot, Sandhurst and on Salisbury Plain, all continued to provide employment across the region. Numerous market towns and regional centres also continued to prosper, such as Salisbury, Devizes, Andover, Basingstoke, Dorchester, Warminster, Taunton, Newbury and Wantage. The position of Southampton as the premier passenger port and liner terminal in the country was firmly established during the period; in 1934 the New Docks were completed with 1½ miles of quays and 40 feet of water even at low tide, while the King George V dry dock could take vessels of up to 100,000 tons. Between 1900 and 1939 the number of passengers travelling via Southampton Docks each year rose from 200,000 to 575,000, and the port also had a significant freight traffic including timber, fruit, grain, motor cars, meat and dairy products.

Bristol with its developing deep-water port at Avonmouth remained one of the most important ports in the country, with an extensive import trade in timber, grain, tobacco, cocoa, paper and fruit. Although some of the older industries of the city such as wool and cotton goods, soap- and glass-making, and coal mining declined or ceased altogether, many other industries became increasingly important in the economic life of the city: tobacco, with the great factory of W. D. and H. O. Wills at Bedminster, cocoa and chocolate produced by several firms of which the most notable was that of J. S. Fry. During the 1920s Fry's moved to a huge new purpose-built factory at Keynsham in the Avon valley between Bristol and Bath. Other important industries included the manufacture of boots and shoes, paper and packaging, printing and chemicals. Most important of all for the future was the establishment in 1910, one year after the first cross-channel flight, of aeroplane construction at Filton on the northern outskirts of Bristol. Sir George White, who was chairman of the company which ran electric trams in Bristol and out to Filton, established an airfield and flying school at Filton, and started the company which was later to be known as the Bristol Aeroplane Company. The company rapidly prospered, especially during the Great War, and by 1919 had over 8,000 workers. During the 1920s and 1930s it produced such famous aircraft as the Bristol Bulldog and the Blenheim, and began a tradition of experimentation and technical advance which eventually led to the great Brabazon and on to the supersonic Concorde.

Postscript: 1939–1974

The hammer-blows of the Second World War, followed by massive redistribution of population, social innovation and economic development have left no corner of the region unaffected, and with such a remarkable acceleration in the pace and scale of change, only a few of the more radical and immediately apparent upheavals can be catalogued here. The geographical position of Wessex meant that it was of major military and strategic importance throughout the War; Portsmouth was the most important royal naval dockyard, military bases, training establishments and major airfields stretched from Aldershot right across the downlands and into the Somerset Levels; Bristol and Southampton were vital in the production of aircraft and aero engines; both ports played a key role in the import of oil, foodstuffs and other commodities essential for the conduct of the war. War also came to Wessex in the most horrendous fashion with the heavy and sustained bombing of the major towns. Large parts of the historic centres of Bristol, Portsmouth, Southampton and other towns were destroyed by enemy action. The villages of Imber in Wiltshire and Tyneham on the Dorset coast were commandeered for military training and the inhabitants were evicted. The whole of the southern coastline was involved in the huge preparations for the liberation of Europe which began in 1944. Southwick House, on the site of the former Augustinian priory three miles from Portsmouth, became the headquarters of General Eisenhower, the Supreme Allied Commander, and it was there that the final momentous decision to launch the attack on the French coast on 6 June 1944 was taken.

After the war the population of several towns increased dramatically; by 1961 Bristol and its suburbs had a population of over half a million, and Southampton had grown to more than 200,000. Even more remarkable was the mushroom growth of those towns which were chosen to accommodate some of the 'overspill' population moved out of London. Thus in twenty years the population of Andover almost doubled:

1951–14,000;   1961–17,000;   1971–26,000.

Even more remarkable was the growth of Basingstoke which was

292

transformed from an agricultural market town whose population in 1931 was only 13,865, into a large new conurbation, with vast new housing estates, modern factories, shops, offices and roads, produced by a partnership between London and Hampshire. The population growth of Basingstoke was as follows:

1951–17,000;　1961–26,000;　1971–52,500.

Similarly Swindon which before the war had been totally dominated by the Great Western Railway, attracted a large number of new industries and employments, ranging from car-body manufacture and insurance offices to the headquarters and distribution centre of several national firms. In 1931 the population of Swindon had been just over 62,000, by 1961 it had grown to more than 92,000.

Alongside population change, massive new industries have been developed. They include nuclear power stations in the Severn valley and at Hinkley Point near Bridgwater, atomic research establishments at Harwell, Aldermaston and at Winfrith on the Dorset heathland, a coal-fired power station near Didcot dominating one end of the Vale of the White Horse, a large chemical works at Avonmouth, cellophane manufacture with its associated peculiar smell at Bridgwater, helicopter building at Yeovil, an oil refinery at Fawley on Southampton Water which was opened in 1951 and is one of the largest refineries in Europe. Military establishments include the modern naval dockyard at Portsmouth, the Admiralty Underwater Research Establishment at Portland, the naval airfield at Yeovilton in south Somerset, military airfields and research establishments at Greenham near Newbury, Lyneham in Wiltshire, Porton Down near Salisbury, and the continuing military occupation of a large part of Salisbury Plain and of the Dorset coast and heath.

In many parts of the region the traditional mixed small-scale family farming has disappeared in the face of elaborate powered machinery needing only a tiny proportion of the workforce once employed in agriculture, but requiring the sort of capital investment that is only possible for large firms and agricultural combines. Much of the chalkland, the heart of Wessex which once supported the great flocks of sheep, has been ploughed, and by the copious use of artificial fertilisers, pesticides and fungicides is made to yield huge annual crops of wheat and barley. The impact of these and other farming changes upon the appearance of the landscape, the population and the social structure of the villages has been immense. The landscape and the society of the region have also been greatly affected by the decline and disappearance of the branch railways, and by the progress of road improvements, with ever more lavish by-pass and road-widening schemes, culminating in the construction of the motorway network. The dramatic impact of the motorways on the landscape is to be seen at many places, in the great bridges and especially the bridges across the Severn and the Avon, and in the Almondsbury interchange north of Bristol, occupying an area of 80 acres, much larger than most medieval towns, at the point where motorways from London, the Midlands, Wales and the west of England converge. Although many of the branch railways have been closed, the greatly increased speed of trains on the main lines has meant that it is possible for people to travel to work in London each day from parts of the region which were formerly remote and self-contained. The electrification of the railway line from Bournemouth to London in 1967 brought Winchester and many parts of the New Forest within an hour's journey from London, with a consequent change in social composition and house prices, while the fast diesel trains on the Bristol and Taunton to London lines have made daily travel to London feasible, not just from Maidenhead, Reading and along the Thames valley, but from Didcot, Newbury, Hungerford, Swindon and even Bath.

Local Government Reorganisation 1974

The drastic reorganisation of the whole ancient administrative framework of the region came into effect on 1 April 1974. A new county of Avon was created, making an unhappy and unpopular union of the ancient city and county of Bristol with large swathes of north Somerset and south Gloucestershire, chosen without regard for geography or even for parish boundaries; Bournemouth, Christchurch and the surrounding parishes were transferred from Hampshire to Dorset, and more than a third of Berkshire, including the historic landmark of the White Horse, were declared to be from henceforth in Oxfordshire, while an arbitrary boundary was drawn across the Berkshire Downs from Lambourn to Streatley. These insensitive changes which completely ignored local feelings of county pride and identity in favour of administrative convenience, and which were carried through in the face of strong and continuing opposition, must now presumably be regarded as permanent. They mark an abrupt break in the steady development and long history of the Wessex region.

Bibliography

Abbreviations

BL	British Library
BRO	Bristol Record Office
DRO	Dorset Record Office, Dorchester
HRO	Hampshire Record Office, Winchester
PRO	Public Record Office
SRO	Somerset Record Office, Taunton
VCH	Victoria County History
WRO	Wiltshire County Record Office, Trowbridge

Addyman, P. V. and Leigh, D. (1972) The Anglo-Saxon village at Chalton, Hampshire, *Medieval Archaeology*, **17**, 1–25.

Albert, W. (1972) *The Turnpike Road System in England 1663–1840*, Cambridge.

Allen, D. G. C. (1952) The rising in the West 1628–31, *Economic History Review*, 2nd Ser., **5**, 76–85.

Aston, M. A. (1977) Deserted settlements in Mudford Parish, Yeovil, *Somerset Archaeological and Natural History Society Proceedings*, **121**, 41–53.

Aston, M. A. (1978) Gardens and earthworks at Hardington and Low Ham, Somerset, *Somerset Archaeological and Natural History Society Proceedings*, **122**, 11–28.

Aston, M. A. and Leech, P. (1977) *Historic Towns in Somerset*, Committee for Rescue Archaeology in Avon, Gloucestershire and Somerset, Bristol.

Atthill, R. (1967) *The Somerset and Dorset Railway*, David and Charles, Newton Abbot.

Atthill, R. (ed.) (1976) *Mendip: A New Study*, David and Charles, Newton Abbot.

Aubrey, J. (1969) *Natural History of Wiltshire*, Ponting, K. G. (ed.), David and Charles, Newton Abbot.

Bamford, F. (ed.) (1936) *A Royalist's Notebook, the Commonplace Book of Sir John Oglander of Nunwell 1622–52*.

Barfield, S. (1901) *Thatcham and Its Manors*, 2 vols, Thatcham.

Barron, R. S. (1976) *The Geology of Wiltshire*, Moonraker Press, Bradford-on-Avon.

Bateman, J. (1876) *Great Landowners of Great Britain* (new edn 1971), Leicester University Press.

295

Bates, E. H. (ed.) (1900) Thomas Gerard's survey of Somerset 1633, *Somerset Record Society*, 15, Taunton.

Bates Harbin, E. H. (ed.) (1908) Somerset Quarter Sessions Records 1625–1639, *Somerset Record Society*, 24, Taunton.

Bath and West of England Agricultural Society *Letters and Papers*, 1780–, Bath (Vol. X, 1805).

Bayley, A. R. (1910) *The Civil War in Dorset 1642–1660*, Wessex Press, Taunton.

Bell, M. (ed.) (1933) Wulfric of Hazelbury, *Somerset Record Society*, 47, Taunton.

Beresford, M. W. (1959) The six new towns of the Bishops of Winchester 1200–55, *Medieval Archaeology*, 3, 187–215.

Beresford, M. W. (1967) *New Towns of the Middle Ages*, Lutterworth Press.

Beresford, M. W. and St Joseph, J. K. (1958) *Medieval England: An Aerial Survey*, Cambridge University Press.

Beresford, M. W. and Finberg, H. P. R. (1973) *English Medieval Boroughs, A Handlist*, David and Charles, Newton Abbot.

Bettey, J. H. (1968–69) Sir John Tregonwell of Milton Abbey, *Dorset Natural History and Archaeological Society Proceedings*, 90, 295–302.

Bettey, J. H. (1970) *The Island and Royal Manor of Portland*, University of Bristol.

Bettey, J. H. (1972) The supply of stone for re-building St Paul's Cathedral, *Archaeological Journal*, 128, 176–85.

Bettey, J. H. (1973–74) Bishop Secker's diocesan survey, *Dorset Natural History and Archaeological Society Proceedings*, 95, 74–5.

Bettey, J. H. (1974) *City and County Histories: Dorset*, David and Charles, Newton Abbot.

Bettey, J. H. (1975–76) The revolts over the enclosure of the Royal Forest at Gillingham, *Dorset Natural History and Archaeological Society Proceedings*, 97, 21–4.

Bettey, J. H. (1977a) *Rural Life in Wessex 1500–1900*, Moonraker Press.

Bettey, J. H. (1977b) The development of water meadows in Dorset during the seventeenth century, *Agricultural History Review*, 25, 37–43.

Bettey, J. H. (1980) *The Landscape of Wessex*, Moonraker Press, Bradford-on-Avon.

Bettey, J. H. (1981) The casebook of Sir Francis Ashley, Recorder of Dorchester, 1614–35, *Dorset Record Society*, 7, Dorchester.

Bettey, J. H. (1982) Calendar of the correspondence of the Smyth family of Ashton Court 1548–1642, *Bristol Record Society*, 35, Bristol.

Bettey, J. H. (1983) Church and community life in Bristol during the sixteenth century, *Bristol Record Society Occasional Publications*, 2, Bristol.

Bettey, J. H. (1984) The cattle trade in the west country during the seventeenth century, *Somerset Archaeological and Natural History Society Proceedings*, 127, 123–8.

Bettey, J. H. and Taylor, C. W. G. (1982) *Sacred and Satiric: Medieval Stone Carving in the West Country*, Redcliffe Press, Bristol.

Biddle, M. (1961–62) The deserted medieval village of Seacourt, Berkshire, *Oxoniensia*, 26–7, 70–1.

Biddle, M. (ed.) (1976) *Winchester in the Early Middle Ages*, Oxford University Press.

Billingsley, J. (1975) *General View of the Agriculture of Somerset*, Board of Agriculture.

Billingsley, J. (1798) The uselessness of commons to the poor, in Young, A. (ed.) *Annals of Agriculture*, **31**.

Bond, S. (1970) The medieval constitution of New Windsor, *Berkshire Archaeological Journal*, **65**, 21–40.

Bonney, D. (1976) Early boundaries and estates in southern England, in Sawyer, P. (ed.) *Medieval Settlement: Continuity and Change*, 72–81, Edward Arnold.

Bossy, J. (1975) *The English Catholic Community 1570–1850*, Darton, Longman and Todd.

Brooks, J. (1969) Eaton Hastings: a deserted medieval village, *Berkshire Archaeological Journal*, **64**, 1–8.

Brown, P. (1981) *Buildings of Britain 1550–1750: South-West England*, Moorland Publishing, Ashbourne.

Buchanan, B. J. (1982) The financing of parliamentary enclosure: some evidence from north Somerset 1770–1830, *Agricultural History Review*, **30**, 112–26.

Buchanan, C. A. and Buchanan, R. A. (1980) *Guide to the Industrial Archaeology of Southern England*, Batsford.

Buchanan, R. A. (1976) Brunel in Bristol, in McGrath, P. and Cannon, J. (eds) *Essays in Bristol and Gloucestershire History*, Bristol and Gloucestershire Archaeological Society, Bristol.

Caird, J. (1852) *English Agriculture in 1850–51*, Longman.

Cam, H. (1930) *The Hundred and the Hundred Rolls*, Methuen.

Carus-Wilson, E. (1941) An industrial revolution of the thirteenth century, *Economic History Review*, **11**, 39–60.

Carus-Wilson, E. (1954; 2nd edn 1967) *Medieval Merchant Venturers*, Methuen.

Carus-Wilson, E. (1975) Medieval Bristol, in Lobel, M. D. (ed.) *Historic Towns: Bristol*, Scolar Press.

Chandler, J. H. (1983) *Endless Street: A History of Salisbury*, Hobnob Press, Salisbury.

Chatwin, C. P. (1960) *British Regional Geology: The Hampshire Basin and Adjoining Areas*, HMSO.

Claridge, J. (1793) *General View of the Agriculture of Dorset*, Board of Agriculture.

Clarkson, T. (1808) *The History of the Rise, Progress and Accomplishment of the Abolition of the African Slave Trade*, Longman.

Clew, K. R. (1968) *The Kennet and Avon Canal*, David and Charles, Newton Abbot.

Cobbett, W. (1912) *Rural Rides*, 2 vols, Everyman edn.

Colchester, L. S. (ed.) (1982) *Wells Cathedral*, Open Books Publications.

Coleman, O. (1960–61) The Brokage Book of Southampton 1443–44, *Southampton Record Series*, **4** and **6**, Southampton.

Colvin, H. M. (ed.) (1963) *The History of the King's Works: The Middle Ages*. HMSO.

Cook, G. H. (1954) *The English Medieval Parish Church*, Phoenix House.

Corley, T. A. B. (1976) Simonds Brewery at Reading, 1760–1960, *Berkshire Archaeological Journal*, **68**, 77–87.

Corrie, G. E. (ed.) (1845) Hugh Latimer's works, *Parker Society*, Cambridge.

Cross, C. (ed.) (1969) The letters of Sir Francis Hastings 1574–1609, *Somerset Record Society*, **69**.

Cunliffe, B. (1972) Saxon and medieval settlement pattern in the region of Chalton, Hampshire, *Medieval Archaeology*, **16**, 1–12.

Curnock, N. (ed.) (1884–85) *The Journal of John Wesley*, Robert Culley.

Darby, H. C. (1973) *A New Historical Geography of England*, Cambridge University Press.

Darby, H. C. (ed.) (1976a) *New Historical Geography of England before 1600*, Cambridge University Press.

Darby, H. C. (ed.) (1976b) *New Historical Geography of England after 1600*, Cambridge University Press.

Darby, H. C. and Campbell, E. M. J. (1962) *The Domesday Geography of South-East England*, Cambridge University Press.

Darby, H. C. and Welldon Finn, R. (1967) *The Domesday Geography of South-West England*, Cambridge University Press.

Davies, D. (1795) *The Case of the Labourers in Husbandry*, Robinson.

Davies, M. F. (1909) *Life in an English Village*, T. Fisher Unwin.

Davis, J. S. (ed.) (1855) English Chronicle, *Camden Society*.

Davis, T. (1794) *General View of the Agriculture of Wiltshire*, Board of Agriculture.

Day, J. (1973) *Bristol Brass, A History of the Industry*, David and Charles, Newton Abbot.

Deane, P. and Cole, W. A. (1967) *British Economic Growth 1688–1959*, Cambridge University Press.

Defoe, D. (1927) *A Tour through England and Wales*, 2 vols, Everyman edn.

Dickinson, J. C. (1976) The origins of St Augustine's Bristol, in McGrath, P. and Cannon, J. (eds) *Essays in Bristol and Gloucestershire History*, Bristol and Gloucestershire Archaeological Society, Bristol.

Donkin, R. A. (1976) Changes in the early Middle Ages, in Darby, H. C. (ed.) *New Historical Geography of England*, Cambridge University Press.

Down, C. G. and Warrington, A. J. (1971) *The History of the Somerset Coalfield*, David and Charles, Newton Abbot.

Driver, A. and Driver, W. (1974) *General View of the Agriculture of Hampshire*, Board of Agriculture.

Dunning, R. (ed.) (1975) *Christianity in Somerset*, Somerset County Council, Taunton.

Dunning, R. (1978) *A History of Somerset*, Somerset County Library, Bridgwater.

Dunning, R. (1980) *Somerset and Avon*, Bartholomew, Edinburgh.

Dunning, R. (1983) *A History of Somerset*, Phillimore.

Durston, C. G. (1981) London and the provinces, *Southern History*, **3**, 39–54.

Earle, P. (1977) *Monmouth's Rebels*, Weidenfeld and Nicolson.

Eden, F. M. (1977) *The State of the Poor*, White.

Edwards, P. R. (1983) The horse trade in Tudor and Stuart England, in Thompson, F. M. L. (ed.) *Horses in European History*, 113–131, British Agricultural History Society, Reading.

Elton, G. R. (1972) *Policy and Police*, Cambridge University Press.

Farr, M. W. (ed.) (1959) Accounts and surveys of the Wiltshire lands of Adam de Stratton, *Wiltshire Archaeological Society, Records Branch*.

Ferris, J. P. (1965) The gentry of Dorset on the eve of the Civil War, *Genealogist Magazine*, **15**, 104–16.

Finberg, H. P. R. (ed.) (1972) *The Agrarian History of England and Wales AD 42–1042*, Cambridge University Press.

Fisher, F. J. (1935) The development of the London food market, *Economic History Review*, **5**, 46–64.

Fowler, J. (1951) *Medieval Sherborne*, Longmans, Dorchester.

Fowler, P. J. (1967) *Regional Archaeologies: Wessex*, Heinemann.

Fowler, P. J. (ed.) (1972) *Recent Work in Rural Archaeology*, John Baker.

Freeman, M. J. (1979) Turnpikes and their traffic: the example of southern Hampshire, *Institute of British Geographers Transactions*, N.S., **4**, 411–34.

Fuller, M. (1964) *West-Country Friendly Societies*, Museum of English Rural Life, Reading.

Fussell, G. E. (ed.) (1936) Robert Loder's farm accounts 1610–1620, *Camden Society*, 3rd ser., 53.

Garmonsway, G. N. (ed.) (1953) *The Anglo-Saxon Chronicle*, Everyman ed.

Gash, N. (1935) Rural Unemployment, *Economic History Review*, **6**, 90–3.

Gelling, M. (1978) *Signposts to the Past*, Dent.

Godfrey, J. (1962) *The Church in Anglo-Saxon England*, Cambridge University Press.

Gough, J. W. (1967) *The Mines of Mendip*, David and Charles, Newton Abbot.

Gras, N. S. B. (1930) *The Economic and Social History of an English Village* (Crawley, Hampshire), Harvard University.

Grinsell, L. V. (1958) *The Archaeology of Wessex*, Methuen.

Grosart, A. B. (ed.) (1886) *The Lismore Papers*.

Hadfield, C. (1955) *The Canals of Southern England*, Phoenix House.

Hall, H. (ed.) (1903) *Pipe Roll of the Bishopric of Winchester 1208–9*, London School of Economics.

Hare, A. J. C. (1872) *Memorials of a Quiet Life*, London.

Hare, J. N. (1981a) Durrington: A chalkland village in the later Middle Ages, *Wiltshire Archaeological Magazine*, **75**, 137–47.

Hare, J. N. (1981b) The demesne lessees of fifteenth-century Wiltshire, *Agricultural History Review*, **29**, 1–15.

Harvey, J. (1983) *The Georgian Garden*, Dovecote Press, Wimborne.

Haskell, P. (1981) Ship money in Hampshire, in Webb, J. (ed.) *Hampshire Studies*, 73–114.

Hatcher, J. (1977) *Plague, Population and the English Economy 1348–1530*, Macmillan.

Havinden, M. (1966) *Estate Villages*, Museum of English Rural Life, Reading.

Havinden, M. (1981) *The Somerset Landscape*, Hodder and Stoughton.

Helm, P. J. (1949) The Somerset Levels in the Middle Ages, *Journal of the British Archaeological Association*, 3rd ser., **12**, 37–52.

Hill, D. (1969) The burghal hidage, *Medieval Archaeology*, **13**, 84–92.

Hinton, D. A. (1977) *Alfred's Kingdom, Wessex and the South 800–1500*, J. M. Dent.

Hoad, M. (1981) The Origins of Portsmouth, in Webb, J. (ed.) *Hampshire Studies*, 1–32.

Hobsbawm, E. J. and Rudé, G. (1969) *Captain Swing*, Lawrence & Wishart.

Hockey, S. F. (1970) *Quarr Abbey and Its Lands*, Leicester University Press.

Hockey, S. F. (ed.) (1974) The Beaulieu Cartulary, *Southampton Record Series*, **17**, Southampton.

Hockey, S. F. (1982) *Insula Vecta, The Isle of Wight in the Middle Ages*, Phillimore.

Holland, A. J. (1971) *Ships of British Oak: The Rise and Decline of Wooden Shipbuilding in Hampshire*, David and Charles, Newton Abbot.

Holt, N. R. (ed.) (1964) *Pipe Roll of the Bishopric of Winchester 1210–11*, Manchester University Press.

Horn, W. and Born, E. (1965) *Great Coxwell Barn*, University of California.

Horn, P. (1976) *Labouring Life in the Victorian Countryside*, Gill and Macmillan, Dublin.

Horn, P. (1981) *A Georgian Parson and his Village, The Story of David Davies 1742–1819*, Beacon Publications, Abingdon.

Hoskins, W. G. and Stamp, L. D. (1953) *The Common Land of England and Wales*, Collins.

Hudson, K. (1965) *Industrial Archaeology of Southern England*, David and Charles, Newton Abbot.

Hudson, K. (1972) *Patriotism with Profit*, Evelyn.

Hudson, K. (1976) *The Bath and West: A Bicentenary History*, Moonraker Press, Bradford-on-Avon.

Hudson, W. H. (1910) *A Shepherd's Life*, Everyman.

Ingram, M. (1984) Ridings, rough music and the reform of popular culture in early modern England, *Past and Present*, 105, 79–113.

Jones, E. L. (1960) Eighteenth-century changes in Hampshire chalkland farming, *Agricultural History Review*, 8, 5–19.

Keil, I. (1961–63) Impropriator and benefice, *Wiltshire Archaeological Society Magazine*, 58, 351–61.

Keil, I. (1965) Farming on the estates of Glastonbury Abbey in the early fourteenth century, *Dorset Archaeological and Natural History Society Proceedings*, 87, 234–50.

Kemp, B. R. (1967–68) The Mother Church of Thatcham, *Berkshire Archaeological Journal*, 63, 15–22.

Kennedy, J. (1970) Laymen and monasteries in Hampshire 1530–1558, *Hampshire Field Club Proceedings*, 27, 65–85.

Kerr, B. (1968) *Bound to the Soil*, John Baker.

Kerridge, E. (1951–52) The notebook of a Wiltshire farmer, *Wiltshire Archeological Magazine*, 54, 416–28.

Kerridge, E. (1953) The floating of the Wiltshire water-meadows, *Wiltshire Archeological Magazine*, 55, 105–18.

Kerridge, E. (1954) The sheepfold in Wiltshire and the floating of the watermeadows, *Economic History Review*, 2nd ser. 6, 282–9.

Kerridge, E. (1958–59) The Revolts in Wiltshire against Charles I, *Wiltshire Archaeological and Natural History Magazine*, 57, 64–75.

Kershaw, I. (1973) The great famine and agrarian crisis in England 1315–22, *Past and Present*, 59, 3–50.

Knowles, D. (1948) *The Religious Orders in England*, Cambridge University Press.

Knowles, D. and Hadcock, R. N. (1953) *Medieval Religious Houses in England and Wales*, Longman.

Knowles, D. (1963) *The Monastic Order in England* (2nd edn), Cambridge University Press.

Latham, R. and Matthews, W. (eds) (1976) *The Diary of Samuel Pepys*, IX, 1668–69, Bell and Hyman.

Leech, R. (1981) *Early Industrial Housing: The Trinity Area of Frome*, RCHM, England.

Leland, J. (1906–10) *Itinerary in England*, Toulmin Smith, L. (ed.), 5 vols, Bell.

Lennard, R. (1959) *Rural England 1086–1135*, Oxford University Press.

Letters and Papers of Henry VIII, ed. J. S. Brewer, J. Gairdner and R. H. Brodie, London, 1862–1932 (Vol VIII, 1885; Vol IX, 1886; Vol XIII, 1892) Parliamentary Papers.

Levett, A. E. and Ballard, A. (1916) The Black Death on the estates of the See of Winchester, *Oxford Studies in Social and Legal History*, 5, Oxford University Press.

Lisle, E. (1957) *Observations in Husbandry*.

Little, B. (1954) *The City and County of Bristol*, Laurie.

Little, E. (1844) The farming of Wiltshire, *Journal of the Royal Agricultural Society*, 5.

Lloyd, A. T. (1969) Salterns of the Lymington area, *Hampshire Field Club Proceedings*, 24, 86–90.

Lobel, M. D. and Carus-Wilson, E. M. (1975) *Historic Towns: Bristol*, Scolar Press.

Longmate, N. (1974) *The Workhouse*, Temple Smith.

Loyn, H. R. (1962) *Anglo-Saxon England and the Norman Conquest*, Longman.

Machin, R. (1976) *Probate Inventories and Manorial Excepts of Chetnole, Leigh and Yetminster*, University of Bristol.

Machin, R. (1978) *The Houses of Yetminster*, University of Bristol.

MacInnes, C. M. and Whittard, W. F. (eds) (1955) *Bristol and Its Adjoining Counties*, British Association.

McIntyre, S. (1981) Bath: the rise of a resort town 1660–1800, in Clark, P. (ed.) *Country Towns in Pre-Industrial England*, Leicester University Press.

Mann, J. de L. (1971) *The Cloth Industry of the West of England from 1640 to 1880*, Oxford University Press.

Marshall, W. (1978) *Rural Economy of the Southern Counties*.

Mathias, P. (1959) *The Brewing Industry in England 1700–1830*, Cambridge University Press.

Mavor, W. (1813) *General View of the Agriculture of Berkshire*, Board of Agriculture.

Meekings, C. A. F. (ed.) (1961) Crown pleas of the Wiltshire Eyre, *Wiltshire Archaeological Society Records Branch*, 16, Devizes.

Meirion-Jones, G. I. (1969–70) Dogmersfield and Hartley Maudit, *Hampshire Field Club*, 26, 111–27.

Miller, E. and Hatcher, J. (1978) *Medieval England 1086–1348*, Longman.

Minchinton, W. E. (1954) Bristol – Metropolis of the West in the Eighteenth Century, *Transactions of the Royal Historical Society*, 5th ser., 4, 69–89.

Mitford, M. R. (1832) *Our Village*, 5 vols, Macmillan.

Monkhouse, F. J. (ed.) (1964) *A Survey of Southampton and Its Region*, British Association.

Moore, J. S. (1979) *Avon Local History Handbook*, Phillimore.

More, H. (1834) *Memoirs of the Life of Mrs Hannah More*, W. Roberts (ed.) London.

Morgan, M. (1946) *The English Lands of the Abbey of Bec*, Oxford University Press.

Morris, C. (ed.) (1949) *The Journeys of Celia Fiennes*, Cresset Press.

Morris, W. A. (1927) *The Medieval English Sheriff*, Manchester University Press.

301

Morton, J. (ed.) (1853) The Ancren Riwle, *Camden Society*, 57.
Orwin, C. S. and Sellick, R. J. (1970) *The Reclamation of Exmoor Forest*, David and Charles, Newton Abbot.
Pantin, W. A. (1957) Medieval Priests' Houses in South-West England, *Medieval Archaeology*, 1, 120–4.
Pares, R. (1950) *A West-Indian Fortune*, Longman.
Parliamentary Papers,
　Report of Poor Law Commissioners on Employment of Women and Children in Agriculture, 510, H.C. 1843, xii.
　Agricultural Statistics (Great Britain), 1875, lxxix, C1303.
　Agricultural Returns of Great Britain, 1899, cvi, C9304.
　Agricultural Returns for Great Britain, 1914, xcviii, Cd 7271.
Parry Okeden, W. H. (1930) The agricultural riots in Dorset in 1830, *Dorset Natural History and Archaeological Society Proceedings*, 52, 75–95.
Pelham, R. A. (1944) The distribution of early fulling mills in England and Wales, *Geography*, 29, 52–6.
Pevsner, N. (1958) *The Buildings of England: South and West Somerset*, Penguin.
Pevsner, N. (1958) *The Buildings of England: North Somerset and Bristol*, Penguin.
Pevsner, N. (1963) *The Buildings of England: Wiltshire*, Penguin.
Pevsner, N. (1966) *The Buildings of England: Berkshire*, Penguin.
Pevsner, N. and Lloyd, D. (1967) *The Buildings of England: Hampshire*, Penguin.
Pevsner, N. and Lloyd, D. (1972) *The Buildings of England: Dorset*, Penguin.
Platt, C. (1973) *Medieval Southampton*, Routledge and Kegan Paul.
Platt, C. and Coleman Smith R. (1975) *Excavations in Medieval Southampton*, 2 vols, Leicester University Press.
Ponting, K. G. (1957) *A History of the West of England Cloth Industry*, MacDonald.
Ponting, K. G. (1971) *The Woollen Industry of South-West England*, Adams and Dart, Bath.
Poole, A. L. (1951) *Domesday Book to Magna Carta*, Oxford University Press.
Postan, M. M. (1952–53) Glastonbury estates in the twelfth century, *Economic History Review*, 2nd ser., 5, 358–77.
Postan, M. M. (1966) Medieval agrarian society: England, in Postan, M. M. (ed.) *Cambridge Economic History of Europe*, I, 1966, 549–99, Cambridge University Press.
Postan, M. M. and Titow, J. Z. (1959) Heriots and prices on Winchester manors, *Economic History Review*, 2nd ser., 9.
Potter, K. R. (ed.) (1955) *Historia Novella*, Nelson.
Potter, K. R. and Davies, R. H. C. (eds) (1976) *Gesta Stephani*, Oxford University Press.
Powell, K. G. (1971) The beginnings of Protestantism in Gloucestershire, *Bristol and Gloucestershire Archaeological Society Proceedings*, 90, 141–157.
Ransome, M. (ed.) (1971) Wiltshire returns to the Bishop's visitation queries 1783, *Wiltshire Record Society*, 27, Devizes.
Reeves, M. (1978) *Sheep Bell and Ploughshare*, Moonraker Press, Bradford-on-Avon.
Renn, D. F. (1968) *Norman Castles in Britain*, John Baker.
Rogers, K. H. (1976) *Wiltshire and Somerset Woollen Mills*, Pasold, Edington.
Rolt, L. T. C. (1969) *Waterloo Ironworks, A History of Taskers of Andover 1809–1968*, David and Charles, Newton Abbot.

Rosen, A. (1981) Winchester in transition 1580–1700, in Clark, P. (ed.) *Country Towns in Pre-Industrial England*, Leicester University Press.

Ruddock, A. A. (1949–50) The decline of Southampton, *Economic History Review*, 2nd ser., **2**, 137–51.

Ruddock, A. A. (1951) *Italian Merchants and Shipping in Southampton 1270–1600*, Southampton.

Salzman, L. F. (1952; 2nd edn 1967) *Building in England*, Oxford University Press.

Sanderson, I. (1971) Abbotstone deserted medieval village, *Hampshire Field Club Proceedings*, **28**.

Sandison, A. (1969) *Trent in Dorset*, Longmans, Dorchester.

Satre, M. C. (1978) *Poverty in Berkshire*, Ann Arbor, Michigan.

Saville, J. (1957) *Rural Depopulation in England and Wales 1851–1951*, Routledge.

Sawyer, P. (ed.) (1976) *Medieval Settlement: Continuity and Change*, Edward Arnold.

Schofield, B. (ed.) (1927) Muchelney memoranda, *Somerset Record Society*, **42**, Taunton.

Sharp, M. (ed.) (1982) Accounts of the constables of Bristol Castle in the thirteenth and early fourteenth centuries, *Bristol Record Society*, **34**, Bristol.

Shorter, A. H. (1951–53) Paper mills in Hampshire, *Hampshire Field Club Proceedings*, **18**, 1–11.

Shrewsbury, J. F. D. (1970) *A History of Bubonic Plague in the British Isles*, Cambridge University Press.

Slack, P. (1972) Poverty and politics in Salisbury 1597–1666, in Clark, P. and Slack, P. (eds) *Crisis and Order in English Towns 1500–1700*, 164–203, Routledge.

Slack, P. (1975) Poverty in early Stuart Wiltshire, *Wiltshire Record Society*, **31**, Devizes.

Slade, C. F. (1969) Reading, in Lobel, M. D. (ed.) *Historic Towns*, I, Scolar Press.

Stedman, A. R. (1960) *Marlborough and the Upper Kennet Country*, Marlborough.

Stenton, D. M. (1952) *English Society in the Early Middle Ages*, Penguin.

Stenton, F. M. (1947) *Anglo-Saxon England*, Oxford University Press.

Stevenson, W. (1812) *General View of the Agriculture of Dorset*, Board of Agriculture.

Taylor, C. (1967) Whiteparish, the development of a forest-edge parish, *Wiltshire Archaeological Magazine*, **62**, 79–102.

Taylor, C. (1970) *The Making of the English Landscape: Dorset*, Hodder and Stoughton.

Temple Patterson, A. (1966) History of Southampton, *Southampton Record Series*, **11**, Southampton.

Temple Patterson, A. (1976) *Portsmouth: A History*, Moonraker Press, Bradford-on-Avon.

Thirsk, J. (ed.) (1967) *The Agrarian History of England and Wales 1500–1640*, Cambridge University Press.

Thomas, D. St J. (1960) *A Regional History of the Railways of Great Britain*, I, *The West Country*, Phoenix House.

Thomas, J. H. (1969–70) Hampshire and the Company of White Paper Makers, *Hampshire Field Club Proceedings*, **26**, 137–48.

Thomas, M. (1984) *The Book of Nailsea*, Barracuda.

Thompson, J. A. F. (1965) *The Later Lollards*, Oxford University Press.

Thompson, F. M. L. (1963) *English Landed Society in the Nineteenth Century*, Routledge.

Thorpe, B. (ed.) (1848–89) *Florence of Worcester*, Rolls Series, London.

Timperley, H. W. and Brill, E. (1965) *The Ancient Trackways of Wessex*, Drinkwater.

Titow, J. Z. (1961) Some evidence of the thirteenth-century population increase, *Economic History Review*, 2nd ser., **14**, 218–33.

Titow, J. Z. (1962) Some differences between manors and their effects on the condition of the peasants in the thirteenth century, *Agricultural History Review*, **10**, 1–13.

Titow, J. Z. (1969) *English Rural Society 1200–1350*, Allen and Unwin.

Titow, J. Z. (1972) *Winchester Yields: A Study in Medieval Agricultural Productivity*, Cambridge University Press.

Tull, J. (1733) *Horse-Hoeing Husbandry*.

Turner, M. (1980) *English Parliamentary Enclosure*, Dawson.

Underdown, D. (1979) The chalk and the cheese: contrasts among the English clubmen, *Past and Present*, **85**, 25–48.

Vanes, J. (ed.) (1975) The Ledger of John Smythe 1538–50, *Bristol Record Society*, 28.

Victoria County Histories London.
 Berkshire, **3**, 1923; **4**, 1924.
 Dorset, **2**, 1908; **3**, 1968.
 Hampshire, 5 vols 1903–14.
 Somerset, **1**, 1906; **2**, 1911; **3**, 1974; **4**, 1978; continuing.
 Wiltshire, 12 vols 1953–83; continuing.

Walker, F. (1972) *Regions of the British Isles: The Bristol Region*, Nelson.

Wanklyn, M. D. G. (1981) Royalist strategy in the south of England 1642–44, *Southern History*, **3**, 55–79.

Watts, D. G. (1967) A model for the early fourteenth century, *Economic History Review*, 2nd ser., **20**, 543–4.

Watts, D. G. (1983) Peasant discontent on the manors of Titchfield Abbey 1245–1405, *Hampshire Field Club Proceedings*, **39**, 121–35.

Webb, J. (1981) *Hampshire Studies*, Portsmouth City Record Office.

Welldon Finn, R. (1971) *The Norman Conquest and Its Effects on the Economy 1066–86*, Longman.

Whetham, E. H. (1964–65) London Milk Trade 1860–1900, *Economic History Review*, **17**, 369–80.

White, G. (1789) *Natural History of Selborne*, Everyman edn 1949.

White, H. P. (1961) *A Regional History of the Railways of Great Britain, II, Southern England*, Phoenix House.

Wigfield, W. M. (1980) *The Monmouth Rebellion*, Moonraker Press, Bradford-on-Avon.

Williams, M. (1970) *The Draining of the Somerset Levels*, Cambridge University Press.

Wood-Legh, K. L. (1953) *A Small Household of the Fifteenth Century*, Manchester University Press.

Wood-Legh, K. L. (1965) *Perpetual Chantries in Britain*, Cambridge University Press.

Worlidge, J. (1669) *Systema Agriculturae*.

Wormald, F. (1959) *The Benedictional of St Ethelwold*, Faber & Faber.

Wright, T. (ed.) (1843) Letters relating to the suppression of the monasteries, *Camden Society*, 26.

Wyndham, K. S. H. (1979) In pursuit of Crown land: the initial recipients of Somerset property in the mid-Tudor period, *Somerset Archaeological Society Proceedings*, **123**, 65–74.

Wyndham, K. S. H. (1980) Crown land and royal patronage in mid-sixteenth century England, *Journal of British Studies*, **19**, 18–34.

Young, A. (1768) *A Six Weeks Tour through the Southern Counties*, Strahan.

Young, A. (1796) *Annals of Agriculture*, **8**.

Young, C. R. (1979) *The Royal Forests of Medieval England*, Leicester University Press.

Ziegler, P. (1969) *The Black Death*, Collins.

Index

Yarmouth, I. of W., 49, 60, 113, 178,
242
Yarnbury fair, Wilts., 147
Yatton, 98–9, 164, 243, 276
Yeo river, 136, 235
Yeovil, 25, 49, 59, 99, 111, 117, 128,
131, 139, 141, 177, 192, 253,
259, 284, 290

helicopter production, 293
market at, 146–7, 233
population, 232, 286
railway, 238
Yerbury family, clothiers, 116, 138,
189, 192
Yetminster, 75, 204, 213, 238, 301
Young, Arthur, 188, 196, 255, 305